Popular Radicalism and the Unemployed in Chicago during the Great Depression

Popular Radicalism and the Unemployed in Chicago during the Great Depression

By Chris Wright

ANTHEM PRESS

Anthem Press

An imprint of Wimbledon Publishing Company
www.anthempress.com

This edition first published in UK and USA 2023
by ANTHEM PRESS
75–76 Blackfriars Road, London SE1 8HA, UK
or PO Box 9779, London SW19 7ZG, UK
and
244 Madison Ave #116, New York, NY 10016, USA

First published in the UK and USA by Anthem Press in 2022

Copyright © Chris Wright 2023

The author asserts the moral right to be identified as the author of this work.

All rights reserved. Without limiting the rights under copyright reserved above, no part of this publication may be reproduced, stored or introduced into a retrieval system, or transmitted, in any form or by any means (electronic, mechanical, photocopying, recording or otherwise), without the prior written permission of both the copyright owner and the above publisher of this book.

British Library Cataloguing-in-Publication Data
A catalogue record for this book is available from the British Library.

Library of Congress Control Number: 2022932206

ISBN-13: 978-1-83999-021-2 (Pbk)
ISBN-10: 1-83999-021-X (Pbk)

Cover Image: Photograph of Ben Shahn, "Unemployed", Artists Rights Society

This title is also available as an e-book.

CONTENTS

Acknowledgments		vi
Introduction		1
Chapter One	Overview	15
Chapter Two	Hardship	37
Chapter Three	Coping	67
Chapter Four	Relief, Part I: "Shelter Men"	107
Chapter Five	Relief, Part II: Governments, Unions, and Churches	135
Chapter Six	Collective Action	193
Conclusion		251
Index		257

ACKNOWLEDGMENTS

Writing is a very solitary activity, but the production of an academic work is never *completely* solitary. This book originated as a doctoral dissertation under the guidance of Leon Fink, whose criticism and advice improved it significantly. Indeed, I benefited greatly from the comments of everyone on my defense committee: Jeff Sklansky, Erik Gellman, Robert Johnston, Lynn Hudson, and Leon. I'm not confident they would be wholly pleased with the final product, but without their input it would doubtless have been unpublishable.

My time at the University of Illinois at Chicago was memorable, and I can scarcely convey how much I learned and grew through contact with excellent professors and thoughtful and collegial graduate students. Philosophy has always been my first love, but the years at UIC taught me (I hope) to think like a historian rather than only an "ideas" guy.

Archival research can be an onerous and lonely task, but with the help of friendly and brilliant archivists it is much easier and even enjoyable. So I have to thank all the archivists at the various institutions I visited: the Chicago History Museum, the University of Chicago, the Newberry Library, the Harold Washington Library, the Tamiment Library at New York University, the Franklin D. Roosevelt Presidential Library, and UIC. Uniformly, they were helpful, kind, encouraging, and insightful when suggesting further avenues of research. I remember being continually (if naïvely) struck by the breadth and depth of knowledge that seems to be a job requirement for archivists everywhere.

The friends and colleagues who commented on the manuscript were generous with their time and mercifully kind in their criticisms. Academia can be a competitive and unforgiving place, but knowing and working with great people makes all the difference. I'm also grateful to the excellent editorial and production team at Anthem Press, who were a pleasure to work with, as well as to several anonymous reviewers.

On a more personal note, I must thank my parents, Mike and MaryKae Wright, who have been unfailingly supportive and to whom the book is dedicated. It is doubtful I could have completed this project without the morale boosts they were happy to give me. Zukhra Kasimova, an impressive scholar in her own right, relentlessly encouraged me to turn the dissertation into a book no matter how defeatist I was about the idea. Lastly, I thank my son Aidan—for existing. He is only a few months old, so he wasn't around to contribute to (or distract from) the writing of this book, but he is, as it were, a nice gift from the universe for my having finished.

ACKNOWLEDGMENTS

In the end, apropos of "acknowledgments," and by way of anticipating the themes of the book, I would simply invoke Peter Marin's notion of the "human harvest," which he describes as follows:

> Kant called the realm of connection the kingdom of ends. Erich Gutkind's name for it was the absolute collective. My own term for the same thing is the human harvest—by which I mean the webs of connection in which all human goods are clearly the results of a collective labor that morally binds us irrevocably to distant others. Even the words we use, the gestures we make, and the ideas we have, come to us already worn smooth by the labor of others, and they confer upon us an immense debt we do not fully acknowledge.[1]

---

1. Peter Marin, "The Human Harvest," *Mother Jones*, December 1976, 38.

INTRODUCTION

Capitalism and mass unemployment are inseparable. Ever since the destruction of the English handloom weavers following the introduction of the power loom in the early nineteenth century, the presence of a "reserve army of the unemployed" has been a permanent feature of industrial capitalist society. Through perpetual structural change and business cycles, capitalism has manufactured unemployment no less reliably than industrial innovation, environmental degradation, and class conflict. The subject of this book is the collective suffering and struggles of the long-term unemployed during one of the great upheavals in American history, the Great Depression.

Unemployment during the Depression is hardly a novel subject of historical inquiry, so the question immediately arises, Why return to a topic that historians have already studied? Can anything new be said? In part, my interest in this old topic has been motivated by ominous parallels between the political economy of the present-day United States and the political economy that eventuated in the Depression. The most obvious parallel, for example, is the extreme income and wealth inequality of the two eras. "U.S. wealth concentration," the economist Gabriel Zucman wrote in 2019, "seems to have returned to levels last seen during the Roaring Twenties."[1] This parallel is rooted, to some extent, in the comparable weakness of organized labor in the 1920s and today. Similar stock market bubbles, too, have helped cause the wealth inequality of the two analogous eras. The income of the working class has, in both cases, stagnated as expansions of consumer credit have been necessary to keep the economy growing. In 1929, the weakness of aggregate demand that had been covered up by massive extensions of credit was largely responsible for the greatest economic contraction in the history of capitalism. It would be reasonable to conclude, in short, that we have a bleak future ahead.

But this fact in itself is hardly sufficient justification to write another social history of the unemployed. Rather, the justification, I hope, is that my interpretation differs from that of earlier scholars. Instead of simply describing the history for the sake of describing it, I want to use it to support a certain point of view about the nature of society. In particular, I want to defend some simple, even vulgar Marxian and anarchist ideas relating to capitalist institutional functioning and, conversely, anticapitalist tendencies in human behavior. As for the choice of Chicago as the city to study, the fact that it was a major site of unemployed activism in the 1930s—being one of the cities hit hardest by the Depression—was what drew my interest. Given the congeries of ethnicities, races,

---

1. Quoted in Jesse Colombo, "America's Wealth Inequality Is at Roaring Twenties Levels," *Forbes*, February 28, 2019.

classes, and political persuasions that constituted Chicago in these years, it would be hard to find a more fascinating and revealing object of study than this city. A local study of such a metropolis—central to the American political economy—would, it seemed, permit a sharper focus and greater depth than if I had undertaken a diffuse study of the entire country.

The social history of the jobless and underemployed masses, an ever-shifting group of people who, despite their teeming numbers, are often invisible and forgotten, is of interest in itself. It provides a lens through which to view some of the most adverse social consequences of capitalism, and it offers insight into how people and communities react to devastating loss—loss of income, loss of identity, loss of stability, loss of modes of sociability and self-expression. It needs interpretation, however; and here is an opportunity to add further interest to the subject.

The interpretation that guides the book amounts to a rejection of the sort of attitude that is all too easy to adopt with regard to scattered and atomized millions of unfortunates like the long-term unemployed. This attitude is expressed in historian William Leuchtenburg's judgment that "most of the unemployed meekly accepted their lot," that the jobless man in the 1930s "spent his days in purposeless inactivity." Society is inclined to sweeping condescension toward those who have lost their livelihood, who have consequently, in a sense, been socially outcast. It is as if they have been rendered passive, hopeless, apathetic, even apolitical. "These are dead men," an observer wrote early in the Depression. "They are ghosts that walk the streets by day."[2] They drift along aimlessly, pitifully acquiescent, the flotsam and jetsam of a turbulent society tossed by economic gales.

Instead, throughout this book I emphasize the realism and resourcefulness, the active resistance, of the millions of families who were, to a large degree, cast aside by an unfeeling world. While despair and "acquiescence" were hardly absent, I prefer to focus on the element of what one might call spontaneity in the consciousness and behavior of the Depression's victims—the element of creativity, freedom, resilience, adaptability, and resistance to dehumanization. That is to say, I emphasize the old Marxian theme of *struggle*, indeed class struggle. My application of this concept of class struggle to the long-term unemployed, a group of people who have rarely been of paramount interest to Marxists, may seem perverse, but I think it is defensible on the basis of a few elementary considerations. First of all, as the historian G. E. M. de Ste. Croix argued long ago, there is no reason that class struggle need entail a lucid class consciousness or explicitly political action, or even collective action at all.[3] Class conflict, and therefore "struggle," is implicit in the very structure and functioning of economic institutions, which

---

2. William Leuchtenburg, *Franklin D. Roosevelt and the New Deal, 1932–1940* (New York: Harper and Row, 1963), 119. See also the various adverse judgments scattered in Arthur M. Schlesinger, Jr., *The Crisis of the Old Order: 1919–1933* (New York: Houghton Mifflin Company, 2003 [1957]), such as his statement that Franklin Roosevelt's inauguration finally awoke a nation from "apathy and daze" (p. 8).
3. G. E. M. de Ste. Croix, *The Class Struggle in the Ancient Greek World, from the Archaic Age to the Arab Conquests* (Ithaca, NY: Cornell University Press, 1981), 44, 57.

are manifestly grounded in the subjugation and domination of one class by another. It is perfectly reasonable to have an "objectivist" understanding of class struggle, and it is doubtless in this sense that Marx made his infamous but broadly correct declaration that the history of all hitherto existing society (meaning class societies, not small-scale tribal ones) is the history of class struggle.[4]

Furthermore, the very efforts of the poor and the unemployed to survive in a hostile world can themselves be called a manifestation of class struggle, being determined by one's location or nonlocation in a set of economic structures. One naturally adopts an antagonistic (or else a prudentially obedient) stance vis-à-vis economic and political authorities; correlatively, efforts to survive and adapt frequently involve collective solidarity, the solidarity of the poor with the poor. I take the feminist slogan "the personal is political" seriously: there can be a kind of political content in the most mundane day-to-day activities. In contexts of severe deprivation, the mere fact of tenaciously surviving can be a type of resistance to dominant social structures, a way of asserting oneself against realities of class and power that are, in effect, designed to crush one under the boot of the ruling class or even to erase one's existence. And out of this mundane resistance can easily emerge more conscious political action: mass demonstrations for expansive unemployment insurance, marches on relief stations organized by Unemployed Councils, and alliances between employed and unemployed workers or farmers and

---

[4]. It is puzzling that generations of intellectuals have found problematic the Marxian claim that economic relations (or production relations), incorporating class conflict, are the foundation or the "base" of society while politics, culture, and ideologies are the "superstructure." One would have thought this statement—admittedly a crude metaphor, but a useful one—to be mere common sense. After all, culture and politics are not somehow the product of spontaneous generation; they are brought into being by actors and institutions, which need *resources* in order to bring them into being. The production and distribution of resources, in particular material resources, takes place in the economic sphere. So, the way that resources are allocated according to economic structures—who gets the most, who gets the least, how the structures operate, and so on.—will be the key factor in determining, broadly speaking, the nature of a given society with its culture and politics. The interests of the wealthy will tend to dominate, but at all times individuals and groups will be struggling by various means, implicitly or explicitly, to accumulate greater resources and power for themselves. This simple argument, which grounds historical materialism or "the economic interpretation of history" in the overwhelming importance of control over resources, strikes me as compelling, however much it has to be fleshed out and dressed up in more "sophisticated" language—and however much it invites casuistic charges of "economism," "reductionism," "oversimplification," and the like. (I might note here, parenthetically, that, as Noam Chomsky sometimes remarks, intellectuals like to make relatively simple things seem complicated because it's how they earn their paycheck—it's a useful service to the ruling class to drown ideas in a flood of verbiage and jargon—and it also permits them the satisfaction of feeling profound and having deeper insight than ordinary people. Left-wing intellectual culture, which often rejects common sense and simple truths in its preference for abstruse and overwrought (though usually intellectually trivial) "theory," can be just as pretentious and anti-democratic as right-wing culture.) For an able defense of materialist common sense, see Vivek Chibber, *The Class Matrix: Social Theory after the Cultural Turn* (Cambridge: Harvard University Press, 2022).

industrial workers. Whether individual or collective, these fights for dignity and survival are all in the mode of class struggle, a concept that thereby becomes of much broader applicability than it might have seemed.[5]

Said differently, in this book I apply James C. Scott's "weapons of the weak" framework to the study of the unemployed. In his 1989 paper "Everyday Forms of Resistance," for example, Scott refers to such acts as "foot-dragging, dissimulations, false compliance, feigned ignorance, desertion, pilfering, smuggling, poaching, arson, slander, sabotage, surreptitious assault and murder, [and] anonymous threats" as characteristic forms of resistance by relatively powerless groups. "These techniques," he observes, "for the most part quite prosaic, are the ordinary means of class struggle."[6] Against the charge that he makes the concept of class resistance overly inclusive, Scott marshals a number of arguments, for instance that when such activities are sufficiently generalized to become a *pattern* of resistance, their relevance to class conflict is clear. Thus, even when workers shirk on the job or when the poor dissimulate to authorities in the hope of obtaining more unemployment relief, class resistance to dominant institutions and inegalitarian values is occurring.

In fact, however "hegemonic" values of capitalism (such as individualistic acquisitiveness), nationalism, and submission to authority may appear when one casts one's glance over a seemingly well-ordered society, implicit opposition to such values and structures is nearly ubiquitous.[7] And it would be a fruitful terrain of study for historians, sociologists, and anthropologists to excavate such latent or explicit opposition. If capitalism, for instance, means private ownership of the means of production, private

---

5. Cf. Julie Greene, "Rethinking the Boundaries of Class: Labor History and Theories of Class and Capitalism," *Labor: Studies in Working-Class History* 18, no. 2 (2021): 99. "Experiences of class," Greene writes, "including class relationships and class struggle, manifest in myriad ways, not just for higher wages or workplace control but also as social movements that may inappropriately be discounted as nonclass or middle-class." She cites "struggles over environmental justice, human rights, anticolonialism, welfare rights, or women's reproductive rights" as possible forms of class struggle.
6. James C. Scott, "Everyday Forms of Resistance," *Copenhagen Papers*, no. 4 (1989): 33–62. See also James C. Scott, *Weapons of the Weak: Everyday Forms of Peasant Resistance* (New Haven, CT: Yale University Press, 1985).
7. The historian Rick Fantasia rebukes "progressive critics of American cultural life [who] tend to sustain the hegemonic myth of culture. Individualism, narcissism, and class subordination read as personal failure," he says, "are often seen as dominant values absorbed and reproduced by the powerless with little recognition of problematic, indeed counterhegemonic, cultural practices and impulses." Rick Fantasia, *Cultures of Solidarity: Consciousness, Action, and Contemporary American Workers* (Berkeley, CA: University of California Press, 1988), 15. For thoughtful critiques of the Gramscian concept of hegemony, see Nicholas Abercrombie et al., *The Dominant Ideology Thesis* (London: George Allen & Unwin, 1980); James Scott, *Weapons of the Weak*, chapter 8; and Vivek Chibber, *The Class Matrix*, chapter 3. For further discussion of these themes, see Leon Fink, *In Search of the Working Class: Essays in American Labor History and Political Culture* (Chicago, IL: University of Illinois Press, 1994), chapter 5, and the Introduction to my own "Down but Not Out: The Unemployed in Chicago during the Great Depression" (Ph.D. diss., University of Illinois, 2017), which is available online.

control by a "boss" over the workplace, production for the single purpose of accumulating profits that are privately appropriated by the owners, and such tendencies as ever-increasing privatization of society, the mediation of more and more human interactions through market processes, and commodification of even human labor power, nature, and ideas, then it can be shown that the large majority of people are profoundly ambivalent or outright opposed to it. Much of labor history has this implication, though it is not always made clear in scholarship.

Even apart from empirical analysis, considerations of a more transhistorical nature support the perspective being sketched here. The late anthropologist David Graeber argued that, notwithstanding appearances of social atomization and cutthroat competition in capitalist society, on a deeper level nearly everyone continually acts in a "communistic" way. He called it "baseline communism." For, if communism means "from each according to his abilities, to each according to his needs" (as Marx defined it), then it simply means sharing, helping, and cooperating—giving to others in need what you're able to give them, even if it is only advice, assistance, sympathy, or some money to tide them over. Friends, coworkers, relatives, lovers, and even total strangers continually act in this way. In this sense, *"communism is the foundation of all human sociability"*; it can be considered "the raw material of sociality, a recognition of our ultimate interdependence that is the ultimate substance of social peace," as Graeber says.[8] Society is held together by this dense anticapitalist fabric, into which the more superficial patterns of commercialism, the profit motive, and greed are woven. Capitalism is thus parasitic on "everyday communism," which is but a manifestation of human needs and desires.

Lest the reader object that Graeber's conceptualization is an inadmissible politicization of the innocuous, unideological facts of spontaneous compassion, altruism, and sociality itself, I would reply, again, that to some degree "the personal is political." The altruistic, democratic, and anarchist ideology of communism, elaborated by such thinkers as Peter Kropotkin, is little but an elevation and generalization of deep-seated "moral" tendencies—propensities of "mutual aid"—in human nature.[9] When socialists or less politically conscious people object to the brutalities of capitalist society, they are doing so on the basis of "unideological" impulses of sympathy and compassion, values of individual self-determination and group cooperation, which are, historically speaking, the heart of anarchist communism. It is therefore hardly far-fetched to perceive the seed of political radicalism in some of the most quotidian practices and emotional impulses of ordinary people, just as radicalism is latently or consciously present in the class struggles of the poor or the relatively powerless.

---

8. David Graeber, "On the Moral Grounds of Economic Relations: A Maussian Approach," *Journal of Classical Sociology* 14, no. 1 (2014): 65–77. See also David Graeber, *Debt: The First 5000 Years* (New York: Melville House, 2011), 94–102.
9. See Peter Kropotkin, *Mutual Aid: A Factor of Evolution* (Mineola, NY: Dover Publications, 2006 [1902]) and *The Conquest of Bread* (Mineola, NY: Dover Publications, 2011 [1906]). Rutger Bregman, *Humankind: A Hopeful History* (New York: Little, Brown and Company, 2019) is a fascinating investigation of the fundamental decency and moral awareness of humanity.

While everyday communism may, informally, be widespread even in the higher echelons of corporate America, historically it has been especially pronounced among the lower classes—the peasantry, industrial workers, struggling immigrants, the petty bourgeoisie—who have relied on it for survival in hard times and even in normal times. Moreover, these classes have simply not been as deeply integrated into commercial structures and ideologies as the upper classes have. Social history has done much to illuminate the "communism" (without calling it that) of the American working class during its many formative decades, through description of the thick networks of voluntary associations that workers created among themselves, and of the "mutualist" ethic to which they subscribed in the context of their battles with employers, and in general of the vitally *public* (antimarket, anti-individualistic, antiprivatized) character of much of their shared culture up to at least the 1940s (in fact beyond).[10] The long-term unemployed as such, however, have tended to be overlooked in this historiography, so I try to remedy that lacuna in the later chapters of this book. For unemployment did not produce only atomization, as is commonly supposed; it also gave rise to the opposite, community and solidarity. And that is what is most interesting to study.

My "agenda" with this book, then, is to highlight the brute material realities and imperatives that structure social life. Rather than focusing on cultural discourses, mass political indoctrination, ideological consent, or the hegemony of the ruling class as forces of social stability, I emphasize the more basic facts of class conflict, economic and political coercion, and ruling-class violence (or its threat) as fundamental to containing the struggles and strivings of subordinate groups. This was true in the 1930s and it is true today, notwithstanding the tendency of contemporary humanistic scholarship to privilege culture or *discourses* over the role of violence and institutional compulsion. (Graeber makes an apt comment in *The Utopia of Rules* (2015): "graduate students [are] able to spend days in the stacks of university libraries poring over Foucault-inspired theoretical tracts about the declining importance of coercion as a factor in modern life without ever reflecting on the fact that, had they insisted on their right to enter the stacks without showing a properly stamped and validated ID, armed men would have been summoned to physically remove

---

10. See, among countless others, Herbert Gutman, *Work, Culture, and Society in Industrializing America: Essays in American Working-Class and Social History* (New York: Alfred A. Knopf, 1976); Herbert Gutman, *Power and Culture: Essays on the American Working Class*, ed. Ira Berlin (New York: Pantheon Books, 1987); David Montgomery, *The Fall of the House of Labor* (Cambridge: Cambridge University Press, 1987); Leon Fink, *The Maya of Morganton: Work and Community in the Nuevo New South* (Chapel Hill, NC: University of North Carolina Press, 2003); Paul Avrich, *Sacco and Vanzetti: The Anarchist Background* (Princeton, NJ: Princeton University Press, 1991); Susan Porter Benson, *Household Accounts: Working-Class Family Economies in the Interwar United States* (Ithaca, NY: Cornell University Press, 2007); Lawrence Goodwyn, *Democratic Promise: The Populist Movement in America* (New York: Oxford University Press, 1976); Charles M. Payne, *I've Got the Light of Freedom: The Organizing Tradition and the Mississippi Freedom Struggle* (Berkeley, CA: University of California Press, 2007); Steve Leikin, *The Practical Utopians: American Workers and the Cooperative Movement in the Gilded Age* (Detroit, MI: Wayne State University Press, 2005).

them, using whatever force might be required."¹¹) It was force, first and foremost, that contained the Depression's mass groundswell, anchored initially in an unemployed constituency, of opposition to basic norms and institutions of capitalism. As we'll see—contrary to liberal verities that have reigned since the postwar era—the popular movements of the early 1930s were in effect quasi-socialist and collectivist in their goals and practices.¹²

It is doubtless true that we all have a "divided consciousness" on questions of social and political organization, commitments to contradictory values—commitments not always conscious but revealed in our behavior—and are susceptible to indoctrination by institutions in the media, politics, and the corporate economy. Scholarship has established this fact beyond doubt.¹³ Since at least the time of World War I and the Creel Committee on Public Information (dedicated to "manufacturing consent" in favor of America's participation in the war), government and big business have devoted colossal resources to molding the public mind in a way friendly to the power of the ruling class. And their efforts have often met with considerable success. On the other hand, the very fact that it is necessary to constantly deluge the public with overwhelming amounts of propaganda, and to censor and marginalize views and information associated with the

---

11. David Graeber, *The Utopia of Rules: On Technology, Stupidity, and the Secret Joys of Bureaucracy* (Brooklyn, NY: Melville House, 2015), 58. For some brief critiques of postmodern idealism, see Chris Wright, *Notes of an Underground Humanist* (Bradenton, FL: Booklocker, 2013), chapters 1 and 2. Charles Tilly states the matter concisely: "The central, tragic fact is simple: coercion *works*; those who apply substantial force to their fellows get compliance, and from that compliance draw the multiple advantages of money, goods, deference, access to pleasures denied to less powerful people." Charles Tilly, *Coercion, Capital, and European States, AD 990–1992* (Cambridge, MA: Blackwell, 1992), 70.
12. On the "liberal verities": Lizabeth Cohen, for example, in her classic *Making a New Deal*, argues that workers wanted nothing more radical than a somewhat stronger state and stronger unions. See Lizabeth Cohen, *Making a New Deal: Industrial Workers in Chicago, 1919–1939* (New York: Cambridge University Press, 1990), chapter 6. Jefferson Cowie, following Alan Brinkley and other historians influenced by the "liberal consensus" school of thought, espouses an even more conventional liberalism with his insistence on the durability of "individualism" even at the darkest moments of the Depression. Jefferson Cowie, *The Great Exception: The New Deal and the Limits of American Politics* (Princeton, NJ: Princeton University Press, 2016), chapter 4. See also the blandly liberal essay he wrote with Nick Salvatore titled "The Long Exception: Rethinking the Place of the New Deal in American History," *International Labor and Working-Class History* 74 (Fall 2008): 3–32, an essay even more "idealistic" than his book in its reliance on tropes of so-called individualism, "a deep and abiding individualism" ahistorically embedded in the core of American culture from Populism through the New Deal to Richard Nixon and George W. Bush. This is a particularly vulgar, essentialist, superficial culturalism.
13. See, for example, Alex Carey, *Taking the Risk Out of Democracy: Corporate Propaganda versus Freedom and Liberty* (Urbana, IL: University of Illinois Press, 1997); Elizabeth Fones-Wolf, *Selling Free Enterprise: The Business Assault on Labor and Liberalism, 1945–60* (Chicago, IL: University of Illinois Press, 1994); Edward S. Herman and Noam Chomsky, *Manufacturing Consent: The Political Economy of the Mass Media* (New York: Knopf Doubleday Publishing, 1988); Patricia Cayo Sexton, *The War on Labor and the Left: Understanding America's Unique Conservatism* (Boulder, CO: Westview Press, Inc., 1991); Neil Postman, *Amusing Ourselves to Death: Public Discourse in the Age of Show Business* (New York: Penguin Books, 1985).

political left, is significant.[14] Why would such a massive and everlasting public relations campaign be necessary if the populace didn't have subversive or "dangerous" values and beliefs in the first place? It is evidently imperative to *continuously police* people's behavior and thoughts in order that popular resistance does not overwhelm structures of class and power.

What is interesting about the 1930s is that the ordinary methods of mass regimentation and indoctrination—methods that at the best of times are only partially successful (as shown, for example, by polls[15])—substantially broke down and the working class had an opportunity to collectively fight for its interests and achieve some limited versions of its goals. Insofar as society in the coming years may see a similar breakdown of established norms and hierarchies, it is of interest to reconsider that earlier time.

The fact is that the political program of a remarkably broad swath of Americans in the 1930s would, if enacted, have constituted a revolution without a "revolution." Upton Sinclair's End Poverty in California campaign, Huey Long's Share Our Wealth program, Father Charles Coughlin's overwhelmingly left-wing radio broadcasts in 1934 and 1935 ("Capitalism is doomed and not worth trying to save"), and the immensely popular though forgotten Workers' Unemployment Insurance Bill, introduced in Congress in 1934 and 1935 in opposition to the more conservative Social Security Act, all amounted to full-on class war against the rich.[16] Again, this is not the received interpretation among historians and social scientists, who have often preferred to emphasize (and puzzle over) Americans' supposed individualism and conservatism relative to, say, the "socialistic" and "class-conscious" Europeans, but in Chapter six I will defend my unorthodox interpretation at some length.[17]

---

14. To take just one example out of thousands, the fact that such a world-famous intellectual as Noam Chomsky has rarely been allowed to appear on mainstream American television or invited to write columns for establishment publications is extremely telling, in fact an eloquent confirmation of his well-known arguments regarding media propaganda and corporate self-censorship. On the Committee on Public Information, see John Maxwell Hamilton, *Manipulating the Masses: Woodrow Wilson and the Birth of American Propaganda* (Baton Rouge, LA: Louisiana State University Press, 2020).
15. See Benjamin I. Page and Robert Y. Shapiro, *The Rational Public: Fifty Years of Trends in Americans' Policy Preferences* (Chicago, IL: University of Chicago Press, 1992). Even in the 1980s, a time of conservative ascendancy, most Americans thought big business and the wealthy had too much power, environmental and safety regulations should be strengthened "regardless of cost," the wealthy should pay more in taxes, and so on.
16. See Robert McElvaine, *The Great Depression: America, 1929–1941* (New York: Three Rivers Press, 2009), 238–40. Also see Eric Leif Davin, "Blue Collar Democracy: Class War and Political Revolution in Western Pennsylvania, 1932–1937," *Pennsylvania History: A Journal of Mid-Atlantic Studies* 67, no. 2 (Spring 2000): 240–97. For example, p. 244: "Fundamentally, the political mobilization of the working class in the thirties was a class war for political and economic equality."
17. For a persuasive argument against this sort of American exceptionalism and in favor of the idea that "there is a history of class consciousness in the United States comparable to that of working-class movements in Britain and on the Continent," see Sean Wilentz, "Against Exceptionalism: Class Consciousness and the American Labor Movement, 1790–1920,"

The book is organized as follows. In Chapter one I provide a brief overview of the Great Depression and its effects on Chicago, and then, at the end, summarize again some of the arguments I'll make in later chapters. The second chapter is different from the others in saying nothing about the *agency* of the unemployed, consisting instead of a litany of the woes they had to endure. While not much is said explicitly about the machinations of Chicago's political and business elite, in its totality it serves as an implied critique of the class priorities of this elite that was happy to sacrifice the well-being of hundreds of thousands on the altar of "lower costs."

The third chapter explores some of the dimensions of people's "activeness," specifically the ways they coped with the tragedies that had befallen them. Having been virtually outcast from many of society's dominant institutions, the long-term unemployed had to reconstruct their lives even in the midst of their collapse. In most cases this would not have been possible if the poor had not been munificent in aiding one another—a feature of Depression life that scholars have still not exhaustively analyzed. In addition, I examine the many ways in which the Depression's victims constructed their own modes of recreation, from sports to gambling to dancing.

The fourth chapter is devoted to "the unattached," who often had to live in flophouses or public shelters because they could not afford their own rooms. Not until late 1935 did Chicago's relief administration provide outdoor relief, or home relief, to most of the unattached, and even then thousands still used the free shelters that remained open or the cheap flophouses in the Hobohemian district. I describe the miserable conditions in which "shelter men" lived, conditions that reveal much about the class-determined priorities of the economic and political elite. Shelter clients, it seems, tended to be well aware of class structures and the conflict between rich and poor that shaped U.S. politics, even organizing with the help of Communists to press for changes in shelter administration. I focus on what these men thought of their situation and on how they adjusted to being the objects of inhumane policies.

In the following chapter I discuss three types of institutions that had an impact on the unemployed: governments, unions, and churches. With regard to the first, I demonstrate what a low priority the well-being of the poor was to the Chicago and Illinois governments by recounting the dreary story of relief financing from 1930 to 1941, which is to say the story of how political authorities singularly failed to provide for the millions of Illinoisans thrown out of work. As a wealthy state that periodically even had budget surpluses, Illinois certainly could have afforded to be more generous than it was in the funds it diverted to relief. (In general, historians have not sufficiently highlighted the degree to which miserly relief policies were a political choice rather than an economic

---

International Labor and Working-Class History, no. 26 (Fall 1984): 1–24. See also Rick Fantasia, *Cultures of Solidarity*; Jeremy Brecher, *Strike!* (Boston, MA: South End Press, 1997); Sharon Smith, *Subterranean Fire: A History of Working-Class Radicalism in the United States* (Chicago, IL: Haymarket Books, 2018); John F. Manley, "Marx in America: The New Deal," *Science & Society* 67, no. 1 (Spring 2003): 9–38. Michael Denning reconstructs the extremely broad cultural appeal and influence of communism, socialism, and Marxism during the 1930s in *The Cultural Front: The Laboring of American Culture in the Twentieth Century* (New York: Verso, 1997).

necessity.) Unions and churches, on the other hand, frequently showed striking compassion for, and solidarity with, the unemployed, although their inadequate resources prevented them from being as effective as they might have been.

The picture I delineate in this chapter might seem too clear-cut, the contrasts (between government and voluntary associations) exaggerated, as if I am simplifying or caricaturing the reality. Such a criticism, indeed, is often made of Marxian or "left-wing" accounts: they are said to be reductive, oversimplifying, too class focused, or one-dimensional. Liberal historians, say, are apt to criticize a work like Howard Zinn's famous *A People's History of the United States* for its one-sidedness or "oversimplifications," unaware that in order to understand the world at all it is necessary to simplify it a bit and explain it in terms of general principles.[18] This is what science does, for example, abstracting from the infinite complexity of a given natural phenomenon in order to formulate a few dominant laws that provide a basis for understanding. There is little point in simply reproducing reality in all its many-splendored complexity; this is mere description for its own sake, not much different from data collection, as opposed to explanation or understanding. While complications must be allowed for and introduced, the writer who "reduces" a confusing mess of phenomena to the principle of class conflict is (if he can support his arguments with evidence) proceeding in a properly scientific way, simplifying the world in order to understand it.[19]

Thus, while I try not to romanticize the functions of unions and churches in relation to the unemployed, I do draw a rather stark contrast between the behavior of local and state governments that were substantially in thrall to the business community and the behavior of more "popular" institutions that to some extent succeeded in breaking away from the values and priorities of the ruling class. The record of unions and churches in

---

18. The celebrated liberal historian Jill Lepore, for instance, expresses misplaced condescension toward Zinn in her *New Yorker* article "Zinn's History," February 3, 2010. See Nathan Robinson, "The Limits of Liberal History," *Current Affairs*, October 28, 2018 (available online) for a brilliant evisceration of Lepore's own attempt at a national history, her bestselling *These Truths: A History of the United States* (New York: W. W. Norton & Company, 2018). Among other weaknesses, she has forgotten that the country has a labor history. This is the kind of oversight predictable when one denies the fundamental importance of class.
19. Karl Kautsky said the same thing when he wrote, "[T]he task of science is not simply a presentation of that which *is*, giving a faithful photograph of reality, so that any normally constituted observer will form the same image. The task of science consists in observing the general, essential element in the mass of impressions and phenomena received, and thus providing a clue by means of which we can find our bearings in the labyrinth of reality." Karl Kautsky, *Foundations of Christianity: A Study in Christian Origins* (New York: Monthly Review Press, 1972 [1908]), 12. "Simplifications," in other words, need not be false or misleading; if they're the right ones (i.e., if they correspond to reality), they can be extremely clarifying. See also Adam Jones's interview with Noam Chomsky titled "The Radical Vocation," February 20, 1990, at https://zcomm.org/wp-content/uploads/zbooks/www/chomsky/9002-vocation.html, where Chomsky explains that being somewhat "black and white" in one's analysis—for example, dividing the world (*to a first approximation*) between, crudely speaking, the capitalists and the workers or the rulers and the ruled—is exactly the rational method, the *scientific* method, the method that's necessary in order to understand how society works.

Chicago was far from morally spotless, but in their aggregate they made a difference in the lives of the economically insecure. I am also interested in how these oppressed people, such as Blacks on the South Side, used their religious life, in part, as a sublimation of struggle, of opposition to dominant values and institutions.

One can certainly interpret religion, in the classical Marxist way, as serving to accommodate people to an oppressive social system by encouraging them to fix their gaze on a fantastical otherworldly paradise that distracts from the imperative project of changing the actually existing world.[20] Similarly, insofar as values of community, love, and altruism may find an outlet in religious life that is frequently denied them in capitalist economic and social life, church attendance can help reconcile people to a harshly competitive, exploitative, and inhumane society. Indeed, a large scholarly literature has established that religion has (often—not always) in the last two centuries been of inestimable benefit to the capitalist class in its obsession with disciplining the working class and subjecting it to the merciless rhythms of industrial production—as well as mobilizing it to support conservative political causes.[21] Nevertheless, I find it of greater interest to puncture these old and undeniable truths by highlighting some of the *contrary* uses of religion, the ways it can serve as a more realistic, if quotidian, means of struggle and self-assertion than, say, the sort of agitation for a hopeless "revolution" that American Communists engaged in during the 1930s. There was a lot of good sense and realism in working-class religion in these years (and not only these years).

I might note here, parenthetically, that, given its interpretive slant, the book contains little discussion of some topics that a "thorough" or all-encompassing social history would touch upon. Such issues as the (very limited) extent to which working-class people may have mobilized in favor of a conservative or fascist politics and the intricacies of Chicago's vast relief administration do not appear in the book. They are not strictly relevant to my arguments. Similarly, if it seems that my negative view of capitalism—and

---

20. See David McClellan, *Marxism and Religion: A Description and Assessment of the Marxist Critique of Christianity* (London: Macmillan Press, 1987); Karl Marx and Friedrich Engels, *Karl Marx and Friedrich Engels on Religion* (Mineola, NY: Dover Press, 2008).
21. Among many others, see E. P. Thompson, *The Making of the English Working Class* (New York: Pantheon Books, 1963); Max Weber, *The Protestant Ethic and the Spirit of Capitalism* (New York: Routledge, 2001 [1905]); E. P. Thompson, "Time, Work-Discipline, and Industrial Capitalism," *Past & Present*, no. 38 (December 1967): 56–97; Paul E. Johnson, *A Shopkeeper's Millennium: Society and Revivals in Rochester, New York, 1815–1837* (New York: Hill and Wang, 2004 [1978]); Charles Sellers, *The Market Revolution: Jacksonian America, 1815–1846* (New York: Oxford University Press, 1991), chapters 7 and 8; Catriona M. Parratt, *"More than Mere Amusement": Working-Class Women's Leisure in England, 1750–1914* (Boston, MA: Northeastern University Press, 2001); Elizabeth Fones-Wolf and Ken Fones-Wolf, *Struggle for the Soul of the Postwar South: White Evangelical Protestants and Operation Dixie* (Chicago, IL: University of Illinois Press, 2015); Kevin Kruse, *One Nation Under God: How Corporate America Invented Christian America* (New York: Basic Books, 2015); Bethany Moreton, *To Serve God and Wal-Mart: The Making of Christian Free Enterprise* (Cambridge, MA: Harvard University Press, 2009); Lisa McGirr, *Suburban Warriors: The Origins of the New American Right* (Princeton, NJ: Princeton University Press, 2002); Darren Dochuk, *From Bible Belt to Sunbelt: Plain-Folk Religion, Grassroots Politics, and the Rise of Evangelical Conservatism* (New York: W. W. Norton & Co., 2011).

foregrounding of working-class opposition to it—is biased or "one-dimensional," I would reply, again, that to conceptualize and understand society it is necessary to pick out dominant tendencies and contrast them with others. Through this sharpening and straightening of lines, *abstracted* from the welter of reality, one achieves a firmer grasp of what is at stake in social dynamics and social analysis. Humanistic scholarship's tendency to revel in ambiguity for its own sake and "problematize" all simplifications or old truths (frequently Marxian or "class reductionist" truths), privileging the *exception* over the *rule*, the *particular* at the expense of the *general*, is liable merely to obfuscate and cloud understanding.[22] (Not coincidentally, it thus serves also to uphold the rule of a dominant class, by distracting from insights into how power works and how working people are continually, albeit sometimes confusedly, engaged in some form of struggle against it. This service of "distraction" and obfuscation is an important function of much liberal and postmodern historiography, and explains why such scholarship, as opposed to critical "materialist" scholarship, has been allowed to become the norm.)

The sixth chapter follows my account of the politics of relief with a discussion of the politics and activism of the unemployed. My main concern, again, is to highlight the realism and frequent militancy of ordinary people, to challenge the notion of their easy acceptance of what Marxists have sometimes called "bourgeois hegemony." Especially when material comforts fall away and people sense that they are being treated unfairly, radicalization can happen very quickly. The "self-blame" of the unemployed, for example, was not such a universal reaction as historians have implied.[23] And even when

---

22. As Chomsky remarks in the abovementioned interview with Adam Jones, "Humanistic scholarship—I'm caricaturing a bit for simplicity—says every fact is precious; you put it alongside every other fact. That's a sure way to guarantee you'll never understand anything. If you tried to do that in the sciences, you wouldn't even reach the level of Babylonian astronomy." It would be unfair of me to cite particular works here as examples of what he means, but suffice it to say that much postmodern scholarship takes a kind of perverse pride in problematizing the indispensable "metanarrative" of the Marxian, class-centric approach to history, preferring to emphasize "contingency," "discontinuity," fragmentary perspectives, diffuse description for its own sake (as if recognition of ambiguity or complexity is the highest scholarly virtue, rather than an analytical nonstarter), the ways that class doesn't explain *everything*, and idealistic focus on "discourses." For an illustration of just how essential a grounding in *class* is, see Peter Mitchell and John Schoeffel, eds., *Understanding Power: The Indispensable Chomsky* (New York: The New Press, 2002). This book will give the reader more insight into the nature of power—and society—than all the works of Foucault put together. (Vivek Chibber, *The Class Matrix*, is another useful rejoinder to postmodern cultural theory.) For more examples of the sort of materialist writing that power structures loathe—because it's too penetrating and subversive—see the (absurdly but predictably neglected) works of Gabriel Kolko, such as *The Roots of American Foreign Policy: An Analysis of Power and Purpose* (Boston, MA: Beacon Press, 1969), *Confronting the Third World: United States Foreign Policy, 1945–1980* (New York: Pantheon, 1988), and his masterful *The Limits of Power: The World and United States Foreign Policy, 1945–54* (New York: Harper & Row, 1972). For general comments on contemporary historical scholarship, see the Introduction to my "Down but Not Out."
23. See, for example, Cowie, *The Great Exception*, 100: "The supposedly collectivist 'red decade' actually featured a long line of individual declarations of self-blame, guilt, doubt, and

there was self-blame, anger at an unjust society was not infrequently present as well. Such anger helped motivate the radicalism that emerged on local and national scales, a radicalism of both "form"—including widespread occupying of private property, sit-ins at relief stations and legislative chambers, continual demonstrations and hunger marches, collective thefts—and "content," which is to say the policy goals many of which were in essence revolutionary.

The question of why these "revolutionary" policy goals, despite their popularity, nevertheless failed can be answered in a number of ways, but what they all boil down to is that the ruling class and its representatives had far more resources than oppositional movements. Through force, media censorship, and the lack of sympathy of national and state-level power centers (Congress, the Roosevelt administration, state legislatures, etc.), it was possible to suppress movements that, in fact, because of their insufficient resources—itself a result of their being contrary to the interests of the owning class—even had difficulty organizing nationally in the first place.[24]

Throughout the book I try to make distinctions between subcategories of the unemployed, such as different ethnicities and income levels. The most obvious distinctions are between Blacks and whites, especially native whites, because the hardships of Blacks were more acute than those of whites. Not surprisingly, then, the former were more frequently militant and "class conscious" than the latter. However, what I found in the course of research was that, despite my attempts to differentiate between groups, having similar class positions tends to homogenize experiences, values, and ideas. I am reminded of what the historian Susan Porter Benson argued in her analysis of working-class family economies in the interwar years: "when it came to confronting the market, ethnicity became a kind of second-order influence; some groups, in some places, turned more to one strategy than to another, but the difference was more one of degree than of kind, and all drew on a common array of strategies."[25] Class was supreme.

It may seem odd for a Marxist to write a somewhat positive account of the long-term unemployed, who have traditionally not been of paramount interest to Marxists. The actively working industrial proletariat has been seen as the most revolutionary class, the unemployed more akin to the despised "lumpenproletariat." In fact, in *Worker Cooperatives and Revolution: History and Possibilities in the United States* (2014) I have argued that the focus on the industrial working class was always rather limited, that any

---

despair. Given the massive economic failure, the ways in which working people internalized the blame for their situation bordered on the pathological."
24. For a study that recognizes the breadth and depth of left-wing support among Americans in the 1930s but credits Roosevelt as almost singlehandedly defeating the prospects of a socialist political party, see Seymour Martin Lipset, "Roosevelt and the Protest of the 1930s," *Minnesota Law Review* 68 (1984): 273–98. Other scholars prefer a more multifaceted analysis of the left's defeats, adducing not only Roosevelt's political genius but also widespread repression, fratricidal war between the AFL and the CIO, and the South's commitment to white supremacy. See, for example, Mike Davis, *Prisoners of the American Dream: Politics and Economy in the History of the U.S. Working Class* (New York: Verso, 1986), chapter 2; and Ira Katznelson, *Fear Itself: The New Deal and the Origins of Our Time* (New York: Liveright Publishing Co., 2003).
25. Benson, *Household Accounts*, 7.

collective agent of "socialist revolution"—a revolution, incidentally, that would have to be *gradual* rather than insurrectionary or completely "ruptural"—would surely include a variety of groups relatively disempowered or exploited by late capitalism, among them service sector workers, the young, the jobless, many peasants and farmers, and so on.[26] It isn't creditable or sensible for Marxists to be scornful of a large and permanent subcategory of the working class (viz., those without work) that will likely continue to grow in the coming years and decades. On the other hand, no group of "the oppressed" should be romanticized either. While I have found it more interesting to try to "problematize" conventional dismissive and negative stereotypes of the unemployed, I hope I have not romanticized or homogenized a very diverse group of people. By reconceptualizing class struggle, for example, I have not meant to ascribe certain conscious ideological beliefs to people many of whom doubtless remained, at least in their own eyes, politically conservative. I have simply tried to apply a more objectivist and, I think, defensible understanding of the concept than the collectivist and subjectivist (involving an elusive thing called "class consciousness") understanding that tends to prevail.

If nothing else, I hope to have partially rehabilitated a category of people who, despite the very real impact they made on American history, have generally elicited far less interest than the industrial workers who a few years later built the Congress of Industrial Organizations. This lack of interest is ironic, for it was the struggles of the jobless in the early 1930s that provoked the most fear among authorities and most threatened the stability of the social order.

---

26. Chris Wright, *Worker Cooperatives and Revolution: History and Possibilities in the United States* (Bradenton, FL: Booklocker, 2014), chapter 4. See also my article "Marxism and the Solidarity Economy: Toward a New Theory of Revolution," *Class, Race and Corporate Power* 9, no. 1 (2021). Both the book and the article are available for free online.

Chapter One

OVERVIEW

In retrospect, it is easy to observe the clouds gathering before the whirlwind was unleashed in 1929–30. In early 1928, the Salvation Army in Chicago had a breadline of 200–600 people every day. "The horde of 'boes and panhandlers infesting the Loop," one writer complained, "makes New York's Times Square parasites seem like a coterie of philanthropists in comparison." A more sympathetic entity, the United Charities, appealed desperately for funds with which to help the unemployed, the many thousands of men in Chicago who had been out of work for months. Eviction notices coming to the attention of the United Charities had, by February 1928, increased from about ten a month to two or three hundred. Job seekers streamed in from Detroit, from the South, from depressed agricultural areas of the Midwest, exacerbating the problem such that already in the fall of 1927 there were at least 100,000 jobless in Chicago. The following March, the Communist Unemployed Council of Chicago led a demonstration of hundreds around City Hall who carried banners declaring "Our Children Are Hungry" and "200,000 Men Out of Work in Chicago." Mounted police swung clubs, yanked speakers down from their perches, and arrested leaders, until the gathering was dispersed and the frightened noonday shoppers could resume their business.[1]

Unemployment lessened that year as the weather warmed, but it was clear, or should have been, that underneath the glittering façade of this second Gilded Age was a deep economic rot that was affecting millions. In the spring of 1928, the American Federation of Labor estimated that an average of 18 percent of its membership was unemployed—12 percent in Chicago, 23 percent in New York, and 36 percent in Cleveland. And since this elite minority of workers could get help from unions in securing and keeping jobs, the percentage among the unorganized was surely higher. A study by the National Resources Committee estimated that 12 percent of workers in 1927 and 10 percent in 1929 were jobless, but many more must have experienced the condition temporarily and even more worked only part-time. Seasonal fluctuations grew especially severe in the late 1920s, but even in "good times" work was unsteady for at least a quarter of the working population. By 1928, intellectuals and social workers around

---

1. "Chicago's Heavy Breadline Tells of Unemployment," *Variety*, February 1, 1928; "Emergency Plea Made in Behalf of Unemployed," *Chicago Tribune*, February 28, 1928; "Unemployment Increases in 'Chi,'" *Pittsburgh Courier*, January 14, 1928; "100,000 Jobless in Chicago," *New York Times*, September 16, 1927; "Police Rout Mob Parading in Loop as Unemployed," *Chicago Tribune*, March 29, 1928.

the country, even internationally, had become alarmed at the growing incidence of joblessness and lengthening of its periods for individuals: the Belgian economist Henri de Man, for example, concluded that one of the most marked characteristics of modern industrialism was the rapidly growing class of permanently unemployed, and a Boston conference of the National Federation of Settlements in June 1928 declared that the greatest threat to the contemporary family was unemployment.[2]

More than a year before the Depression began, a researcher collected hundreds of harrowing case studies of unemployment in a book, *Some Folks Won't Work*, that became a national bestseller. Typical of them is the following laconic set of notes on a Black family in Chicago:

> Painter and decorator. Two children, one married. Son aged nineteen, truck driver, unemployed. Fine couple, hard working and provident. Formerly always able to weather dull seasons with savings. Had been able to pay $2000 down on $5000 house, and had paid off all but $1700 in monthly installments when unemployment struck them. [...] Wife has helped by cooking out and taking care of confinements. Took in boarders. Car laid up. Payments on house and union dues lapsed. [...] Enough money borrowed from friends to save house. Food cut to $4 a week for three people.[3]

So it went for many millions of people in 1928 and 1929 (and earlier).

Why was the prosperity of the "Roaring Twenties" so fragile and superficial as all this? Why was it to culminate in the greatest depression in the history of capitalism? The main reasons, arguably, were already understood by liberals and, especially, leftists of the time, years before John Maynard Keynes systematized some of their ideas. Central to them was the growing inadequacy of mass purchasing power in the United States, in large part a consequence of the sickly state of organized labor.[4] Income and wealth inequality, for example, were acute, with the top 0.1 percent of families in 1929 receiving as much as the bottom 42 percent. The top 0.5 percent of Americans also owned 32.4 percent of all the net wealth of individuals. Poverty was widespread, 12 million families—more than two in five—having incomes below $1,500, which itself was (according to the Brookings Institution) $500 below the income required to supply basic necessities.

---

2. "Union Unemployment Keeps at High Mark," *New York Times*, April 30, 1928; "American Trade-Unions and the Problem of Unemployment," *Monthly Labor Review*, March, 1928: 8–27; David Weintraub, "Unemployment and Increasing Productivity," in National Resources Committee, *Technological Trends and National Policy* (Washington, DC: United States Government Printing Office, 1937), 70; Irving Bernstein, *The Lean Years: A History of the American Worker, 1920–1933* (Baltimore, MD: Penguin Books, 1966), 60; Robert McElvaine, *The Great Depression: America, 1929–1941* (New York: Three Rivers Press, 2009), 22; Clinch Calkins, *Some Folks Won't Work* (New York: Harcourt, Brace and Company, 1930), 17–19.
3. Calkins, *Some Folks Won't Work*, 44, 45.
4. Trade union membership had by 1929 declined from a wartime peak of 5 million to less than 3.5 million—out of a labor force of 49 million. David M. Kennedy, *Freedom from Fear: The American People in the Great Depression* (New York: Oxford University Press, 1999), 25; Bernstein, *The Lean Years*, 55.

Seventy-one percent of families in 1929 earned less than $2,500. The weakness of consumer demand implied by such facts contrasted ominously with the impressive rise of productivity during the 1920s, manufacturing output per labor hour leaping 72 percent and output per unit of capital 52 percent. With productive capacity increasing precipitously and aggregate demand much more slowly, capacity utilization was inevitably declining—excess capacity rising, in other words—and markets were becoming saturated by the end of the decade. Sooner or later, out of businesses' efforts to maintain profits, these trends had to manifest themselves in reduced investment and heightened cost-cutting, which meant, for example, employee layoffs and wage reductions, which only reinforced the underlying macroeconomic problem of low demand. A vicious circle thereby developed, in which the capitalist solution to the problem of shrinking markets served to exacerbate the problem. By mid-1929, this process, and the resultant downturn in business activity that would usher in the Depression, was underway.[5]

Communist analyses of the economy in the late 1920s were prescient and of lasting value. They were grounded in the insight that—in Marxian language—"the most basic contradiction of capitalism [is] the contradiction between the growth of productive forces and the lagging behind of the markets." Out of their compulsion to increase profits lest they be swallowed up by competitors, businesses generally have to raise labor productivity relentlessly, which is accomplished through technical and organizational innovations that make possible the employing of fewer workers, the deskilling and thus cheapening of the labor power that remains, the speeding up and intensifying of the work process, successful offensives against labor unions, and other means of reducing costs and increasing output. The dysfunctional consequence of these imperatives is that fewer and fewer people have the money to buy the greater output that is possible, a fact that, as was just mentioned, causes businesses to cut back investment and squeeze workers even *more* in order to maintain profits. (It is at this point, as liberals argued, that the government has to step in to boost demand and so keep capitalism functioning, which, in the context of the Great Depression, it finally did on the necessary scale during and after World War II.)[6]

The fantastic technological achievements of the 1920s, which included electrification, mass automotive transport, and mass production innovations, were therefore partly responsible for the precarious foundations of the economy and the resultant severe depression of the 1930s. "Technological unemployment"—that is, people's loss of work due to mechanization and automation—was bemoaned by commentators from the political center to the far left. William Green, head of the AFL, observed in 1929 that

---

5. Maurice Leven, Harold G. Moulton, and Clark Warburton, *America's Capacity to Consume* (Washington, DC: Brookings Institution, 1934), 55, 56; McElvaine, *The Great Depression*, 38, 39; Richard Du Boff, *Accumulation and Power: An Economic History of the United States* (Armonk, NY: M. E. Sharpe, Inc., 1989), 85–89. See also James Devine, "Underconsumption, Overinvestment, and the Origins of the Great Depression," *Review of Radical Politics Economics* 15, no. 1 (Spring 1983): 1–27; and Paul Burkett, "Forgetting the Lessons of the Great Depression," *Review of Social Economy* 52, no. 1 (Spring 1994): 60–91.
6. N. Ross, "A Note on the Development of Post-War Capitalism in the U.S.," *Communist*, September 1929: 512–28; Du Boff, *Accumulation and Power*, 91–106.

in the steel industry seven men could now cast as much pig iron as 60 could before, and one man could as efficiently operate open-hearth furnaces as 42 under old methods. In the machinist industry one unskilled worker could replace 25 skilled ones, while in textiles, 3,000 replaced 5,100. Because of such tremendous productivity advances, manufacturing employment in the 1920s not only didn't noticeably expand but may even have shrunk, as did the labor force in the extractive industries such as agriculture and mining. Work in the white-collar and service sectors, by contrast—which was frequently more insecure, low paying, and temporary than in manufacturing—expanded 45 percent. This was, however, far from sufficient to absorb industrial workers laid off by mechanization and other causes, as a Brookings Institution study in 1928 concluded. Of 754 workers surveyed who had been laid off in the preceding 12 months, 344 had still not found permanent employment, and the large majority of the total had been out of work for more than a quarter of the year. The temporary jobs secured by 234 included road building, selling newspapers, clerking in stores on Saturdays, and mowing lawns.[7]

Exacerbating the problem of finding employment was the huge influx of rural inhabitants into cities. The agricultural depression that had begun in 1921, a result of global overproduction of crops, forced millions off the land—according to some estimates about four million between 1920 and 1929. Again, advances in productivity ironically had deleterious consequences, in that the increased use of trucks and tractors on farms made superfluous a large proportion of the agricultural labor force. These years also witnessed Blacks' Great Migration north, which brought tens of thousands more people to Chicago's overflowing Black Belt, and many more to Detroit, New York, St. Louis, Philadelphia, Cleveland, and other cities. Indeed, it was primarily large cities, not smaller towns, that attracted rural migrants, which of course put extra pressure on the job market, wages (downward), and welfare agencies in these places. More and more, people had to shift from city to city in search of work.[8]

One of the factors that enabled economic growth to continue for years despite the growing size of this "precariat" (as it might be called today) was the enormous expansion of credit. Buying products in monthly or weekly installments because one could not afford them became a widespread practice for the first time. By the end of the decade, 60 percent of cars and 80 percent of radios were sold on credit. Neighborhood shopkeepers routinely had to extend credit to their loyal customers, trusting that their bouts of unemployment would be temporary. The superabundance of credit in the U.S. economy (and the Federal Reserve's easy-money policy in 1927) also encouraged rampant speculation in the stock

---

7. Du Boff, *Accumulation and Power*, 85; William Green, "Prosperity and Unemployment," *New York Herald Tribune*, September 1, 1929; Beulah Amidon, "Busy Machines—and Idle Men," *Survey Graphic*, April 1, 1929: 14, 15; Jay Lovestone, "The Present Economic Situation," *Communist*, February 1928: 83; Bernstein, *The Lean Years*, 55; "Labor-Absorbing Power of American Industry," *Monthly Labor Review*, June, 1929: 1402–404.
8. Sumner H. Slichter, "Recent Employment Movements," *Survey Graphic*, April 1, 1929: 16; St. Clair Drake and Horace Cayton, *Black Metropolis: A Study of Negro Life in a Northern City* (New York: Harcourt, Brace and Company, 1945), 77; "Unemployment on Increase in North," *New York Amsterdam News*, February 22, 1928.

market, highly leveraged buying of stocks just to resell them at a higher price, a game that proved so lucrative and became so elaborate in its rules that Wall Street consumed mountains of surplus capital from around the world that could have been more usefully invested in productive enterprises. America's millions of superfluous workers would have appreciated more factories as opposed to more speculative gambling. But it was out of the question to build factories on the scale required, particularly in light of saturated markets and ever-lower rates of return on productive investment. So the gambling continued and the self-feeding confidence bubble expanded, until finally in late 1929 it popped, when the stock market crashed. Colossal amounts of wealth were destroyed, business confidence was shattered, credit contracted, bankruptcies began to spread as profits declined, hundreds of thousands of workers were laid off as investment fell, and the "deflationary spiral" slowly dragged the economy almost to a standstill in early 1933.[9]

The depression was deepened and lengthened by a remarkable confluence of factors—intra- and inter-national—that are too numerous and involved to review in depth here. Unprotected and unregulated corporate and banking structures were highly vulnerable to a stock market collapse and its repercussions in the curtailed spending and investment of the wealthy, in addition, more generally, to the possibility of devastating bank runs. American businesses' cutting back of purchases of raw materials from other countries had a disastrous impact on their economies and their own ability to serve as foreign markets. The international tariff war set off by the United States' Smoot–Hawley Act of 1930 further hampered world trade and discouraged recovery. The political and economic legacies of World War I helped cause the depression as well: in particular, the postwar reparations and war debts problems created instability and imbalances in the international economy, which the United States only aggravated when its lending abroad—which during the 1920s had boosted foreign economies and their capacity to import American products—declined starting in 1928, as a result of the Federal Reserve's increasingly restrictive monetary policy. Moreover, the restoration of the international gold standard in the mid-1920s ultimately proved quite damaging, by forcing central banks to defend their currency's gold parity. This entailed, for instance, the Federal Reserve's deflationary policy of raising interest rates in the early 1930s, which discouraged investment and deepened the depression. Only after countries had left the gold standard did they have the freedom to enact expansionary fiscal and monetary policies. In short, the Great Depression resulted from (1) certain endemic tendencies of capitalism, notably overproduction and underconsumption; (2) the breakdown of the relatively unregulated and un-Keynesian form of capitalism that had been more appropriate to conditions in the nineteenth than the twentieth century; and (3) unfortunate aftereffects of the world war combined with constraints imposed by the gold standard.[10]

---

9. Lovestone, "The Present Economic Situation," 80–81; McElvaine, *The Great Depression*, 40–41, 44–6; Lizabeth Cohen, *Making a New Deal: Industrial Workers in Chicago, 1919–1939* (New York: Cambridge University Press, 1990), 234.
10. Needless to say, this account is vastly oversimplified and would hardly be uncontroversial. See John Kenneth Galbraith, *The Great Crash* (Boston, MA: Houghton Mifflin, 1954), 177–87; John A. Garraty, *The Great Depression: An Inquiry into the Causes, Course, and Consequences*

As already stated, however, things were bad enough even before the Depression began. This was obvious from a Senate committee's hearings held in the winter of 1928–29 to investigate the causes and possible remedies of unemployment, by then a subject of national concern. Among the committee's final recommendations were that adequate statistics of unemployment be collected, that government at all levels plan ambitious public works to stabilize employment, that the feasibility of a system of old-age pensions be studied, and that the federal government coordinate the building of efficient employment exchanges on state and municipal levels. The necessity of a more effective organization of such exchanges, intended to bring together businesses looking for workers and workers looking for a job, was clear from testimony given at the hearings. For example, an industrial relations expert testified that in Pittsburgh he had seen "hundreds, if not thousands, of job seekers milling around, hour after hour, and day after day, from one factory gate to another, in the utmost of despair and with frequent exclamations against society in general and the Government in particular—yet all the time with other factories hardly a mile away looking for workers!" The hearings thus illuminated both the urgency of the unemployment situation and the chaotic, haphazard nature of the country's response to it. Nevertheless, it appears that the committee's findings were almost wholly ignored.[11]

The year when the economy was to start its downward spiral began fairly auspiciously, though not magnificently. The steel industry was booming in early 1929, with capacity utilization rates of nearly 100 percent in Chicago. Railroads were doing vigorous business, and the retail sector was showing more activity than the previous year. More telling, however, was the sorry state of the construction industry, which, together with automobiles, was a major foundation of American economic growth. Building construction in Chicago for the first six months of the year was 35 percent less than at the same time in 1928, when it hadn't been stellar. High unemployment rates among Chicago's 112,000 building workers led to unions' (unsuccessful) demands for the 5-day, 40-hour week, which they expected would make jobs available to a greater number of workers than had them at present. By August the nation's biggest industries, motor vehicles and iron and steel, were scheduling cutbacks in output, since in their earlier optimism they had acquired larger inventories than they could now dispose of. Because of numerous forward and backward linkages, these cutbacks tended to shrink the country's economic

---

of the Worldwide Depression of the Nineteen-Thirties, As Seen by Contemporaries and in the Light of History (Garden City, NY: Anchor Books, 1987), chapter 1; McElvaine, The Great Depression, 33–50; Barry Eichengreen, Globalizing Capital: A History of the International Monetary System (Princeton, NJ: Princeton University Press, 2008), chapter 3; Charles P. Kindleberger, The World in Depression, 1929–1939 (Los Angeles, CA: University of California Press, 1986); Barry Eichengreen, Golden Fetters: The Gold Standard and the Great Depression, 1919–1939 (New York: Oxford University Press, 1995); Nicholas Crafts and Peter Fearon, "Lessons from the 1930s Great Depression," Oxford Review of Economic Policy 26, no. 3 (Autumn 2010): 285–317; Michael A. Bernstein, "The Great Depression as Historical Problem," OAH Magazine of History 16, no. 1 (Fall 2001): 3–10.

11. Bernstein, The Lean Years, 63; Senate Committee on Education and Labor, Unemployment in the United States: Hearings before the Committee on Education and Labor, 70th Congress, 2nd session, 1928–29, xv, 167.

activity as a whole, a process that fed on itself until, after the stock market crash, the situation grew dire in the winter. In fact, already in the spring of 1929 the family welfare societies in industrial cities were staggering under an increasing load of unemployment relief. "Not in years," reported one administrator, "have charitable organizations been so burdened with the care of needy families in their own homes." By the following spring things were far worse.[12]

Unfortunately, statistics on unemployment of the time are so unreliable that, even after decades of scholarship on the subject, all we can give are educated guesses. Sifting through the many estimates that have been proposed since the 1920s makes for intolerable confusion. U.S. Bureau of Labor Statistics figures, which have been accepted by most historians, are as follows. (The numbers are in thousands.)

Table 1 Labor force participation

Year	Labor force	Employed	Unemployed	Unemployed rate
1929	49,180	47,630	1,550	3.2%
1930	49,820	45,480	4,340	8.7%
1931	50,420	42,400	8,020	15.9%
1932	51,000	38,940	12,060	23.6%
1933	51,590	38,760	12,830	24.9%
1934	52,230	40,890	11,340	21.7%
1935	52,870	42,260	10,610	20.1%
1936	53,440	44,410	9,030	16.9%
1937	54,000	46,300	7,700	14.3%
1938	54,610	44,220	10,390	19%
1939	55,230	45,750	9,480	17.2%
1940	55,640	47,520	8,120	14.6%
1941	55,910	50,350	5,560	9.9%

These numbers seem too low. For one thing, they contrast wildly with estimates by the National Resources Committee in 1937. Some difference between the two is to be expected, since the latter excludes from the labor force "enterprisers, self-employed, and unpaid family workers on farms," taking account only of people who would ordinarily be paid by someone else. On the other hand, other methodological parameters of the NRC study would tend to understate the number of unemployed; for instance, it was not possible to include all the people who had dropped out of the labor force—or simply didn't try to enter it—because of discouragement. In any case, the NRC's unemployment percentages for the years 1929–35 are, respectively, 10, 19, 32, 45, 47, 42, and 41. Indeed, given the massive numbers of women and children who in the 1930s tried and would have liked to obtain employment—because of the primary wage earner's difficulty in doing so—but much of the time were unable to, it does not seem outrageous to

---

12. "Industry Speeds Up in Chicago District," *New York Times*, March 11, 1929; Lovestone, "The Present Economic Situation"; "Chicago Reports Sharp Drop in Six Months' Construction," *New York Herald Tribune*, July 8, 1929; "Urge Five-Day Week in Chicago Building," *New York Times*, June 24, 1929; Du Boff, *Accumulation and Power*, 89; Galbraith, *The Great Crash*, 174; Jacob Billikopf, "The New Unemployment," *New York Times*, June 1, 1929.

conclude that fully half of the nation's (potential) labor force in the 1930s was regularly jobless or worked only a couple of days a week.[13]

Historical precedents also cast doubt on the standard estimates of Great Depression unemployment. In 1900, a year of relative prosperity, unemployment affected 22 percent of the labor force, with a mean duration of 3.6 months. Between 1908 and 1922, the average jobless rate for unionized workers in Massachusetts was 7.7 percent. Between 1896 and 1926, the jobless rate in manufacturing, transportation, and the building trades was 10 percent—12 percent from 1920 to 1926. Similarly, Robert and Helen Lynd's classic *Middletown* (1929) revealed that in the "typical" American city of Muncie, Indiana, more than a quarter of a sample of workers had been laid off in the prosperous year of 1923, while during the first three-quarters of 1924—a year of recession—62 percent had at some point been jobless. It is hardly credible, then, that unemployment in 1929, for example, was only 3.2 percent, especially considering that social workers across the country complained about being overwhelmed by demands for relief even in the spring.[14]

Franklin Roosevelt's Committee on Economic Security, whose numbers are somewhat more reliable, estimated that 15,071,000 people were jobless in March 1933, the worst month for unemployment in U.S. history. Irving Bernstein states that "on the day that Hoover left the presidency, March 4, 1933, one out of every three wage and salary earners in the United States was totally without work and there is no way of knowing what proportion of the others were on part time."[15]

Heavy industry was hit hardest in the 1930s, and so Chicago, being a center of industry, suffered terribly. During the worst times it practically ceased to function. Its construction industry was utterly decimated: nationally 82 percent of construction jobs were lost between 1929 and 1933, and the number was higher in Chicago. Only 137 residential units were built in 1933, and only 8,000 in the entire period between 1931 and 1938. Already in October 1931, 624,000 Chicagoans were out of work—an astounding 40 percent of the labor force, making Chicago's plight far more severe even than New York City's.[16]

---

13. Weintraub, "Unemployment and Increasing Productivity," 69, 70.
14. Alexander Keyssar, *Out of Work: The First Century of Unemployment in Massachusetts* (New York: Cambridge University Press, 1986), 304, 305; Isador Lubin's testimony, Senate Committee on Education and Labor, *Unemployment in the United States*, 491; Harry W. Laidler, *Unemployment and Its Remedies* (New York: League for Industrial Democracy, 1931), 9; Robert and Helen Lynd, *Middletown: A Study in Modern American Culture* (New York: Harcourt, Brace and World, 1929), 56, 57.
15. Bernstein, *The Lean Years*, 254, 316, 317; Anne Page, *Employment and Unemployment, 1929 to 1935* (Washington, DC: Office of National Recovery Administration, 1936), 12, 13; Jerome B. Cohen, "The Misuse of Statistics," *Journal of the American Statistical Association* 33, no. 204 (December 1938): 664.
16. William Green, "Unemployment," *Weekly Newsletter*, Illinois State Federation of Labor, February 22, 1930; Illinois Department of Labor, "Statistical Indexes and Summary Tables," *Labor Bulletin* XXII, no. 7 (January 1933): 142, 145; Robert G. Spinney, *City of Big Shoulders: A History of Chicago* (DeKalb, IL: Northern Illinois University Press, 2000), 193;

Illinois was savaged by the Depression, more so than most states. Out of a total of 3,185,000 gainful workers, the number of unemployed rose from about 300,000 in the spring of 1930 to more than 1,500,000 in January 1933. Only Michigan and a few other states had this official rate of approximately 50 percent unemployment. Aside from some ravaged mining areas downstate, nowhere were things worse than in Chicago, which in early 1933 had probably over 850,000 jobless out of 1,560,000 gainful workers. Perhaps a third of the others—throughout the state and the country, in fact—worked only part-time. Payrolls plummeted even more steeply than employment because of both this use of part-time labor and drastic reductions in wage rates. Admittedly, not all industries were equally affected: in Illinois, among the ones that suffered least were food, chemicals, and textiles; printing, clothing, and trade were harmed more; and metals, machinery, and wood products had the sharpest declines in payrolls and employment. Nevertheless, the unfolding cataclysm touched everyone and destroyed many.[17]

The differential impact on various categories of people illustrates the raging social and economic inequalities of the time. In Chicago, while Blacks were about 7 percent of the population in 1932, they constituted over 20 percent of the unemployed. In many cases they were laid off specifically so whites could be hired. In the bleakest months of the Depression, Chicago's Black Belt was a cauldron of misery and poverty, with unemployment approaching 90 percent in some sections. Bank failures were more widespread and devastating there than elsewhere in the city, causing the already tiny Black middle class to further shrink. Nor was the situation helped by the fact that 40,000 more Blacks entered the city during the 1930s, fleeing the collapse of the Southern cotton economy and rampant discrimination in the administering of relief. For most of them, not even the traditional low-status, low-paid jobs of servant work and manual labor were available. In 1935, almost half of Black domestic servants, a third of semiskilled workers, and at least a fourth of the unskilled were still without jobs. Indeed, even in 1940, when the country was benefiting from Europe's war boom, 26 percent of Black men above 14 years of age were seeking work while being supported by local relief or the WPA, or simply the generosity of friends and neighbors. Only the United States' entry into World War II would finally banish, for a time, the chronic unemployment and underemployment Chicago's Blacks had endured not only since 1929 but in fact since they first made the trek up north years earlier.[18]

Illinois Department of Labor, "Unemployment Estimates for Chicago as of October 15, 1931," *Labor Bulletin* XI, no. 5 (November 1931): 82; Albert Romasco, *The Poverty of Abundance: Hoover, the Nation, the Depression* (New York: Oxford University Press, 1965), 155.

17. *First Annual Report of the Illinois Emergency Relief Commission* (Chicago, IL, 1933), 33, 36; Kennedy, *Freedom from Fear*, 87; "Growth of Annual Average Employment and Payrolls, 1929–1934," *Review of Employment and Payrolls of Illinois Industry*, March 22, 1935.

18. "The Negro in the Industrial Depression," *Monthly Labor Review*, June, 1931: 60–62; St. Clair Drake and Horace Cayton, *Black Metropolis: A Study of Negro Life in a Northern City* (New York: Harcourt, Brace and Company, 1945), 214–18; Harold F. Gosnell, *Negro Politicians: The Rise of Negro Politics in Chicago* (Chicago, IL: University of Chicago Press, 1967), 321. See also William A. Sundstrom, "Last Hired, First Fired? Unemployment and Urban Black Workers during the Great Depression," *Journal of Economic History* 52, no. 2 (June 1992): 415–29.

Blacks were far from the only disadvantaged minority in Chicago, though they were the worst off. The foreign-born, who made up a third of Chicago's population, were likewise in dire condition. As elsewhere in the country, the fact that immigrant workers were disproportionately uneducated and unskilled, not to mention frequently untutored in English, made them and their families especially vulnerable in the case of an economic downturn. On average they were already poorer than native whites, and because fewer of them belonged to unions their jobs were more insecure and seasonal. Thus, for example, the large Eastern European community was almost wholly sucked into the economic mire. No systematic and reliable data exist on immigrants in Chicago, but impressionistic accounts from knowledgeable observers paint a grim picture. Out of about 220 Bulgarian families scattered in the city, it was reported in 1935 that only 10 were in "comparatively good" condition, the rest—40 of which were on relief—being "miserable." The larger Yugoslav population—of "well over 60,000"—was similarly scattered in small groups around Chicago, and perhaps as a result seems to have been a little worse off than the Polish and Czechoslovak communities, which were more tightly knit. The number of Lithuanian stores, factories, and workshops in Chicago fell by half during the Depression, and the Lithuanian Alliance of America was forced to evict countrymen who had defaulted on their mortgages. Many of the Poles, Lithuanians, Slovaks, and Mexicans who worked in the meatpacking industry were not immediately affected by the downturn in 1930, because meatpacking did not collapse to the degree that steel and the agricultural equipment industry did. However, *underemployment* quickly became a major problem for these packinghouse workers, as companies adopted "share-the-work" plans—called "share-the-misery" plans by their employees—that entailed reduced hours and extended layoffs.[19]

Mexicans were treated even worse by the Depression than other immigrant groups. In 1930, there were 20,000 of them in Chicago, concentrated in three neighborhoods: Back of the Yards, the Near West Side, and the smokestack-filled South Chicago. By 1940, due to voluntary and coerced repatriation, 20 percent had returned to Mexico. No other immigrant group in Chicago had a higher rate of unemployment than Mexicans, but in addition they had to deal with the evil of aggressive nativism. Conservative organizations like the American Legion and the Immigrant Protective League negotiated cheap train fares to Texas in order to facilitate removal of Mexicans, and everyday incidents of discrimination increased as Americans blamed Mexicans for "taking our jobs." For instance, when a family applied for relief, the caseworker assigned to them was apt to discuss how much happier they would be in their own country; and

---

19. Leland Collins DeVinney, "The Relation of Educational Status to Unemployment of Gainful Workers in the City of Chicago, 1934" (PhD diss., University of Chicago, 1944); anonymous and untitled report, Ernest Burgess Papers, Special Collections Research Center, University of Chicago Library, box 131, folder 3; "Yugoslavs in Chicago and Depression" and miscellaneous papers, ibid., folder 4; Robert A. Slayton, *Back of the Yards: The Making of a Local Democracy* (Chicago, IL: University of Chicago Press, 1986), 190; Rick Halpern, *Down on the Killing Floor: Black and White Workers in Chicago's Packinghouses, 1904–54* (Chicago, IL: University of Illinois Press, 1997), 99, 100; "Voice of the People," *Chicago Tribune*, January 19, 1936.

landlords sometimes resorted to removing the doors and windows of apartments with Mexican tenants in order to encourage them to move without having to pay for a court notice. Given the enormity of their plight, what is surprising, perhaps, is only that more Mexicans during the 1930s did not voluntarily leave Chicago.[20]

Other "disadvantaged" groups in the city and country included women, the very young, and those older than about fifty. Actually, the unemployment rate for women was often less than for men, in part because much fewer women were in the labor force—about a quarter of them on the eve of the Depression—but also because they could more easily get part-time and seasonal jobs. Thus, in early 1931, 24 percent of Chicago's working women were jobless, a lower number than for men, which after 1933 got even lower (at times) as the domestic service and clerical occupations partially recovered. Needless to say, there was a discrepancy between the races: in early 1931, about 20 percent of native white women were without work versus 59 percent of Blacks.

Qualitative accounts of the early Depression in Chicago are scattered through historical scholarship, but they bear repeating in our own age of historical amnesia and threatened economic and social collapse.[21] Briefly, between 1930 and 1933 a near apocalypse occurred in Chicago and comparable industrial cities. In later chapters we'll discuss the city's total incapacity to meet the crisis, in part a consequence of endemic fiscal woes and long delays in tax collection, but even anecdotal testimonies give a sense of the calamity. By late 1930 even the mainstream press was admitting that hundreds of women, mostly between 50 and 70 years of age, were sleeping on park benches, under bushes, in doorways and hallways. Having lost their livelihood, they had been evicted by landlords and were forced to wander the city desperate for a meal and some shelter, eating out of garbage cans behind restaurants. Thousands of men were sleeping in parks on the lakefront or on the cold concrete underneath Wacker Drive. Too poor to pay 15 cents for a bed in a flophouse, they clustered together beneath the highway by the hundreds and built small fires with bits of broken wood picked up on vacant lots. As an observer picturesquely remarked,

> Many of these men are hungry; those who have food share it with their friends under the rule of the road. As they huddle by their feeble fires, or sit, coat collar turned up and cap pulled low, staring at the blackness which is the river, there is a steady, quiet hum from overhead, where the automobiles skim smoothly along, carrying well fed men and women

---

20. Michael Innis-Jiménez, *Steel Barrio: The Great Mexican Migration to South Chicago, 1915–1940* (New York: New York University Press, 2013), 55, 144; Gabriela F. Arredondo, "'What! The Mexicans, Americans?' Race and Ethnicity, Mexicans in Chicago, 1916–1939" (PhD diss., University of Chicago, 1999), 73–78, 124–34.

21. See, for example, Robert Brenner, *The Economics of Global Turbulence: The Advanced Capitalist Economies from Long Boom to Long Downturn, 1945–2005* (New York: Verso, 2006); John Bellamy Foster and Robert McChesney, *The Endless Crisis: How Monopoly-Finance Capital Produces Stagnation and Upheaval from the U.S.A. to China* (New York: Monthly Review Press, 2012); David Harvey, *The Enigma of Capital, and the Crises of Capitalism* (New York: Oxford University Press, 2011); Richard Heinberg, *The End of Growth: Adapting to Our New Economic Reality* (Gabriola Island, Canada: New Society Publishers, 2011).

from one busy moment to another in their prosperous lives. Wealth on the upper level, hunger and misery below.[22]

As has been amply related by historians, "Hoovervilles" sprang up in cities all over the country. In Chicago, one of them even sprouted in the city's front yard, in and around Grant Park. It elected its own "mayor"—a disabled former railroad brakeman and miner—and had its Prosperity Road, Easy Street, and Hard Times Avenue. "Building construction may be at a standstill elsewhere," the mayor remarked, "but here everything is booming. [...] Ours is a communistic government. We pool our interests and when the commissary shows signs of depletion, we appoint a committee to see what leavings the hotels have." Notwithstanding the prime real estate around Grant Park, it was more common to find Hoovervilles in garbage dumps. In 1932, for example, "every single place where food remains were dumped" was an attraction for the city's starving thousands.[23]

Meanwhile, the city bristled with breadlines at charities, churches, and shelters, by late 1930 at least 16 of them that each had from several hundred to several thousand men a day, shuffling along silently to get a bowl of "slop" or a two-day-old piece of bread. Even after the peak of the Depression had passed, 20,000 homeless men were still regularly living in the 20 public shelters that Chicago provided. The buildings used for these shelters were schools, warehouses, abandoned factories, and even the old county jail, all typically located in dilapidated areas of the city near the central business district.

As regards this glitzy business district—"the Loop"—the Depression half-emptied it out, as it emptied out houses and factories all over the city. Most of the Loop's office floor space and many of its stores were unoccupied in 1933, such that Chicago's elite grew anxious lest the city present an unflattering façade to the millions of international visitors congregating for the "Century of Progress" world's fair. The mayor had a clever solution to this problem: he called on property owners and tenants to dress up vacant windows with either merchandise or exhibits of some sort, and to keep the windows lighted until at least 2:00 a.m. every night.[24]

It is hard to imagine in the twenty-first century what the city must have been like and looked like in those dreary years of the early Depression and later in the decade too. In newspapers one reads of groups of hundreds of homeless being driven in the freezing October night air to sleep in free shelters that quickly became overcrowded, such that hundreds had to curl up on the cold floor. Others were turned away and, shivering, trudged on, finally finding shelter in police stations and other public buildings, where

---

22. *Daily Worker*, October 30, 1930; Bruce Bliven, "No Money, No Work," *New Republic*, November 10, 1930.
23. *New York Times*, November 12, 1930; *New Frontier*, February 8, 1933.
24. *New Frontier*, March 4 and 22, 1933; *Daily Worker*, December 13, 1930; Edwin H. Sutherland and Harvey J. Locke, *Twenty Thousand Homeless Men: A Study of Unemployed Men in the Chicago Shelters* (New York: Arno Press, 1971/1936), 1; Margaret Marshall, "Chicago: Two Exhibits," *Nation*, June 28, 1933.

sometimes they were served coffee and sandwiches by the staff and housewives who had come to help. So ubiquitous were breadlines, panhandlers, and "professional beggars" already in early 1931 that civic and business groups in the North Loop started a campaign to rid Michigan Avenue of them. "It is getting so that a person can hardly walk a block without being approached for money," one man complained, going on to blame the public's "mistaken ideas of charity" for the proliferation of beggars. (Giving them money only encouraged them, he argued.) The campaign had considerable success: within a couple of months all the breadlines on the North Side had closed.[25]

In general, things only got worse as the years passed. More and more buildings had to be used to house men and women who were being evicted by the thousands every month; nor did it help that Chicago became a Mecca for many thousands of transients from all over the country, who often seemed to have a more cheerful attitude than unemployed locals did. As one (immigrant) said, "They feed you at the old county jail. [...] If you got a dime you get meals, soup, bread, coffee, and a spring bed, for a week. If you got no dime, they feed you anyway, but you sleep on the floor." A reporter remarked of the hundreds of men living at Grant Park in 1931 that "most of the out-of-towners seemed carefree and confident of a winter that's 'at least better than working.' There were, on the other hand, many hard luck stories from Chicagoans."[26]

We'll explore some of those hard-luck stories in the following chapters, as well as conditions inside the shelters. A major factor influencing both of these things was the set of relief policies by the city and the state. While transients may not always have known it or been personally troubled by it, there was in fact an almost continuous relief crisis in Chicago during the early 1930s—and after 1935 too, when the federal government withdrew from "this business of relief," as Roosevelt disdainfully called it. In this respect, Chicago was little different from most industrial cities in the country, and most towns and rural communities. The only difference, perhaps, was in the severity of its financial crisis. Of all cities in the country, it was likely the one least prepared for the Depression, because of its chaotic finances, delayed tax collection due to legal controversies, and absurdly high rates of tax delinquency among the wealthy. In June 1930, for example, there was a tax payment backlog of 20 percent for 1928, 40 percent for 1929, and 50 percent for 1930, causing the city to be on the verge of bankruptcy. It could not even afford to pay its employees, much less offer adequate relief to the poor; schoolteachers, firemen, policemen, and others went unpaid for months at a time. A disproportionate burden of relief, therefore, fell on private organizations like United Charities, Catholic Charities, the Salvation Army, the American Red Cross, and the Jewish Social Service Bureau. They were overwhelmed.[27]

---

25. *Chicago Tribune*, October 21, 1930; March 5 and 15, February 22, November 24, 1931; December 24, 1932.
26. *Chicago Tribune*, October 1, 1931.
27. Dwayne Charles Cole, "The Relief Crisis in Illinois during the Depression, 1930–1940" (PhD diss., St. Louis University, 1973), 4; Roger Biles, *Big City Boss in Depression and War: Mayor Edward J. Kelly of Chicago* (DeKalb, IL: Northern Illinois University Press, 1984), 22, 23.

It may be useful here to give a brief, anticipatory overview of the contours of relief in Chicago throughout the decade. As industry after industry collapsed in 1930 and 1931, the relief needs of hundreds of thousands of applicants became so unmanageable by the city and county that the state had to step in in manifold ways; in particular, in early 1932 it created the Illinois Emergency Relief Commission (IERC) to oversee the finances and administration of relief. Soon even this agency, not having enough money at its disposal, proved inadequate to the task, so Mayor Cermak of Chicago desperately appealed to the federal government, panicking lest social unrest reduce his city to chaos. "It would be cheaper," he pointedly remarked, for Congress "to provide a loan of $152,000,000 to the City of Chicago, than to pay for the services of Federal troops at a future date." Chicago did not get nearly that much money, but by the spring of 1933 it and Illinois had received about $55 million from the federal government's Reconstruction Finance Corporation, more than any other state. It was very far from sufficient: thousands of state residents were near starvation and thousands more would experience that condition in the following years, despite the various state taxes and bond issues that were passed to pay for relief. The federal government, too, renewed its commitment to alleviating states' distress in May 1933, when, under the Roosevelt administration, it formed the Federal Emergency Relief Administration (FERA) to give grants and establish uniform national regulations for the administration of relief. The IERC estimated that in October 1933, 402,000 Chicagoans (and 866,000 Illinoisans), or 12 percent of the city's population, were receiving relief of some kind. Many more needed it but, voluntarily or involuntarily, did not get it.[28]

Fearing another winter of unbearable suffering and civic unrest, the federal government created the Civil Works Administration (CWA) in November 1933. Not exactly a work relief program because it did not require that the people hired be on relief rolls, it nonetheless gave jobs to over four million unemployed men and women until it was phased out (despite its great popularity) in the spring. It was so successful that it inspired, in 1935, the even grander Works Progress Administration, which continued until 1943. Over 100,000 people in Cook County, and 225,000 in Illinois, found employment with the CWA, which not only lessened the burden on relief agencies but also injected some much-needed purchasing power into the economy. Until the end of 1935, FERA continued to subsidize and help administer both direct relief (i.e., the provision of cash or, more often, grocery orders directly to "clients") and work relief, thus preventing the system from sinking into sustained crisis—although for the inundated caseworkers who each attended to 100 or 200 families on relief, it must have seemed like it was always on the verge of doing so.[29]

The years after 1935 were characterized by great success and dismal failure, in fact tragedy on an epic scale. The Works Progress Administration has been justly celebrated

---

28. *New York Times*, June 22, 1932; Biles, *Big City Boss*, 23, 24; *Second Annual Report of the Illinois Emergency Relief Commission* (Chicago, IL, 1934), 36, 81.
29. Ibid., 46; Jeff Singleton, *The American Dole: Unemployment Relief and the Welfare State in the Great Depression* (Westport, CT: Greenwood Press, 2000), chapter 5; "New Federal Work-Relief Program," *Monthly Labor Review*, July 1934: 38–40.

for its many concrete achievements, including taking a total of 8.5 million people off the relief rolls and putting them to productive work. On the other hand, its successes disguised great failures. The unemployed population on relief had been divided into two categories: the employable and the unemployable, for example, the elderly, the disabled, and orphaned children. Only the employable were to be hired by the WPA, the others being forced to turn to state and local public assistance agencies for whatever help they saw fit to give. This was not a great change from the situation before the New Deal, when such "deserving" poor had traditionally been cared for—inadequately—by their communities. With the early New Deal, many of them, as well as the able-bodied unemployed, had received federal emergency relief; but this ended in 1935, when the WPA was created, FERA was dissolved, and the federal government withdrew from administering and providing grants for direct relief. Once the provisions of the Social Security Act of 1935 were implemented, the situation of some of these unemployables did improve, since federal grants were now given to states in order to assist the aged, the blind, orphaned and disabled children, and poor single (mostly white) mothers. (Federal benefits were also given *directly* to some people over 65 years of age who fulfilled certain conditions—which was the aspect of the law that has come to be known colloquially as "Social Security.") Aside from the "Social Security" program, though, each state was allowed to give whatever level of assistance it desired: for example, in December 1939 Arkansas gave $8.10 every month to families with dependent children, whereas Massachusetts gave $61.07. So, depending on where one lived—and what race one belonged to—one was given either miserly or munificent grants by the state. Moreover, several categories of people were exempt from the old-age benefits program, including domestic workers, agricultural laborers, casual workers, and public employees.

Arguably, however, the greater tragedy than the federal government's semineglect of "unemployables"[30] was what happened to the able-bodied unemployed who were not hired by the WPA (or PWA or CCC): they, too, were left to the mercy of states and localities. The Roosevelt administration simply washed its hands of them. Nor were they a negligible minority: even at its peak, the WPA left millions of employable people on the local relief rolls, being unable to hire them because of its insufficient budgets. All these people, in addition to the many millions of able-bodied unemployed who were not on relief at all, were consigned to a hell somewhat reminiscent of that they had endured from 1930 to 1933, before the federal government had stepped in to fund the large majority of relief nationwide. It is true that the Social Security Act contained provisions for unemployment insurance; unfortunately, just as much discretion was left to the states as in the case of grants to "unemployables." Each state could determine how much compensation to give and whom to give it to, with the consequence that large numbers of the jobless ended up not being eligible for insurance at all. Illinois did not even start giving

---

30. Many of these people, such as the malnourished, those who suffered from nervous strain, and others whose ailments were temporary and had been caused largely by the Depression itself, were quite employable.

benefits until mid-1939, and in many cases their inadequacy was such that they had to be supplemented with relief anyway.

In short, after 1935, the unemployed could only hope that the elites of their state and community would help them in even remote proportion to their plight—which was impossible, or not desired, in many places that either could not handle the financial burden or chose not to. New Jersey actually resorted simply to issuing licenses to beg.[31]

Thus, federal oversight of relief was abandoned in the second half of the 1930s, and Illinois, once again, was left to fend for itself, which it did badly. It turned out to be quite incapable of taking care of its unemployed, partly because its industrial economy effectively did not recover until the 1940s. Of course, neither did the country's economy as a whole. Between 1935 and 1937 business conditions briefly improved, but the upswing was decidedly less pronounced for the middle and lower classes. Some of the best commentary on these matters was provided by the Communist Party—affiliated Labor Research Association, whose work historians have almost wholly ignored. The group's monthly *Labor Notes* observed, for instance, that labor productivity in manufacturing was, on average, 23 percent higher in 1935 than in 1929, as a result of better machinery and the increasing speed and intensity of work. In part because of such improvements in productivity, but more because of the New Deal's stimulating effect on economic activity, corporate profits steadily rose from 1935 to early 1937; even Chicago's steel industry began to recover. With orders from the automotive industry rising, steel's capacity utilization rose to 80 percent in late 1936, much higher than at any time in the previous five years.[32]

It seems, however, that the effects of this business upturn on employment were not as marked as one might think. If people on federal work relief—WPA, PWA, and CCC—are counted as unemployed, the Labor Research Association measured the numbers of the jobless from late 1932 to early 1938 (see Table 2)[33]:

Table 2 Total unemployed population

Date	Unemployed	On federal work relief	Unemp., excluding those on work relief
November 1932	16,783,000	—	16,783,000
November 1933	16,138,000	599,000	15,539,000
November 1934	16,824,000	3,007,000	13,817,000
November 1935	16,658,000	2,486,000	14,172,000
November 1936	14,751,000	3,792,000	10,959,000
November 1937	14,825,000	2,223,000	12,602,000
March 1938	16,456,000	3,462,000	12,994,000

---

31. For the previous two paragraphs: Josephine Chapin Brown, *Public Relief, 1929–1939* (New York: Octagon Books, 1971/1940), 165–70; Frances Fox Piven and Richard A. Cloward, *Regulating the Poor: The Functions of Public Welfare* (New York: Vintage Books, 1993/1971), chapter 3; Singleton, *The American Dole*, chapter 6; Social Security Act of 1935; *Chicago Tribune*, June 23, 1939.
32. Labor Research Association, *Labor Notes* 4, no. 12 (December 1936): 1; *Chicago Tribune*, December 21, 1936.
33. Labor Research Association, *Labor Notes*, vol. 6, nos. 1 and 6 (January and June 1938).

Even according to the lower numbers in the right-hand column, the proportion of unemployed never fell below about 20 percent of the labor force in the second half of the decade.

As is well known, the limited recovery of the country's economy came to a crashing end in late 1937 and 1938, because of the government's return to fiscal conservatism, the Federal Reserve's tightening of credit, and the beginning of the Social Security payroll tax in 1937, which took $2 billion out of the pockets of consumers. The stock market plummeted, corporate profits plunged nearly 80 percent, steel production sank to one-fourth of its mid-1937 level, and unemployment rose to about 25 percent (notwithstanding the government's lower estimates). In desperation, Washington reintroduced deficit spending, for example by expanding the WPA, and eased credit, which restored some measure of economic vitality in 1939. The prescriptions of liberals and leftists were thus strikingly validated, and the ideas of fiscal conservatives apparently refuted. Nevertheless, because the world is ruled not by ideas but by economic interest and power, the agenda of big business and its representatives in Congress quickly came to the fore once again: in late 1939, Roosevelt and Congress rediscovered the virtues of retrenchment of social spending and cut appropriations for work relief and other social programs. For instance, a rule was instituted that people who had worked on WPA projects for 18 consecutive months had to be terminated, which led to the laying off of 775,000 workers. (A survey showed that three months later, 87 percent of them had still not found private employment.) Instead of social spending, Washington rallied around an issue with bipartisan support: the increase of military appropriations, in preparation for possible entry into the European war. This—and the war itself—was of benefit to the economy, preventing it from sinking again into the doldrums of 1938, but it was of far greater benefit to the corporate sector than to the unemployed or the poor (that is until the United States entered the war in late 1941).[34]

These *misérables* were now, indeed, no longer "the forgotten men"; they were remembered—but repudiated. Much has been said in historical scholarship about the federal government's consistently scandalous treatment of agricultural and domestic workers, but less attention has been devoted to the fate of the long-term jobless as such in the late 1930s.[35] In few places, surely, were they worse off than in Chicago or Illinois. Both state and city were wildly irresponsible in caring for the destitute, refusing to provide the

---

34. Kennedy, *Freedom from Fear*, 350; McElvaine, *The Great Depression*, 297, 298, 306–308; "Nice for Corporations," *Social Work Today*, March 1940, 25.
35. In addition to standard histories cited above, see, for example, Anthony Badger, *The New Deal: The Depression Years, 1933–40* (New York: Hill and Wang, 1989); Irving Bernstein, *A Caring Society: The New Deal, the Worker, and the Great Depression* (Boston, MA: Houghton Mifflin Company, 1985); T. H. Watkins, *The Hungry Years: A Narrative History of the Great Depression* (New York: Henry Holt and Company, 1999); William R. Brock, *Welfare, Democracy, and the New Deal* (New York: Cambridge University Press, 1988); Raymond Wolters, *Negroes and the Great Depression: The Problem of Economic Recovery* (Westport, CT: Greenwood Publishing Corp., 1970); David Eugene Conrad, *The Forgotten Farmers: The Story of Sharecroppers in the New Deal* (Urbana, IL: University of Illinois Press, 1965).

necessary finances and administrative apparatus to make possible efficient and effective relief. The relatively successful relief policies and financing between 1933 and 1935, when FERA was in substantial control and periodically came to the rescue of the poor when the state refused to, ended in late 1935, from which point Illinois entered a period of semichaos in the provision of relief. Starting in July 1936, the administration of relief was devolved from the IERC to 1,454 local units (towns, cities, and counties) throughout the state, and the state legislature took measures to compel localities, particularly Chicago, to assume a fair share of the financial burden. As one historian observes, the Chicago City Council had been "blatantly negligent" in paying for its own relief needs, and for the remainder of the decade, even when deprived of state funds, it continued to show little compassion for the poor—except when forced to by the threat of public disorder. The city and state lurched from crisis to crisis, barely managing to scrounge up more money whenever it appeared that thousands would starve to death if something drastic were not done, somehow navigating the muddle of relief agencies and jurisdictions that constituted the state's welfare system. In July 1938, the IERC regained some supervisory authority over the wasteful and inefficient local relief jurisdictions, but the system remained decentralized, hence subject to periodic crisis and the whims of local authorities. Finally in 1943, too late to deal with the emergency of the Depression, some sanity was restored when the Illinois Public Aid Commission—which had succeeded the IERC in 1941—took over administration of Old Age Assistance, Aid to Dependent Children, and the county welfare departments, thus effectively ending the fiasco of decentralized relief.[36]

Unfortunately, many human casualties were littered along this tortuous road to sanity. There is no telling how many people needed relief from hunger and poverty, but between July 1936 and July 1938, an average of 500,000 Illinoisans were on the relief rolls each month (not counting those dependent on the WPA, CCC, or NYA [National Youth Administration] or receiving mothers' aid pensions, Old Age Assistance, or aid for the blind. The corresponding number for Chicago was approximately 217,000. These numbers mean little, though; more important are the conditions in which relief recipients (and others less favored) lived. They were not exactly sumptuous. The Chicago Relief Administration (CRA) had established that the absolute minimum to sustain a family of five was $59.65 per month; accordingly, this was set as the "100 percent relief budget."[37] As it happened, though, in the later years of the 1930s this minimum budget—or "the 100% skeleton budget," as a Chicago church committee

---

36. Donald S. Howard, "Worse than Forgotten Men," *Social Work Today*, May 1940, 13; Cole, "The Relief Crisis in Illinois," chapters 8, 9, 12, and 13; *Biennial Report of the IERC, Covering the Period July 1, 1936 through June 30, 1938* (Chicago, IL, 1938), 21; Frank Z. Glick, *The Illinois Emergency Relief Commission* (Chicago, IL: University of Chicago Press, 1940), chapter 7; *Chicago Tribune*, June 18, 1943.
37. The United Charities determined that $81 was necessary for subsistence for the same-sized family that the CRA allowed $44, which made the CRA budget 54 percent of the UC budget. The latter, in turn, was 65 percent of the "health and decency" budget of the U.S. Children's Bureau.

called it—was rarely granted to relief recipients. Instead, they were expected to survive on anywhere from 65 to 85 percent of it, an expectation that tended to produce a public outcry that occasionally convinced the City Council to appropriate more funds. Even so, the starvation, malnourishment, and many cases of rickets, pellagra, beriberi, and scurvy that proliferated among the Chicago poor led the City Club, a top business group, to denounce the "appalling picture of distress and suffering." "[Those on relief] would get more if they were prisoners," the organization said in a report. That is surely no exaggeration, as the following typical description suggests:

> William Linneman and his family [...] have been on relief for about three years and have gone through the usual course of misery most families on relief experience: not enough food, shortage on grocery orders, refusal of special diets when needed, gas shut off—no stove all last winter, poor living quarters, continual fighting for clothing, shoes; always fighting for the bare necessities of life almost always denied them by the relief authorities. This all contributed to and brought about the present condition of Mr. Linneman.
>
> He is suffering from anemia—malnutrition and other diseases. He is 6 feet tall [and] weighs 96 pounds (the weight of a normal child of 12).[38]

The uninterrupted disaster of collective deprivation in Chicago's "economic basement" from 1929 (indeed earlier) until 1942 was not passively accepted by the deprived. Irving Bernstein was right to call the 1930s "the turbulent years," but he was wrong to limit that designation to the New Deal period. The first three years of the decade were just as turbulent, as protest-charged, as the later years, in some respects more so. The Communist Party was by far the most active organizer of unemployed protest, chiefly by means of its thousands of Unemployed Councils all over the country, but other entities played an important role as well. In Chicago, the Workers Committee on Unemployment, initially organized by members of the Socialist Party, emerged in 1931 as an important rival of (and occasional collaborator with) the Unemployed Councils, helping people resist evictions, publicize relief grievances, pressure government for more generous relief policies, and agitate for passage of radically social democratic laws at the state and national levels. Together, at their peak in 1932–33 these Communist and Socialist organizations had between 100 and 200 locals in Chicago and tens of thousands of members, with tens of thousands more followers who participated regularly in gigantic demonstrations and eviction "riots." We'll observe later the attacks of fear and panic that seized the city's wealthy when such disorder crested at the trough of the Depression—reactions that were an effective indication of the very real militancy of the poor.

Nationally, while the Socialist Party was much less involved in unemployed organizing than the Chicago Workers Committee, other institutions proved effective at harnessing discontent. Around the time of the Bonus March to Washington in the summer

---

38. *Biennial Report of the IERC*, 43, 125; Relief Commission of the Council of Hyde Park and Kenwood Churches, *Report on Relief in Illinois* (Chicago, IL, 1940); *Hunger Fighter*, August 1935.

of 1932, Father Cox's Jobless-Liberty Party was a serious contender for the allegiance of the cast-off multitudes. The Industrial Workers of the World established Unemployed Unions in industrial centers like Chicago and New York, though the group's lack of resources prevented it from achieving the success of the Communists. More consequential were the organizations with which A. J. Muste was associated, the Conference for Progressive Labor Action (CPLA) and the later American Workers Party. The many Unemployed Leagues that the CPLA helped found were concentrated in Ohio and Pennsylvania rather than Illinois, with smaller statewide federations in West Virginia, North Carolina, and New Jersey. In addition to all these regional or national organizations were the thousands of smaller bodies around the country, most of them self-constituted by the jobless with no imprimatur of higher-level political parties, that had up to thousands of members or followers and engaged in self-help, protest, neighborhood-wide sharing of resources, organized cooperation, looting, theft, bootlegging (especially of coal), and any other necessary activity not countenanced by the authorities. The nationwide totality of this activity amounted to a society in semiupheaval.[39]

In the second half of the 1930s, some of these groups lost strength and others were born. In particular, the Workers Alliance of America (WA) was formed in March 1935 to bring together all the major unemployed organizations in the country and coordinate their activities. It was judged more efficient to end the fragmentation, competition, and political sectarianism, and in any case this was in the Communist Party's Popular Front period, so even the Unemployed Councils set aside their differences with the Socialists and Musteites and joined the federation in 1936. The various state Workers Alliances that already existed—the Illinois one had grown out of the Chicago Workers Committee—and the Unemployed Leagues, Relief Workers Unions, CWA unions, and nonpartisan local and state groups, all united in a grand alliance encompassing 400,000 or more people. It had many successes, though, arguably, not momentous ones. Relief everywhere remained subpar, WPA wages were generally low, and federal and state governments later on ignored the protests and pleas of the WA and repeatedly cut funding for relief. Ultimately, after the Communists gained control of the WA in 1939, some organizations split off in disgust to form the Workers Security Federation—and the Illinois Workers Alliance (IWA) became the Illinois Workers Security Federation. This change, however, did not increase its effectiveness. In the end, both the WA and the WSF petered out ingloriously in 1941.[40]

---

39. *Blue Shirt News*, June 25, 1932; *Industrial Worker*, August 2, 1932, and July 4, 1933; Roy Rosenzweig, "Radicals and the Jobless: The Musteites and the Unemployed Leagues, 1932–1936," *Labor History* 16, no. 1 (Winter 1975): 52–77; Bernstein, *The Lean Years*, 416–25. On the Musteites, see also Leilah Danielson, *American Gandhi: A. J. Muste and the History of Radicalism in the Twentieth Century* (Philadelphia, PA: University of Pennsylvania Press, 2014), 144–50, 184–86, 193.
40. James Lorence, *Organizing the Unemployed: Community and Union Activists in the Industrial Heartland* (Albany, NY: State University of New York Press, 1996), 96, 97; Illinois Workers Security Federation, *Proceedings of the Sixth Annual State Convention*, October 28–29, 1939; IWSF bulletins and correspondence, Frank McCulloch Papers, Chicago History Museum, Research

Notwithstanding the many tragic defeats that the unemployed movement suffered, the number and variety of people and institutions it united in struggle are staggering. Not only leftists or the poor, but also unions, churches, charities, settlement houses, Black institutions like the Urban League, liberal groups and politicians, and many in the middle class joined the movement. It was a time of authentic populism, focused not merely on union organizing of industries or Black rights in the South but *the abolition of economic insecurity itself*, as manifested first and foremost in joblessness. This is indicated, for example, by the nationwide outpouring of support for the radical Workers' Unemployment and Social Insurance Bill introduced in Congress by Representative Ernest Lundeen in 1934 and 1935, written by members of the Communist Party, and intended as an alternative to what became the Social Security Act. It provided for unemployment insurance for workers and farmers (regardless of age, sex, race, or political affiliation) that was to be equal to average local wages but no less than $10 per week plus $3 for each dependent; people compelled to work part-time (because of inability to find full-time jobs) were to receive the difference between their earnings and the average local full-time wages; commissions directly elected by members of workers' and farmers' organizations were to administer the system; social insurance would be given to the sick and elderly, and maternity benefits would be paid eight weeks before and eight weeks after birth; and the system would be financed by unappropriated funds in the Treasury and by taxes on inheritances, gifts, and individual and corporation incomes above $5,000 a year. It easily rivaled the most social democratic laws ever proposed in Europe. It was endorsed by "more than 2,400 locals [in fact about 3,500], and the regular conventions of five International and six State bodies of the American Federation of Labor; practically every known unemployed organization; thousands of railroad and other independent local and central bodies, fraternal lodges, veterans', farmers', Negro, youth, women's and church groups [...] [and] municipal and county governmental bodies in seventy cities, towns and counties," in addition to millions of individual citizens who signed postcards and petitions in support of it. The terror it inspired in the wealthy ensured that it never had much chance of becoming law, but the point is that it united millions of Americans approximately along class lines and across barriers of race, ethnicity, sex, occupation, region, and even political ideology. In itself, however, its popularity was but a spectacular manifestation of the immense movement, the veritable crusade for social and unemployment insurance that swept up millions in class struggle.[41]

For the 1930s in the United States were not defined only by dismal economics, wretched poverty, and the whole litany of human degradation sampled in this chapter.

Center, box 5, folders 5–10; Frances Fox Piven and Richard A. Cloward, *Poor People's Movements: Why They Succeed, How They Fail* (New York: Pantheon Books, 1977), chapter 2.

41. Clarence Hathaway, "The Minnesota Farmer-Labor Victory," *Communist*, December 1936; Gene Dennis, "The Wisconsin Elections and the Farmer-Labor Party Movement," ibid.; McElvaine, *The Great Depression*, chapter 9; *Hearings before a Subcommittee of the Committee on Labor, House of Representatives*, 74th Congress, 1st session, February 1935, 1, 2; "Call to a National Congress for Unemployment and Social Insurance," *Unemployment Insurance Review*, vol. 1, 1935.

At least as importantly, the decade was defined by an upsurge of anticapitalist values: sharing, community, solidarity, the rejection of acquisitive individualism, the struggle for a *moral* economy. These years were the twentieth century's great backlash against the driving capitalist forces of privatization, marketization, and property rights over human rights—the backlash that grew out of this economy's crash into literal and moral bankruptcy. For a time, the advance of privatization was interrupted, even reversed. Thus, far from universally atomizing, mass unemployment also united, drawing people out of isolation to help each other and create shared public spaces.

In the following, accordingly, I will focus not only on the dreariness and horrors of Depression life in Chicago, or the failure of policy to ensure compassionate care for the destitute, or the oligarchical structure of Chicago's political economy that determined policy priorities. More positively, as mentioned in the Introduction, I will examine the shift in popular values and practices that occurred, including the eruption of a nearly anarchist—antiauthoritarian—populism among the downtrodden and the institutions that came to represent them. Doubtless the social discontent was most often channeled into relatively "nonrevolutionary," non-Communist outlets, for most Americans had a healthy skepticism of the Communist Party—their rejection of it tended to grow out of an eminently rational analysis of social and political possibilities in the United States. Given their correct understanding of the realities of power, the majority of the unemployed were in fact surely less deceived than many of the radical activists who sought to rouse them to revolution.[42]

Still, as we'll see, Americans, ostensibly a conservative and individualistic people, rejected the prevailing political economy to an incredible extent.

---

42. On the impressive lack of realism of the Communist true believer, see Aileen S. Kraditor, *"Jimmy Higgins": The Mental World of the American Rank-and-File Communist, 1930–1958* (New York: Greenwood Press, 1988).

Chapter Two

HARDSHIP

"Any city, however small, is in fact divided into two, one the city of the poor, the other of the rich." So said Plato in fourth century BC; so say many social critics in the twenty-first century AD. And so was certainly the case in the 1930s, of no city more than of Chicago. At the same time as the *Daily News* was reporting on high society and high fashion—embroidered dinner frocks, gold mesh peplums, debutantes attending balls dressed in gowns of white chiffon with silver sequins—the *Daily Worker* was reporting of Chicagoans dropping dead from "pure hunger," police officers killing Black men protesting an eviction, and thousands of children suffering from acute malnutrition and disease. The jobless and the poor were not likely to receive much consideration from a city legendary for its political corruption, its gangsterism, its violence and police brutality, where the wealthy class of bankers and businessmen was largely refusing to pay its taxes in the early 1930s—so much so that in one year, for example, Silas Strawn, head of the U.S. Chamber of Commerce and a multimillionaire, paid a property tax of only $120, and many other businessmen paid taxes as low as $20—a city where, for the sole purpose of preventing a rise in taxes to pay for relief and social services, "a group of bank presidents, department-store heads, and chiefs of manufacturing companies" could openly take control of the government for a brief period in 1932 and force cuts in "extravagant" expenditures. In such a city, it is not surprising that the suffering among the jobless should be "immeasurably worse than in any other section or city" in the country, to quote a contemporary observer. Nor is it surprising that, in light of the blithe disregard of the wealthy, "the real burden of this crisis [should be] borne not by any relief agency, but by the poor sharing with the poor," as stated in a 1932 report by the Chicago Workers' Committee on Unemployment (WCU). "Small merchants, landlords, milkmen, school teachers, who have little or nothing themselves, are straining their own resources to the breaking point to help their neighbors, relatives, and friends."[1]

Before considering the means by which the second city, the city of the poor, tried to keep body and soul together, it is necessary to describe exactly what that city had to endure. Of course, it was not a homogeneous entity; it was divided into races, sexes,

---

1. Plato, *The Republic*, Book IV; *Chicago Daily News*, January 6, 7, 8, 1932; Mauritz Hallgren, *Seeds of Revolt: A Study of American Life and the Temper of the American People during the Depression* (New York: Alfred A. Knopf, 1933), 123–27; James Mickel Williams, *Human Aspects of Unemployment and Relief, with Special Reference to the Effects of the Depression on Children* (Chapel Hill, NC: University of North Carolina Press, 1933), 6.

ethnicities, and occupations. Since this is a book on the unemployed and not exclusively the poor, we'll also have to consider the experiences of middle-class professionals who temporarily lost their jobs because of the economic downturn. Their physical deprivation was not always as extreme as that of "blue-collar" workers, but mentally their suffering—their frequent loss of status and self-respect, their boredom and frustration with a workless existence—could be even worse.

Chicago's economy did not fully recover until 1943, more than a year after the United States had entered World War II. The cumulative experience of the city's industrial workers is emblematic, revealing in perhaps exaggerated form trends in the broader economy. From 550,000 employed industrial workers in 1929, the monthly average shrank to 332,000 in 1933, then climbed, painstakingly and with interruptions, up to almost the 1929 level in 1937, after which it collapsed again the following year. In 1939, finally, a cyclical upturn began that, despite some hiccups in 1940, was comparatively resilient, leading into the dynamism of the war years and the steep decline of the relief rolls between 1941 and 1943. In the periods of expansion, culminating in the expansion of the early 1940s, payrolls tended to grow more dramatically than employment, which indicates that much of the work being done in stagnant years was on a part-time basis (and often at extra-low wages). All this goes to show that from 1930 until about 1941, the situation of the average industrial worker, whether in steel or printing or chemicals, was very precarious, characterized by long spells of unemployment interrupted by part-time or, mercifully, full-time work, which at any moment could lapse back into unemployment.[2]

Even workers in the packing industry, which was somewhat less depressed than most, were granted no dispensation from the hardships and uncertainties of insecure employment. The meatpacking "underemployment" problem mentioned in the last chapter persisted, off and on, through the whole decade (as, indeed, it had earlier). As one man recalled, employees would sometimes report for work only to find the doors locked. "No notice, nothing, just tough luck fellows. That's the way it was and it happened more than once. Two weeks, three weeks, sometimes only three days, but you never knew when and for how long." With the exception of Black workers, who had no security whatsoever, work for the 25,000 men and women employed in Chicago's stockyards and packinghouses was typically more regular but not much more secure than for other manufacturing employees. For example, in March 1933, when Chicago's manufacturing employment as a whole was at 59 percent of its monthly average between 1923 and 1925, it was at 76 percent in meatpacking.[3]

The plight of Black workers, however, made that of whites seem enviable. The increased willingness of whites during the Depression to take unskilled jobs in the wretched meatpacking industry led to a substantial loss of Black labor in the one industry where, proportionately, it had been significantly overrepresented. The percentage of

---

2. *Chicago Tribune*, October 22, 1939, December 15, 1940, January 18, 1942, March 27 and November 6, 1943, January 2, 1944.
3. Robert Slayton, *Back of the Yards* (Chicago, IL: University of Chicago Press, 1986), 189; Rick Halpern, *Down on the Killing Floor* (Chicago, IL: University of Illinois Press, 1997), 100; *Chicago Tribune*, August 30, 1935, January 19, 1936, January 21 and May 8, 1938.

Black workers in Chicago's packinghouses and stockyards fell from over 30 in 1930 to less than 20 in 1940. But this sharp decline was not confined to meatpacking or even manufacturing: in every sector of the economy, the loss of Black labor in the 1930s was much more pronounced than the loss of white labor—five times more pronounced in the case of professional and managerial work. Racist discrimination was so extreme that in years of economic expansion, when the mainstream press was full of employers' complaints about a dearth of skilled labor, some of these same employers refused to hire skilled Black craftsmen. Largely because of such endemic racism, Black women continued through the 1930s to have better chances of finding a job than their menfolk, since domestic work was more open to them. This alone, however, could not keep families afloat. Approximately 5 out of 10 Black families in Chicago remained dependent on some type of government aid in 1940; and of people receiving direct relief the following year, 41 percent were Black. "Between 1935 and 1940," the authors of the classic *Black Metropolis* sum up, "the Negro proletariat seemed doomed to become a *lumpen-proletariat*."[4]

One way to gain insight into the characteristics of the unemployed, in terms of their industry, occupation, and duration of unemployment, is to extrapolate from data on relief recipients. In Chicago their number was never even close to the total employable jobless, but the data on them are at least suggestive. In particular, a study that the federal government conducted in May 1934 of workers on relief in 79 cities, including Chicago, is illuminating. If one corrects for probable differences in composition between the unemployed on relief and those not on relief, it was found, for example, that both in Chicago and nationally, occupations in the manufacturing and mechanical industries, especially building and construction, were overrepresented among the jobless population; the clerical, professional, public service, and trade occupations were underrepresented; and the incidence of unemployment was, predictably, higher among unskilled than skilled workers. In Illinois in February 1935, 83 percent of workers on relief were manual workers—which helps explain why half of Blacks and a third of Mexicans were on relief, compared to less than a fifth of whites.[5]

A Chicago study based on census figures in 1931, before things got *really* bad, gives more detailed information, summarized in Tables 3, 4 and 5. (In the later months of the year, the numbers of unemployed were higher than those listed.)[6]

---

4. Walter A. Fogel, *The Negro in the Meat Industry* (Philadelphia, PA: University of Pennsylvania, 1970), 48–51; St. Clair Drake and Horace Cayton, *Black Metropolis* (New York: Harcourt, Brace and Company, 1945), 217, 88, 89; *Chicago Tribune*, December 26, 1940, May 18, 1941; "Unemployment among Nonwhites in the United States, March 1940," *Monthly Labor Review* (May 1941): 1181–84.
5. Gladys L. Palmer and Katherine D. Wood, *Urban Workers on Relief* (New York: Da Capo Press, 1971/1936), passim; Louise Ano Nuevo Kerr, "The Chicano Experience in Chicago: 1920–1970" (PhD diss., University of Illinois at Chicago Circle, 1976), 78; Elizabeth A. Hughes, *Illinois Persons on Relief in 1935: A Report of a Project Sponsored by the Illinois Emergency Relief Commission and Conducted under the Auspices of the Works Progress Administration, Illinois* (Chicago, IL, 1937), xvi, xliii.
6. Grace Lee Maymon, "An Analysis of the United States Census Figures on Unemployment in Chicago, 1930 and 1931" (MA thesis, University of Chicago, 1934), 34, 12.

Table 3 Total unemployed in Chicago in 1931, by industry

	Gainful workers	Unemployed workers	Percent unemployed
All industries	1,558,949	450,244	28.9
Agriculture, forestry, fishing	3829	1765	46.0
Extraction of minerals	1,221	344	28.2
Manufacturing and mechanical	624,951	251,884	40.3
Transportation	180,489	42,253	23.4
Trade	360,526	64,757	18.0
Public service	31,383	5,258	16.8
Professional work	111,470	10,611	9.5
Domestic and personal	187,248	53,199	28.4
Industry not specified	57,832	20,173	34.9

Table 4 Men unemployed in Chicago in 1931, by occupational group

	Gainful workers	Unemployed workers	Percent unemployed
All occupations	1,152,108	353,980	30.7
Proprietors and managers	123,926	8,752	7.1
Professionals	35,171	5,158	14.7
Clerks and kin	227,392	41,107	18.1
Skilled workers	260,818	105,305	40.4
Semiskilled workers	197,894	72,414	36.6
Unskilled workers	167,313	95,749	57.2
Domestic servants	63,019	16,950	26.9

Table 5 Women unemployed in Chicago in 1931, by occupational group

	Gainful workers	Unemployed workers	Percent unemployed
All occupations	406,750	96,264	23.7
Proprietors and managers	9,702	481	5.0
Professionals	34,700	2,114	6.1
Clerks and kin	176,160	31,173	17.7
Skilled workers	7,400	1,502	20.2
Semiskilled workers	87,801	31,057	35.4
Unskilled workers	8,463	2,853	33.7
Domestic servants	69,002	26,034	37.7

The distribution of (former) occupations and industries among the unemployed stayed roughly the same through the decade.[7]

Information on the duration of unemployment is equally interesting. Data on relief recipients are instructive (though a bit skewed, since, as a rule, only people who had

---

7. C. R. Thompson, "Analysis of Occupational Characteristics of Employable Persons Receiving Relief from Chicago Relief Administration during the Month of September, 1937" (Illinois State Department of Labor, 1937), 9.

been jobless for more than a couple of months made the wrenching decision to give up their independence and apply for relief). A 1937 survey of the Chicago relief rolls determined that half of the cases had been on relief for more than four years, most of them without any break. It is true that some of these people were, or had become, "unemployable" (from old age, disability, mental illness, or the need to stay at home to take care of children), but the data show, at any rate, that unemployment was apt to last a brutally long time. By 1939, thousands of men had been out of work for six or seven years.[8]

White-collar workers may have been better off than most in the industrial sector, but this fact was of little consolation to the many who did suffer. Teachers, clerks, architects, engineers, musicians—thousands of all these relatively "privileged" Chicagoans were laid off, sometimes for years. Or they simply didn't receive pay for months at a time. The saga of public school teachers in the early 1930s (as of many other municipal employees) is especially tragic. Tax collection had been suspended between 1927 and 1929, as taxable property was being reassessed, but the city had continued to spend money from the sale of tax anticipation warrants, thereby accumulating large deficits. They were further accumulated by the reassessment's lowering of property valuations in Chicago, which meant there was less taxable income when collection was finally resumed. Worst of all, a tax strike by large property owners from 1929 to 1932 utterly crippled the city's finances, so exacerbating deficits and starving Chicago's treasury—which was simultaneously under attack from the economic crisis—that in April 1931 the city declared it could not pay its 14,000 teachers. Between May 1931 and May 1933 they were paid for only *four months*, while continuing to work and indeed paying for hungry schoolchildren's lunches. Teachers placed much of the blame for their years-long ordeal on the banks, which up to April 1933 were refusing to buy the tax anticipation warrants that were, for the moment, the only way for the city to pay its employees. Even after the new mayor Ed Kelly prevailed on banks to lend the Board of Education some money in April 1933, it was to give teachers but a fraction of what they were owed. Only in August 1934 was Kelly finally able to give them all their back pay, when he secured a loan of $25 million from the Reconstruction Finance Corporation.[9]

And yet the teachers' trials were far from over, for the city proceeded to impose years of austerity budgets on the school system, pleading high deficits. It closed junior high schools and two-year colleges, reduced the number of kindergarten classes by half, increased teaching loads 40 percent and enlarged class sizes, shortened the school year by a month, cut teachers' salaries and laid off over a thousand, and curtailed physical education and music instruction. These cuts were but one piece of a citywide program

---

8. Benjamin Glassberg and Alexander J. Gregory, "How Long Are Clients on Relief?" (Chicago, IL: American Public Welfare Association, 1938), 8–11, 29. See also Richard J. Jensen, "The Causes and Cures of Unemployment in the Great Depression," *Journal of Interdisciplinary History* 19, no. 4 (Spring 1989): 553–83.
9. Roger Biles, *Big City Boss in Depression and War: Mayor Edward J. Kelly of Chicago* (DeKalb, IL: Northern Illinois University Press, 1984), 22–24; Lyman B. Burbank, "Chicago's Public Schools and the Depression Years of 1928–1937," *Journal of the Illinois State Historical Society* 64 (Winter 1971): 365–81; *New York Herald Tribune*, August 26, 1934. See also John F. Lyons, "Chicago Teachers Unite," *Chicago History* 32, no. 3 (Spring 2004): 32–47.

of retrenchment, which also involved the closing of nearly all evening schools, the ending of summer schools, the abolition of community centers, and the reduction of playgrounds. Such trends operated all over the country, but Chicago was a particularly egregious case.[10]

One writer concluded that "public education is threatened with something little short of an absolute breakdown in vast areas of the country." Just between 1931 and 1933, school budget reductions in small cities outside the South averaged 33 percent, even as nationwide enrollment was increasing by almost 200,000 students. Whether the continually invoked justification of "fiscal health" necessitated such austerities is debatable: more than one knowledgeable commentator attributed the cuts to a hostility among the wealthy to public education as such, noting that most of them sent their children to private schools and that the costs (in high taxes) of these expanding public schools "had become unendurable to those who had no use for them. The crash of '29," he suggested, "provided the pretext for the declaration of war." Tax delinquency was an enormous problem throughout the Depression: many cities and towns around the country collected but a quarter to a third of the taxes levied. Nor, in most cases, did they do anything to raise taxes on those who could most afford to pay. In any event, these severe cutbacks—which ironically helped stimulate popular protest, supported by Franklin Roosevelt, for an expansion of the federal government's role in society—had clear consequences with respect to the earnings and employment of many thousands of workers around the country.[11]

In fact, it bears emphasis that the misery of the poor and the unemployed in the 1930s was made possible by one circumstance above all: the *unwillingness* of government on the local, state, and federal levels to provide aid in sufficient amounts. "The public clamor for tax reduction and economy in government in some sections of the country," a liberal writer remarked in 1932, "has risen to the point of hysteria. 'Business can no longer stand the burden of government.' So goes the popular refrain all too frequently." The gospel of "economy" (austerity) and budget balancing that was preached by Chambers of Commerce, Businessmen's Associations, the National Association of Manufacturers, Real Estate Boards, "taxpayers' associations" like the Civic Federation of Chicago, and lobbying groups for bankers, and was echoed by their media mouthpieces like the *Chicago Tribune*, became a near-religion for local and state governments. When even police forces, schools, health departments, and libraries were being downsized, there was little chance that relief for the poor would be expanded sufficiently to meet the crisis. The federal government, too, was deeply susceptible to balanced-budget thinking,

---

10. Biles, *Big City Boss*, 25, 26; Burbank, "Chicago's Public Schools," 373–75; *New York Times*, July 19, 23, 1933; *Chicago Tribune*, September 17, 1933; Milton S. Mayer, "How to Wreck Your Schools: The Destruction of Education in Chicago," *Forum and Century*, May 1937; William Carr, quoted in Eunice Langdon, "The Teacher Faces the Depression," *Nation*, August 16, 1933.
11. Langdon, "The Teacher Faces the Depression"; "Schools Badly Affected," *Weekly News Letter*, Illinois State Federation of Labor, December 30, 1933; Mayer, "How to Wreck Your Schools"; Howard P. Jones, "The Crisis in Local Government," *Survey*, October 15, 1932.

as historians have observed—not only in the Hoover years but also the Roosevelt years, especially the last third of the Depression decade.[12]

Up to the 1940s, Chicago's budget was subject to the discipline of austerity. Substantially raising taxes on the rich, or even collecting all the money that had been lost through tax delinquency, was off the agenda. Thus, in 1938 Mayor Kelly boasted before a meeting of business leaders that that year's corporate fund expenditures—that is, funding for such services as public safety, public health, sanitation, and transportation—were lower than their level in 1927, despite the population increase of 350,000. And he promised an austere 1939 budget. As we'll see in Chapter five, the CRA, which oversaw relief in the second half of the decade, was continuously starved of funds—not because of Illinois's poverty, for it was one of the wealthiest states in the country, but because adequate unemployment relief was simply not a priority for the city's and state's governing institutions.[13]

One last thing to note before we consider the hardship of Chicago's economic outcasts is the level of overall unemployment from 1930 to 1939. Table 6 gives (conservative) government estimates of monthly averages for Illinois, which we can assume are a few percentage points below the levels in Chicago[14]:

Table 6 Monthly averages of unemployment in Illinois

	Estimated unemployed	*Percent unemployed*
1930	468,728	16.5
1931	810,221	28.4
1932	1,214,746	42.4
1933	1,170,821	40.7
1934	945,896	32.7
1935	884,984	30.5
1936	732,599	25.2
1937	511,473	17.5
1938	891,828	30.4
1939	798,494	27.1

No wonder it seemed to people that precarious living was the new *permanent* condition.

Physical Hardship

Hunger and disease

In January 1932, in the depths of the Depression, the Chicago WCU organized a series of public hearings to draw attention to the suffering of the jobless multitudes. Almost

---

12. Jones, "The Crisis in Local Government"; *New York Times*, January 6, 1930, March 26, 1932, January 3, 1933, November 29, 1935, January 15, 1939; *New York Herald Tribune*, September 27, 1936; *Chicago Tribune*, April 11, 1940; *Washington Post*, March 20, 1932.
13. *Chicago Tribune*, November 11, 1938, April 21, 1939.
14. Illinois Department of Labor, Division of Statistics and Research, *Review of Employment and Payrolls for Illinois Industries and Cities* (Chicago, IL, 1940), 24.

two hundred people testified from the Humboldt Park area, South Chicago, the South Side and the West Side Black districts, as well as several other heavily affected areas. The testimonies, some of which were reported in Chicago newspapers and subsequently summarized in a WCU report titled "An Urban Famine," are valuable for giving human content to the statistics mentioned above.

The first and most obvious condition spotlighted was the lack of physical necessities. "The situation," the Workers' Committee reported, "bears all the earmarks of a famine. [...] Malnutrition is prevalent and starvation is far from unusual." Needless to say, this was the case all over the country. In 1935, for example, the United States Department of Labor reported that 25 percent of American children were undernourished, in some areas 70 percent. Children, in fact, suffered the worst. One Chicago charity official noted that "we find such evidences of malnutrition as poor posture and lack of muscle tone, and eyes no longer bright"; rickets ("soft bones"), anemia, diphtheria, scurvy, and tuberculosis became more common. As early as 1931, it was reported that perhaps 35 percent of Chicago schoolchildren were suffering from malnutrition. "Nothing is more heartrending," a health expert remarked, "than to see the malnourished, hungry child, in spite of this physical defect and the pangs of hunger, making a futile effort to concentrate on his lessons with dizzy head and gnawing appetite." Luckily, teachers' compassion could sometimes come to the rescue[15]:

> It is heart breaking [said one teacher] to watch the children at recess look longingly at their favorite luxury, a "hot dog." I saw several ragged children watching the more fortunate ones eating them the other day. They seemed so hungry and wistful. I reached down in my pocket for several nickels and fed the lot of them. They had a real feast.[16]

Such generosity was possible even when teachers had not been paid for a few months; but after eight months or more of absent paychecks, famished schoolchildren had either to suffer stoically or hope that private institutions would undertake a fundraising campaign on their behalf. The *Chicago Tribune*, for example, sponsored a Hungry School Children's Fund to solicit donations from the public—tens of thousands of dollars. Unfortunately, none of this money was available for Chicago's unpaid teachers, who were left to waste away. Such stories abounded as of a single woman living for weeks on graham crackers and milk. By the summer of 1932 (or earlier), hundreds of teachers were walking to school every day or hitchhiking because they could not afford transportation; hundreds were rushing to second jobs immediately after class ended; and at least six hundred were "in the hands of charity organizations—and were it not for these

---

15. "An Urban Famine," Frank McCulloch Papers, Chicago History Museum, Research Center, box 4, folder 1; statement by Israel Amter, *Hearings before a Subcommittee of the Committee on Labor, House of Representatives*, 74th Congress, 1st session, February 1935, 215, 216; Robert McElvaine, *The Great Depression*, 80; Katherine Kelley, "Infant Welfare Society Wars on Malnutrition," *Chicago Tribune*, October 28, 1933; *Chicago Tribune*, June 19 and December 26, 1931.
16. "Too Little Food Makes Joe Dull Boy in School," *Chicago Tribune*, October 7, 1932.

charity organizations, they would be starving in the streets," as the editor of the *Chicago Herald and Examiner* put it.[17]

There have been many accounts of the misery of the 1930s, but somehow one does not fully appreciate the apocalyptic character of those years, particularly before the New Deal, until immersing oneself in documents from the time. It was simply ludicrous when Herbert Hoover declared, "No one is actually starving." In reality, as early as October 1930, the head of Chicago's Bureau of Public Welfare admitted that 12,000 Chicagoans were starving—this in the "world center of the surplus of foodstuffs," as an outraged writer commented. By 1932, there were at least 20,000 men in flophouses and breadlines every day, a number that continued to rise. Hospitals around the city became so overcrowded with hunger patients that sick workers and their children were constantly turned away.[18]

As we know, conditions kept worsening up to 1933. Relief had to be cut repeatedly because of lack of money and lack of "political will" to address the problem—a euphemism, as we'll see, for the business elite's desire to keep relief at low levels. The costs of this policy in lost lives and social disruption, which continued to accumulate, were such that between 1931 and 1933 even the press and prominent politicians repeatedly insisted that hundreds of thousands were on the verge of starvation. One reads headlines—sometimes exaggerated—like "Chicago Crisis Worst Since the Fire of 1871" and "Half a Million in Chicago May Face Early Starvation." But even these alarmist headlines contained some truth. Daily, people were dying of hunger and resultant disease in flophouses, hospitals, shacks, and claustrophobic apartments, in neighborhoods from the steel-working South Chicago to the meatpacking Back of the Yards to the Loop-laboring Near North Side. Some families had to resort to such barbarities as eating their cat. Garbage-eating, too, was a continually practiced device for staying alive, and for feeding one's family—though the city looked upon it none too kindly. To discourage the poor, the city was apt to run big tractors over staple foods dumped in landfills to mash them up, making them inedible to the hundreds of starving people hoping for scraps.[19]

The plight of single men, friendless and homeless, frequently compelled to roam the country in search of a job, has been much discussed in the scholarship on the Depression, but that of single unemployed women less so. They often had it even worse. "According to the reports of social workers," we read in one account, "food is the first thing that goes when a woman is up against it, and appearance and clothes are the last. [...] They know that 60 percent of their chances of getting a job depend on their

---

17. *Chicago Tribune*, October 4 and 20, November 2, 1931, and April 10, 1933; Biles, *Big City Boss*, 23; testimony by Victor Watson, *Hearing before a Subcommittee of the Committee on Manufactures on S. 4592*, Senate, 72nd Congress, 1st session (June 4, 1932), 40; *Daily Worker*, October 16, 1931.
18. Frank Palmer, "12,000 Starving in Chicago," *Federation News*, October 18, 1930; *Hearings before a Subcommittee of the Committee on Manufactures on S. 4076*, Senate, 72nd Congress, 1st session (June 20, 1932), 15, 16; *Daily Worker*, April 18 and September 10, 1931.
19. *New York Times*, January 25, 1932; *China Press*, January 16 and July 13, 1932; Bill Gebert, "The Reign of Hunger and Terror in Chicago," *Daily Worker*, January 26, 1932; *Hunger Fighter*, January 9 and April 23, 1932.

appearance." Disdaining breadlines and soup kitchens as "degrading," many of these independent women, formerly middle class, even "postponed medical care when it was urgently needed." Bread, coffee, an occasional fruit, and whatever else they could find constituted their daily fare.[20]

Even the jobless who were lucky enough to have homes rarely had an adequate diet. For those who had been unemployed more than a couple of months, starchy foods were the mainstay. In Back of the Yards, for example, many families subsisted on potatoes, stale bread dampened with water and covered with sugar or mustard, and sauerkraut (especially among Poles). People who qualified and were willing to go on relief often did better than others, for, when the relief budgets were low, food was the last thing to be sacrificed. By 1932, with the help of state funding, the Cook County Bureau of Public Welfare gave a monthly ration of staples, canned goods, milk, beans, oatmeal, and so on, plus two grocery orders each month. It was a monotonous diet—and the way the monthly ration was disbursed, through a "commissary" system, was especially humiliating—but on the whole it kept families from being tortured with hunger, most of the time. Still, the public need and the relief apparatus were so gigantic that families constantly complained about inadequacies, such as food orders that had not been received or ration boxes from the commissary that had rancid bacon and coarse flour.[21]

As the Depression progressed and the state and federal governments stepped in with more funds, more of the unemployed were able to go on relief. In Chicago, only 11 percent of families whose heads were unemployed were on relief in April 1930; this number rose to 32 percent in January 1932. With interruptions, it continued to increase thereafter. These families, then, tended to have at least a minimal amount of food security, although the nutritional component was usually substandard. The situation improved with the establishment of the FERA, especially after October 1933, when the government started distributing surplus foods to relief clients, in addition to the food they were already receiving. The surplus foods program lasted the rest of the decade.[22]

That circumstance was fortunate, for there were moments in the second half of the 1930s when Chicago relief was virtually shut down and the only things families had to eat were the surplus commodities distributed by the federal government. In the fall of 1937, food allowances were cut by a third: they averaged nine cents per meal per

---

20. Betty Hansen, "The Effect of Unemployment on the Personality and Attitudes of Women," 1934, Ernest Burgess Papers, box 146, folder 5; Emily Hahn, "Women without Work," *New Republic*, May 31, 1933.
21. Slayton, *Back of the Yards*, 190; testimony by Edith Abbott, *Hearings before a Subcommittee of the Committee on Manufactures on S. 5125*, Senate, 72nd Congress, 2nd session (January 1933), 264; *Chicago Tribune*, November 4, 1932; "Reports of Studies of Families Living on the Budget of the Unemployment Relief Service of the Cook County Bureau of Public Welfare," April 1932, Mary McDowell Papers, Chicago History Museum, box 3, folder 16; Laura Friedman, "A Study of One Hundred Unemployed Families in Chicago, January, 1927 to June, 1932" (MA thesis, University of Chicago, 1933), 173.
22. "Estimate of Minimum Relief Requirements for Chicago for Fiscal Year October 1, 1931– September 30, 1932," United Charities Papers, Chicago History Museum, box 8, folder 2.

person, which was less than that provided for dogs at animal shelters. After the federal government in late 1935 stopped financing direct relief, average monthly relief grants in Chicago fell dramatically, in some years to around 75 percent of the budget that the CRA had declared the minimum for subsistence.[23]

A Chicago alderman estimated in 1939 that over two hundred thousand people in the city were slowly starving because of inadequate relief. Large families from South Chicago to the Near West Side sometimes received only $30 or $40 per month, which did not even cover their food budget, much less rent and everything else. Black families on the South Side survived on neck bones and dried beans. Even men who had been lucky enough to get off direct relief and take a WPA job frequently found it difficult or impossible to pay for rent, clothing, light, gas, and food for their family on the pitiful monthly wage of $55 for unskilled workers.[24]

Such tragic tendencies were not unique to Chicago. Contrary to old liberal myths of steady progress for the poor under the New Deal, one-third of the nation was still "ill-housed, ill-clad, and ill-nourished" in 1940. Indeed, according to a study by the Citizens' Committee of Planned Parenthood, about a third still lived at or below a *bare subsistence* level 10 years after the 1929 crash. Another study, in 1939, concluded that "few even of the *middle* third [of the country, in income] are able to enjoy what is customarily called an American standard of living."[25]

As already stated, mass hunger was typically attended by mass malnutrition and (less so) disease. Like most things associated with the Depression, this fact was most dramatically and suddenly manifested in the early years. The head of the Jewish Charities of Chicago, one of the best-funded agencies that took good care of its clients, said in December 1931 that visiting nurses were discovering in almost every home "a problem of illness that is unmet." The inadequacy of health facilities—and of relief resources devoted to medical care—remained a major problem in metropolitan Chicago throughout the 1930s, though it was especially acute in the years of crisis that

---

23. Dwayne Charles Cole, "The Relief Crisis in Illinois during the Depression, 1930–1940" (PhD diss., St. Louis University, 1973), 376–78, 367; *Washington Post*, May 17, 1938; Arthur P. Miles, "Relief in Illinois without Federal Aid," *Social Service Review* XIV (June 1940): 283–300; Relief Commission of the Council of Hyde Park and Kenwood Churches, *Report on Relief in Illinois* (Chicago, IL, 1940), 9; "Public Hearing on the Relief and WPA Situation in Chicago" at the Humboldt Park Methodist Church, February 21, 1938, in Frank McCulloch Papers, box 56, folder 1.
24. To understand how inadequate that wage was, consider that the minimum standard income for a family of three—and most working-class families were larger—was generally considered to be $1,500 per year. That translates to $29 per week, or $116 per month. So, $55 for an unskilled WPA job was not exactly munificent. Alice Theresa Theodorson, "Living Conditions of Fifty Unemployed Families" (MA thesis, University of Chicago, 1935), 8, 9. Sources for the text above include a speech by Alderman Paul H. Douglas, August 8, 1939, in Frank McCulloch Papers, box 6, folder 1; *Chicago Defender*, October 21, 1939; "Public Hearing on the Relief and WPA Situation in Chicago"; "Meeting of District Supervisors," July 24, 1939, and letter from Joel Hunter to Governor Henry Horner, October 31, 1939, United Charities Papers, box 10, folder 2; *Chicago Tribune*, October 17, 1940.
25. *Chicago Defender*, April 15 and December 23, 1939.

bookended the decade (1930–33 and 1938–40). For one thing, the city and county had not a single public clinic for the ambulatory sick in need of general care, unlike New York City, Los Angeles, Boston, Philadelphia, and Minneapolis, which had extensive municipal clinic facilities. Inadequate private clinics were left to care for the large majority of the ambulatory sick poor. These people frequently had to travel long distances to stand in line for hours, just to be told, sometimes, that the place was too crowded to accept them. For many, it was only when they became seriously ill that they could be taken care of: a police patrol wagon might then be called to take them to Cook County Hospital.[26]

As for the number of poor people needing care, it is partly indicated by the fact that visits to the 12 clinics that ministered most to poor outpatients doubled within a few years after the Depression began, reaching almost a million visits in 1935 and staying at that level for the rest of the decade. This, of course, does not include hospital visits, at-home care, or the many thousands who needed help but did not receive it. Even for simple cases, as opposed to patients who needed X-rays, laboratory work, or the like, hospitals were so overcrowded from 1938 to 1940 that they regularly had long waiting lists, which meant that sick people might have to wait months or over a year for care. This was similar to the Depression's early years, except that "the ridiculous anomaly of the economic system"—tremendous unused supplies despite tremendous need to use them—was more obvious in the first half of the decade. Even in 1934, government hospitals were still overflowing at the same time that nongovernment hospitals were half-empty, because of patients' inability to pay for service.[27]

Especially before the state and federal governments had taken over responsibility for relief, spending on medical care by many (not all) welfare agencies was pathetically insufficient. Of necessity, most of the money they gave went for food. The United Charities, for example, which in 1928 provided medical care and clothing, had by 1931 practically eliminated those items from relief. Such financial exigencies, which persisted in a milder form even after the federal government had begun to fund relief, led to the "desperate" plight of patients needing dental care or dentures. Teeth removed, dentures were denied. Clients in pain regularly had to wait up to a year or two to get a referral to a dentist. In 1936, it was estimated that 90 percent of Chicagoans were afflicted with dental disease, and only 25 percent received adequate care. These problems replicated national trends, for according to a 1936 survey by the American Dental

---

26. Testimony by Samuel Goldsmith, *Hearings before a Subcommittee of the Committee on Manufactures on S. 174 and S. 262*, Senate, 72nd Congress, 1st session (December 1931), 36; "Chicago's Sick and the Lack of Clinic Facilities," October 5, 1938, Raymond Hilliard Papers, Chicago History Museum, box 77, folder 4.
27. "Chicago's Sick and the Lack of Clinic Facilities"; Mary Diran, "Medical Care Given to a Group of Clients of the Unemployment Relief Service" (MA thesis, University of Chicago, 1935), 6; Babette S. Jennings, "Health Services in Chicago," in *Social Service Year Book, 1934*, eds. Linn Brandenburg et al. (Chicago, IL: Council of Social Agencies, 1934), 54.

Association, between 87 and 99 percent of all elementary school children in the United States had decayed teeth and were in need of treatment.[28]

In fact, even during the era of FERA, from mid-1933 to 1935, knowledgeable commentators declared it an "indisputable fact" that at least half the country was without adequate medical care. Things were especially bad, of course, for minorities and low-income groups, such as Mexicans. Garbage was infrequently collected in Chicago's Mexican neighborhoods; according to one physician in 1930, "insufficient food, poor housing, crowding, [...] everything is ideal for the development of many diseases, among which tuberculosis occupies the most important place."[29]

As usual, however, no one suffered worse than Blacks. For the whole decade, outpatients had one main resource, a clinic at a private hospital on the South Side (Provident Hospital), which could not meet more than a small fraction of the need. The situation was especially pitiful considering Blacks' high susceptibility to illness, because of their poverty. For instance, a reporter for Harry Hopkins, head of FERA, observed in 1934 that the incidence of tuberculosis was remarkably high among Chicago's African Americans. The average jobless person, he said, "has no money for medical service at the incipiency of his disease; moreover, he is compelled to double up in already overcrowded houses which have no running water, are insufficiently ventilated and devoid of sunshine, and have only one unspeakably filthy toilet for several families." It is no surprise, then, that the death rate from tuberculosis among Blacks in Chicago was 7 times that of whites, 290 per 100,000 people.[30]

As relief standards in Illinois deteriorated after 1935, so did the health of hundreds of thousands of people. The high caseloads of Chicago's public relief workers, as many as two hundred or more cases per person, ensured that clients' medical needs would be neglected. Few home visits, either for investigation or for the rendering of specialized services, were possible. The situation was aggravated by the fact that medical workers, too, had huge caseloads. When a physician finally did write an order for a client to take to a relief station so that it would give him a special diet or shoes or a mattress, it was far from guaranteed that the client would receive the item or service even after months of fighting and badgering the station. He was told to come back the following week or to wait in the office for hours for a supervisor who

---

28. Clorinne McCulloch Brandenburg, "Chicago Relief and Service Statistics, 1928–1931" (MA thesis, University of Chicago, 1932), 70, 72; "Chicago's Sick and the Lack of Clinic Facilities"; Diran, "Medical Care Given to a Group of Clients of the Unemployment Relief Service," 74; Mary E. Murphy, "Health Services in Chicago," in *Social Service Year Book, 1936*, 77; *Chicago Daily News*, August 18, 1936.
29. *Chicago Tribune*, December 3, 1934; "The Effects of Unemployment on the Personality of Women," 4; Mark Reisler, *By the Sweat of Their Brow: Mexican Immigrant Labor in the United States, 1900–1940* (Westport, CT: Greenwood Press, 1976), 107, 122.
30. "Chicago's Sick and the Lack of Clinic Facilities"; John F. Bauman and Thomas H. Coode, *In the Eye of the Great Depression: New Deal Reporters and the Agony of the American People* (DeKalb, IL: Northern Illinois University Press, 1988), 64, 65; *Chicago Defender*, August 3, 1935; Drake and Cayton, *Black Metropolis*, 204; Mary-Jane Grunsfeld, *Negroes in Chicago* (Chicago, IL: Mayor's Committee on Race Relations, 1944).

never showed up. If he went to the relief station day after day to solicit help for a sick daughter or wife at home, he was lucky if a nurse was eventually sent to his home to examine the patient.[31]

In late 1939, the Chicago Committee on Adequate Relief published an open letter that, in its outrage at the immorality of civilization, could almost have been written by one of the Old Testament prophets. Noting "MILLIONS OF DOLLARS ARE BEING SPENT IN CHICAGO AND ILLINOIS FOR SPACIOUS HIGHWAYS, BEAUTIFUL PUBLIC BUILDINGS, [AND] EXPANDED PUBLIC IMPROVEMENTS," it condemned authorities for the fact that, according to the Illinois State Health Department, death rates were on the rise. Among other circumstances, it reported the findings of a recent study that had compared 800 fee-enrolled students at the University of Chicago with 7,000 relief family enrollees with the Civilian Conservation Corps. "The 800," it summarized, "had good postures, good complexions, sound teeth, firm muscles," while "the 7,000 were rampant in defective teeth and hearing, curvature of the spine, pallid complexions," and signs of scurvy and rickets.[32]

One could cite similarly damning reports ad nauseam. But such facts as have been surveyed here should already suggest that, whatever they may have thought about their own intentions and motivations, political and economic authorities regularly acted with little regard for the poor. Particular officials may well have been dismayed at widespread suffering, but the institutional context in which they were embedded, organized as it was around a political economy of (objective) "class struggle," prevented them from diverting sufficient resources to social welfare programs.

We should keep in mind, incidentally, that the low standards of health and nutrition in the Depression were not a dramatic departure from the past. The health of those with a low income was certainly worse than it had been, but it had never been up to decent standards. According to a 1925 study, over two-thirds of unskilled or semiskilled workers in Chicago did not make enough money to give their family a standard of living equal to the minimum relief budget. And that was in a year of prosperity! Even when supplementary earnings by a wife or children were included, 45 percent of families surveyed were still unable to meet the requirements of the relief budget. In other words, a large number of people would have been better off if they had left their jobs and gone on relief.[33]

---

31. Glick, *The Illinois Emergency Relief Commission*, 217–23; Harriet A. Byrne and Cecile Hillyer, *Unattached Women on Relief in Chicago, 1937* (Washington, DC: Government Printing Office, 1938), 9, 10; "Public Hearing on the Relief and WPA Situation in Chicago."
32. "Open Letter and Report of the Chicago Committee on Adequate Relief," November 1939, Committee on Adequate Relief, Graham Taylor Papers, Chicago History Museum, box 53, folder 2378.
33. Leila Houghteling, *The Income and Standard of Living of Unskilled Laborers in Chicago* (Chicago, IL: University of Chicago Press, 1927), 86, 97–103.

Shelter and clothing

In the abovementioned WCU report on the 1932 hearings is a succinct paragraph that sums up the housing woes of hundreds of thousands in that dark time:

> The housing situation is critical in at least two aspects, eviction and crowding. People have been unable to pay rents for many months and landlords cannot carry them any longer. Evictions hang over the heads of thousands of families. Many families have already been forced to move a number of times. Charities are very seldom paying any rents. Many families have been forced to move into very small quarters or have moved in with other families with resultant serious overcrowding.

Behind those colorless sentences was a level of chaos and misery to which only Charles Dickens could have done justice.[34]

First of all, even before the Depression, the housing conditions of most Chicagoans were awful or mediocre. To quote an investigator, in the 1920s no less than the 1930s, "great masses of people still live[d] in very miserable homes and in conditions of almost unbelievable discomfort for this modern period—without the accepted conveniences of modern life, without bathrooms, without a single private toilet for family use, with broken and frozen plumbing, occasionally without a sink, [...] in rooms many times illegally overcrowded." The sprawling tenement districts on the West Side, the North and Northwest Sides, the South Side, South Chicago, and the Calumet region, submerged in palls of smoke and safely segregated from the pleasant wealthier neighborhoods, home to working-class Blacks, Mexicans, Poles, Jews, Slovaks, Lithuanians, Greeks, and over a dozen other nationalities—these tenement areas may have been less infamously congested than the tenements of New York, but they were not less dilapidated, or congested *inside*. In most areas, well over 75 percent of the tenements still inhabited in the 1930s had been built before 1902, and so were largely unaffected by a tenement-house code enacted in that year that was meant to improve conditions. Instead, the buildings deteriorated year after year, landlords refusing to modernize them as they awaited the "business invasion" that would raise land values and require the demolition of old houses. Frame tenements in particular, as opposed to brick-and-stone dwellings, had often been built hastily after the Great Fire of 1871 and so were unpainted, dingy, dark, and "unfit for the kind of homes that twentieth-century standards of decent living demand."[35]

These wood frame dwellings constituted a large proportion—from 45 to 95 percent—of the housing in many neighborhoods, such as Back of the Yards, the Hull House area, the Lower North Side, and, in the northwest, the Polish St. Stanislaus district. Wood is ravaged by time and weather, and so "everywhere [were] rickety porches, stairs, and sheds, rotting clapboards and shingles, grimy [and] smoke covered," in addition to ubiquitous vermin and the scourge of rats. Some families in the Hull House neighborhood,

---

34. "An Urban Famine," Frank McCulloch Papers.
35. Edith Abbott, *The Tenements of Chicago: 1908–1935* (Chicago, IL: University of Chicago Press, 1936), 479, 179–82, 184.

which was populated mostly by Italians and Greeks, actually slept with guns under the bed to shoot the rats in the night and hung food from the ceiling to protect it. It is true that sanitation had improved since 1900, with more adequate plumbing facilities. On the other hand, in 1925, most low-income houses and apartments canvassed did not have bathrooms, so all the water for cleaning and bathing was carried from the sink (often located in the hall). In the mid-1930s almost a third of apartments still had no toilet, contrary to regulations.[36]

For many families, most modern conveniences were lacking. Central heating was frequently absent, in the winter necessitating that families huddle around the coal stoves in their kitchen, the only heated room in the apartment. Some lived in the basement, damp and dark and poorly ventilated. These evils were often magnified in the case of furnished rooming houses, which provided accommodation (usually temporary) in rundown apartments of one or two rooms, and which by the 1930s had colonized large sections of the city. The buildings—sometimes old deteriorated homes of the wealthy—might be huge, housing 60 or a 100 families, but most of them offered far from desirable abodes, especially for children. Many without electricity and gas, filthy and vermin infested, full of dark halls and dirty, broken furniture, provisioned by one or two common toilets and sinks for the whole building, these apartments epitomized the "city of the poor." Nor was it morally uplifting that rooming houses could be located in the vice districts, so that, as one investigator said, "little children saw prostitutes and their so-called patrons coming and going through the common hallways."[37]

Over six hundred thousand Chicagoans regularly lived in rooming houses in the late 1920s, and probably more during the Depression. Irregular employment and financial necessity were common reasons for people to live there, as well as the desire for freedom, or for drink and drugs. It seems that American-born whites and Blacks, and not immigrants, were most likely to inhabit these degraded places; "transients" were frequently found there, and clerical workers, and "all sorts of shipwrecked humanity." This was notably the case in the "Hobohemia" that lent a colorful and cosmopolitan character to the outskirts of the Loop. Around West Madison Street near the river, North Clark Street, and South State Street, in districts overlapping with slums, tens of thousands of the most diverse nonconformists congregated and lived, a marvelous panoply of humanity—hoboes, peddlers, bootleggers, artists, soapbox orators, migratory workers, "dope fiends," prostitutes, bohemians of every conceivable provenance. Amid the cabarets and saloons, the dance halls and bars, the radical bookstores, the welfare agencies and employment agencies, were scores of ramshackle lodging houses, flophouses where guests slept on the floor or in bare wooden bunks, and homeless shelters for single men. One gets a sense of the scale of these Loop-proximate slums from the fact that even

---

36. Ibid., passim.; Houghteling, *The Income and Standard of Living of Unskilled Laborers*, 111; Elizabeth A. Hughes, *Living Conditions for Small Wage-Earners in Chicago* (Chicago, IL: Department of Public Welfare, 1925), 30.
37. Abbott, *The Tenements of Chicago*, 206, 222, 230, 403–407, chapter 10; Mary Faith Adams, "Present Housing Conditions in South Chicago, South Deering and Pullman" (MA thesis, University of Chicago, 1926), 46; *Chicago Tribune*, September 1, 1937.

before the Depression, around 400,000 migratory men passed annually through these districts, which—on the Near North Side and in "Little Hell," east of Goose Island—were also the home of small colonies of Persians, Greeks, Poles, Jews, and Sicilians. A sociologist has left us a memorable description of Little Hell in 1929:[38]

> Dirty and narrow streets, alleys piled with refuse and alive with dogs and rats, goats hitched to carts, bleak tenements, the smoke of industry hanging in a haze, the market along the curb, foreign names on shops, and foreign faces on the streets, the dissonant cry of the huckster and peddler, the clanging and rattling of railroads and the elevated, the pealing of the bells of the great Catholic churches, the music of marching bands and the crackling of fireworks on feast days, the occasional dull boom of a bomb or the bark of a revolver, the shouts of children at play in the street, a strange staccato speech, the taste of soot, and the smell of gas from the huge "gas house" by the river, whose belching flames make the sky lurid at night and long ago earned for the district the name Little Hell—on every hand one is met by sights and sounds and smells that are peculiar to this area, that are "foreign" and of the slum.[39]

Such was the world that is gone, the bursting-with-energy but stricken-with-poverty world. One can easily imagine the chaos of housing conditions in such a world, a not-yet-standardized place that thrilled with the kinetic energy of heterogeneity.

In addition to rooming houses and flophouses and cheap hotels was the widespread phenomenon, popular among immigrants and Blacks, of a family's taking in lodgers. In 1925, for example, a study found that over 40 percent of Mexican and Black one-family households had lodgers, as did a third of low-income native white households. This practice only intensified in the Depression, as unemployment made it even harder to pay rent. A housing shortage, moreover, had plagued Chicago for decades, as tens of thousands of men and families streamed in from the Old World and the American South, offering up their bodies and their lives to the leviathan corporations that refused to invest in adequate housing for their workers. Homeless men, laborers by day and wanderers by night, shacked up in boarding houses or flophouses or a small room set aside for them in some family's apartment. Strange men might sleep in the same room as the daughters of the household, two or more people might sleep in the same bed, or the kitchen might be converted into a bedroom at night. The housewife, of course, would have much more work to do if she took in lodgers, but it was judged worthwhile if they could help pay the rent.[40]

---

38. *Chicago Tribune*, December 9, 1926; *New York Times*, February 6, 1927; Abbott, *The Tenements of Chicago*, 327, 337; Harvey Warren Zorbaugh, *The Gold Coast and the Slum: A Sociological Study of Chicago's Near North Side* (Chicago, IL: University of Chicago Press, 1929), chapters 4, 6, 7, 8; Nels Anderson, "The Hobo: The Sociology of the Homeless Man" (PhD diss., University of Chicago, 1925), chapters 1 and 3.
39. Zorbaugh, *The Gold Coast and the Slum*, 159, 160.
40. Hughes, *Living Conditions for Small Wage-Earners*, 13; Abbott, *The Tenements of Chicago*, chapter 11; Reisler, *By the Sweat of Their Brow*, 106.

Conditions in some of the Chicago slums were so bad that politicians and the mainstream press took chagrined notice of them, bewailing their mutilation of the city's image. Visitors entering Chicago on trains would get a "closeup of Chicago's worst—abandoned shacks, backyards full of rubbish, chimneys that lean at crazy angles, broken windows stuffed with rags, trash heaps in unkempt alleys, and homes that have little to distinguish them from the trash heaps." These slummy areas, again, were not a negligible portion of the city: they constituted a third or more of it, according to one estimate in 1941. In fact, in the 1940s the Black Belt, an area less than five square miles on the South Side, had the highest population density in the world, higher than Calcutta, India: 90,000 people per square mile.[41]

In short, both before and after the Depression, Chicago's housing situation was not exactly exemplary. It was even worse, however, in the 1930s, given the surge in evictions. Historians and even casual readers are familiar with the stories of bailiffs throwing families' furniture onto the street as the children or women cried and men pleaded, despairing of the future; but these cases of sensational drama accounted for a small minority of the tens of thousands of people who were forced out of their homes. Usually the process was more peaceful, if almost equally tragic. Sometime after the tenant had failed to pay his rent, the landlord would give him an ultimatum: hand over the rent within five days, or you have to leave. If he still received no rent, he filed a suit with the Renters' Court, which issued a summons that specified when the tenant would have to appear in court for a hearing. Rarely did the tenant attempt a defense; the judge, therefore, had no choice but to order him to leave his home, giving him from 5 days to 15 or 20. If he disobeyed the judge's orders, the landlord could file a writ of restitution with the bailiff's office, which was then served on the tenant to inform him that he would be dispossessed within 24 hours. The landlord had to pay a fee to actually have the bailiffs evict a family; if he could not afford the fee, as was frequently the case, there was no way to enforce the writ, and the tenant was able to stay.[42]

The most poignant commentary on the human dimensions of mass evictions may be the report of a settlement worker in 1933 after visiting a nursery school. "Some sort of game was going on," she recounted, "to the accompaniment of make-believe tears, groans and harsh orders and much violent shifting around of toys. 'It's Eviction,' explained [a] worker ruefully. 'They're playing Eviction. They don't play keeping-house any more or even having-tonsils-out. Sometimes they play Relief, but Eviction is the favorite—it has more action and they all know how to play it.'"[43]

How it happened that, apparently, few families spent a night or two literally on the street is explored more in the next chapter, but, in brief, it was usually the generosity of neighbors, friends, and relatives that came to the rescue. In one case a family's furniture

---

41. *Chicago Tribune*, May 5, 1929, November 3, 1941; *Washington Post*, May 19, 1929; Mary Faith Adams, "Present Housing Conditions," 20, 21; Thomas A. Guglielmo, "White on Arrival: Italians, Race, Color, and Power in Chicago, 1890–1945" (PhD diss., University of Michigan, 2000), 286; *Chicago Defender*, August 7, 1943.
42. Abbott, *The Tenements of Chicago*, 426–30.
43. Gertrude Springer, "Shock Troops to the Rescue," *Survey*, January 1933.

lay on the street for two days as its owners stayed with a friend; in another, a neighboring landlady took pity on the forlorn group sitting on the sidewalk and let them stay in a vacant room for the weekend. "There were many illustrations," wrote an investigator, "of the old saying that 'only the poor are kind to the poor, and those who have little give to those who have less.'"[44]

Those who had much, however, were especially cruel to Blacks, who, throughout the Depression, suffered evictions more often than other groups. Landlords (mostly absentee) on the South Side sometimes had it easier than those in white neighborhoods, because they did not always have to go to court to evict Black tenants. Instead, they colluded with bailiffs, likely with the help of small bribes, to evict people without having to go through the legal hassles. No wonder that "eviction riots"—large protests and coordinated resistance to the casting of furniture into the street—were more common and militant in Black neighborhoods than white. The situation was especially explosive in the summer of 1931, when rampant evictions on the South Side culminated in a massive demonstration that left three men dead, killed by police. Finally awoken to the desperation of the poor, supposedly being roused to insurrectionary fervor by Communists, Mayor Cermak declared a temporary moratorium on all evictions. They resumed again soon enough, increasing in frequency until 1933.[45]

Fortunately, the relief agencies' rent moratorium did not last the whole of the Depression. Officially, their rent policy was liberalized somewhat in May 1933, 15 months after the IERC had taken over administration of statewide relief. In practice, rent payments remained inadequate until November 1934, when FERA insisted that they be considered a regularly budgeted item. Even after this, the usual $25 maximum monthly allowance for a family's rent varied according to the availability of funds. At times payments almost ceased altogether, for example in May 1935, when FERA temporarily withdrew funding from Illinois because of the state's shameless irresponsibility in paying for its own relief needs. Again in the winter of 1935, rent payments were reduced. And yet again payments ceased briefly in the fall and winter of 1936 and 1937, due to yet more relief crises. This pattern continued in the following years, whenever the state and local governments were once more struggling to scrape together a few more millions of dollars, meanwhile doing whatever they could to shift the blame and the burden to each other. In most of these cases, bailiff-conducted evictions of "delinquent" tenants shot up, to as many as a hundred or more every day in November 1937; evictions from rooming houses were even more frequent. The Black Belt suffered the worst, which provoked huge protests on the South Side in 1937. But by then the brief and relatively humane era of FERA had come to a premature end, so little was done to

---

44. Meeting between Chicago Workers' Committee on Unemployment and the Illinois Relief Commission, May 18, 1934, p. 11, in Frank McCulloch Papers, box 4, folder 3; Edith Abbott and Katherine Kiesling, "Evictions during the Chicago Rent Moratorium Established by the Relief Agencies, 1931-33," *Social Service Review* IX (March 1935): 34-57; Abbott, *The Tenements of Chicago*, 455.
45. Minutes of superintendents' meeting, August 6, 1931, United Charities, box 8, folder 1; *Daily Worker*, August 5, 1931; *Chicago Tribune*, August 5, 1931.

address protesters' grievances. Delinquent unemployed tenants continued to be evicted en masse from 1938 to 1940, if rarely on quite the level of 1932, and many landlords continued to receive only half the rent or none at all, depending on the state of relief finances that month.[46]

The Depression's eviction epidemic was not only a terrible problem in itself; it also contributed to that other crisis, the appalling conditions of housing for the poor and the long-term unemployed. Compounding overcrowding was the common practice, especially in the Black Belt, of landlords' partitioning apartments into two or three or seven tiny "kitchenettes"—with one or two rooms—for one or more families each, so as to bring in more rent. If overcrowding was bad in the 1920s, it was dreadful in the 1930s. But now a new element was added: landlords who were receiving no rent or inadequate rent might not make repairs on their buildings, so plumbing stayed out of order, janitor service might be withdrawn, toilets and sinks and ceilings leaked badly, furnaces and pipes were not fixed. The city of the poor rotted, as the city of the rich closely guarded its riches.[47]

The quintessential city of the poor was Chicago's Black Belt. And the quintessential symbol of the Black Belt was the kitchenette apartment. Let us defer to Richard Wright in describing it:

> The kitchenette, with its filth and foul air, with its one toilet for thirty or more tenants, kills our black babies so fast that in many cities twice as many of them die as white babies.
>
> The kitchenette is the seed bed for scarlet fever, dysentery, typhoid, tuberculosis, gonorrhea, syphilis, pneumonia, and malnutrition.
>
> The kitchenette scatters death so widely among us that our death rate exceeds our birth rate, and if it were not for the trains and autos bringing us daily into the city from the plantations, we black folks who dwell in the northern cities would die out entirely over the course of a few years.
>
> The kitchenette, with its crowded rooms and incessant bedlam, provides an enticing place for crimes of all sorts—crimes against women and children or any stranger who happens to stray into its dark hallways. The noise of our living, boxed in stone and steel, is so loud that even a pistol shot is smothered.[48]

"Innumerable killings, particularly throat-cuttings," took place in some of these dark buildings, where drugs and moonshine were peddled, sometimes by children on behalf

---

46. Cole, "The Relief Crisis in Illinois during the Depression," 89, 90, 259, 260, 367; *First Annual Report of the Illinois Emergency Relief Commission*, 66; *Chicago Tribune*, November 7, 1935, September 8, 1937; *New York Herald Tribune*, December 2, 1935; *New York Times*, October 4, 1936; *Chicago Daily News*, November 9, 1937; *Chicago Defender*, November 27, 1937; "Public Hearing on the Relief and WPA Situation in Chicago," 2, 3.
47. Abbott, *The Tenements of Chicago*, 464–68; Mary-Jane Grunsfeld, *Negroes in Chicago*; *Chicago Defender*, October 2, 1937.
48. Richard Wright, *12 Million Black Voices* (New York: Thunder's Mouth Press, 1988), 105–108.

of their parents. Buildings meant for 6 families might house 24 instead, parents sleeping in the same bed as children, in rooms barely ventilated. Meanwhile, because of the housing shortage, these unlivable apartments were exorbitantly expensive.[49]

The third major physical consequence of poverty and unemployment, after hunger/malnutrition and inadequate shelter, was the deterioration or absence of clothing. This curse did much to shatter self-esteem, disrupt children's recreation and school life, and impede even adults' social and work lives. A thorough monograph has yet to be written on all the dimensions and repercussions of the mass clothing crisis of the 1930s.

Impressionistic accounts are not hard to find. "In the cities," an author observed in 1932, "in the cold months, children have had to wait days and sometimes weeks for shoes. Frequently children are found wearing misfit second-hand shoes, which injure their feet, forced on them by the public welfare office. Older children are prevented from working for lack of shoes." Frequently children were too ashamed to go to school because of their shabby clothes, or they could not go because the soles of their shoes were worn through. When they did go, they were apt to fight over safety pins or other clothing items. "A safety pin is very precious now," a Chicago social worker testified before Congress in 1933. "[Children] need pins to pin themselves together because their clothes are vastly more ragged than has ever been known in any city before and they have to pin together their wretched clothes and children quarrel over the possession of a pin."[50]

The situation was not always much better after a family had gone on relief. A study in 1940 of families in New York (not including Blacks) who were on home relief and the WPA found that 50 percent could not clothe themselves adequately. This was a severe handicap in job searches: "men came to the office for an interview wearing patched trousers, frayed collars, and shoes with holes in the socks." (The next sentence in the study is striking: "Many men were further handicapped by lack of teeth.") Some people recalled that when they were on home relief it was "practically impossible" for them to get clothing, since the monthly allowance in their budget for clothes was from $0 to $5, even in the case of a family of eight.[51]

The humiliation of being without adequate clothing—or adequate shelter, food, or health—leads into our next subject, the psychological pain that the long-term unemployed had to endure.

---

49. "Effect of the Depression in the Area Bounded by 47th, 51st, South Park, and the New York City Tracks," Burgess Papers, box 134, folder 1; *Hearings before a Subcommittee of the Committee on Manufactures on S. 5125*, 262; Edith Marie Hunter, "The Evolution of Chicago's South Side within the Last Fifty Years" (MA thesis, Northwestern University, 1942), 85; David Ward Howe, "Why Raise Rents?," *Chicago Defender*, April 1, 1939; *Atlanta Daily World*, April 29, 1937.
50. Williams, *Human Aspects of Unemployment*, 63; Friedman, "A Study of One Hundred Unemployed Families," 152; testimony of Edith Abbott, *Hearings before a Subcommittee of the Committee on Manufactures on S. 5125*, 264.
51. Eli Ginzberg, *The Unemployed* (New York: Harper, 1943), 59, 123.

Mental Hardship

The physical suffering of the jobless was bad enough, but in some respects the mental suffering may have been even worse. It doesn't require profound imaginative powers to consider the psychological implications of being without paid work for months or years. *Homo sapiens* is not like other species of animal, content to loll about aimlessly when not eating or sleeping, satisfied as long as its stomach is full. Uniquely, human beings are *restless*, driven toward self-confirmation, self-activity, a kind of ceaseless urge to "objectively" confirm their sense of self-worth. They need a purpose, something that gives their life meaning; they need to feel like a useful member of the community, be it the small community of the family or the great community of humankind. In a capitalist world structured around the virtual necessity to have a job in order both to make money and to participate in social life, these deep-seated human desires will be satisfied (especially for men) typically through employment—not least because this allows one to provide for one's family. If employment is not forthcoming, neither, most likely, is sustained psychological validation. Life may become suffused with despair.[52]

A vast sociological and psychological literature on the unemployed has accumulated since the Great Depression, which I cannot review in depth here. Writers have suggested typologies of the long-term unemployed, psychological explanations of their behavior, and "stages of adjustment" that people experience after months of being economically outcast. The usefulness of all this scholarship, particularly for historical writing, is debatable. In the 1930s, for example, one writer described three types of unemployed: the anxious, who suffered mostly from the fear of future insecurity; the "apathetic," who had lost confidence and appeared to have become "indifferent"; and the unresigned, who refused to accept unemployment and were critical of society. Another distinguished "the unbroken" from "the broken" (resigned) and "the distressed" (bitter and hopeless). More elaborate classifications have been proposed as well.[53]

Perhaps more interesting than such typologies are the stages of adjustment that have been theorized. According to a study in 1938, "all the writers who have described the course of unemployment seem to agree on the following points: First there is shock, which is followed by an active hunt for a job, during which the individual is still optimistic and unresigned; he still maintains an unbroken attitude. Second, when all efforts fail, the individual becomes pessimistic, anxious, and suffers active distress. [...] And third, the individual becomes fatalistic and adapts himself to his new state but with a narrower scope. He now has a broken attitude." Some of this language, in being value-laden and overly general, is objectionable and has been abandoned by more recent research; the

---

52. See Karl Marx, *Economic and Philosophic Manuscripts* (1844); Chris Wright, *Notes of an Underground Humanist* (Bradenton, FL: Booklocker, 2013), chapters 1 and 3; R. D. Laing, *The Divided Self* (New York: Pantheon Books, 1969); Peter Kelvin and Joanna E. Jarrett, *Unemployment: Its Social Psychological Effects* (New York: Cambridge University Press, 1985).
53. Philip Eisenberg and Paul Lazarsfeld, "The Psychological Effects of Unemployment," *Psychological Bulletin* 35, no. 6 (June 1938): 358–90.

"stage" model has tended to persist, though. "Optimism–pessimism–fatalism" has been the usual longitudinal classification of the mentality of the long-term unemployed.[54]

A study of families in a previous depression, that of 1921–22, summed up certain consequences of unemployment rather well: "[Lowered morale] was a persistent phenomenon that permeated every manifestation of the Depression. Among the jobless breadwinners of families it took a variety of forms under different circumstances: strain and friction within the family, loss of ambition to seek work, occasionally desertion of family, temperamental upheavals, loss of mental balance even to the point of insanity, development of lawless habits, begging, the fostering of bitterness against the government and social institutions in general, or sheer laziness from the discontinuance of sustained application." A collection of case studies a few years later summed it all up in this terse statement: "What, above all, unemployment does to people is to take the spring out of them."[55]

For families, a common cause of conflict was the shift in gender roles sometimes consequent upon the father's loss of a job. As with so many things in life, gender is determined in part by control over material resources. When the father made the money, he had the most prestige and authority; when he lost his job and his wife or children brought home the money instead, he tended to lose his authority. For example, with respect to the Polish district in Chicago west of Goose Island, it was observed that the "autocratic domination" of the father had been "profoundly shaken" by the Depression. As a high school principal put it, "the prestige of the former wage-earner is lowered by asking working women or children for spending money—for beer, cigarettes, or carfare." Chafing against their loss of status, husbands might become "more inclined to quarrel, more brutal, and irritable," as wives complained, or they simply grew sullen and withdrawn. In some cases they sank so low in the eyes of their wife and children that they were not even consulted regarding family decisions and were all but ignored most of the time. "I certainly like my mother lots more," one girl told an investigator, "for she buys me everything." The men did not always rebel against their loss of status, becoming instead pliable and passively resigned, as in the sad case of this Bulgarian man:[56]

> [T]he father does not count anymore in the family [after four years of unemployment]. The children call him now by his first name and the father has resigned to his new position and

---

54. Eisenberg and Lazarsfeld, "The Psychological Effects of Unemployment," 378; Kelvin and Jarrett, *Unemployment*, chapter 2; Norman T. Feather, *The Psychological Impact of Unemployment* (New York: Springer-Verlag, 1990), chapter 3; Graham Stokes and Raymond Cochrane, "A Study of the Psychological Effects of Redundancy and Unemployment," *Journal of Occupational Psychology* 57, no. 4 (December 1984): 309–22.
55. Philip Klein, *The Burden of Unemployment* (New York: Russell Sage Foundation, 1923), 37; Williams, *Human Aspects of Unemployment*, 38; Marion Elderton, ed., *Case Studies of Unemployment* (Philadelphia, PA: University of Pennsylvania Press, 1931), xxxvi.
56. Miscellaneous reports from 1934 and 1935, Ernest Burgess Papers, box 131, folders 3 and 4; E. Wight Bakke, *Citizens without Work* (New Haven, CT: Yale University Press, 1940), 137–39; Mirra Komarovsky, *The Unemployed Man and His Family: The Effect of Unemployment upon the Status of the Man in Fifty-Nine Families* (New York: Arno Press, 1971/1940), 39.

seems to be content, only hoping that he will die soon so he would not eat the children's food, so there would be more for them. Whenever I [a friend] visit the family and I offer to buy something for him, the father refuses to accept it, saying "better save it for my funeral."

For men more attached to traditional notions of masculinity, the psychological shock of emasculation could be unendurable. After all, to quote an investigator, the unemployed man usually saw himself as "fail[ing] to fulfill the central duty of his life, the very touchstone of his manhood—the role of family provider. The man appear[ed] bewildered and humiliated. [...] [Before the Depression,] every purchase of the family—the radio, his wife's new hat, the children's skates, the meals set before him—all were symbols of their dependence upon him. Unemployment changed it all." The feeling of being superfluous drove some to that final tragic act, suicide. One Polish man, for instance, could not abide the contempt of his wife and daughter-in-law, and asked for 10 dollars from his wife so as to leave the city. When she refused, he killed her and then himself.[57]

It was not only Poles or Eastern Europeans who had patriarchal traditions and suffered from the deterioration of accepted gender norms. These norms were remarkably similar across cultures, ethnicities, races, and regions of the United States. While patriarchal attitudes varied in strength between nationalities and, especially, individual families, it was common for the man's frequent loss of status and authority—whether partial or complete—to result in a dysfunctional marital relationship. This aspect of unemployment in the Depression has been so widely studied that we need not go into detail here. The litany of marital woes is long: some wives of unemployed husbands lost respect for them, grew disgusted and irritated by the man's constant presence in the home, decided he had no personality and was uninteresting, resented him for supposedly not trying hard enough to get a job, and so forth. Husband and wife "scolded and nagged" each other over petty issues, fought more frequently over treatment of the children, and even became prone to violent outbursts of long-suppressed rage and frustration. Not uncommonly, sexual activity was cut down or eliminated, usually on the wife's initiative but sometimes on the husband's. One Jewish woman, for example, "had always hated 'it' but never felt that she could do anything about it. But now, 'thank God,' it was possible for her to sleep apart from her husband."[58]

Comments made to social workers were revealing. One woman, an Anglo American, said bluntly that "when a man cannot provide for the family and makes you worry so, you lose your love for him. A husband has to have four qualifications—first, second, and third he should be able to support the family, and fourth he should have personality." Her own husband had none of these qualifications. Things were even worse in another family, in which the father told an interviewer he didn't "care a damn anymore. [...]

---

57. Komarovsky, *The Unemployed Man and His Family*, 74, 75; Ruth Shonle Cavan and Katherine Howland Ranck, *The Family and the Depression: A Study of One Hundred Chicago Families* (Freeport, NY: Books for Libraries Press, 1969/1938), 129–31.
58. Eli Ginzberg, *The Unemployed*, 77. See also—in addition to works cited immediately above—Samuel Stouffer and Paul Lazarsfeld, *Research Memorandum on the Family in the Depression* (New York: Social Science Research Council, 1937).

As far as I am concerned the kids can do what they please, and the wife, too, for that matter. It's just like I said, 'Love flies out of the window when money goes.'" One study of 471 husbands in Chicago found that 25 percent of marriages that had been afflicted by unemployment for less than a month were unhappy, while 40 percent were unhappy if unemployment had lasted more than six months. On the other hand, some researchers argued that families that became dysfunctional during the Depression had in most cases not been stable or healthy to begin with. Thus, another Chicago study concluded, perhaps with a touch of oversimplification, that "well-organized families, even when greatly affected by the Depression, continued organized; unorganized or disorganized families became further disorganized." In fact, "the family that was harmoniously organized became *more* unified [by the Depression] and the members *more* loyal."[59]

In the less fortunate families, alienation between husband and wife could become so extreme that separation or divorce was the only solution. The number of divorces in Cook County actually decreased between 1930 and 1933, then rose again, by 1935 reaching approximately its level before the Depression and staying there for the rest of the decade. But the decline in divorce was a result of couples' lack of money, not of marriages' becoming happier. Social workers felt that separations increased in the early years of the Depression, and statistics showed that fewer children in 1933 than in 1930 lived in two-parent households. The number of new marriages plummeted in the first four Depression years, then rose to a peak in 1937, then plummeted again in the next two years, because young men could not hope to support a wife if they could not get a job.[60]

In many families, the man's relationship not only with his wife but also with his children suffered. Having lost the power of money, he lost some or all of his power over his kids, especially the adolescents. Even when they still respected him, there was some disappointment and even shame. "One of the most common things," one man remembered decades later, "was this feeling of your father's failure. That somehow he hadn't beaten the rap. Sure things were tough, but why should I be the kid who had to put a piece of cardboard into the sole of my shoe to go to school?"[61]

In 1934, students at the University of Chicago studied how the Depression had affected immigrant families in Chicago. People with connections to the Yugoslav community, for instance, reported that, since the vast majority of immigrants had been poor peasants before they came to Chicago, they were able to tolerate present difficulties "with much resignation and good will." Less easy to tolerate was children's habitual

---

59. Komarovsky, *The Unemployed Man*, 132, 46; Cavan and Ranck, *The Family and the Depression*, viii; Ernest Burgess, "The Effect of Unemployment upon the Family and the Community," 4, Burgess Papers, box 52, folder 1.
60. *Chicago Tribune*, June 2, 1939; "Broken Homes," Burgess Papers, box 81, folder 4. See Matthew J. Hill, "Love in the Time of the Depression: The Effect of Economic Conditions on Marriage in the Great Depression," *Journal of Economic History* 75, no. 1 (March 2015): 163–89.
61. Interview with Larry Van Dusen, in Studs Terkel, *Hard Times: An Oral History of the Great Depression* (New York: Pantheon Books, 1970), 120.

disobedience, starkly different from how the parents themselves had acted as children in Yugoslavia. "Prior to Depression [*sic*]," said one knowledgeable Yugoslav, "when father was the sole bread winner and children much younger, he was ordinarily able to exercise much of his parental authority. At present, when his chances for employment are nil and children are the bread winners, situation is entirely different. There are few Yugoslav homes where parents still have the last word, although as a rule Yugoslav children are more home loving than for instance Polish." While "affectional ties" in Yugoslav families had, in general, "loosened" because of the Depression, it was typical for extended families to stand by their members and help them despite their own troubles. This was the case, of course, for many immigrant communities. The following observations, as well, apply to more than just Slavs or Yugoslavs:

> The most depressing thought of Yugoslavs in this city, as well as of other Slavic groups, is feeling of social insecurity. While in the old country, on their small farms, although often hungry and never dressed well, they felt security of their soil, their little gardens and homesteads. They realize industry here is not able to give them such security and with much despair think of fatal "forty" when they are "too old" to work. Some of them, however, are confident that this prolonged depression will solve the question of social security—through proper legislative measures.[62]

Most did not have such far-sighted confidence and so suffered from a scourge dreadful to the human mind: a dearth of hope. Social workers found this to be just as true of Anglo Americans as of immigrants. For many mothers, one author concluded, "the most serious strain was their gnawing fear that they would never escape from their present predicament." The future was a wasteland of "constant harassment": walking long distances to save a penny or two on purchases; helping children to get along on very little; washing and ironing everything, even heavy sheets, themselves; constantly repairing clothing and furniture fabric; trying to cheer up their disconsolate husbands.[63]

An unemployed social worker wrote a description of her experience that is worth quoting at length for providing a middle-class perspective. It is the more poignant in that she had no dependents, was not responsible for parents or wife or children, and did not face the dreaded choice of starvation or charity, like so many others.

> I kept telling myself, "Here is the leisure you have been craving for so long. [...] Now if ever is the time to learn the stores and to enjoy window-shopping, to bring your correspondence up to date, to visit your friends.
>
> But somehow the savor had gone out of everything. It was hard to settle down to reading. Why write to friends till you had something to tell them? It was the same with visits. You grew tired of saying, "Nothing yet"; it touched your pride. [...]

---

62. "Yugoslavs in Chicago and Depression," Burgess Papers, box 131, folder 4.
63. Ginzberg, *The Unemployed*, 80, 81.

You understood now the basis for the complaints of a friend who taught English to foreigners. Her classes always fell off when work was slack. She had never been able to see why. "That is the very time they should come. They're not tired. They could come to class fresh and rested and have lots of time for home study. Instead, they don't come at all. Just shiftless, I call it. If they had any real ambition—! And then when they get jobs they come stringing back!" You could explain it to your friend now. The poor souls, of course they couldn't settle down to study, worried and uneasy as they were!

[...] [More than a month passed.] A dead weight hung in my chest. It took away the taste for food. Sleeping became difficult. My weight reached a new low. A failure, done for, finished! The years ahead looked very dark—just down and down.[64]

In this discussion of mental suffering it remains only to address two more topics: the rise in social atomization that grew out of mass unemployment and some of the negative consequences of unemployment for the mental well-being of children and young adults. These topics are closely related, for, with fewer opportunities to interact with peers, to go to movies or concerts or buy nice clothes for dances or go on dates, the youth could grow restless, depressed, and profoundly "alienated." And insofar as children were unable to go to school or to participate in extracurricular activities, their social integration and mental development were likewise handicapped.

On the most general tendencies of atomization, an investigator in 1940 had this to say: "[Unemployment] cancels many of the opportunities usually related to leisure. No social role is substituted for those gone with the job. [...] The reality of citizenship has been reduced by the loss of contact with organizations which participate to some extent in the larger interests of the community." A study specifically of Chicago observed that "families that previously attended church regularly stopped because they lacked appropriate clothing and had no money to contribute. Club memberships were dropped, motion pictures became an impossible luxury, and friends and relatives could not be visited unless they were within walking distance, as there was no money for carfare." It was even worse in winter, when people would huddle in bed all day for lack of fuel and clothing. Outside, a deathly silence hung in the streets.[65]

Trends of atomization were accentuated by the economic storm's battering of the ethnic community, which had been so vital and vibrant years earlier. Lizabeth Cohen expounds on this thesis in her classic *Making a New Deal* (1990), arguing that the weakening of ethnic and religious institutions in the 1930s helped usher in the age of industrial unionism and the welfare state. The former institutions no longer provided the security or sense of collective identity they once had, and the latter institutions took their place. Implicit in this argument is recognition of the epochal social change that heralded the heyday of the nation-state era of history between the 1930s and the 1970s: the relative decline of local and "personalistic" attachments in comparison to the rise of a broader

---

64. Anonymous, "How It Feels," *Survey*, February 15, 1932, 529, 530.
65. Bakke, *Citizens without Work*, 16, 17; "The Effect of Unemployment upon the Family and the Community," 3, Burgess Papers, box 52, folder 1; Edward Robb Ellis, *A Nation in Torment: The Great American Depression, 1929–1939* (New York: Kodansha International, 1995), 236.

but more atomized and diffuse sense of national belonging. These trends had been operating for centuries, but with the crisis of the 1930s and its resolution in the corporatist-Keynesian political economy of the 1940s and after, they reached their culmination. Political, corporate, and union bureaucracies manifested an unprecedented gigantism, extending their tentacles into every corner of society to regulate and control it, trying to indoctrinate populations with ideologies that subordinated all else—ethnicity, religion, occupation, local community—to the claims of nation and capitalism. Thus, insofar as the Great Depression and mass unemployment partially atomized and undermined the semi-insular ethnic community, this dovetailed with, and helped bring about, the maturation of the corporatist nation-state. That is to say, "the unemployed" were not the only ones who suffered the fragmentation of community; ultimately everyone did, with the decline of localism and the eventual consolidation of sprawling national bureaucracies.

The demise of many neighborhood shopkeepers is a well-known example. In the 1920s, Karl Marx's predictions about the dismal fate of most of the petty bourgeoisie still could have seemed mistaken, given the proliferation of local merchants and storekeepers who were frequently good friends with their customers. By the 1940s, however, it was clear, or should have been, that Marx had been largely right all along: most of the petty bourgeois eventually succumbed to wage labor, and the economy came to be utterly dominated by oligopolies.[66] Between 1930 and 1935 in the United States, for instance, 750,000 independent enterprisers in industry, trade, and the professions were wiped out (about one in five), including 500,000 storekeepers. This translated into a partial loss of the vitality of local ethnic life, as—among other things—the chain store supplanted the neighborhood merchant who could no longer afford to extend credit.[67]

It is easy, however, to overestimate the waning of ethnic and racial ties—clubs, churches, charities, the many immigrant "societies" that existed for every conceivable function—that took place under the two shocks of the Great Depression and the United States' restriction of immigration in the early 1920s. The membership of many of these noncommercial organizations did decline in the 1920s and especially the first half of the 1930s, but rarely was the decline catastrophic. It was even partly reversed in the late 1930s and 1940s. Civil society remained vibrant, with frequent parades, festivals, public picnics, union events, and constant church activities (there were 500 churches in the Black Belt alone). To some extent the Depression even stimulated these, as we'll see. Those who suffered from material deprivation invented their own modes of association and rebelled in their own ways against the atomizing tendencies of unemployment.[68]

---

66. Where Marx went wrong was in his failure to predict the welfare state and Keynesian stimulation of demand, which emerged as capitalist remedies to these trends of class polarization and working-class immiseration. See my *Worker Cooperatives and Revolution*. Now that social democracy is in decline across the West and class polarization is peaking again, it has become clear that the real problem with Marx was that, in a sense, he was almost two hundred years ahead of his time.
67. "Middle Class Hit by Crisis," *Labor Notes*, September 1935.
68. Eugene McCarthy, "The Bohemians in Chicago and Their Benevolent Societies: 1875–1946" (MA thesis, University of Chicago, 1950); St. Clair Drake, *Churches and Voluntary Associations in*

Nevertheless, these tendencies were indeed prominent, affecting not only the jobless themselves but also their children. In fact, even apart from the intrinsic consequences of unemployment, Chicago youth were driven toward atomization by the Depression, in particular by the policies that the Depression provided a pretext for government to impose on the city. Closing playgrounds, excluding children four to five years old from kindergarten, and enacting all the other conservative policies mentioned earlier certainly did nothing to enhance social integration. Juvenile delinquency increased in the early years of the Depression, although statistics from the time may not be reliable. What is certain is that Chicago's Black Belt had the highest juvenile crime rate in the city—21 percent of youth delinquents in 1930 were Blacks, and over 20 percent of Black boys between 1933 and 1940 were involved in delinquency. When asked by city officials in the 1930s why the youth were committing more crimes than ever, a minister in Bronzeville replied curtly, "wipe out vice and give my people jobs!"[69]

The Depression's most tragic effect on youth was that it disrupted life paths and career paths. It was a colossal wall suddenly erected between the present and ambitions for the future. The young may not always have been immediately resentful for having to drop out of school to help support their family, but if they were still working in a dead-end job two or three years later, unable to resume their education or get married, they were likely to be bitter. Relief agencies frequently required that if a family were to receive relief, the children who were of an appropriate age had to financially contribute, so as to reduce the burden on the agency. This amounted to a demand that the child postpone independence.

Consider, for example, the story of Mary O'Rourke:

> She left school after the eighth grade, found a job, and helped support the family for a year. Then she fell in love and married. Her husband's income was sufficient to support himself and his wife, and he objected to Mary's working, but her family needed her help, so she took a job against his wishes. Presently his business took him to another city. Mary was torn between the desire to go with him and to stay by her family. She stayed. After a year and a half she lost track of her husband, and three years have now passed since she heard from him. She is bitter and her frustration is reflected in her work and in her social relationships.[70]

In addition to the despair of seeming to have no future was the stifling of *present* desires, which must have been made even more painful by consciousness of the *unfairness* of it all, of the fact that other young people were satiating their hearts' desires even while

---

the *Chicago Negro Community* (Chicago, IL: Works Progress Administration, 1940), 3.
69. Graham Taylor, "Our Public Schools in Progress and Reaction," *Survey Graphic*, February 1934; Annette Baker, "The Effect of the Depression on Juvenile Delinquency," paper for a sociology course, June 8, 1934, in Ernest Burgess Papers, box 146, folder 5; *Washington Post*, January 22, 1933; *Chicago Tribune*, May 25, 1932, and March 3, 1940; Drake and Cayton, *Black Metropolis*, 202, 203, 684.
70. Coral Brooke, "Youth Engulfed," *Survey*, January 1935.

one had to restrict one's own consumption to little more than subsistence levels. One young woman, for example, complained that while working for the American Medical Association at $60 a month, she had in the past two years been able to buy for herself precisely four things: a pair of shoes, a summer dress, a blouse, and a hat. All the rest went to her family. "Would you," she asked her caseworker, "or any other girl of 21 like to live on this budget for two years? Wouldn't you like to be able to see a show with the girls you work with once in a while? So would I, but I can't." The relief agency insisted that she tolerate this existence indefinitely.[71]

All this illustrates the familial disruption and disorientation that could attend the father's unemployment, and illustrates, once again, how a simple change in class conditions has immeasurable repercussions for other spheres of life. Gender norms are disrupted, authority patterns are upset and new ones established, emotional conflicts multiply and intensify, and old values may wither away. To a large extent, the poor live in a different universe than the rich; and Plato was right to contrast the city of the poor with that of the rich.

---

71. Ibid. See Lois Rita Helmbold, "Beyond the Family Economy: Black and White Working-Class Women during the Great Depression," *Feminist Studies* 13, no. 3 (Autumn 1987): 629–55.

Chapter Three
COPING

Many commentators during and after the 1930s were inclined to make sweeping negative generalizations about the long-term unemployed. They were seen as almost universally passive, apathetic, despairing, and atomized, something like an inert mass of lost souls. One observer in 1933 wrote, "The acquiescence of the unemployed [...] is what impresses us. To be sure, there are mutterings and bursts of sullen resentment and an occasional riot, but the prevailing attitude up to the present time has been submissive." Another declared baldly that "the unemployed man and his wife have no social life outside the family. The extent of the social isolation of the family is truly striking. This refers not only to formal club affiliations but also to informal social life."[1]

As we have seen, such interpretations are by no means wholly false. They have a kernel of truth, but they state it in a tendentious and exaggerated form. Some of the long-term unemployed did, of course, succumb to abject despair and even suicide, but most did not. In fact, there are historians who draw almost the opposite conclusions from those just quoted. Anthony Badger, for instance, insists that "what characterised the American workers' response to unemployment was tough-minded realism. Such stoicism and resilience might militate against political radicalism but it did not signify self-blame, indifference, or hopeless despair."[2]

In this chapter, accordingly—and in later ones—we'll consider Chicago's Depression-era unemployed from the perspective of their *activity*, unlike in the previous chapter. Because of what they had to endure, they were frequently compelled to adopt a courageous stance, for the sake of loved ones. In the tasks of survival and day-to-day living, the socially disadvantaged are, on both implicit and explicit levels, continually resisting, improvising, calculating, cooperating, and rationally using whatever means are available to take what they can get from a callous world. The struggle of living-while-poor is a *class* struggle—in fact a direct and immediate outgrowth of "the" class struggle, the conflict between elite and subordinate classes—and as such is essentially opposed to the dominant society. It need not entail a lucid or sophisticated "class consciousness," inasmuch as such consciousness is not always necessary or useful to people in their everyday

---

1. James Mickel Williams, *Human Aspects of Unemployment and Relief, with Special Reference to the Effects of the Depression on Children* (Chapel Hill, NC: University of North Carolina Press, 1933), 8; Mirra Komarovsky, *The Unemployed Man and His Family* (New York: Arno Press, 1971 [1940]), 122.
2. Anthony Badger, *The New Deal: The Depression Years, 1933–40* (New York: Hill and Wang, 1989), 41.

lives; but, arguably, the struggle does tend to entail at least an implicit awareness of oneself as belonging to a group or groups that have grievances and interests in common, as against the privileged and the rich. As we'll see in Chapter six, it does not take much for the seed of this awareness to flower into a more militant class consciousness.

Later I will also discuss some of the ways that the long-term unemployed were able to enjoy themselves despite their troubles. In the company of others, they tried to ward off the evils of ennui and despair that were apt to arise from unemployment and poverty; and the vitality of life in the poorer areas of Chicago during this time of even-greater-than-usual poverty indicates that to a large extent they succeeded. For example, the Mexican colony in South Chicago overcame the atomizing effects of unemployment by embracing a shared passion for sports, particularly baseball, softball, and basketball. In fact, sports tended to unite communities—Irish, Italian, German, Hungarian, and Greek—all over the city.

There is one significant type of "recreation" that I do not address in this chapter: religion. The chapter is simply too long to include a section on religion. I save that section for Chapter five, in which I discuss the reciprocal interest that churches displayed in the poor and the poor displayed in churches.

Surviving

The strategies of staying alive, of continuing to find ways to eat and drink and have a shelter over one's head even while being treated as "redundant" and unnecessary, were not much different in the 1930s than they had been in the 1880s. Indeed, they were not much different from devices resorted to even now in the absence of unemployment insurance: using up one's savings, relying on earnings from a spouse or children, borrowing from relatives or friends or moving in with them, picking up odd jobs here and there, moving to a cheaper home, and taking in lodgers. There were also avenues of institutional relief, whether public or private. In an "abstract" way we already know all this, the manifold ways people managed to persevere when mainstream society had turned its back on them. In an abstract way we know that the human species is resourceful. What is interesting, though, is the concrete reality of this "scraping by" and the intimate realities of people's resourcefulness and pride.[3]

A couple of short descriptions of how people adapted to long-term unemployment may serve to introduce the subject. Take, for example, the Buenger family, who lived in the Stockyards neighborhood. The father was laid off from a pipe manufacturing company in November 1930. "His wife found a job scrubbing floors at the Chicago

---

3. Alexander Keyssar, *Out of Work: The First Century of Unemployment in Massachusetts* (New York: Cambridge University Press, 1986), chapter 6; Lizabeth Cohen, *Making a New Deal: Industrial Workers in Chicago, 1919–1939* (New York: Cambridge University Press, 1990), chapter 5. The secondary literature is full of descriptions of people's strategies for survival, on which I'll embellish in this chapter. See, for instance, Cheryl Lynn Greenberg, *"Or Does It Explode?" Black Harlem in the Great Depression* (New York: Oxford University Press, 1991), chapter 7; and Ruth Milkman, "Women's Work and Economic Crisis: Some Lessons of the Great Depression," *Review of Radical Political Economics* 8, no. 1 (1976): 73–97.

Civic Opera for $21.50 a week. For three months the family managed on the mother's income. In addition they accumulated debts with the grocer, who was a godfather of one of the children. They also borrowed small sums from friends. During this period they moved to a cheaper apartment. [...] The location was almost the same, but in the new place there were only four rooms for eight persons." After three months they applied for, and received, financial assistance from a settlement house, and began to receive food rations from the county, while continuing to accumulate debts for groceries and meat. The oldest daughter found part-time work that paid from $3 to $5 each week.[4]

Many people were able to go without charity entirely, for years. For example, Ralph, 53 in 1937, had been a carpenter but lost his job early in the Depression. With his savings soon gone and his wife ill, he sent her to live with relatives on a farm in Indiana and began to look for work. As stated in an article in the *Chicago Tribune*,

> When he walked past restaurants he knocked on the windows. If no work was forthcoming he picked up a broom and began sweeping the sidewalk.
>
> He had one regular job: Emptying ashes each Friday night for two elderly spinsters. He walked four miles to their home, and the first night he received 75 cents in payment. "Shucks," he said, "it ain't wuth [*sic*] that much," and returned 50 cents. The spinsters told their friends, and soon he was emptying a dozen ash cans.
>
> No matter how menial the labor, Ralph took it. When he had a handyman's job-for-a-day at $1, he became exultant. And for four years he existed. If at times he went hungry he never complained. Instead he proudly displayed seven cents in his wallet—car fare to the next job, when it came. It came a month ago, a regular job as janitor at $15 a week. And he sent for his wife.[5]

In short, each household met the Depression in its own unique way, although we can point to similarities and patterns in their approaches.

***

Naturally, the first recourse of any household whose head was no longer employed was to use up some or all of the savings that had been accumulated. Among manual workers, it was rare for savings to be substantial, because of the hand-to-mouth existence and the typically large families. Nearly all had saved less than $200, in addition to having insurance policies of one form or another, often several per family. But even when hundreds of dollars had been set aside in banks—painstakingly accumulated over many years, years of scrimping and scraping, self-denial, and frugal living to build up some security for the future—the money became useless when the banks failed in 1931 and 1932. What had required endless effort to create was destroyed with the closing of two august doors, as

---

4. Genevieve Ann Lensing, "An Unemployment Study in the Stockyards District" (MA thesis, University of Chicago, 1932), 62–64.
5. *Chicago Tribune*, August 13, 1937.

people outside cried and begged for them to reopen. Some even thought that, in their geographical area at least, the collapse of the banks was more of a catastrophe than the widespread unemployment itself, because the bank closings wiped out middle-class savings. Dempsey Travis, a young Black man living on Chicago's South Side, remembered later what had happened to his uncle when the Binga State Bank was closed in August 1930. "Thrifty Uncle Otis became destitute with the turn of the examiner's key in the front door of the bank. Otis Travis died in 1933, broke and broken-hearted, without having recovered one penny of his savings."[6]

The majority of the long-term unemployed had at least some small savings they could initially draw on: certainly more than one-fourth had bank accounts, and at least three-fourths had insurance policies they might be able to borrow on or cash in. Many also, wisely suspicious of dominant institutions, had stashed away money at home. However, of a hundred unemployed blue-collar families interviewed in June 1932, only one still had any bank or home savings left, and 76 no longer had any insurance at all. They had either borrowed up to the limit, cashed the policies in, or let them expire, and several fathers who had belonged to fraternal insurance societies had dropped out. Such societies had become much less useful now that so many of their members had ceased to pay dues; in fact, as Lizabeth Cohen describes in *Making a New Deal*, most ethnic societies either collapsed early in the Depression or had to dramatically curtail the benefits they offered members. The Slovene National Benefit Society, for instance, reduced benefits for sickness, injuries, and surgical operations as its funds depleted and its membership shrank (from almost 64,000 in 1930 to 48,000 by spring 1933). In general, then, insurance does not seem to have been of great value to most of the unemployed.[7]

The decision to use up all or nearly all of one's savings—in the desperate effort to avoid being a charity case—must have been agonizing for these people whose years of thrift had been directed toward a definite end, and not *this* one. An Italian man who came to a relief agency to beg for work had lived for six months on money he had spent two years accumulating, money with which he had hoped to bring his wife and two children to the United States. A Jewish man had to exhaust the $80 that had taken him four years to save. Another had saved $1,500, but this he, too, consumed on rent, food, household expenses, and doctors' bills before applying for relief.[8]

---

6. Friedman, "One Hundred Unemployed Families," 120–22; Slayton, *Back of the Yards*, 190; Dempsey Travis, *An Autobiography of Black Chicago* (Chicago, IL: Urban Research Institute, 1981), 33; Marquis Childs, "Main Street Ten Years After," *New Republic*, January 18, 1933.
7. Jeanette Margaret Elder, "A Study of One Hundred Applicants for Relief the Fourth Winter of Unemployment" (MA thesis, University of Chicago, 1933), 47, 52, 53, 78, 80; Eli Ginzberg, *The Unemployed* (New York: Harper, 1943), 29; Friedman, "One Hundred Unemployed Families," 142, 143; Cohen, *Making a New Deal*, 227–30; Theodorson, "Living Conditions of Fifty Unemployed Families," 53; Ewan Clague and Webster Powell, *Ten Thousand Out of Work* (Philadelphia, PA: University of Pennsylvania Press, 1933), 103.
8. Erma Clementine Janssen, "A Study of 363 Unemployment Cases in a Residential Suburb" (MA thesis, University of Chicago, 1932), 62; Lensing, "An Unemployment Study," 19.

While savings were of use in the short term, in the long term—and immediately—the most essential adjustment was to cut down on expenses. As soon as a family saw it would be difficult for its chief wage earner to get hired again, it was apt to stop paying union dues and to end payments on installment goods. As mentioned in the last chapter, working-class families quickly had to sacrifice many high-quality, expensive foods, instead eating starches and sugars. It was not uncommon, in fact, for families—at least in the early stages of unemployment—to try to pay all their large bills first, such as rent, coal, and gas, spending only the leftover money on groceries. "Payment of rent comes before anything else," remarked one mother, "and I would rather have that clear than sufficient food." As the months wore on, though, and savings depleted, these fears lost their battle with reality: it was frequently the largest bills, particularly rent, that had to be sacrificed, since nothing was more necessary than food.[9]

The ways that most of the deprived economized have, unfortunately, been lost in the fog of history, memorialized only occasionally in the scattered remarks of journalists, social workers, memoirists, and letter writers. The Bennett family bought a kerosene stove, cut in half their two-quart milk order, and "managed on one ton of coal this winter [1932]." The Flemings decided that if they slept late, two meals a day would be enough. The Sumner family "lived on crackers" for a year, while the Parkers used no gas for seven years and could not afford ice in the summer or repairs on household equipment. In most cases, it quickly became necessary to forego such luxuries as clothes-shopping, movie-watching, book-buying, and church-donating. In addition, "laundry formerly sent out was done at home; dental work was delayed; needed operations and medical treatment were postponed; baking was done at home; telephones were dispensed with." Sooner or later, whatever *could* go *did*.[10]

As custodians of the family economy, women were in charge of much of the economizing. A Polish woman who worked as a domestic laborer observed that her daughter needed good clothes for high school: "I make all the clothes for her—make things over if I get some nice dresses from my employers. Yes, I always see to it that Viola looks nice and the same way with every one in my family—no matter how poor." Another woman remembered, many years later, a series of never-ending chores: "Sewing, patching, darning, mending. Handing down, cutting down, and making over. [...] Ripping seams and remodeling old suits and dresses. Unravelling sweaters and using the wool to knit other sweaters as the children grew. [...] Patching worn places, and then patching the patches." Such resourcefulness was necessary even for good housekeeping, since it was by no means easy to keep things looking nice when one lacked money for replacements. The few free minutes a woman had every day might be spent repairing old furniture. One study found that 70 percent of women whose families were on relief were "good" housekeepers (as opposed to "poor" or "passable"), an impressive proportion that may be explained in part by what an interviewer said of one Mrs. Horowitz: "She had always

---

9. Lensing, "An Unemployment Study," 13, 14, 16.
10. Elder, "A Study of One Hundred Applicants for Relief," 93; Ruth Cavan and Katherine Ranck, *The Family and the Depression* (Freeport, NY: Books for Libraries Press, 1969/1938), 85.

taken a good deal of pleasure in her home, and now it was almost her only pleasure. Her furnishings were lovely and looked like new, although Mrs. Horowitz said that she had had them for nineteen years."[11]

An indication of the gulf that World War II and the postwar period created between the old world and the new is given by the conditions, and the survival strategies, of the unemployed. From the 1880s to the 1930s, they did not significantly change. As in the 1880s, so in the 1930s "clothing was patched rather than replaced, insurance policies were dropped, sick children were treated with home remedies. Fuel expenses were reduced by keeping rooms unheated, by scavenging the streets for coal and wood, and by switching from electric to kerosene lamps or from lamps to candles." These quotations are from Alexander Keyssar's *Out of Work*, which is about Massachusetts in an earlier era, but they could equally apply to Chicago in the Great Depression. The following *New York Times* article from 1933 could have been written in the 1890s[12]:

> Residents of Chicago within a radius of several miles from Lake Calumet are solving their fuel problem this Winter by helping themselves to a considerable supply of peat recently discovered along the northern shore of the lake. Each day the stream of traffic to and from the swamp increases and every kind of conveyance is used for transporting the peat.
>
> [...] The neighborhood of the bog is dotted with huts built by men who were left unemployed when the surrounding factories stopped production. The huts have been constructed from materials gathered from the near-by dump. The peat fuel has been a godsend to this colony. It is removed in blocks or sods about three by four feet in dimension. After the blocks are dried in the sun to remove excess moisture, they are stacked in piles to be cut into chunks for burning as needed.

Thus, in general, every imaginable expedient was resorted to—sometimes on the basis of strangers' kindness. Some families were allowed to live in basements or rear apartments in exchange for taking care of furnaces, doing odd painting or carpentry jobs, or just looking after an unoccupied house. And many families, especially African American, lived rent-free in buildings that had been condemned but not yet torn down. The most notorious of these was the so-called Angelus Building, a seven-story building on the Near South Side that had served as a popular hotel during the World's Fair of 1893 but now housed "the most forlorn and destitute of all of Chicago's great population of hungry and miserable people." As an investigator wrote, "going from floor to floor and through one dark hall after another, searchlight in hand, one could only think of Dickens and places like Tom-All-Alone's in London in the middle of the nineteenth century; and it became necessary to remind one's self often that this was the twentieth century in one of the greatest and wealthiest cities of the world." Scores of families lived

---

11. Elderton, *Case Studies of Unemployment*, 229; Lara Campbell, *Respectable Citizens: Gender, Family, and Unemployment in Ontario's Great Depression* (Toronto, ON: University of Toronto Press, 2009), 35; Ginzberg, *The Unemployed*, 80.
12. Keyssar, *Out of Work*, 161, 162; *New York Times*, January 22, 1933.

in this dark, cold, fire-hazardous, waterless building, secure at least from the threat of eviction, if nothing else.[13]

The ranks of the truly extreme "economizers" included thousands, surely, who could relate to the experience of a "little old country Irish woman" in Chicago who lived for almost a week on a single quarter that a kindhearted girl had given her. "It was this way," she explained. "I bought a 9 cent can of tea and a 5 cent loaf of bread, and I got half a pound of sausage for 10 cents—you buy it just as you go over the bridge at Madison Street. And I had a nickel left, so I got a 5 cent tin of milk, and you see a spoonful of that will do for a meal."[14]

Of course, it was not enough to economize. It was necessary to raise money in whatever ways one could. One method was to pawn belongings, from jewelry to furniture. In order to pay their rent, the Haymans, for example, pawned two diamond rings, two watches, a suit, and three coats. It was imperative that they keep up with their rent because they lived in furnished rooms, out of which the landlord could lock them at any time. Some families resorted to commercial loan companies and "loan sharks," typically because they could not rely on relatives as others could.[15]

Whether in the city or its suburbs, whether working class or middle class, Black or white, the jobless regularly had to sell off their belongings one by one as they tried to eke out an existence for a few more months. A radio, an automobile, furniture, clothes, a wedding ring, another wedding ring, perhaps a store if they owned one, even (among many Blacks) the mattresses on which they slept—piece by piece they parted with their past lives. Under pressure from their agencies, relief workers often insisted that every possible resource be used up before the family could be accepted for relief, a demand that could simply add insult to injury. One family was forced to sell a diamond ring that had been passed down for generations. "It was either that or get put off relief," the father said, "but believe me I would almost rather beg on the streets than to have sold that ring. [...] Really, it seemed to me that our whole family was represented by that diamond ring."[16]

Needless to say, the most effective and popular way to raise money was to find any job one could or to have one's family members find a job. Single young women were perhaps the most courageous and determined of all. Frequently, at least in large cities, "white-collar girls" seem to have been even more loath to accept charity than most adult men, so proud were they and so highly did they prize their independence. Day after day they rose early in the morning to trudge the streets, spending as little as possible on food and transportation. According to one reporter, such a woman

---

13. Friedman, "One Hundred Unemployed Families," 146; Edith Abbott, *The Tenements of Chicago: 1908–1935* (Chicago, IL: University of Chicago Press, 1936), 468–73.
14. Kathleen M'Laughlin, "Jobs Pour In, but Many More Must Still Be Found," *Chicago Tribune*, October 22, 1930.
15. Elder, "One Hundred Applicants for Relief," 86.
16. Janssen, "A Study of 363 Unemployment Cases," 63; Elder, 66; Friedman, 151, 152; Bakke, *Citizens without Work*, 209.

lives as long as possible on her savings, trying all the time to find more work and going without enough food to save money for clothes. Then she turns to her friends—private borrowing is not quite so shameful—until she becomes too much of a burden. There are girls who for the past few months have risen every morning before dawn, to be first in the lines of applicants for any job that has been advertised, and when the early-morning rush is over and it is too late to hope for success, they must look for a place to sit, to wait until the day is over. That place is not easy to find, particularly in winter.[17]

Some rode the subway all night because they had no money for rent: "you can stay on the subway indefinitely for a nickel, if you know the right places to change." Or they rested during the day in the lounges of department stores, week after week. Meanwhile, the stresses under which they labored were grinding away at their mental stability, so that when they finally did accept relief, one of the agencies' greatest expenses was to provide them with psychiatric treatment.[18]

And yet, externally, they were still able to maintain their appearance, on which everything depended. "They always manage somehow," according to an observer, "to fix themselves up at the Salvation Army for about a quarter. It is pretty marvelous how vivid life stays in a woman, how she always washes her stockings and looks pretty clean, and has some powder for her nose, no matter how pinched and miserable she is. Women sometimes have an indestructible lust for living that is pretty hard to douse."[19]

For all job seekers, there was the same condition of day-after-day-after-day disappointments and slowly eroding hope. The diary of Olive Devies, divorcée, Chicago mother of a 19-year-old girl, provides a glimpse of the dreary repetitiveness of this life. Mrs. Devies did not work, instead spending her days sewing, visiting friends, going to church, and pursuing her hobbies (e.g., stamp collecting). Her daughter worked as a typist downtown but was laid off in March 1940. In the following weeks, her mother's daily journal entries typically begin in exactly the same way: "Marion left the house at 8 a.m. and spent the day in the loop looking for a job." Almost every day. Weeks later: "Marion left the house at 8 a.m. and spent the day in the loop looking for a job." Until 6 p.m. every day. One can picture this young woman wandering alone from employment office to employment office, scanning newspapers for promising job advertisements, windowshopping for "Help Wanted" signs, filling out applications, hungry and tired—and then getting up early the next day to do it all over again, for the twentieth time. At last, she secured an interview with the Belson Manufacturing Company, which hired her the next day. Sweet deliverance![20]

Few were so lucky. The sociologist E. Wight Bakke, who studied the behavior of unemployed men in England and the United States throughout the 1930s, found pretty

---

17. Emily Hahn, "Women without Work," *New Republic*, May 31, 1933.
18. Ibid.; Marlise Johnston, quoted in Betty Hansen, "The Effect of Unemployment on the Personality and Attitudes of Women," 1934, Burgess Papers, box 146, folder 5.
19. Ibid.
20. Diary of Olive Devies, entries in March and April 1940, Special Collections, Harold Washington Library.

much the same thing wherever he looked. At first, confident belief that the unemployment would be temporary (except in 1932 and 1933, very dark years). While they were not always confident that the same firm would hire them back, they usually thought it would not be long before they found a job in the same industry. (This belief was certainly less common among Blacks.) The positive attitude might last up to six months for about a third of the men, especially if they were skilled workers, even as the daily tramping and line-waiting and advertisement-answering ate away at their initial buoyancy. Some walked ten or more miles a day. For skilled workers, it was a very gradual process for them to accept that they would have to "take anything," however low the job's status and wages were. But, after months of "up at five-thirty or six in the morning to start out again"—for the best time to find a job was in the morning—acquiescence in the need to lower one's standards was almost inevitable. One man, a truck driver, spoke for all of them: "*It isn't the hard work of tramping about so much, although that is bad enough. It's the hopelessness of every step you take when you go in search of a job you know isn't there.*"[21]

Some job seekers, both male and female, tried their luck with the private and public employment agencies. The applicant first registered at the central desk, after which he or she was referred to the proper division for the kind of work he was seeking. He was then interviewed regarding his experience and qualifications. His registration card would be placed in the "active" file for two weeks or a month, and then—if a job hadn't been found—it would be placed in the "inactive" file. Meanwhile, the agency was continually receiving orders for work, not only from businesses but also from housewives in need of domestic labor. And it would solicit employment orders as well, through phone calls and personal visits to businesses. A placement officer selected from the active file one or more of the best qualified candidates for a particular job offer and then called them, to interview them one more time regarding this particular job offer. Frequently the employer was not satisfied with the applicant, and a new one had to be selected.[22]

While they were useful institutions, employment agencies were not very popular. Only a minority of the unemployed used them, and the agencies were able to place only a minority of the applicants. For example, in a typical week in the second half of 1931, the Illinois public employment agency in Chicago received over two thousand applicants but secured jobs for only about seven hundred. The service did get more effective with time, as more workers became familiar with it and business conditions improved in the second half of the decade. In 1936, for instance, it was able to provide jobs for 74,000 of the 118,000 people who registered with it for the first time, while in 1937 it placed 92,000 registrants.[23]

---

21. E. Wight Bakke, *The Unemployed Man* (London: Nisbet and Co., Ltd., 1933), 64–67; *Chicago Tribune*, November 1, 1930; Bakke, *The Unemployed Worker: A Study of the Task of Making a Living without a Job* (New Haven, CT: Yale University Press, 1940), 239, 240. Italics in original.
22. Willard E. Parker, "Renewals, Orders, and Cancellations in a Public Employment Exchange," *Personnel Journal* 7, (February 1933): 312–24; "Public Employment Services," *Monthly Labor Review*, January, 1931: 10–32.
23. *Chicago Tribune*, October 6, 1931; Anne S. Davis, "Employment and Vocational Guidance," in *Social Service Year Book, 1936*, eds. Linn Brandenburg et al. (Chicago, IL: Council

There were eight public employment agencies in Chicago, scattered in various neighborhoods around the city. Blacks used a separate branch on the South Side, which was located in two poorly ventilated, badly equipped narrow store buildings—until late 1935, when it was moved to a larger and better-equipped office building. Major improvements in the employment service took place that year and in 1936, as more money flowed in from the federal and state governments: staffs were enlarged, standards and procedures improved, and facilities expanded. More businesses and workers became aware of the service as it publicized itself extensively. It even helped people with disabilities find jobs, and, in alliance with the NYA and other New Deal programs, gave vocational counseling to people between 16 and 20 years of age. A number of other organizations in Chicago supplemented the work of the Illinois State Employment Service, including the Jewish Vocational Service, the YMCA and YWCA, the Masonic Employment Bureau, and the National Reemployment Service. Nevertheless, despite this social infrastructure, most of the jobless continued to use their own informal methods of seeking employment.[24]

The most popular way was to inquire with former employers, since they tended to hire men who had already worked for them. But the implication of this fact was obvious: in the worst years of the Depression, there was little point in applying for a job if the company did not already know you. Over and over again, men were asked, "Do you know anybody inside?" "No." "Well there's not much use in you filling out this application then, but you can try." And men did keep trying, for years on end. In 1940, people who had been on relief for seven years were still trying. "I'm a-lookin' all the time for my husband to get something to do," a Black mother of six told a reporter in late 1940. "He still goes a-lookin' all the time. He ain't got no soles on his shoes, walkin' and walkin' and walkin.'" To earn his relief money he worked 10 days a month "wrappin' up rat poison." After seven years, discouragement still had not gotten the best of this family. "That's all we can do—just live in hopes, that's all."[25]

In most cases, if men found a job at all it was only part-time or temporary work. Usually this amounted to little more than an "odd job," or, say, a week- or two-week-long version of such. Undertaken usually through the initiative of the sufferers themselves, but not infrequently through the initiative of friends, relatives, neighbors, or simply concerned citizens who wanted to help a stranger, odd jobs proliferated across Chicago

---

of Social Agencies of Chicago, 1936), 42; Frances L. Karlsteen, "Employment and Vocational Guidance," in *Social Service Year Book, 1937*, 46; Dinah Connell, "Employment and Vocational Guidance," *Social Service Year Book, 1938*, 49; Arthur Carstens, "Employment and Vocational Guidance," *Social Service Year Book, 1940*, 45.

24. "Minutes of Meeting of the Chicago Local Advisory Council of the Illinois State Employment Service," June 25, 1935, and "A Few Informal Notes Regarding Cook County Activities Since July 1, 1935," n.d., Graham Taylor Papers, box 52, folder 2344, Special Collections, Newberry Library; Davis, "Employment and Vocational Guidance," 39–47; Karlsteen, "Employment and Vocational Guidance," 40–47.

25. Marcia Winn, "Negro Mother's Plea: Give My Husband a Job!" *Chicago Tribune*, October 17, 1940.

in the 1930s like never before or since. People routinely called employment agencies to report little jobs they needed done, such as windows washed, bookcases made, furniture painted, or having storm windows put in.[26]

Unfortunately, there was not an efficient way to connect the city's tens of thousands of little tasks that needed doing with the men who could do them. A *Tribune* investigation in January 1933 found that "the door-to-door method of asking employment [could] no longer be used by men looking for temporary work," because housewives refused to open their doors to strangers. As one woman said, "the newspapers are filled with stories of housewives or maids who have opened their doors to strangers and found themselves held up." Mayor Cermak was so impressed by the *Tribune* report that a few days later he ordered the city's 40 district police stations to serve as the intermediary: people could call the station, and the police would assign the job to a "person of good character" they knew who was in need of work.[27]

Still, in this relatively unbureaucratized age, most of the activity happened through informal channels. In studies from the time we read of one man who occasionally put in window panes for neighbors for 50 cents and another who was able to earn hundreds of dollars periodically painting houses and doing repair jobs. Black men sometimes picked up bottles and "junked," as they called it (selling them for a penny or two to the "junk man"), while white men were more apt to hang around garages, hoping to get a job parking cars, washing windshields, or changing tires. One energetic young electrician made $48 in four months: $30 he earned from rewiring the telephone system in a bank, $8 from shoveling snow, and $10 from catching rats with his hands in a large dairy, at five cents apiece.

Some men, on the other hand, became household entrepreneurs: one earned a dollar a week making "paper novelties" out of tissue and cardboard, assisted by his five children. They usually worked (at home) from noon to two or three in the morning. An unemployed Polish architect made and sold pieces of furniture, while his wife found part-time work in a tailor shop and accepted orders for making dresses and coats. An electrician sold ferns that he dug up in the forest.[28]

As we have seen, however, despite all the efforts of the chief wage earner to find work, his wife and children often had to help provide for the family. They could find part-time and temporary jobs more easily, since more low-paid service occupations were open to them than to adult men. For boys between about 13 and 16 years of age paper routes seem to have been the most popular job, while many girls secured work as mothers' helpers. Young girls were preferred as domestic help over women in their 30s or 40s—for older women were "set in their ways," while girls could be molded—but girls rarely enjoyed working as servants. They would rather have worked in factories and had

---

26. *Chicago Tribune*, November 1, 1930, February 1, 1931.
27. Ibid., January 1, 3, 4, 1933.
28. "Chicago Hearings on Unemployment," January 6, 1932, p. 15, Graham Taylor Papers, box 53, folder 2380; miscellaneous reports, n.d., Burgess Papers, box 131, folders 3, 4; Ruth Strine, "A Study of 119 Families Receiving Relief from the Grovehill District of the Unemployment Relief Service" (MA thesis, University of Chicago, 1933), 35.

freedom at the end of the day. In fact, strangely enough, there was sometimes a shortage of domestic help in Chicago during the Depression decade, because the wages most housewives offered—$6 a week or less—were too low to interest young applicants (while the older women who would have accepted them were not wanted). Other common occupations for young women included stenographer, telephone operator, saleswoman, and waitress.[29]

It was not rare for boys even younger than 13 to contribute to their family's income. One survey found that a third of young boys in Back of the Yards earned money to give to their parents, even if only 2 cents or 10 cents a week. Some collected and sold brass, copper, iron, rags, and paper, taking a wagon through alleys to pick up whatever junk they could find, which they would sell to the "junk man." Others would steal bags of newspapers and bulletins from men hired to distribute them—when their backs were turned—and sell them a couple of months later to the "paper man." Many Black boys worked all night on milk wagons, carrying the milk to each house because the drivers were "too lazy" to do it, according to one report. The consequence was that in school the next day they tended to sleep through classes, exhausted from the previous night's work.[30]

Typically, families derived more income from the mother's work than the children's. Not that women were usually paid much. By 1940, one-fifth of all women in the country who worked for wages were domestic servants, who on average earned less than $8 per week even in New York City, where they were paid the highest. Wage discrimination against women was endemic. A Polish woman in the stockyards district scrubbed the floors of Union Station for $10 a week; another helped support her family by sorting pickles at $15 a week (for two months in the summer of 1930); a third worked as a waitress for $15 a week, when her husband had formerly earned $50 as a railroad car repair man. It was common for immigrant mothers to work part-time at night cleaning downtown offices, a not-very-remunerative job.[31]

Black women had it worst of all. In 1940, almost half of the women who did domestic service in Chicago were Black; most of these were supplementing their relief checks with surreptitious "day's work" that paid very little, in part because of the additional competition from white women who wanted such jobs. It was common for Black women

---

29. Janssen, "A Study of 363 Unemployment Cases," 57, 58; Virginia Gardner, "Women, 35, 'Too Old' for Maids, Say Housewives," *Chicago Tribune*, May 29, 1935; Cavan and Ranck, *The Family and the Depression*, 162, 165.
30. E. Clinton Belknap, "Summer Activities of Boys Back of the Yards in Chicago" (MA thesis, University of Chicago, 1937), 38, 39; "The effect of the depression in the area 47th to 51st, South Park to the New York Central tracks, as reported by Mrs. Margaret Bradburn, truant officer for the Colman and Farren schools," Burgess Papers, box 134, folder 1.
31. McElvaine, *The Great Depression*, 183; Lensing, "An Unemployment Study," 39; Janssen, "A Study of 363 Unemployment Cases," 57; "Family Life and the Depression," and report by Father Victor, Burgess Papers, box 131, folder 4. For many more examples of women's work to support the family, see Lois Rita Helmbold, "Beyond the Family Economy: Black and White Working-Class Women during the Great Depression," *Feminist Studies* 13, no. 3 (Autumn 1987): 629–55.

in the Depression to have a "regular" job that might pay them $6 or $8 a week, then to supplement this with one or more domestic service jobs at $1 or $2 a week, and on top of this, perhaps, to get relief, because of their husband's unemployment. Others were not fortunate enough to have a regular job, instead being forced to offer their services at so-called slave markets—"street corners where women congregated to await white housewives who came daily to take their pick and bid wages down."[32]

Black women were also the most likely to try that other, socially maligned option: prostitution. The number of professional prostitutes (employed by well-organized brothels) in Chicago had decreased by around 70 percent in the two decades before 1933, and even in Black neighborhoods it declined during the Depression, following business trends. But many more young women, sometimes as young as 12 or 13, temporarily became "amateur" prostitutes in the 1930s, to earn a few cents or a dollar here and there. One police officer estimated in 1932 that prostitution in Bronzeville had increased by 20 percent in the previous two years, an average of a hundred girls being picked up by police every month. But this number far understates the extent of the activity, since it was constantly going on in the dark corners of kitchenette apartments, sometimes by housewives in the presence of their children. It could even be sanctioned by husbands. Sociologists estimated that every building in lower-class areas of the Black Belt was likely to contain some prostitutes, who, according to disapproving housewives who lived in the same buildings, might even "stop in the entrance or any place and have a man!"[33]

For some women there were other motivations to sell their bodies than simply the need to eat or the inability to get a job because of their skin color. High-school students who were arrested for "street-walking" complained that the only work they could get was as maids or waitresses, or in hotels, and this, because of the low status and the low wages, was far from appealing. "When I see the word *maid*," said one, "—why, girl, let me tell you, it just runs through me! I think I'd sooner starve." Another woman, who had lost her white-collar job during the Depression, tried working as a maid but soon turned to prostitution: "I didn't want to do housework," she said. "Here I had been in some kind of office since I was fourteen years old. Now why should I start scrubbing floors at this late date in life? I tried first one thing and then another, and I couldn't make a hit of it, so …" From this perspective, the turn to prostitution seems less like tragedy than an assertion of individuality, a *refusal* to be thrust into the degradation to which society would consign one. For hardly any work at all, one could make more money than from hours of filthy, backbreaking scrubbing of floors or servile serving of meals to white people; and one could then buy some of the finery that this same white society judged as a criterion of human worth. For some women, certainly, it was desperation that drove them to occasional prostitution, but for others it was pride.[34]

---

32. Drake and Cayton, *Black Metropolis*, 242–49.
33. *Chicago Tribune*, January 3, 1933; "Effects of the depression on prostitution" and other reports, Burgess Papers, box 134, folder 1; Drake and Cayton, *Black Metropolis*, 596–99.
34. Drake and Cayton, 598.

Disregard for social conventions and legal straitjackets was not confined to some women's embrace of prostitution. It was far more widespread than that. Across the country, petty theft and bootlegging of coal and other materials shot up in the early years of the Depression, though they declined after 1933. We'll never know the extent of "criminal" activities undertaken by those who had lost a stable means of income, since most of the petty property crimes did not make it to the attention of the police—and even those that did were usually not reported by the press, for fear of emboldening other would-be defilers of the sanctity of property. But from scattered hints, we know that Chicago overflowed with working-class defiance of the laws of the rich.[35]

One simple form of defiance occurred in people's own homes: when companies turned off the gas and electricity because of nonpayment of bills, residents broke open the padlocked outlets and got the services for free. Usually this act was accompanied by a sense of entitlement rather than shame. One study stated bluntly, "such purloining from an impersonal business concern was not considered dishonest." At public hearings on unemployment in 1932 and 1933, men even spoke with pride of their flouting of the law. "The other day my gas was shut off," one said. "I went to work and shut the meter off and plugged in and got gas. I have stolen coal," he continued. "You may wonder how that has affected my mind. A year or two ago if I had seen somebody holding up somebody else I might have risked my life to stop it. Today, I would say, 'I hope he has a big fat politician by the neck and kills him or a big fat banker.'" We cannot know how many families illegally used gas or electricity in their homes, but the fact that men were willing to brazenly admit to it in public hearings suggests the practice was not uncommon. Even when people were unwilling or unable to do it themselves, the local Unemployed Council or some other group might come in and do it for them.[36]

More frequent, and more frightening to authorities, was theft that occurred outside the home. A writer for *The Nation*, for instance, reported the following from Detroit, in the summer of 1932:

> There have been minor riots and threats of worse disturbances. Petty thievery is increasing. Windows of small retail shops are smashed at night and relieved of their goods. Children from the poorer districts have taken to snatching bundles from customers coming out of grocery stores. They run off to barren homes with their booty, or eat it themselves in out-of-the-way alleys. More frequently, grown men, usually in twos and threes, enter chain stores, order all the food they can possibly carry, and then walk quietly out without paying. Every newspaper in town knows of this practice and knows that it is spreading, but none mentions it in print.[37]

---

35. S. J. Duncan-Clark, "Chicago Records Big Drop in Crime," *New York Times*, December 1, 1935; *Chicago Tribune*, October 24, 1939.
36. Friedman, "One Hundred Unemployed Families," 149; Cavan and Ranck, *The Family and the Depression*, 66; "An Urban Famine: Summary of Open Hearings Held by the Chicago Worker's Committee on Unemployment, January 5–12, 1932," p. 12, Graham Taylor Papers, box 36, folder 1950.
37. Mauritz A. Hallgren, "Grave Danger in Detroit," *Nation*, August 3, 1932.

As a much larger city than Detroit, Chicago certainly saw far more thievery—which was probably the main reason Mayor Cermak made his famous remark in 1932 that the federal government had a choice: it could send either relief or troops.

A Communist leader of the jobless later observed that "mass street demonstrations and other gatherings of the unemployed were followed by their participants swarming into nearby restaurants, eating their fill, and then departing with advice to the cashier to 'charge it to the mayor.'" Some of the more spectacular thefts included food riots in New York City and occasions such as an incident when over a thousand men waiting in a Salvation Army breadline saw bakery goods being delivered to a nearby hotel and promptly raided the trucks to help themselves. In St. Paul, Minnesota, a group of unemployed workers invaded a packinghouse and made off with hundreds of hams and sides of bacon. In Oklahoma City in January 1931, hundreds of men charged into a grocery store and took all the food, having just paraded through the city in protest at authorities' failure to distribute relief. Such collective thefts were frequent in the early 1930s.[38]

Later, we'll consider the activities of "gangs" of youth, who were responsible for some of the more serious thefts but who were more often motivated by the desire for excitement and adventure than the necessities of survival. Their crimes, however, constituted a minority of the total. Even in places where there were few or no organized gangs, including many areas on Chicago's South Side, such forms of theft as purse snatching, pickpocketing, stealing packages from trucks, and ganging up on peddlers and storekeepers were relatively common, especially in 1931 and 1932. It was usually young people who committed these kinds of crimes, but adults were not above thievery if it would help their families. Immigrant mothers told of shoplifting stockings or even curtains from department stores, and of asking their children to steal things. Sometimes the thefts went awry, in which case the press might report them. For example, in two separate incidents on one day in November 1930, two fathers—"driven to desperation by the hunger of their children"—were killed trying to steal turkeys for Thanksgiving, one by police bullets as he fled the butcher's shop, the other by the proprietor as he crawled through a window he had smashed with a brick. In 1935, a teenager was shot dead trying to steal a bottle of milk off a porch for his infant nephew, who had been crying for two days out of sheer hunger.[39]

Significantly, theft was "quite generally approved" in communities on the South and West sides, as social workers reported and as was evident from interviews and public hearings. Contemplating crime was the new norm. "People are ready to take money,"

---

38. Franklin Folsom, *Impatient Armies of the Poor: The Story of Collective Action of the Unemployed, 1808–1942* (Niwot, CO: University Press of Colorado, 1991), 240, 241; *Daily Worker*, January 14, 21, 1931.

39. "The effect of the depression in the area 47th to 51st, South Park to the New York Central tracks," Burgess Papers, box 134, folder 1; John Evans, "'Gangs of Boys Part of City's Poverty Growth,'" *Chicago Tribune*, December 11, 1931; Friedman, "One Hundred Unemployed Families," 177; Report by Harriet Lesniak, Burgess Papers, box 131, folder 4; report by president of Local #5 Unemployed Council, December 24, 1934, ibid.; *New York Times*, November 27, 1930; *Washington Post*, August 4, 1935.

an unemployed father said in 1932. "They say they are going out to do this and that. I am often tempted to go myself, but I think, 'I have a family. What if I am pinched?' So I don't go, but you can hear talk of robbery on any street corner. Not one would refuse to steal a ten-dollar bill if he saw a man walking down the street with one." Another: "I wouldn't mind taking money from a wealthy employer who has wrenched money from his employees." Race and ethnicity were of little consequence here: the combination of physical hunger and moral outrage tends to level distinctions, so that inconvenient social norms are sloughed off and all that remain are the realities of class and the imperatives of survival.[40]

"Everyday communism"

We have yet to consider probably the most important factor in enabling people to cope with the 11-year-long crisis: the commitment of relatives, friends, neighbors, and the poor to helping each other. Sometimes, it's true, they would steal from one another, as just mentioned; much more often, they gave to one another. Of course, this was not some sudden efflorescence of generosity with no precedents in history. Rather, it grew out of the most durable and necessary dynamics of human history, the tendencies mentioned in the Introduction that the anthropologist David Graeber dubbed "baseline communism." The fetish of "privatization" that has, in a whirlwind of "creative destruction," remade the world in recent centuries has had to be *forced* on those at the bottom, who resisted it—arguably never more than in the 1930s.

In every region of the country and every social context—urban or rural—suffering people showed a striking degree of compassion and, often, solidarity. In a book of personal histories, for example, a woman from Ivyland, Pennsylvania, states, "My memories from the Great Depression are of unbelievable love, courage, and sharing"—as in the case of the neighbor who fed the woman's family once a week for years or the other neighbor who cut down every tree on his property to provide firewood for several families. In Lakeland, Florida, there is the story of the old woman who owned a general store along a highway, where she frequently saw individuals and entire families shambling along, pieces of old automobile tires tied to their feet in place of shoes; so she would invariably invite them to her house and give them a meal and goods from her store, until finally she could not keep the store anymore because it had been almost emptied out. One person simply states that "families were a lot closer [than they are now]." A Mexican man from South Chicago recalls, "At that time people were more together. Mexican people would help each other without expecting anything in return." A woman from Selma, Alabama, sums up: "I'll never forget those years: neighbors helping neighbors, sharing whatever good fortune came their way; doctors rendering services regardless of patients' finances; and worship with friends whose faith far outdistanced their troubles."[41]

---

40. "An Urban Famine," 1932, p. 11, McCulloch Papers, box 4, folder 1; Friedman, 177, 178.
41. Deb Mulvey, ed., *"We Had Everything But Money"* (New York: Crescent Books, 1995), 33, 22, 26; Ardyth Ann Stull, "Stories of the Children of the Great Depression: What I Learned

Indeed, "everyday communism" was so ubiquitous and taken for granted it is hard to make interesting distinctions regarding its practice between races and ethnicities, or to do more than merely give examples of what was happening constantly all over Chicago and the United States. Statistics about such things as how often and in what ways friends and relatives helped each other are not available. Insofar as generalizations are possible, they may be only of the sort exhibited by these comments by a welfare association on Polish families in Chicago, in 1934: "The depression appears to have little effect upon family bonds. [...] [E]ach individual family reacts differently, but as a whole, the Polish family displays a marked consciousness of responsibility towards each of its members." This was just as true of other immigrant peoples, as well as of Anglo Americans and Blacks.[42]

For example, people who lived in the countryside regularly provided their city-dwelling relatives with milk, eggs, butter, and fresh vegetables—frequently hundreds of dollars' worth over just a few months. Working-class parents on Chicago's West Side told investigators of receiving up to $300 in cash from family members and friends, often as gifts, not loans. More typical were gifts in the form of food and clothing, but even then, this might represent a substantial drain on the resources of the givers, who not infrequently were themselves unemployed. A survey in 1933 of 119 jobless families found that 49 had received this kind of help from friends and relatives, in addition, sometimes, to receiving shelter. Of 363 families in Evanston, 50 percent had received help of some kind from relatives, 13 percent moving in with them—by April 1931, that is. It is likely that in the following years the proportion of people receiving shelter increased.[43]

The sharing of shelter usually proved mutually advantageous. A 20-year-old woman who moved in with her widowed older sister, the mother of three young children, was able to escape from an unpleasant stepmother, while the rent she paid was of use to her sickly and sporadically employed sister. They "help[ed] each other out, as can," the young sister said. Altogether, in working-class areas of Chicago, shared housing was virtually the norm, especially among women: a 1932 study of women employed in the slaughtering and meatpacking industry, for instance, found that 31 percent lived in two-family dwellings and 60 percent in multifamily dwellings. The historian Susan Porter Benson comments that, while in some respects less flexible than single-family housing, "multiple-unit dwellings allowed kin and friends to live in close proximity without directly sharing living space, making it easier to pool domestic labor such as laundry, child-minding, cooking, and house-cleaning."[44]

---

from My Parents" (PhD diss., Iowa State University, 2013), 2; Jesse John Escalante, "History of the Mexican Community in South Chicago" (MA thesis, Northeastern Illinois University, 1982), 20; Elderton, *Case Studies of Unemployment*, 132, 182, 223, 361.
42. Report by the Polish Welfare Association, Burgess Papers, box 131, folder 3.
43. Lensing, "An Unemployment Study," 20; Janssen, "A Study of 363 Unemployment Cases," 56, 59, 60; Strine, "A Study of 119 Families," 38, 39.
44. Susan Porter Benson, *Household Accounts: Working-Class Family Economies in the Interwar United States* (Ithaca, NY: Cornell University Press, 2007), 81, 100, 101.

Similarly, it was most frequently among women that goods were shared or exchanged, because women were in charge of the household economy. Both during and before the Depression, in the more "prosperous"—or rather, less depressed—years of the 1920s and earlier, working-class female friends and relatives were munificent in their exchanges of gifts. The experiences of the Allen family are representative:

> A friend who worked in the stock yards [in the early 1930s] brought them bacon and inexpensive cuts of meat; another friend gave them a dozen cans of macaroni; someone else supplied ice. A friend gave Mrs. Allen a coat that had been left at her house and never called for. Mrs. Allen's sister also came to her aid and, through an exchange of services, both benefited: Mrs. Allen mended for her sister, and the sister made clothes for her; the sister bought fruit, and Mrs. Allen canned all of it, retaining some for her work [as an amateur cook]. Money was also borrowed from friends and relatives to the extent of about $900.[45]

Friends and relatives were far from being the only recourse. A survey of 100 unemployed families in Chicago found that 75 had received gifts both from people close to them and from landlords, neighbors, bakeries, grocery stores, former employers, church organizations, societies and various national alliances, and even the *Chicago Daily News*. A survey in 1934 of almost two thousand single women on relief found "ample evidence of the consideration shown by landlords, more frequently landladies," since all but a handful of the women were in rent arrears of from 1 to 12 months. In a case in Chicago, a family's gas had been shut off, and the neighbor, who didn't know them, sent in money for the gas bill "so they could heat the baby's milk." In another case neighbors collected $105 on behalf of a family that was about to be evicted. This type of help was extremely common: Communists working in Unemployed Councils reported that "in many instances we found neighbors collecting money among themselves to help a family threatened with eviction." Sometimes neighbors provided unemployed families with food for the holidays; or they regularly gave them food baskets, with food collected from around the community. But so as not to hurt the recipients' pride, they might do it in an oblique way: they would set the basket down at the front door at night, and knock on the door and quickly leave.[46]

In general, the importance of neighborly magnanimity cannot be overstated. When relief ran out, it was often neighbors who kept each other alive. The findings of a study in 1932 of 400 Philadelphian families are worth quoting, since they apply to neighborhoods in Chicago as well:

> [Regarding the provision of food,] the outstanding contribution has been made by neighbors. The poor are looking after the poor. In considerably more than a third of the four

---

45. Cavan and Ranck, *The Family and the Depression*, 118, 119.
46. Friedman, "One Hundred Unemployed Families," 156, 157; Earl G. Harrison, "Without without Work," *Survey*, March 1934; Elder, 82; Sam Nesin, "Weaknesses in Unemployment Work and How to Overcome Them," *Daily Worker*, June 16, 1931; Stull, "Stories of the Children of the Great Depression," 177, 178.

hundred families the chief source of actual subsistence when grocery orders stopped was the neighbors. [...] This help was the more striking since the neighbors themselves were often close to the line of destitution and could illy spare the food they shared. The primitive communism existing among these people was a constant surprise to the visitors. More than once a family lucky enough to get a good supply of food called in the entire block to share the feast. There is absolutely no doubt that entire neighborhoods were just living from day to day sharing what slight resources any one family chanced to have.[47]

Such practices constituted, in effect, a benign and unconscious type of resistance to acquisitive and individualistic values. Mutual support and solidarity like this were certainly in no way emanations of the dominant culture; they had autonomous, organic roots in the lives and communal heritage of subordinate classes; and, as we'll see in a later chapter, were easily manifested as explicit collective resistance to the ruling class.

It was common in many parts of Chicago for families to grow food in gardens, whether in their backyard or in public spaces cleared for that purpose. In South Chicago, Mexican families grew tomatoes, corn, squash, and hot peppers on a large public plot of land, which was also used by whites and Blacks to pick mushrooms and mustard leaves. At harvest time, family fiestas were held in which the fruits of their labor were shared with neighbors and friends, the remaining crops to be canned for use in the winter.[48]

Institutional, as opposed to personal, generosity was almost equally striking—except among political and large business organizations, that is, the dominant power structures. Churches, settlement houses, charities, fraternal societies, trade unions, and hundreds of civil society organizations that united in groups like the Federated Council of Professional and Business Women to aid the unemployed (by providing food, clothes, meals, and temporary jobs) all had, in the aggregate, a momentous effect on the well-being of the poor—even into the later years of the decade, when the government had taken over most relief functions. Even the Renters' Court sometimes gave money to the families who appeared before it day after day. One year the judge collected from his friends over $2,000, from which he paid the rent for some families, while for others a collection might be taken in the courtroom. From 5 to 15 dollars a day was raised by passing the hat.[49]

The "communism" that enabled people to survive and even to stay off relief extended, in a sense, to neighborhood storekeepers. As Lizabeth Cohen has emphasized, thousands of unemployed families in Chicago relied on the local merchant to extend credit, as he regularly had in the 1920s. This was one of the reasons they continued to shop at his store instead of the cheaper chain stores that were springing up around the country. The amounts of credit that grocers gave—and not only to their fellow countrymen—often

---

47. Ewan Clague, "When Relief Stops What Do They Eat?" *Survey*, November 15, 1932.
48. Escalante, "History of the Mexican Community in South Chicago," 23.
49. Roberta Nangle, "Chicago Clubs Offer United Aid to Unemployed," *Chicago Tribune*, January 10, 1932; *Chicago Daily News*, February 2 and March 16, 1932; Katherine Frances Kiesling, "The Problem of Rents and Evictions in the Depression Period" (MA thesis, University of Chicago, 1933), 59.

with little expectation that they would be repaid, beggar belief. We read of an Italian family getting $184 worth of groceries on credit, a German family getting $125, and a Polish family getting $325. Storekeepers reported giving credit to 50 families over two-and-a-half years and of being owed $3,500. Mexicans in South Chicago were able to get most of their goods on credit through the entire Depression, including from merchants of a different ethnicity than they. To some extent it was in the interest of grocers to keep giving more credit, since if they discontinued it they might lose customers, but it is clear that it was often done out of a sense of loyalty, duty, and compassion for people who were experiencing a crisis, and with whom relationships had been built over years. As Alexander Keyssar says, extending credit was an "expression of social bonds and conventions, of a culture that valued mutual aid and mutual obligations." The cold logic of the chain store was not that of the neighborhood merchant, enmeshed in ethnic networks and communal ties, animated by other impulses than insatiable pecuniary gain. The following stories from Philadelphia in 1932 would have been familiar to hundreds of merchants in Chicago[50]:

> John Nigro, a baker, was sued for debt a few days ago. His accounts receivable totaled $5,000. He could collect none of them; he knew when he was letting these bills run up that he was dispensing charity, but he continued to provide relief for his neighbors until he himself went to the wall. In the same neighborhood another shopkeeper, pointing to a bill of $200 that was owed him, said: "Eleven children in that house. They've got no shoes, no pants. In the house, no chairs. My God, you go in there, you cry, that's all. What can you do? Let them go hungry?"[51]

Still, by the fourth winter of unemployment, as many independent shopkeepers themselves were in dire condition because customers continued not to pay their bills, credit had in most cases dried up.

It was not only extending credit that depleted the resources of merchants; it was also their continual provision of free goods to people, outside any commercial context at all. Grocers all over the city fed several people every day during months of acute crisis, when there was even more begging than usual. Milk wagon drivers were another group that was noted for its generosity. One driver explained the usual practice: "We donate every week through the union. The unemployed milk drivers are paid first and what is left goes to the milk fund. In addition to that, we often help out some of the families on our routes. I have figured for the last five months [that is, the second half of 1931] that four or five dollars a week goes out. I leave the milk. It goes into the book and I pay for it."[52]

Some of the most impressive generosity existed among the poorest of the poor, such as Blacks in the slums of Chicago's Black Belt. The communal mentality went beyond the simple sharing of resources, which was the norm even in many middle-class

---

50. Cohen, *Making a New Deal*, 234, 235; Elder, "A Study of One Hundred Applicants for Relief," 76, 81; Janssen, 59; "An Urban Famine," 16, Graham Taylor Papers, box 36, folder 1950; Escalante, "History of the Mexican Community," 23; Keyssar, *Out of Work*, 163, 164.
51. Mauritz Hallgren, "Mass Misery in Philadelphia," *Nation*, March 9, 1932.
52. "An Urban Famine," 17; *New York Times*, July 12, 1931.

neighborhoods. Social workers sometimes were struck by the scarcity of "wild children" in the slums, children with no guardians, especially in light of the family desertions—usually by fathers—that happened in the area. The explanation is that Black families regularly took in stray children and adopted them as their own, adding them to the unruly brood already crammed into a small home. Whether or not this practice was a heritage of rural living in the South, it was certainly unusual, for very few whites acted similarly. Indeed, so "communal" was the environment in many Black neighborhoods that stray children would simply wander into apartments and, a little while later, be added to the family. Somehow, ways were found to feed them and take care of them.[53]

People who had been evicted frequently found solace in the homes of neighbors. One young woman returned from giving birth in a hospital to find she had been dispossessed and her husband had left her, taking most of the household goods with him. Fortunately a neighbor, who was herself receiving relief, opened her door to the deserted, homeless girl, and shared everything she had with this young mother and her child. Such compassion among fellow sufferers ensured that very few evicted families ever spent a night outside or were consigned to the hell of homelessness.[54]

One must also mention the "communism" that existed within the immediate family. Needless to say, a communist mentality—"from each according to his ability, to each according to his need"—is the very foundation of a healthy family life, as it is of a healthy social life; for cooperation, love, sympathy, and the sharing of resources are present in any nondysfunctional relationship. But in families that were not torn apart by the Depression, these things became even more pronounced than they had been. This was most obvious with regard to children's sharing of income with their parents. But they also frequently took on more household duties, especially if their mothers had to work. Even working-class boys participated in domestic chores, large percentages (30, 50 percent) washing floors and dishes, sweeping the sidewalk, emptying the garbage, chopping wood to be stored for winter, caring for younger children, and "keeping Dad from getting drunk while mother is at the Yards working." The participation of boys in these activities sometimes defied gender stereotypes and showed how adaptable families could be.[55]

Their adaptability, however, was especially indicated by *fathers'* willingness to take part in "feminine" domestic tasks. A Chicago study published in 1938 found that "men who had never before helped about the house and who perhaps belonged to cultural groups that regarded housework as derogatory to a man's status welcomed housework and became able assistants to their wives." Apparently, a large proportion of men from even the most patriarchal of cultural backgrounds, such as Eastern Europe, soon grew willing to do laundry, go shopping, help with cooking, and take care of the children,

---

53. "The effect of the depression in the area 47th to 51st, South Park to the New York Central tracks, as reported by Mrs. Margaret Bradburn," Burgess Papers, box 134, folder 1.
54. Lillian Wald, excerpt from *Windows on Henry Street*, in *Women of Valor: The Struggle against the Great Depression as Told in Their Own Life Stories*, eds. Bernard Sternsher and Judith Sealander (Chicago: Ivan R. Dee, Inc., 1990), 39.
55. Belknap, "Summer Activities of Boys," 39, 40; Glen H. Elder, Jr., *Children of the Great Depression*, 64–69.

activities they may (in some cases) have considered hopelessly beneath them only months earlier. Some, indeed, welcomed them, as things to occupy their time. It was not rare for unemployment actually to improve family ties, as the father developed greater respect for his wife's duties and abilities, and as family members spent more time with each other. "Unemployment itself," a sociologist wrote, "frequently acts as a stimulus to a more successful organization of family life than formerly existed." It is known, after all, that in moments of crisis communities are as apt to unite as to disintegrate, displaying impressive solidarity while drawing on deep reserves of psychological resilience.[56] Testimony after testimony from the 1930s gives witness to the durability and frequent intensification of family ties under the impact of the Depression. "For the Polish family," a Chicago priest said in 1934, "depression time is the time for sharing the most essential things in life; therefore, generally speaking, I will say that the family affectional ties are strengthened not weakened by the depression."[57]

A working-class Polish woman remarked, "The days that I work my husband stays home and takes care of the housework and gets the meals ready. He helps me wash clothes in the evening and Viola [the daughter] does the ironing after school." An Irish father took on all the heavy housework such as scrubbing the floors and washing clothes (though he refused to hang them out to dry, afraid of people seeing him). Mr. Page, a former truck driver, was "helpful in the house, devoted to [his wife], cheerful, and a great help with the children." "Of course [his wife] wants him to get a job," an interviewer noted, "but she hates to think of losing his companionship during the day."[58]

Information on these matters is sketchy, but it seems that, depending on the category (ethnicity, employed or not, etc.), between perhaps 20 and 40 percent of working-class husbands in urban contexts provided substantial help with household chores, especially cleaning, dishwashing, and childcare. Eastern Europeans were often particularly helpful, Germans and Italians a bit less so, and English and Jewish immigrants, it seems, least of all. Susan Porter Benson concludes that in the 1920s and 1930s, "working-class men participated in housework to a far greater degree than conventional historical wisdom allows."[59]

There has always been a tendency for commentators and historians to emphasize the family- and community-fragmenting aspects of the Depression, because those were the most obvious and dramatic. But far more interesting, and equally or more important, were the "communal" phenomena that have been briefly surveyed in this section. With regard to any particular context, such tendencies as these should be of great interest to the social historian and the anthropologist, since it is these that are conventionally

---

56. See Rebecca Solnit, *A Paradise Built in Hell: The Extraordinary Communities That Arise in Disaster* (New York: Penguin Books, 2009).
57. Cavan and Ranck, *The Family and the Depression*, 87; Friedman, "One Hundred Unemployed Families," 74; Ginzberg, *The Unemployed*, 75, 76; Bakke, *Citizens without Work*, 241; report by Father Victor, Principal of Holy Trinity High School, Burgess Papers, box 131, folder 3.
58. Elderton, *Case Studies of Unemployment*, 230, 189, 343; Komarovsky, *The Unemployed Man*, 78, 79; Ginzberg, *The Unemployed*, 75, 76.
59. Benson, *Household Accounts*, 45–49.

underemphasized—being contrary to dominant ideologies in a capitalist society—and that are, ultimately, what keep society functioning.

***

Through all the means that have been discussed here, people were able to postpone reliance on relief for very long periods. For many, that was the categorical imperative: *not to beg for relief. Maintain independence and self-respect.* Despite the hardships, despite the frustrations of looking for work endlessly and having to take odd jobs whenever one could and having to scrounge, and even requiring that one's wife and children play the masculine role by working, *deny the need for charity.* For that, supposedly, was to admit defeat. Some men even killed themselves rather than apply for relief.

As we saw earlier, some people who had lost their jobs were able to stay off relief the whole Depression, through ingenuity, luck, and spartan living. But those cases were exceptional. According to a survey of 101 families that had previously earned good wages, 29 had experienced over a year of unemployment before applying for relief, 14 had been unemployed between 6 months and a year before the relief application, and the rest (57 families) accepted relief after less than 6 months of unemployment. Another survey of 87 blue-collar Chicago families found that 18 managed to go longer than a year before asking for relief. So, in general, it is safe to say that a substantial minority, perhaps a quarter or a third, of unemployed white Americans and immigrants in Chicago did not turn to relief for a year or more, sometimes three or four years. (The situation was different for most Blacks, who had fewer resources.) This may even be an underestimate, for according to E. Wight Bakke three-quarters of the unemployed in New Haven did not apply for relief until they had been out of work two or more years.[60]

One might argue that this extreme reluctance to go on relief was merely a manifestation of Americans' "traditional individualism" and inability to create an alternative working-class culture.[61] More charitable, though, would be to argue that independence and self-reliance—where self is defined not individualistically but in terms of family, extended kin, friends, neighbors, community, and fellow workers—were hallmarks of a relatively independent working-class culture that were not incompatible with the latter's traditional ethic of "mutualism" (to quote the historian David Montgomery). In a broader sense, to value independence from institutions that pry into one's most intimate personal affairs in a degrading and condescending way, as relief agencies did, with the implication that one is incapable of financial responsibility, is neither "bourgeois" ("individualistic") nor working class but simply *human*, arising out of the natural desire to freely determine oneself.

---

60. Elder, "A Study of One Hundred Applicants for Relief," 63; Strine, "A Study of 119 Families," 33; Friedman, "One Hundred Unemployed Families," 161; Frances Fox Piven and Richard A. Cloward, *Poor People's Movements* (New York: Vintage Books, 1979), 56.
61. See, for example, Melvyn Dubofsky, "Not So 'Turbulent Years': A New Look at the 1930s," in *Life and Labor: Dimensions of American Working-Class History*, eds. Charles Stephenson and Robert Asher (Albany, NY: State University of New York Press, 1986), 223.

And yet despite popular hostility toward intrusive authorities such as relief agencies, we'll see in Chapter six that it was possible for millions of people very early in the Depression to demand statist collectivism on a scale that would have been scarcely conceivable a year or two earlier. Their valorization of self-reliance did not prevent tens of millions from advocating a system that in some respects would have been quintessentially socialist.

"Re-creating"

Informal recreation

Contrary to what one might think from reading some reports of the time, recreation for most families severely affected by insecure employment during the 1930s did not consist only of sitting at home and staring at the wall. Lack of money did not entail lack of recreation, although it did limit the forms of fun that could be indulged in. Fortunately, it isn't only the financially secure who are able to enjoy life.

Writing a paper on the topic, a student at the University of Chicago summed up the transformation from 1929 to 1934 in one sentence: "Play and recreation," she observed, "have become more simple and wholesome." This was true even for families that had some (small) means of income. Before the Depression there was an element of "grandeur" to recreation, as formal dinner dances were, for many young people, weekly or biweekly occurrences, and groups would have dinner at a hotel and then spend the night "gadding about" (as the student put it) to night clubs. "*Now*," she said, "a crowd gathers at someone's home, plays bridge or dances, has a simple lunch and calls it an enjoyable evening." Such changes symbolize that which perhaps most set the Depression decade apart from the rest of the twentieth century: it was the era of (partial) decommercialization, decommodification, and deprivatization.[62]

One way this anticommercial spirit manifested itself was in the frequent substitution of outdoor activities for indoor activities. Whereas a few years earlier, young people had favored night clubs, movie theaters or plays, and other kinds of commercial entertainment, now they substituted "nature play" (as one young woman put it)—if, that is, they had access to nature of some sort, whether parks or rivers or forests. In the environs of Chicago, it was common for children and teenagers to pack up some food and hike to a spring to have a picnic or go on a jaunt through the woods and splash around in a river, maybe frog-hunting. Hiking grew popular, as did camping (with the encouragement of settlement houses and New Deal programs). A "bicycle craze" sprang up as well, in part because many could no longer afford automobiles or the fare for streetcars.[63]

The city had a quite extensive network of recreational facilities and relevant social institutions. For example, the Depression-stricken Near West Side (largely Italian) had eight public playgrounds, five parks, three public libraries, about 130 churches, 24 public schools, and several settlement houses (most famously Hull House). Not even

---

62. "Recreation and Depression" (a student paper), 1934, Burgess Papers, box 177, folder 2.
63. Miscellaneous student papers, ibid.; *Chicago Tribune*, March 6, 1937.

Black neighborhoods on the South Side were altogether deprived of such resources: for instance, Washington Park had at least thirty-four churches, several youth organizations such as Boy Scouts, and its enormous namesake park, which included 11 baseball diamonds, 15 softball fields, an archery range, hockey fields, 25 tennis courts, and other facilities. Churches, too, frequently had indoor and outdoor recreational facilities, such as gymnasiums, club rooms, volleyball courts, playgrounds, baseball diamonds, and ping-pong tables. Despite all this, however, the Chicago Recreation Commission found in its four-year-long investigation in the late 1930s that a "very considerable number of community areas" lacked recreational facilities, and that the city's park and play facilities "should be multiplied several-fold in order to conform to well-accepted standards."[64]

Another inadequacy was that, partly because of budget cuts, there were relatively few organized recreational programs for youth and children at public institutions. Most public schools did not offer summer programs, and when they did they didn't always include the workshop or handicraft classes that most appealed to boys. Programs in parks were not much more satisfactory. In Back of the Yards, for example, the lack of personnel meant that sometimes the only "program" younger children could participate in was swimming. And because only a limited number of people were allowed in the pool at any given time, kids often had to stand in line for hours in the hot sun, waiting for the precious 30 minutes that they would be allowed to swim in the pool. Public libraries, likewise, had insufficient funds to buy new books or offer exciting programs. Such were the fruits of government retrenchment.[65]

So, to a great extent, it was left to the young to create their own fun. A 1937 study of Back of the Yards gives detailed information on how young boys—Mexican, Polish, Irish, and German—spent their free summer hours, when they were not helping with housework or earning a little money for the family. About half of the boys interviewed had access to tools around the house, which they used to make such things as two-wheel scooters, wooden guns, foot stools, model airplanes, and dog houses. Most of the boys also had pets of some sort—dogs, cats, pigeons, guinea pigs, rabbits, and chickens. Their enjoyment of these animals fed their yearning to live in the countryside. "In de country a guy can be around de animals," said one, while others followed up with "You can ride horses," "Have fun chasin' the chickens," and "Feed the pigs." "In the country—more fun. You can play baseball better there—no cars in the way and you don't bust a window like we did a week ago." Children tolerated the congestion of urban neighborhoods, but they did not always enjoy it. (And no wonder, considering this description of Back

---

64. Louis Wirth and Margaret Furez, eds., *Local Community Fact Book, 1938* (Chicago, IL: Chicago Recreation Commission, 1938); Arthur J. Todd, *Chicago Recreation Survey 1937, Vol. IV: Recreation by Community Areas in Chicago* (Chicago, IL: Works Progress Administration, 1939); Arthur J. Todd, ed., *Chicago Recreation Survey, Vol. V: Recommendations Adopted by the Chicago Recreation Commission, and Summary of Findings* (Chicago, IL: Works Progress Administration, 1940), 5, 9, 16, 17; "Notes on Recreation, Informal Education, and Group Work in Chicago," May 1938, Welfare Council Papers, box 167, folder 4, Chicago History Museum.
65. Belknap, "Summer Activities of Boys Back of the Yards in Chicago," 23–29.

of the Yards: "The streets, the alleys, the vacant lots, 'along the tracks,' the parks, the University of Chicago Settlement playgrounds, every place is jammed with boys and girls, large and small!")[66]

In addition to all the unorganized street and park activities—innumerable games (including card games, hopscotch, tag, hide and seek, kick the can, "rolling hoops," and "Push 'em in de Hell"[67]), wood-crafting, swimming, roller-skating, street hockey, and the like—were such indoor activities as reading and listening to the radio. Girls, both older and younger, tended to stay inside more than boys, in part because they were given less freedom by their parents. If they had material, some high-school-aged girls liked to make hats and dresses and do embroidery. Across the city, it was common for teenage girls to read magazines and books for pleasure; fewer, but still a sizable minority, enjoyed listening to the radio—and it was not rare for financially struggling families to have radios. More girls played baseball in lower-income neighborhoods than in wealthier areas like Lakeview (where it was more usual for them to play tennis).[68]

Not all the youth's fun was "simple and wholesome," however. Gangs of teenage and younger boys proliferated in the 1930s as in the 1920s, especially in low-income areas. Most gangs did not routinely engage in crime—they were simply peer groups from around the block, which had sprung up around shared interests and frequently a common ethnicity—but it was not unusual for their activities to straddle the line between licit and illicit. In between playing baseball and basketball, or lounging on street corners or playing marble and dice games, they might fight members of another gang who had wandered into their territory. Gang rivalries could be fierce, so much so that merely going to a drugstore in another gang's territory might get one beaten up. This had especially been the case in the 1920s and earlier, when teenagers told interviewers of times when they had lain in wait for hours for one of the "enemy" to invade the local block on his way to the meat market. By the 1930s these rivalries were waning, but even so, ethnic differences, as between Mexican gangs and Polish gangs, perpetuated a degree of hostility and suspicion.[69]

Stealing was another favored form of recreation among gang members. Given the "gambling spirit" that inspired many gangs—the zeal for taking chances, for outwitting the law and "getting something for nothing"—stealing was a way of achieving status within the group, and of expressing the common ethos of opposition toward the established order. Shoplifting at department stores, for example, provided adventure. One technique was for a couple of kids to attract the attention of clerks while others filled

---

66. Ibid., 104.
67. An 11-year-old described this game as follows: "try to push someone into the street; then the fellow that's 'it' comes along and tickles you, sometimes maybe five minutes, if you laugh you go to hell—if you don't laugh you go to heaven." Belknap, "Summer Activities," 86.
68. Irene Smith Barlow, "Leisure-Time Activities of Two Hundred High School Girls in Chicago" (MS thesis, University of Chicago, 1934), passim.; Escalante, "History of the Mexican Community in South Chicago," 28.
69. James J. Gentry, "Bronzeville in Chicago," *Chicago Defender*, June 12, 1937; *Chicago Tribune*, July 10, 1932; Belknap, "Summer Activities of Boys," chapter 6.

their shirts or sweaters full of merchandise, which they passed to friends outside the door, who then dashed away as the first group returned to load up again. The more enterprising and prolific shoplifters were able to make a lot of money by reselling the stolen goods. On the South Side and in South Chicago, it was also popular to rob fruit trucks. One or more boys would "hop" the back of the truck when it stopped at a railroad crossing, throw off fruit to companions stationed along the road as the truck continued driving, and then jump off at the next crossing. The fruit was usually sold to get money for cigarettes, a dance, or seeing a movie.[70]

More serious was the epidemic of car thefts in the early 1930s, and the theft of spare tires and other parts. The press reported that several thousand cars were stolen by "wayward boys" every month, until in 1934 a new municipal court was established just to deal with the problem. Even into the late 1930s, property crimes were committed by many different sections and strata of the population, but none more so than the impecunious youth. WPA researchers observed that their young interview subjects were apt to have pockets bulging with small things like knives, pencils, whistles, and toys they had snatched from stores; and some teenagers—Mexican, Black, Polish, etc.—told of stealing bikes, skates, and even coal from sheds (a rather elaborate project that required cooperation and advance planning). "Holdups" remained common the whole decade and were frequently reported in sensationalist terms by the press. Why did so many of the young turn to crime? "Easy money," was the laconic reply. "Nothing to it," said one boy. "You stick a hand in your pocket and make 'em think it's a gun. Then you stick a hand in their pockets and get their dough."[71]

These trends toward a greater incidence of juvenile delinquency were already clear in 1931, and—partially excepting the middle years of the decade, when the economy improved—continued into 1940 and beyond, particularly in Black neighborhoods. "There has been an increase in armed robbery," the Black-owned *Chicago Defender* noted in 1940, "and bands of young hoodlums roam the streets insulting and attacking women, with little fear of arrest." Murders were on the rise. Gambling flourished, hordes of teenagers bought liquor, knife fights and "shooting frays" were common, and discipline in public schools—which were severely overcrowded—was tenuous. "Lawlessness within the schools," the *Defender* complained, "has reached the point where students, even husky young athletes, have their coats, hats, and other property stolen and are afraid to identify the thieves even though they know them. Young hoodlums think nothing of entering the schools on occasion and actually running the classes." Just in the previous few weeks, a student had been stabbed to death, boys had thrown acid on a teacher, a janitor had been shot, and "a teacher who had the temerity to take a gun away from a

---

70. Edward Jackson Baur, "Delinquency among Mexican Boys in South Chicago" (MA thesis, University of Chicago, 1938), 119–25, 172, 173; Belknap, "Summer Activities of Boys," 61–63.
71. *New York Times*, January 21, 1934, December 1, 1935; *Chicago Tribune*, April 15, 1933, March 8, 1938; Baur, "Delinquency among Mexican Boys," 122, 172, 173.

pupil was forced to return the gun at the point of a knife." Such were the conditions and attitudes fostered by civic breakdown on the South Side.[72]

Aside from criminal activity, boys on the South and West Sides had a colorful repertoire of modes of adventurism. Many liked to swim in Lake Michigan, but since they lacked money they would sneak rides on streetcars to the lake, or they would try the riskier tactic of "flipping a ride." This meant jumping onto the back bumper or the spare tire of a car when it stopped at a red light, then jumping off when the boy's destination was reached or the car turned off his desired road. Children as young as five years old would hitch rides on the back of streetcars, sometimes seven or eight hanging on at a time. Another risky activity was the popular one of visiting the stockyards, which was forbidden and could be dangerous. According to an investigator,

> Some [boys] liked to watch the cattle and play with the sheep and hogs; others liked to watch the "cowboys" as they herded animals from one pen to another or fed them hay or grain; some liked to dig in the debris to the north and west of the Racine Avenue entrance to find steers' horns which could be taken home and made into useful or ornamental articles; others collected old brass and copper, which they smuggled out.[73]

One way to get in was to sneak through the gates when a shift ended and workers were flooding in while others flooded out. More creatively, "another group discovered that if they washed their faces, combed their hair, put on clean shirts, and then told the watchman at the gate that they were to meet a party of people at a certain packing plant in the Yards and make an educational tour through one of the plants, the trick was accomplished, and the watchman glowingly let them pass."[74]

From the perspective of moralizing authorities, one of the most deplorable consequences of the Depression was the rise in sexual promiscuity, another form of recreation that so-called wayward youth and adults indulged in. Again, it was in parts of the city where social regulation had most broken down, particularly in the Black Belt, that "morals" were loosest. Between 1928 and 1933, more than 2,000 of the 25,000 Black babies that were born in Chicago were illegitimate. Even before the Depression, between 1923 and 1928, from 10 to 15 percent of the Black maternity cases in Cook County Hospital were unmarried mothers. But in the 1930s, "sexual delinquency" followed the trends in petty theft and violence, except more so: males and females, of whatever age, for whom marriage was not a suitable option, whiled away the weary hours in fondling and sex, seeking comfort and companionship in the warm body of a fellow human being.[75]

***

---

72. *New York Times*, March 1, 1936; David Ward Howe, "Bad Housing, Unemployment Breeds Young Criminals in Chicago," *Chicago Defender*, May 18, 1940.
73. *Chicago Tribune*, August 11, 1933; Belknap, 66.
74. Ibid., 67.
75. Drake and Cayton, *Black Metropolis*, 589; E. Franklin Frazier, "The Negro Family in Chicago" (PhD diss., University of Chicago, 1931), 213.

Adults tended to be less adventurous and determined in their quest for recreation than the young, but they, too, were by no means content to sit idly at home continuously and without end. It is true that one of the chief means of entertainment, as already stated, was home-centered: namely, listening to the radio. Boys, girls, and adults together regularly relied on the radio for much of their intellectual and emotional stimulation, as people in more recent times have relied on the television. The family's radio was enjoyed in the 1920s, but it was often cherished in the 1930s, as shown by the fact that the number of households owning radios increased rapidly between 1930 and 1935. In 1936, one in four Black migrant families from the South owned a radio. Fathers and sons were likely to listen to the ball game, and immigrant parents liked to listen to programs in their own language—to the great frustration of their children, who preferred American programs like *Amos 'n' Andy*, *Tarzan*, and *Buddy Rogers*. Boys complained in interviews that their parents tended to monopolize the radio or only let them use it occasionally.[76]

Whether reading, among the unemployed and insecurely employed, increased or decreased during the Depression is unclear, for conflicting tendencies were at work. Some studies reported that it declined, largely because people could no longer afford to buy books and magazines, but also because some unemployed men were too depressed to do much reading anyway. On the other hand, many libraries reported that their services were in greater demand than ever—even as budgets and personnel were being cut, especially in the early Depression. Between 1929 and 1932, 33 cities saw a 37 percent increase in demand for public library books, most notably for books on unemployment and industrial planning. Said one head librarian, "people are reading more and better books and a vastly greater number of people are reading."[77]

Adult men who were not well educated or had not been in the habit of reading books before the Depression typically found other ways to spend their time, when not brooding at home. Unemployed Blacks were not much different from whites: common answers to interviewers' questions of what they did all day included playing cards, listening to the radio, "just sitting at home," and "foolin' around," which covered such activities as dancing in informal house groups, congregating on street corners and in taverns and barbershops, "sex-play" in kitchenettes or elsewhere, and "waiting tensely for the policy

---

76. "Personal Observations of the Effects of the Depression upon Family Recreation," Burgess Papers, box 177, folder 2; Jesse F. Steiner, *Research Memorandum on Recreation in the Depression* (New York: Social Science Research Council, 1937), 42; Wallace D. Best, *Passionately Human, No Less Divine: Religion and Culture in Black Chicago, 1915–1952* (Princeton, NJ: Princeton University Press, 2005), 178; Belknap, "Summer Activities of Boys," 46, 47.
77. Bakke, *Citizens without Work*, 14; *New York Times*, December 29, 1932; *New York Herald Tribune*, February 13, 1933; Belknap, "Summer Activities of Boys," 47, 48; Eric Novotny, "'Bricks without Straw': Economic Hardship and Innovation in the Chicago Public Library during the Great Depression," *Libraries and the Cultural Record* 46, no. 3 (2011): 258–75; Barlow, "Leisure-Time Activities of Two Hundred High School Girls," 19, 27, 32. See also Douglas Waples, Leon Carnovsky, and William M. Randall, "The Public Library in the Depression," *The Library Quarterly: Information, Community, Policy* 2, no. 4 (October 1932): 321–43; and Margaret M. Herdman, "The Public Library in Depression," *The Library Quarterly: Information, Community, Policy* 13, no. 4 (October 1943): 310–34.

drawings three times a day." This last was indeed largely unique to the Black Belt and an important focus of intellectual and emotional energy for the entire community.[78]

The game called "policy" was a form of lottery, and as such was illegal, but by the 1930s it was such an enormous "racket" and was so integral to the South Side community that to abolish it was hopeless. Political bosses, court officials, lawyers, police officials, and the "ward machine" received hundreds of thousands of dollars in bribes every year from the businessmen who owned and operated the 500- or so policy stations (where bets were made) on the South Side. Many people even argued, not implausibly, that policy was good for the Black Belt economy, since it sustained hundreds of local businesses and provided employment to more than 6,000 people (many of them women), including clerks, accountants, doormen, janitors, bookkeepers, "bouncers," and "writers."[79]

The most numerous policy employees were the so-called writers, who collected bets and wrote receipts for them that would be necessary to verify winnings later on. Some of them walking from door to door to solicit bets and others situated in the policy stations, writers collected anywhere from pennies to dollars from people who gambled that a certain combination of numbers would be drawn from a drum-shaped container, called a "wheel," that contained numbers from 1 to 78. The wheels were scattered around the South Side at strategic spots. Drawings from each of the wheels took place three times a day: 12 numbers were drawn from the lot of 78 inside. Depending on how many particular numbers one had gambled would be drawn—and bets were usually for three numbers, such as 4, 11, and 44—winners were paid at odds of from 100:1 to 3,500:1. But the real odds were much worse than this, and it was very rare to win. Even so, the game was wildly popular on the South Side, practically a collective obsession, with policy stations on virtually every block (though often hidden, because of their illegality). A huge and complex infrastructure existed to operate the game, and both policy stations and wheel locations were kinetic spaces overflowing with all the different kinds of operatives and excited players and paid-off policemen and bouncers to keep order. "Almost everybody on the South Side plays policy," remarked one man, likely exaggerating; "if I could prove it, you'd find that eight out of every ten people puts in at least two plays [out of a possible three] a day."[80]

In a time as bleak as the Great Depression, it is understandable why people would become enamored of a form of gambling as cheap as policy, in which a thrill could be had for as little as a penny. Women were at least as fond of the game as men, sometimes

---

78. Drake and Cayton, *Black Metropolis*, 606.
79. Ibid., 481–484; Will Cooley, "Moving Up, Moving Out: Race and Social Mobility in Chicago, 1914–1972" (PhD diss., University of Illinois at Urbana-Champaign, 2008), 105–10.
80. Lewis A. H. Caldwell, "The Policy Game in Chicago" (MA thesis, Northwestern University, 1940); Elizabeth Schlabach, "'Fancy Gigs,' 'Adjuncts to the Faith,' and Spiritualists: African American Female Mediumship in Bronzeville" (2015), unpublished manuscript; Mark H. Haller, "Policy Gambling, Entertainment, and the Emergence of Black Politics: Chicago from 1900 to 1940," *Journal of Social History* 24, no. 4 (Summer 1991): 719–39.

gambling away money that would have been better spent on food. For instance, it was usually women who patronized spiritualists and séances in order to learn what numbers would be best to play. Hundreds of spiritualists dotted the social landscape of the South Side, sometimes giving séances for free, in incense-soaked rooms with Persian rugs and plush furniture. After prayers and mystical atmosphere-conjuring, the Madame in charge walked slowly around the table and spoke in hushed tones to each member of the audience. "The spirits bring me in touch with you, young man," she might say to someone; "they give me a moving condition. [...] Would you recognize an uncle in the spirit world? His name is William and he died because of some sort of lingering ailment. The spirits want you to take care of William." As a participant commented in a report, "this is the visitor's cue to play the numbers [in policy] for the name William. The fact that he has never had an uncle named William is immaterial." "Dream books" were published for policy players to interpret in numerical terms such names, as well as to interpret actual dreams, which players frequently used to divine what numbers to bet on.[81]

Church authorities and various social organizations complained, year after year, about the effect of policy on the community, but little was done about it. "Every neighborhood in many sections of our city," the National League of Justice lamented, "is infested. The laws and church yards are strewn with policy slips. Women take the last nickel or dime to play policy rather than buy a loaf of bread for their children. The conditions [...] are deplorable." One woman expressed a common opinion: "Policy is a great detriment to our people. [...] It tends to encourage other forms of gambling. In the alleys around here you'll find little kids shooting craps. What can you expect when their parents play policy?"[82]

The other "socially destructive" activity that the discouraged unemployed, especially men, periodically indulged in was alcohol consumption. I will say more about this in the next chapter, but here it may be noted that alcoholism was less common than one might think. The main reason, of course, was that people lacked money to drink regularly. A study of one hundred Chicago families observed that drink "rarely became a permanent method of escape, perhaps because increased poverty and the system of the relief agencies, whereby grocery orders and food boxes were supplied but no cash, forced a reform in the habits of some of the habitual drinkers." Another study found that alcoholism was much less common among Depression relief clients than pre-Depression clients: among the latter, 12 percent were severely alcoholic, compared to 2 percent among the former. These numbers reflect the fact that a higher proportion of relief clients in the Depression than in the 1920s came from socially "well-adjusted" backgrounds.[83]

---

81. Caldwell, "The Policy Game in Chicago," 31, 36–39, 50; "A report on the status of spiritualism in the area between 47th, 51st, South Park and the New York Central Tracks, as reported in an interview with R. F. C. Tonelle," Burgess Papers, box 134, folder 1.
82. Caldwell, "The Policy Game in Chicago," 73; Drake and Cayton, *Black Metropolis*, 490–92.
83. Cavan and Ranck, *The Family and the Depression*, 107; Bernard Sternsher, "Victims of the Great Depression: Self-Blame/Non-Self-Blame, Radicalism, and Pre-1929 Experiences,"

There is one last, very prominent type of recreation for the unemployed we should mention here, albeit only in passing. A contemporary investigator described it in colorful terms. In addition, she said, to maybe planting a garden, making furniture, making toys for the children, even making a bike in one case,

> A man could also talk. He could stand at a street corner and talk. He could drop in to a friend's house and talk. [...] Meetings and street gatherings were also time-consuming. They served as an outlet for discouragement, bitterness, and unconsumed energy. They served, too, as a bolsterer of egos. It gave a man a sense of importance to stand in front of a crowd and to shout, to be on the organization committee, to tell other people what to do. And then it gave him a sense of direction. His feeling of living in an aimless, impregnable, unfeeling universe was forgotten when he was appointed delegate to such and such a gathering, and when he planned this and that sort of a protest meeting.

The enticements of political agitation or serving on some committee or other—perhaps one of the 40 or 50 community councils that existed in Chicago in the 1930s—were very real, not only to some marginal malcontents but also to many thousands of men and women from every ethnic background. We'll save this discussion, however, for the chapter on political activity.[84]

Organized Recreation

While most recreation, as always, was informal, such institutions as settlement houses, churches, charities, and New Deal agencies did orchestrate an incredible expansion of organized recreation for the public, until by the end of the Depression decade a whole new "regime of play" (to coin a term) had evolved. By 1940, the intricate and extensive networks of cooperation between the federal government, local public recreation bodies, and private social agencies bore little resemblance to what had been the case only eight years earlier. Indeed, the relative lack of coordination of Chicago's recreational programs between 1930 and 1932 was already beginning to change by 1933, under the impact of the New Deal and the increased flow of money it entailed. What follows is a brief overview of some of the institutional innovations that evolved under Roosevelt's administration, after which we'll look in more depth at settlement houses, whose programs were representative of broader trends.

In late 1933 the Civil Works Educational Service was created, as part of the Civil Works Service. While lasting only until May 1934, when the Civil Works Service was discontinued, it developed 18 nursery schools for children under 6 years of age and established a free junior college to replace Crane Junior College, which had been closed the previous year because of budget cuts. After the end of the Civil Works Educational

---

Social Science History 1, no. 2 (Winter, 1977), 161; Garland O. Ethel, "Soup Line in Seattle," *Nation*, February 25, 1931.

84. Friedman, "One Hundred Unemployed Families," 174, 175; map of Chicago's community councils, April 29, 1933, Lea Taylor Papers, Chicago History Museum, box 21.

Service in early 1934, a new program called the Children's Leisure Time Service—later the Chicago Leisure Time Service—was initiated under the aegis of the IERC. In brief, it was a work relief project: hundreds of workers were assigned to dozens of social agencies in order to do such things as clear vacant lots for community gardens and playgrounds, and help administer summer camps and other activities later in the year. In the first summer alone, 61,000 children were enrolled in activities, 82 lots were cleared for playgrounds, and 250 community gardens and 686 backyard gardens were planted.[85]

Meanwhile, the federal government invested in adult education with its Emergency Educational Program, which in 1934 employed almost a thousand out-of-work teachers in hundreds of locations in Chicago. The program continued in succeeding years, though with periodic interruptions due to lack of funds. One of its priorities was Workers' Education, the major goals of which were to arouse a sense of community among workers, "to reach unorganized workers [...] to stimulate social action," and to foster critical thinking about society and cultivate neighborhood leaders. This program lasted until 1939; and while continually attacked across the country by conservatives and business interests as being Communist and pro-unions, on the whole it met with striking success in Chicago. Labor groups, unions, religious organizations like the Jewish People's Institute and the YWCA, and settlement houses all enthusiastically participated. English classes and citizenship classes were among the most popular, hundreds of Mexicans, for example, taking advantage of them in the Hull House, Chicago Commons, and the Mexican Social Center on the Near West Side. Also popular were the many specialized classes in subjects like labor laws, labor problems, "training for union leadership," economics, U.S. labor history, theater and the arts, and—for women—cooking and sewing. Unemployed workers regularly attended these classes, such as the young shipping clerk who had been fired after participating in a strike, and who brought his wife to a labor class so she could better understand why he was unemployed.[86]

Some courses, in fact, were exclusively for people who were out of work, such as the YWCA's Practice School for Unemployed Office Workers, which had 3,000 students in 1934. With the help of New Deal money, moreover, programs that had already existed for older youth and adults were expanded. Some of the most important were the Boy Scouts, Girl Scouts, and Camp Fire Girls; the Young Men's Jewish Charities and the Catholic Youth Organization, both of which offered, for example, forums, classes, and vocational and professional guidance; the YMCA, which increased services to young

---

85. "Recreation and Informal Education," *Social Service Year Book: 1934*, 70–73; Edwin S. Lide, "The Social Composition of the CWES Junior College in Chicago," *The School Review* 43, no. 1 (January 1935): 28–33.

86. "Recreation and Informal Education," *Social Service Year Book: 1934*, 70, 73; Judith Ann Trolander, *Settlement Houses and the Great Depression* (Detroit, MI: Wayne State University Press, 1975), 114, 115; Louise Ano Nuevo Kerr, "The Chicano Experience in Chicago: 1920–1970" (PhD diss., University of Illinois at Chicago Circle, 1976), 98–100; Dick Richards, "Chicago Commons and Its Neighbors," 19, term paper for Social Work 201, March 13, 1940, Chicago Commons Papers, Chicago History Museum, box 27, folder 3; *Chicago Tribune*, August 13, 1934.

adults; and settlement house programs. Workers' Education deepened and broadened in 1936 and 1937, as the Chicago Labor College, the Affiliated Schools for Workers, the Workers' Alliance (a national organization that represented the unemployed), and the Workers' Education Committee of the Chicago Federation of Labor coordinated their activities and interests through a new Chicago Workers' Education Council. The public library, church organizations, men's and women's clubs, and universities all helped lead the "unprecedented" expansion of adult education in 1936, by organizing forums, discussion groups, lecture series, and tours that related to "social issues of the day."[87]

Thus, by 1935–36, a byzantine but highly coordinated structure had evolved to organize much of Chicago's noncommercial recreation and extracurricular education. The Division on Education and Recreation of the Chicago Council of Social Agencies oversaw a sprawling network of programs, while cooperating with the newly established WPA and NYA, both of which provided much of the (formerly unemployed) manpower to run the activities. The Chicago Leisure Time Service, for instance, became a work project under the WPA, in early 1937 supplying 750 recreation leaders to over 70 private agencies. Every year, the Chicago Park District offered many classes in physical education, arts, and crafts, in addition to more specialized and experimental programs like "garden clubs," in which children and adults used plots of land in the parks to grow gardens. Facilities continued to expand on the basis of the New Deal's largesse—more playgrounds being built, library space added to boys' clubs, thousands of city lots cleared for play use, and so on. Despite the unpredictability of government funding in the later years of the decade, ever more people took advantage of the programs on offer.[88]

Even workers' education, increasingly under attack after 1937, continued to grow until 1939, along with adult education as a whole. In 1939, for example, the Amalgamated Clothing Workers was able to organize a concert-lecture series for its members (including those without work), and the WPA's supply of teachers helped keep many other programs that were run under union auspices growing until around 1939. In adult education more generally, 1938 and 1939 saw much greater tapping of the potential of radio, scores of Town Hall of the Air "listening groups" being organized by the Adult Education Council. Public forums and vocational education classes—both financed mainly by the federal government—likewise grew more numerous in these years, on occasion park facilities being used even for the discussion of controversial political issues. Through the Community Forum Service, in 1939 almost a thousand speakers were furnished to 300 organizations practically without cost.[89]

---

87. Elizabeth C. Jenkins, "Recreation and Informal Education," in *Social Service Year Book, 1934*, 73; Arthur J. Todd, *Chicago Recreation Survey, Vol. III: Private Recreation* (Chicago, IL: Works Progress Administration, 1938), 69–71; Florence M. Eldridge, "Recreation and Informal Education," in *Social Service Year Book, 1936*, 57, 58.
88. Reports by the Chicago Federation of Settlements, Welfare Council Papers, box 167, folders 2 and 4; E. P. Gissenaas, "Recreation, Group Work, and Informal Education," in *Social Service Year Book, 1939*, 64, 65, 67; Marguerite K. Sylla, in *Social Service Year Book, 1937*, 63, 64; Eldridge, "Recreation and Informal Education," 61.
89. Gissenaas, "Recreation, Group Work, and Informal Education," 69; Harleigh Trecker, "Recreation, Group Work, and Informal Education," in *Social Service Year Book, 1938*, 73.

All this flowering of a mature civil society, this quasi-improvisatory fashioning of a new mode of institutional structuring of recreation—which would, of course, continue to evolve and change in the 1940s and afterward, frequently in less "public-spirited," less worker-friendly, more corporatist and privatized ways than in the 1930s—could not but affect even the more marginal groups in Chicago, the poor, the unemployed, the insecurely employed. Increased resources for every facet of public recreation meant increased opportunities for unemployed people and their families to resist alienation and atomization. In fact, the majority of programs just mentioned—and I have scarcely hinted at the sheer abundance of them—were aimed at underprivileged groups.[90]

But there was one exception: Blacks. Much less was done for them than for groups closer to the mainstream, including immigrants, even Mexicans. A report by the Council of Social Agencies in 1935 stated the point concisely: "Organized recreational facilities are conspicuous by their absence in the Negro areas of Chicago." Elaborating, it observed that "the institutional facilities are limited to the work conducted by church groups, a very limited number of small community centers, the YMCA, the YWCA, and the community services offered by the school and library systems." Even public parks were lacking: for the city as a whole, the population per acre of park space in 1925 was 507, while for black communities—with the exception of a couple of neighborhoods on the South Side—it was anywhere from 1,000 to 7,400 people per acre. Only one or two underfunded settlement houses were located in predominantly Black neighborhoods, and the ones that served neighborhoods in which there was a small Black population, such as South Chicago and the Near North Side, catered mainly to whites.[91]

African Americans' virtual exclusion from settlements is all the more unfortunate in light of the vitality of these institutions in the 1930s, the decade that—at least in terms of the sheer volume of activity—was perhaps their heyday. There were several dozen settlement houses in Chicago, located in the disadvantaged neighborhoods they served; among the more famous were Hull House, Chicago Commons, Association House, and the University of Chicago Settlement. Most were intimately involved in relief efforts, and many functioned as a center of neighborhood life. Chicago Commons, for example, located on the Near Northwest Side in a primarily Italian and Greek (but also Polish, Irish, and Mexican) neighborhood was held in high regard by the thousands of people who lived nearby and could benefit from its services and leadership. It had several departments, including Mothers' Clubs, Adult Education, Nursery and Kindergarten, Camp, Group Work, and Family Service, which dealt most directly with problems of unemployment relief. With the help of volunteers, its residents and staff were able to

---

90. Belva Overton, term paper for Sociology 358, January 10, 1935, "The Effect of the Depression upon the Recreational Activities Offered at the Wabash Avenue YMCA," Burgess Papers, box 177, folder 4.
91. Howard D. Gould, "The Negro in Chicago," in *Social Service Year Book, 1935*, 90, 91; Todd, *Chicago Recreation Survey, Vol. III*, 10, 11; Thomas Lee Philpott, *The Slum and the Ghetto: Neighborhood Deterioration and Middle-Class Reform, 1880–1930* (New York: Oxford University Press, 1978), chapters 13 and 14.

maintain a tightly packed daily schedule of activities, in addition to the invaluable relief services they provided to individuals and families.[92]

The work with young people (aside from very young children) was organized around clubs and classes, such as folk dancing, drama, dressmaking, handicrafts, music, and newspaper editing. Field trips were frequently taken to places of civic or cultural interest, and in the summer there were camping trips to Michigan, where hundreds of kids could stay in cottages for a few weeks. Year-round, play groups for young children were organized in the afternoons. We have already seen the offerings in adult education, but the mothers' clubs provided hundreds of women with additional support, a haven from the harassment of being a working-class mother during the Depression. As a reporter said, "The weekly meeting of a Mothers Club"—and there were usually about 10 such clubs at this settlement—"is in many cases the only chance a Mother has to leave her family and apartment and forget her complex problems." The activities varied according to the women's interests; for example, the Polish mothers' club enjoyed choral singing, while in other clubs women sewed or played games or invited speakers to talk about important issues of the day. With such a busy schedule, Chicago Commons was full of people—sometimes to the point of near-pandemonium—from early in the morning to late at night almost every day.[93]

In fact, one author estimated that in 1933–34, about 333,000 people, or 900 every day, participated in activities or used the facilities—four floors plus a basement. Outside groups and neighborhood organizations held meetings at the house, as many as 250 groups making regular use of it. Like other settlement and neighborhood houses, Chicago Commons was truly a pillar of social life, not some marginal institution run on a shoestring by a few idealistic do-gooders. (Its budget, paid largely by donations and fundraising events, was about $50,000, no paltry sum in the Depression years.) Every afternoon as soon as school ended the house flooded with children and teenagers who would excitedly run to their clubs and classes or use the playground or game rooms. Very young children were so attracted to the Commons—and to Hull House and others—that they would sometimes spend the entire day there, just hanging around shyly in the background, in order to escape an unpleasant or boring home life. A worker at the University of Chicago Settlement remarked, in a not too flattering comparison, that "children gather like flies to the warmth and comfort of our rooms," about a thousand attending clubs and classes every week, in addition to the many who just used the game rooms or enjoyed the house's atmosphere.[94]

---

92. "Three Months' Work at Chicago Commons," 1934, Commons Papers, box 26, folder 1; Richards, "Chicago Commons and Its Neighbors."
93. Richard Crews and Kevin Donlan, "A Study of Chicago Commons," 1940, Graham Taylor Papers, box 53, folder 2385; "Chicago Commons Schedule of Typical Week—1931–32," Commons Papers, box 25, folder 1; Richards, "Chicago Commons and Its Neighbors," 21.
94. Crews and Donlan, "A Study of Chicago Commons"; "Unemployment Among Our Neighbors" and "Unemployment at the University Settlement," Mary McDowell Papers, box 3, folder 16; Lea Demarest Taylor, "Chicago Commons and the Challenge of Today,"

A *Chicago Tribune* feature article on settlements in 1932 gave a sense of the changes that had taken place since the Depression began. It reported an "almost incredible increase of activity." A huge corps of volunteers at the main houses worked three days a week to handle the overflow of people idled by the crisis; much of the work consisted of relief, such as giving them clothes made by other unemployed people in emergency workshops. Overall, attendance in clubs had doubled, or in some, such as the Italian women's club at Hull House, sextupled. "Sewing and cooking instruction is clamored for by young and old," the article reported. "English classes are tremendously popular, the library is always crowded, and the gymnasium and shower baths are kept in use almost incessantly." Unemployed men gathered at the Hull House gymnasium each morning for exercise and then used the showers; frequently they returned at night for games, folk dancing, singing, and refreshments.[95]

It was not only Anglo or European whites who were welcome at most settlement houses; Mexicans were as well. Work among Mexicans at the University of Chicago Settlement (in Back of the Yards) grew "by leaps and bounds" in the early years of the Depression, as one social worker said. Already in 1932, Mexican groups at the settlement included two orchestras, a banjo-mandolin club, an art class, two adult athletic clubs, classes in the girls' and boys' gymnasiums, a mothers' club, and courses in English and business arithmetic. In addition, the Polish unemployed men's group inspired Mexicans to create their own such group, which soon had a membership of 600. In fact, by the late 1930s, Mexicans were the largest ethnic group using the settlement's facilities. "I practically lived there," recalled a man years later; "they had such terrific programs. [...] It was a very important part of our lives"—for it was the only place in all of Back of the Yards that accepted Hispanics without reserve. The South Chicago Mexican colony, unlike the colonies in the Near West and Back of the Yards, did not have a large settlement to help organize its recreation; as a result, many of its youth regularly went up north to participate in activities at the Hull House and University of Chicago Settlement. Some of the most popular were team sports, especially baseball, softball, and basketball.[96]

Sports, indeed, were a crucial mode of entertainment for Chicagoans idled by the Depression. Among their indispensable functions was not only providing an outlet for pent-up youthful energies and giving participating individuals and families something to be proud of; they also helped unite and define communities, reinforced ties of friendship

---

in *Chicago Commons through Forty Years*, ed. Graham Taylor (Chicago, IL: Chicago Commons Association, 1936), 207–36.
95. Kathleen M'Laughlin, "Keep Up Morale! Is Settlement Workers' Motto," *Chicago Tribune*, April 20, 1932.
96. Mollie Ray Carroll, "Maintaining Morale in a Crisis: The University of Chicago Settlement, 1931–32," McDowell Papers, box 3, folder 16; "Record of the Development of the Clubs for Unemployed Men and Women," McDowell Papers, box 20, folder 1; Slayton, *Back of the Yards*, 186; Michael Innis-Jiménez, "Persisting in the Shadow of Steel: Community Formation and Survival in Mexican South Chicago, 1919–1939" (PhD diss., University of Iowa, 2006), 194, 208.

and extended family, and allowed people to rebel against enforced passiveness and the daily indignities of being poor. A Mexican man in South Chicago, laid off from steelworking, recalled what sports meant to him in the 1930s: "There was nothing, no work, no nothing. The only recreation was playing baseball and more baseball, basketball and more basketball. So we turned out a lot of great baseball players and basketball players." "The entire [Mexican] community turned to sports," a historian writes. Pickup games were very common, and both young people and adult community leaders organized leagues centered in Bessemer Park. Mexicans had avoided this South Chicago park in the 1920s because of intimidation by other ethnic groups, but by the 1930s the flood of unemployed families who valued it for its beauty and its many facilities was irresistible. Baseball and basketball teams even traveled to other areas of the city and played against different ethnicities, which expanded young people's mental horizons. Over the course of a few years an impressive sports infrastructure developed in South Chicago, with junior teams (playing other junior teams from around the city) coached by older boys who had their own leagues, adult men organizing their own teams, at least one all-girls league, and interneighborhood tournaments organized by the staff and volunteers at the Chicago Park System, the Community Center, local churches, and the WPA-affiliated project Common Ground. These sorts of initiatives and activities were replicated in other Chicago neighborhoods.[97]

It is a striking fact that despite the inadequacy of institutional and financial resources in the Depression, more people than ever participated in sports. In the early 1930s, public parks—used for baseball, basketball, volleyball, swimming, and so on—were more popular than ever, though they lacked funds for proper maintenance. Beaches and pools, in particular, grew crowded. A government survey in 1937 found scores of athletic clubs and hundreds of unsupervised social athletic clubs that young people had organized, called "basement" clubs because their headquarters were usually rooms on the ground floor of residential or store buildings. Archery clubs in parks had grown in popularity, as had bowling, with an incredible 900 leagues and 9,000 teams in Chicago. Hundreds of independently organized softball, soccer, and basketball leagues, and thousands of local "scrub teams" like those in South Chicago, lifted teenagers and adults out of the tedium of unemployment and poverty.[98]

In addition to the unparalleled vitality of sports, and the vitality that sports leagues helped impart to communities, it is worth remembering that the ethnically segmented clubs and societies were to a large extent still able to withstand the encroachments of mass culture in the 1930s. The same government survey just mentioned uncovered some

---

97. Michael Innis-Jiménez, "Beyond the Baseball Diamond and Basketball Court: Organized Leisure in Interwar Mexican South Chicago," in *More than Just Peloteros: Sport and U.S. Latino Communities*, ed. Jorge Iber (Lubbock, TX: Texas Tech University Press, 2014), 83; Escalante, "History of the Mexican Community," 24; Anita Edgar Jones, "Conditions Surrounding Mexicans in Chicago" (MA thesis, University of Chicago, 1928), 72; Innis-Jiménez, "Persisting in the Shadow of Steel," chapter 5.
98. Todd, *Chicago Recreation Survey, Vol. III*, 117–24; Jesse Steiner, *Research Memorandum on Recreation in the Depression*, 41, 42.

telling statistics. The Council of Polish Organizations had an aggregate of more than 300,000 member agencies in Chicago (many of them commercial, however), from arts clubs and singers' alliances to athletic groups, from welfare associations to churches. The Ukrainian Central Committee represented approximately eighty cultural, social, and economic organizations, while the city's 52,000 Norwegians had over fifty such. For the Czechoslovak population there were 500 clubs and societies; Italians had several hundred mutual benefit societies alone, still alive in 1937 despite the financial devastation of the Depression. Dozens of folk dance groups from many different nationalities proudly exhibited their country's traditions in festivals that the city sponsored.[99]

All this gives some indication of how dense and vibrant civil society was in these years of economic stagnation. Indeed, in some respects the stagnant economy *contributed* to communities' vitality, not only by encouraging the sharing of resources but also, as I've noted, by interrupting the forward march of privatization, marketization, and commercialization.[100] The Depression precipitated a huge expansion of the twin vocations of volunteering and social work, as millions of people embraced the opportunities to help their fellow man that the crisis and delegitimization of capitalism had created. Popular institutions such as settlement houses took advantage of the weakened state of the economy to press forward their agenda of working-class empowerment and communal self-expression.

In short, even the relatively mundane practices of working-class survival and recreation were, in some respects, implicitly grounded in radical humanistic values. In the sphere of informal recreation, the working-class culture to which so many of the unemployed and insecurely employed belonged had a notable cultural independence or "spontaneity"; in the sphere of organized recreation, similarly, the popular movements that will be examined in Chapter six were able to push the state so far to the left that, arguably for the first time, it sponsored genuinely democratic educational and recreational programs.

As we'll see in the next chapter, men who were consigned to public shelters likewise asserted themselves against both destitution and the authoritarian regime of relief to which they were subjected.

---

99. Todd, *Chicago Recreation Survey, Vol. III*, 90–94; Vytautas F. Beliajus, "Folk Dancing in Chicago," *Recreation* 30, no. 6 (September 1936): 309, 310.
100. On this "forward march" and the inevitability of periodic backlashes against it, see Karl Polanyi, *The Great Transformation* (New York: Farrar & Rinehart, 1944).

Chapter Four
RELIEF, PART I: "SHELTER MEN"

I got my first taste of shelter life at 758 West Harrison, where application for admission to the shelters is made. I had to stand around outside a while before the doorman would let me in. When I got inside the building I found a lot of men sitting on benches. They were cursing the shelter, the shelter men, and the case workers. One old man sitting near me complained with curses, "There's too much cock-eyed red tape around this place. It's getting worser and worser every time I come up here." A younger man confided to me, "It took a lot of courage for me to come into this place; in fact I came up here three times before I went in and then only when a couple of friends came along who had been in before."[1]

So begins an undercover investigation of the Chicago shelters in the spring of 1935. The picture that emerges from this and similar accounts is, to say the least, damning. One reads of incredibly filthy bathrooms in one shelter, "plain dirt all over the floor, while urine that was old and strong smelling was running in small streams everywhere." Garbage cans, overflowing and pungent, were placed beside the long breadlines in which the men shuffled to get meals, many of the shufflers regularly expectorating into filthy spittoons that were placed in prominent locations. Sleeping every night in a packed room with 25 other men was another hardship, especially considering the cacophony of "snoring, sneezing, moaning, sleep-talking, and coughing" that kept one awake for hours. "Last night one man coughed so loud and so long that he woke everyone up. Finally a fellow told him, 'For Christ's sake shut up or get the hell out of here!'" The blankets seemed to another reporter to be made of paper, which left the men shivering all night from drafts. Bedbugs and lice, fond of this environment, bit and crept all over their prey.[2]

There is good scholarship on the homeless in the Depression, but more can still be said about the conditions of shelters and inhabitants' responses to them, in particular their *resistance* to their treatment.[3] The purpose of this chapter, then, is to humanize a

---

1. Edwin H. Sutherland and Harvey J. Locke, *Twenty Thousand Homeless Men: A Study of Unemployed Men in the Chicago Shelters* (Chicago, IL: J. B. Lippincott Company, 1936), 2.
2. Jesse Walter Dees, Jr., *Flophouse* (Francestown, NH: Marshall Jones Company, 1948), 96, 97; Sutherland and Locke, *Twenty Thousand Homeless Men*, 3, 4, 8.
3. For example, see Charles Hoch and Robert A. Slayton, *New Homeless and Old: Community and the Skid Row Hotel* (Philadelphia, PA: Temple University Press, 1989); Kenneth Kusmer, *Down and Out, On the Road: The Homeless in American History* (New York: Oxford University Press, 2002); Todd DePastino, *Citizen Hobo: How a Century of Homelessness Shaped America* (Chicago, IL: University of Chicago Press, 2003); Joan M. Crouse, *The Homeless Transient in the Great Depression* (Albany, NY: State University of New York Press, 1986).

category of people who were, and are, often treated as less than human merely because they lacked property. How did Chicago's shelter men live, what were their backgrounds, what were their opinions and attitudes, how did the city's relief policies evolve, and how did those subjected to these policies fight against them? Even the supposedly class-unconscious, apolitical, listless homeless population was capable of assertiveness.

The chapter will proceed as follows. First, I will give some information on the neighborhoods in which the homeless of Chicago mainly lived, near the Loop, after which I'll sketch the relief administration as it applied to these "unattached" men and women. The bulk of the chapter, however, is focused on conditions in the men's public shelters and how clients responded to them, how through individual and collective struggle they tried to make their lives more bearable.

Relief Administration

For decades, Chicago had teemed with the homeless. Hundreds of thousands of "tramps," "hoboes," and "bums" passed through the city every year, the distinction between the three categories being defined by the famous radical Ben Reitman in a pointed way: "the hobo works and wanders, the tramp dreams and wanders, and the bum drinks and wanders." In addition to these types were the thousands of local homeless (many of them considered "bums"), who, like the traveling hordes, lived alternately in flophouses, shelters, lodging houses, cheap hotels, and the like. Many were casual laborers working regularly or irregularly at unskilled work, day labor, and odd jobs, but large numbers were unemployable due to physical or psychological disabilities. At any given moment, the number of homeless men in Chicago (including nonresidents) ranged from 30,000 to 60,000, reaching 75,000 or more in times of recession.[4]

These numbers might not seem very high in a city of 3 million, but their concentration in a few areas around the Loop made the homeless and semihomeless quite a visible population. One might even say that several prominent neighborhoods on all four sides of the Loop belonged to the (semi-)homeless. There was the West Madison Street district near the Chicago River, known to the denizens of "Hobohemia" as the slave market because it was here that most employment agencies were located, where the men sought information on jobs near and far. Beggars, peddlers, the disabled, gamblers—illegal gambling houses were often located on the second floor of taverns or furniture stores—bootleggers, casual laborers, and other such types all mingled here, where virtually no women or children were to be seen. It was to South State Street that the men went when they desired the company of women, for here was the playground: burlesque shows, cabarets, "Oriental" dancers. Men living in the cheap hotels and flophouses along this street and Van Buren or South Clark Streets were apt to take short jobs around the city periodically, a few hours a day, to accumulate just enough money to live on—vagabonds who had settled down and retired from the nomadic life, the "home guard" as they were

---

4. Nels Anderson, *The Hobo* (Chicago, IL: University of Chicago Press, 1967/1923), 87, 96.

contemptuously called by younger men still in thrall to wanderlust. This was also the area to which the relatively few homeless Black men gravitated.[5]

A third branch of Hobohemia was on North Clark Street and a few streets nearby, up north to Washington Square Park. Institutions that catered to the homeless and the "queer and exiled types" of the neighborhood proliferated: taverns, pawnshops, secondhand stores, cabarets, dozens of rooming houses and run-down hotels, pool halls, barber shops, and innumerable small dance halls where prostitutes picked up customers or lonely men might buy a 10-cent ticket to dance with a girl. "At night," reported an investigator in 1929, "North Clark Street is a street of bright lights, of dancing, cabareting, drinking, gambling, and vice." Washington Square Park was full of life as well, presenting quite a different aspect from its sanitized appearance today[6]:

> By day its benches are filled with men reading newspapers, talking, or just sitting in the sun. But at night, crowded along its curbstones, are gathered groups of men, often as many as a hundred in a group, listening to the impassioned pleas of the soap-box orator, the propagandist, and the agitator. All their arguments come down to one or the other of two propositions: the economic system is all wrong, or there is no God. [...] After getting down from the soap box the speaker often will pass the hat, making his living by reading up on some subject or other in the library during the day, and speaking at night. [...] Because of the constant and violent agitation from its soap boxes, night after night, Washington Square has come to be known as "Bughouse Square."[7]

In fact, while North Clark Street was the main drag of Hobohemia, much of the entire Near North Side swarmed with "derelicts" only a step or two ahead of outright homelessness. Bohemians, hoboes, prostitutes, and other types of nonconformists all rubbed shoulders with "marooned" families in rooming houses and immigrant families in tenement apartments, forming a great mass of unsettled humanity.[8]

East of the Loop, too, were encampments of homeless men. Hoboes lived in little "jungles" of improvised shacks behind the Field Museum, next to the lake, and Grant Park was a popular place to sit in the summer and talk or read the papers—or, on the section facing the lake, to wash one's clothes, bathe, sew, and mend shoes. As we saw in the first chapter, these traditions continued in the early Depression but on a larger scale, when Hoovervilles colonized the park.[9]

On the eve of the Depression, then, there were several well-established communities of "the unattached" north, south, east, and west of the Loop—in addition to the hundreds of more atomized homeless people scattered around other neighborhoods,

---

5. Ibid., 4–8; Kusmer, *Down and Out, On the Road*, 157.
6. Harvey Warren Zorbaugh, *The Gold Coast and the Slum* (Chicago, IL: University of Chicago Press, 1976/1929), chapter 6; Paul G. Cressey, *The Taxi-Dance Hall: A Sociological Study in Commercialized Recreation and City Life* (Chicago, IL: University of Chicago Press, 1932); Anderson, *The Hobo*, 8–10.
7. Zorbaugh, *The Gold Coast and the Slum*, 115.
8. Ibid., chapter 7.
9. Anderson, *The Hobo*, 10, 11.

particularly on Chicago's west side. To help provide for (some of) these men, free shelters were maintained in the 1920s and earlier by welfare organizations and religious agencies, such as the Salvation Army, the Christian Industrial League, and the Central Bureau of Catholic Charities. The religiously affiliated shelters were known as missions, since in return for food, beds, and some clothing the men were subject to appeals that they accept God in their lives, repent of their dissolute ways, and convert. Intermittently there were also municipal lodging houses run by the Department of Public Welfare, where men received a bed, two meals daily, and medical care. Until 1930, Chicago managed to make do on this somewhat haphazard arrangement.[10]

It was in autumn of 1930 that the swelling numbers of men applying for assistance necessitated a change in policy. A Clearing House for Homeless Men was established in late 1930, the function of which was to register the men who applied for assistance and assign them to a particular shelter. Civic groups and police distributed thousands of cards to panhandlers and unemployed men around the city directing them to the new Clearing House, with the result that a deluge of men soon descended upon the agency. Based on a short interview, each man was directed to one of the city's permanent shelters or the seven emergency shelters operated by religious organizations and the Chicago Urban League, which ran one for Blacks. By late 1932, Chicago had 25 shelters for men, maintained by both private and public agencies and financed by the new IERC. Most of them were located in the vicinity of West Madison Street's Hobohemia.[11]

The number of people being cared for in these public shelters climbed from 12,000 in late 1931 to 35,000 in early 1933. Later in the decade it declined, to as few as 5,000 in June 1935 and only 100 a year later, when one shelter remained open in Chicago. It wasn't that the economy was doing amazingly well by this point; rather, the administration of relief had changed. For one thing, some men had been transferred to WPA work camps. More importantly, nearly all were placed on home relief instead of shelter relief, because this was seen as less demoralizing than being herded like sheep in warehouses, old factory buildings, schools, and "cage hotels."[12]

Statistical studies conducted at the time indicate who these men were who found themselves suddenly living (in most cases) in the old neighborhoods of Hobohemia, in many cases surrounded by alien elements—flophouses, burlesque houses, and

---

10. Dees, Jr., *Flophouse*, 40–51; Alvin Roseman, *Shelter Care and the Local Homeless Man* (Chicago, IL: Public Administration Service, 1935), 4.
11. Clearing House for Men, *Men in the Crucible* (Chicago, IL: Illinois Emergency Relief Administration, 1932), 1; Robert S. Wilson, *Community Planning for Homeless Men and Boys* (New York: Family Welfare Association of America, 1931), 114, 115; Roseman, *Shelter Care*, 4; Robert W. Beasley, "Homeless Men—Chicago: 1930–31," *Social Service Review* 5, no. 3 (September 1931): 439; *First Annual Report of the IERC* (Chicago, IL, 1933), 75.
12. *First Annual Report of the IERC*, 75; Clearing House for Unemployed Homeless Men, "Report for the Month of December, 1931," Welfare Council Papers, box 444, folder 2; Lenore G. Levin, "Care of Resident Non-Family Men and Women, and Care of Transients and Non-Residents," in *Social Service Year Book, 1934*, ed. Linn Brandenburg (Chicago, IL: Council of Social Agencies, 1934), 28; *Biennial Report of the IERC, Covering the Period July 1, 1934 through June 30, 1936*, 101–105.

pickpockets. A report in 1935 suggests that around 10 percent were the old type of beggar and bum, 20 percent were a somewhat "higher" class of migratory laborer, and the rest were mostly skilled and unskilled workers based in Illinois. This heterogeneity of the shelter population necessitated attempts at classification and distribution of groups of men to particular shelters. Young men and boys were assigned to one shelter, middle-aged and able-bodied men to another group of shelters, white-collar workers to yet others, and so forth. The system was far from perfect, however, as a variety of men could be found in most of the shelters (except for the white-collar ones, where inhabitants were treated better and on a more individualized basis).[13]

While men constituted the vast majority of the "homeless," thousands of women, too, were left adrift by the economic tsunami, which necessitated expansions of shelter care. Such care was known to be demoralizing, however, so as soon as the financial situation improved—with the entrance of the IERC and then, especially, FERA into the relief-financing business—the Service Bureau for Unemployed Women began to end the use of shelters and pay for its clients to live in their own domiciles until they found a job.[14]

Women's shelters were quite different from men's, far less impersonal and unpleasant. For one thing, they were smaller, frequently being women's residence clubs that had been transformed for the purpose. More like dormitories than warehouses, they were relatively home-like, comfortable, and clean, in part because the residents themselves did housework in connection with their recreational and occupational therapy programs. They ate three meals a day, the same meals the staff were served. In fact, these shelters were generally pervaded by "a spirit of kindliness and consideration and an atmosphere of freedom" that male shelter clients could scarcely have imagined in their wildest dreams. What made such decent treatment possible was the fact that at any given time only hundreds, not tens of thousands, of nonfamily women were housed there.[15]

Chicago's relief administration, like the entire country's, was in flux the whole decade, as policymakers and bureaucrats managed the conflicting demands of the business community on the one hand, which desired lower costs and more niggardly relief, and the unemployed and their advocates on the other, who fought for humane policies. In 1935, the latter group had a significant victory: most shelters were closed and the Service Bureaus for Men and Women abolished, their former "clients"—about 17,000

---

13. *Men in the Crucible*, vi; Roseman, *Shelter Care*, 9–11, 52; Robert W. Beasley, "Care of Destitute Unattached Men in Chicago with Special Reference to the Depression Period Beginning in 1930" (MA thesis, University of Chicago, 1933), 31, 32, 83.
14. "Shelters for Women—Findings and Conclusions," 1932, Graham Taylor Papers, box 38, folder 1982; Olive Walker Swinney, "Provisions for the Care of Destitute Non-Family Women in Chicago" (MA thesis, University of Chicago, 1937).
15. Ibid., 58, 83–94; "Shelters for Women—Findings and Conclusions"; Robert Beasley and Mary Gillette Moon, "Care of Non-Family Men and Women," in *Social Service Year Book, 1932*, 30; Helen Cody Baker, "A Home for Mary Lou," *Survey*, March 15, 1932, 669, 670; Service Bureau for Women, "Service Report for the Month of June, 1933," Welfare Council Papers, box 444, folder 3.

people at that point (almost all men)—being transferred to home relief, and hence to individual care. In principle, at least, this change was supposed to return single people to a more normal status in the community at the same time that it improved the quality of their care. The Unemployment Relief Service took over responsibility for the employables, while the Cook County Bureau of Public Welfare became responsible for the so-called unemployables.[16]

While relief administration evolved again in 1936, these changes of 1935 were permanent. There was never a return to the time when many thousands of men had to endure the miseries of "congregate care" in a few overcrowded buildings. From 1935 to 1942, only one or two public shelters remained; after 1942, even these were closed. The entire relief load of homeless men—only a few hundred by then—was again taken over by private agencies such as the Chicago Christian Industrial League and the Salvation Army, both of which maintained high-quality lodging houses with individualized treatment.[17]

In the following chapter we'll consider the shameful history of Chicago and Illinois's financing of relief, which demonstrates what a low priority the well-being of the unemployed was to the state's political and economic elites. For now, let us turn to the experiences of the unfortunate men who found themselves confined to shelters.

Shelter Life

If this book is essentially a case study in the truth that class conflict is the fulcrum of society, then a look at the conditions in Depression-era shelters is a case study in the callousness of the ruling class. Whatever the subjective intentions of policymakers might have been, their institutions functioned so as to treat the poor as criminals or animals, to punish them for the crime of being poor and thus potentially dangerous. A graphic illustration of this guiding value occurred in 1938, when the Chicago mayor and high officials in the CRA and the police department endorsed the idea of fingerprinting all "inmates" (as they called them) of public shelters. It was thought that at least half the 2,100 men in the CRA's two shelters would leave immediately if a fingerprinting expert appeared on the premises. The proposal was not enacted—probably because of questions about its legality or simply the difficult logistics of carrying it out—but a month later Evanston put it into practice, quickly netting two one-time convicts. "Lock them up," a police lieutenant ordered, "until we find out if they are wanted for crime." This was a somewhat backward logic, but it is illustrative of authorities' attitude toward the poor.[18]

It has long been known that one of the main functions of relief is to discipline the labor force. That is to say, the frequent miserliness of relief policies, the degradation into

---

16. Margaret D. Yates, "Family Service and Relief," in *Social Service Year Book, 1935*, eds. Linn Brandenburg et al., 9–11; Florence Nesbitt, "Family Service and Relief," in *Social Service Year Book, 1936*, 5; *Biennial Report of the IERC, July 1, 1934 to June 30, 1936*, 103–106.
17. Dees, Jr., *Flophouse*, 143–49.
18. *Chicago Tribune*, January 8, 9, 11, 12, and February 10, 1938.

which they have forced those among the poor who could not find employment, has—in the words of political scientists Frances Fox Piven and Richard A. Cloward[19]—served the purpose of enforcing work norms. "Work hard, work constantly, and get by on your own resources," the lower classes are admonished, "for if you don't, this is what awaits you!" Indeed, historically provisions for poor relief and for punishment of criminals have often overlapped.[20] It should hardly surprise us, therefore, that even in the mid-1930s, when mass popular unrest was forcing expansions of public welfare programs, relief remained grotesquely inadequate. Nor is it surprising that this fact was most dramatically manifested in the case of the "dangerous" population of unattached men who had lost the means to live in their own home.

The reader can doubtless imagine that life in Chicago's shelters was no utopia, but it may be worthwhile to give some details. One way to characterize these institutions is that they were, in effect, designed to turn their residents into "bums," as a *Tribune* article put it. Given that few major changes were ever made in these shelters, the natural conclusion is that they successfully served their purposes as determined by the governments that funded them and the relief administration that ran them, an administration that itself was subject to pressures from the conservative business community. To the degree that it occurred, the transformation of men from active shapers of their own destinies into hopeless derelicts whose self-worth had been crushed not only crippled the spirit of rebellion in a disaffected group of men; it also provided a pretext to publicly demonize them (as the *Tribune* did, for example), to demonize public relief itself and argue for its dismantling, and to tar and feather, by association, the lower classes in general. It reinforced class prejudice and the Social Darwinistic self-justifications of the wealthy at the same time that it made more docile and compliant tens of thousands of men. From this perspective, shelter relief exemplified class politics.

Consider the testimony, from 1935, of an "inmate" of Chicago shelters:

> Here [in shelters] privacy is a forgotten word. On a cold or rainy day, or during the evenings, men are crowded into the basement or assembly room—German, colored, Pole, Greek, Mexican, American, Irish, Russian, and every nationality. [...] Here also are degenerates, drunks, working men, bums, clerks, old men with all ambition gone, young men whose every ideal has been crushed, all herded together. One almost tastes the stench of unclean bodies, and the sulphur odor from fumigated clothes. For quite a while this lack of privacy nearly drove me nuts.[21]

---

19. Specifically, in their classic *Regulating the Poor: The Functions of Public Welfare* (New York: Vintage Books, 1971), xv.
20. See, for example, Georg Rusche and Otto Kirscheimer, *Punishment and Social Structure* (New York: Columbia University Press, 1939); David Rothman, *The Discovery of the Asylum: Social Order and Disorder in the New Republic* (Boston, MA: Little, Brown & Co., 1971); H. C. M. Michielse and Robert van Krieken, "Policing the Poor: J. L. Vives and the Sixteenth-Century Origins of Modern Social Administration," *Social Service Review* 64, no. 1 (March 1990): 1–21.
21. *Chicago Tribune*, June 15, 1935.

It is true that some people received better treatment. The few white-collar clients, mostly clerks and salesmen, lived in buildings that had been designed for residential purposes, and so were relatively comfortable. One or two men might sleep in a room, in some cases the kind of room in certain flophouses: a square wooden cubicle with chicken-wire mesh on top to prevent stealing and to let in air. These tiny rooms were the opposite of luxury, but at least they afforded *some* privacy. Furthermore, the beds actually had mattresses, sheets, and pillows. Men in the non-white-collar shelters had to sleep on an uncomfortable canvas army cot, usually without a sheet or a pillow; and when they did have a sheet, it was unlikely to have been washed in months and might be soiled with blood or fecal matter. For a short period (until funding ran out) some white-collar men were even allowed to live in their own rooms and were given $4 a week in return for one day's work, so as to reintegrate themselves into their community. And yet despite such perquisites, caseworkers remarked that these higher-status clients were apt to have an even more adverse reaction to shelter life than those with more humble backgrounds.[22]

Shelter inmates' hardships began immediately as soon as they stepped inside the intake center and began the hours-long wait for a two-minute medical examination. Interrogation by a caseworker was the next step—a rather pointless step in light of the fact that nearly every applicant was always accepted. One applicant gave a spirited complaint about this procedure: "Hell, they want to know when your grandmother died, what she died of, and why did ya let her die. They ask you a few questions, get up and chew the fat with someone, then maybe come back and ask a few more questions. Boy, when you go through all that red tape to get in here and swear that pauper's oath, and swear you've told the truth when you have told several lies, you've touched bottom. There's no pride left."[23]

The physical facilities of most shelters, bare and dreary, were not calculated to lift the spirits. Typically there was a recreation room in which people could sit and play cards or dominoes or other games, or stand or sit on the floor because the room was overcrowded, full of all types of men packed together—native and foreign-born, the bum and the skilled tradesman, the ex-clerk and the ex-convict, Black and white.[24] Not much recreating went on here, though, as is clear from the following description of one such room (which was written, admittedly, in that most terrible year 1932):

> In the auditorium was [a] group of men. If one walked among them, one was conscious of their apathy. One could feel their hopelessness and misery. Some were dozing on the seats. Others were lying asleep on the platform. A few checker games were in progress. Infrequently, a card game went on in a corner. [...] One noticed a certain stillness in the place. It did not seem possible that so many men could be gathered together without some

---

22. Roseman, *Shelter Care*, 14, 15, 26, 34; Hoch and Slayton, *New Homeless and Old*, 47; Dees, Jr., *Flophouse*, 137, 138.
23. Sutherland and Locke, *Twenty Thousand Homeless Men*, 2.
24. While there was a separate shelter for Black men, every shelter had some whites and some Blacks.

noise. Then the thought struck home that these men, for the most part, were not talking. They were sitting in dejected silence, and those who were talking did so quietly.

The day's search for work had proved hopeless. There was nothing to do but tramp the streets or sit and brood, no money to buy amusement for the empty hours.[25]

The recreation room, however, could be called pleasant compared to the "bull pen," a dark, damp, dismal place located in the basement. Littered with cigarette butts, wads of chewing tobacco, and discarded clothing, it had no furniture except some backless benches. Here was where men could escape supervision, where they could smoke, spit on the floor, drink, or sleep off a hangover. It was also where men were sent to be punished, if, say, they had failed to show up for fumigation that night or if they had returned to the shelter intoxicated. During the day, the bull pen was frequently occupied by 50 or a 100 men dozing on the benches or the floor because they had been unable to sleep the previous night. "The great majority of them," reported an investigator, "do not appear to be sleeping off a drunk, but rather merely so weary in body and in spirit that the oblivion of sleep offers them a haven."[26]

The sleeping rooms were so densely packed with cots that it was sometimes necessary for the occupant to crawl in from the head or the foot of the bed—which violated state health regulations. And then, having gone to bed at 8:00 or 9:00 p.m., the occupant spent the night trying to get to sleep, until awoken at 5:30 or 6:30 a.m. Among the annoyances he would have to endure were the stuffiness of the air, the stench, the cold drafts from outside, the sizzling and cracking of steam in the pipes, the quarrels over opening or closing a window—"Put that window down!," "Put that damn window up!"—and of course the lice. If he was sick in the morning he would be forced out of bed anyway and denied access to the sleeping room until 7:00 p.m., when it was opened again.[27]

The health service seems to have been fairly well organized, though the care provided was not always satisfactory. Each shelter had an infirmary, where a physician worked up to two hours a day and an orderly was present 24 hours daily. Medicine could usually be obtained from supplies at the infirmary, where there was also some (inadequate) provision for bed care. The Clearing House opened a small central infirmary in November 1931 for emergency cases and convalescents from all the shelters; by 1934, it had more resources than all the shelters' infirmaries combined. A psychiatrist was even added to the staff that year, in recognition of the thousands of shelter inhabitants who were mentally unbalanced or depressed; but the large majority of these cases could not even be examined, much less treated. There is reason to think, too, that a great many

---

25. "The Drifting Unemployed: A Study of the Younger Unemployed at the Newberry Shelter," 1932, 15, 16, Welfare Council Papers, box 233, folder 5.
26. Sutherland and Locke, *Twenty Thousand Homeless Men*, 5–8; Roseman, *Shelter Care*, 10; Dees, Jr., *Flophouse*, 97, 103, 104. These documents and page numbers are the sources for the following paragraph as well.
27. Beasley, "Care of Destitute Unattached Men in Chicago," 34, 35; Sutherland and Locke, *Twenty Thousand Homeless Men*, 8, 9.

undiagnosed cases of tuberculosis existed among the shelter men, in light of the constant spitting and coughing of many of them.[28]

In addition to medical care, clients were offered miscellaneous personal services for free, such as barber service, shoe repair, and tailor service. Unfortunately, they were never adequate to meet the needs of the majority, especially since the staff had privileged access to them. The shoe repair service, for example, must have been constantly overcrowded, because the shoes that the men were supplied with were of low quality, causing blisters and infections. Clothing, too, was of "extremely poor quality," to quote the Director of the Clearing House for Men, even after a Central Clothing Depot had been set up in May 1932. Prior to this, the clothing issued by the various shelters had been ill-fitting; the establishment of a central depot at least helped address this problem. But even then, clothing appropriations amounted to a dollar per year for each man—$50,000 for 50,000 men during the year 1931–32. What this meant concretely was described in 1934[29]:

> Even the most casual observer of the men in the shelter must notice how ragged the clothing of a large proportion of the men is. Some of them appear almost scarecrow-like; with knees visible through trouser legs too far worn to repair; with trouser seats patched and repatched with contrasting colors; with shirts so frayed and tattered that it is difficult to understand how they remain in one piece; and coats or sweaters so threadbare as to be no protection at all against the cold. [...] Fully three-quarters of the men in [one] shelter appeared to be so disreputably clothed that their appearance would label them as "bums."[30]

Meal service, too, tended to be inadequate the whole decade. Until November 1934, most shelters served only two meals a day, at 6:30 a.m. and 5:30 p.m. It was assumed that if the men got hungry in the interim, they could go out and beg for food or find odd jobs. One Chicagoan wrote of his experience early in the Depression:

> After breakfast at our [shelter] we would hurry over to another charity where we got some more soup and bread. Then we legged it forty-seven blocks to the South Side where a church dispensed coffee and bread. From thence we rushed back nineteen blocks to another church which started feeding [lunch] at eleven. If lucky, we got around in time to get a second [lunch] at another place two miles further uptown. That left us about two hours in mid-afternoon to rest, to panhandle tobacco money, or to read such scraps of old newspapers as we were able to pick up.[31]

The quality of the food served at shelters was uneven. Particularly in the early years of the Depression, it was common for the food to be rotten or bug-ridden. On paper,

---

28. Roseman, *Shelter Care*, 30–32; *Second Annual Report of the IERC*, 145; Dees, Jr., *Flophouse*, 56–59; *Men in the Crucible*, 15–17.
29. Beasley, "Care of Destitute Unattached Men," 37, 54, 55; Roseman, *Shelter Care*, 18, 19; *Men in the Crucible*, 34.
30. Roseman, *Shelter Care*, 18.
31. Roseman, *Shelter Care*, 15–17; France Bunce, "I've Got to Take a Chance," *Forum and Century*, February 1933, 108–12.

the menu could look appealing, featuring fish, potatoes, beef, biscuits, vegetables, and coffee. In practice, it tended to be bland at best, as a reporter described his supper of cold beets, a tin soup bowl of beef stew, a tin mug of weak coffee, and unbuttered bread. Under tremendous pressure from social workers, activists, and the shelter men themselves, meal service was improved in 1934, most significantly by the addition of lunch, but also by providing a more varied menu. Nevertheless, the essence of the whole depressing meal-time experience remained: a man had no choice in what to eat; he was assigned to a particular seat (a spot on one of the long backless benches in the dining room), possibly next to people whose table manners he found revolting; he simply shoveled in the food quickly and without conversation, mindful of the men still waiting outside; and to eat, he first had to shamble along in a serpentine line for up to two-and-a-half hours, three times a day.[32]

All things considered, the central fact of shelter life was *regimentation*. One author summed it up: "When the man enters the shelter he learns the meaning of the word 'line.' He is a 'linesman'; he lines up to see the caseworker; he lines up for his meals; he lines up to fumigate [every two weeks] and then to bathe; he lines up to wash, to shave, to use the toilet, and to go to bed. 'I spend,' said one man, 'half my waking hours either standing and waiting for something or sitting and waiting for someone.'" "Why in hell don't they line us up against the wall and shoot us and get it over with," grumbled one inmate. Watchmen were always present to intimidate and challenge the men, especially drunks, who were frequently beaten—with clubs, sawed-off baseball bats, or lead pipes—and forced outside even in the cold night air. Signs posted on the walls warned, "Don't Loiter Here—This Means You," "Keep Quiet and Listen," and "Keep Out," this last with an illustration of a fist striking a nose. "The place has approximately the same effect as a jail," remarked a reporter. "It is the individual against the world. The monotony of the same old faces, ideas, arguments, line, nothing to do but sit, finally gets under the skin."[33]

An observer of shelter life might have concluded that the whole point of the program was to infantilize the men, to deprive them of initiative and individuality. A total bureaucracy regulated every aspect of their lives, except in the hours every day that they spent on the streets. To make sure that inmates did not have to use their mind even to remember procedures and duties, bulletins with instructions were posted all over the building. The structural ideal was a kind of totalitarianism, power's penetration of every recess of the mind to break down the personality and reduce it to the lowest common denominator, the apathetic former job seeker, the inarticulate bum, the broken old man—to isolate and make anonymous, to fill with resentment and consciousness of inferiority. In some cases, "spies" even circulated among the inmates to learn of opinions and happenings, a fact that only heightened the atmosphere of distrust and suspicion.

---

32. Roseman, *Shelter Care*, 15–17; *Men in the Crucible*, 36, 37; *Chicago Hunger Fighter*, December 26, 1931, February 27, 1932; Dees, Jr., *Flophouse*, 105–108; *Chicago Daily News*, October 20, 28, 1932; Sutherland and Locke, *Twenty Thousand Homeless Men*, 3–5.
33. Roseman, *Shelter Care*, 7, 8; Dees, Jr., *Flophouse*, 121–25, 134; Sutherland and Locke, *Twenty Thousand Homeless Men*, 7, 14; Glenn H. Johnson, *Relief and Health Problems of a Selected Group of Non-Family Men* (Chicago, IL: University of Chicago Press, 1937), 33.

The rule of impersonality so shaped the men's minds that they seldom cared to learn each other's names, seldom inquired of past lives or personal business. Many preferred not to talk at all but to sit alone, as they worried there was no escape from the "hopeless maelstrom." Perhaps ironically, the non-Hobohemians—the white-collar workers, the skilled tradesmen, the steady unskilled workers—were frequently more despondent about the future than the habitual Hobohemians. Their fate, it seemed, was to become "shelterized," to internalize the bureaucracy.[34]

Even work relief, which social workers and some administrators hoped would empower and help "rehabilitate" clients, often did not have the desired effect. Beginning in June 1932, it took the form of projects for the Cook County Department of Highways and the Chicago Bureau of Streets, maintenance work done in the shelters, and, in the case of some white-collar clients, clerical and professional work for the Chicago Public Library and the Board of Education. All men except the disabled and those who served on the shelter staff were required to work one 5-hour day for each 13 days of meals and lodging. Technically their five hours of labor got them $3.25 in credit for shelter relief plus 25 cents in cash, but since they had already been receiving shelter relief for free in the preceding years, it seemed to many that they were really being paid only 5 cents an hour. They considered themselves slave laborers. "[This is] worse than slavery," a Black man complained to a labor reporter. "The officials order us around like prisoners. Slaves were worth money. The owners wanted them to live so they could work. Here they don't care if you're sick or if you die." Nor did it help that the character of the work was not exactly edifying: even many white-collar men, not to mention the others, had to do such "made-work drudgery" (as they disgustedly called it) as cleaning spittoons, sweeping floors, shoveling snow, and cleaning trash-filled alleys. This work relief program continued until the summer of 1935.[35]

It is true that some men appreciated the opportunity to feel at least moderately useful. And they all did appreciate the 25 cents with which they could buy a razor, soap, a lunch, or, in some cases, alcohol and sex with a prostitute. In an environment as degraded as the one described here, the little pleasures that could be bought with 25 cents would assume outsized importance, as precious links to the world of the living.

The Men

While the shelters tended to function, in effect, as devices of dehumanization, the men who found it necessary to live in them did not thereby cease to be men. At times they even organized to change practices, with some success; and their experiences gave most of them a definitely left-of-center political consciousness. They did not become only an

---

34. Sutherland and Locke, *Twenty Thousand Homeless Men*, 14, 15, 144–58; Dees, Jr., 124; "The Drifting Unemployed," 46; Samuel Kirson Weinberg, "A Study of Isolation among Chicago Shelter-House Men" (MA thesis, University of Chicago, 1935), chapter 4.
35. Beasley, "Care of Destitute Unattached Men," 38–44; Roseman, *Shelter Care*, 20; Dees, Jr., *Flophouse*, 82–85; *Worker's Voice*, October 15, 1932; Sutherland and Locke, *Twenty Thousand Homeless Men*, 101.

undifferentiated mass of cattle, as they were frequently thought of, but remained individuals with their own distinctive pasts and futures, and personalities.

So, first of all, what were their pasts? Who were these men? By 1932, there were over fifty different nationalities and cultural groups represented in the shelters; 60 percent of the people were American, after which the most common group, constituting 7 percent, was Polish. Of all the continental European immigrants, who were about 30 percent of the total, the Central European peasant was most highly represented. On the whole, half of the men had already been accustomed to the Hobohemian culture, being either "bums" (habitual drunks, beggars, etc.), migratory laborers, or casual laborers rooted in Chicago, nearly all of whom had lived in flophouses and lodging houses in the main stem of Hobohemia. For the other half, including the steadier type of unskilled worker, it was more or less traumatizing to find themselves suddenly living with bums or—if he was an American—"damn foreigners."[36]

As we have seen, the Hobohemians' background was of raw living in the kaleidoscopic neighborhoods of West Madison, North Clark, and South State Streets. All ages, nationalities, and occupations, including some skilled and white-collar workers, were seen here—indeed, were seen even just on West Madison Street, which had a magnetic energy that both repelled and attracted. Its habitués were apt to swear, "I'm going to get off this goddamn street soon"—away from the petty racketeers, the drug peddlers, the drunks and their predators the jack-rollers (whose pastime consisted of beating up drunks and stealing from them)—and they might even succeed in getting away for a couple of weeks, but almost always they returned, with the self-reproach, "I'll be damned if I can stay away—what it is, I don't know." Part of it was the inexpensiveness of the area, where meals could be had for 15 or 20 cents. More important, though, was the companionship that could be found in the hotels and lodging houses, and the hash houses and restaurants. "Who the hell wants to stay out in a furnished room by himself?" remarked one man. "I'd die of lonesomeness."[37]

The people who lived on such streets were likely to prize their independence, thinking of themselves, in fact, as much more free and independent than their socially esteemed "betters" in the middle class, who were tied down by marriage and the whole mundane existence of the mainstream. Often traveling all over the country, working as harvest hands, railroad laborers, lumberjacks, truckers, waiters in cheap restaurants, stevedores, or just panhandling and doing odd jobs, the young and middle-aged men were wont to have a sort of defiant pride, a "don't-give-a-damn" attitude (tinged with a certain sensitivity) about how the outside world viewed them. Conscious that they were seen as low-lifes, they regularly insisted to themselves and others, "I ain't a damned bum!" This stubborn pride and love of freedom manifested itself in Hobohemians' sometimes being even more intolerant of the regimentation and dependence of shelter

---

36. *Men in the Crucible*, 62; S. Kirson Weinberg, "The Problem of Unattachment of Shelter House Men," 1934, term paper for Sociology 310, Ernest Burgess Papers, box 184, folder 1, pp. 1, 84.
37. "West Madison Street," 1934, Burgess Papers, box 135, folder 2.

life than non-Hobohemians: whenever they could, they left the shelters for flophouses or lodging houses, where they didn't have to wake up, go to bed, and eat at prescribed times, or stand in long lines most of the day. This was especially true of "professional beggars" (technically a different category than bums)—who, incidentally, worked as hard at their jobs as many a skilled worker.[38]

Having had less exposure to indoctrination by the dominant culture than many non-Hobohemians, these people tended, arguably, to be more independent minded and realistic in their views about life and society than their formerly middle-class counterparts were. Their attitudes had emerged relatively organically from their material conditions and persisted through the years spent in shelters. Living hard, precarious lives ever on the edge of want, familiar with the policeman's glare and even his truncheon, expert in the ways of individualized and improvisatory class struggle, "hobos" and their kin built their worldview on the foundation of a granite cynicism. Everything was a "racket"—religion, politics, business, and relief administration. Missions, for instance, were not at all popular for their treatment of their homeless beneficiaries as a captive audience that had to endure hours of sermons and prayers in order to get mediocre food. "Something that should be put out of business," grumbled one shelter inmate, a middle-aged American who had been a migratory steam shovel operator, "is all missions and churches. What the hell good are they anyway? They don't produce nothing. They are just like banks. They're parasites." The fact that, according to one study, about 40 percent of men in shelters seldom or never attended church because of disbelief or indifference to religion (as opposed to the 40 percent who had other reasons for not attending, such as poor clothing and lack of money) suggests just how antireligious Hobohemia was; for the skilled and unskilled workers with steadier jobs more regularly attended church, at least when they had work.[39]

Politics may have been even more an object of derision than religion. In the political sphere, the deeply materialistic and realistic worldview of most Hobohemians was manifested in two different attitudes: a far-left hostility to the dominant social order, and a cynicism about getting involved with politics at all. In the rare cases when these men voted, for example, they were apt to sell their vote to the highest bidder. "I might as well give my vote to the one who will pay me the most, for what does it matter?" one protested. "You'll only get a rimming either way. They have you coming and going. The poor man doesn't have a chance in this country; the cards are stacked against him."[40]

The other political attitude, the left-wing radicalism, had been most pronounced in the heyday of Hobohemia before the 1920s, when the IWW was at its height. A dense and vital counterculture had thrived nationwide, nourished by radical newspapers (*Appeal to*

---

38. Kusmer, *Down and Out*, 160, 161; "West Madison Street"; interview with J. P. Smith, November 13, 1934, Burgess papers, box 135, folder 2; Harvey J. Locke, "Unemployed Men in Chicago Shelters," *Sociology and Social Research* 19 (May–June 1935): 420–28; Dees, Jr., *Flophouse*, 140.
39. Anderson, *The Hobo*, chapter 11; interview of Carl Kolins by John Oien, 1934, Burgess Papers, box 135, folder 2; Weinberg, "A Study of Isolation among Chicago Shelter-House Men," 43; Sutherland and Locke, *Twenty Thousand Homeless Men*, 67.
40. Sutherland and Locke, *Twenty Thousand Homeless Men*, 67, 68.

Reason, Industrial Worker, Hobo News, Solidarity, Liberator, Voice of Labor, etc.); socialist literature (migratory workers were smitten with Jack London but also read Marx and Engels, Lewis Morgan, Paul Lafargue, Antonio Labriola, and the like); songs by Joe Hill and other Wobblies, an entire folklore that glorified manly independence and resistance; and such institutions as left-wing unions, radical bookstores, Bughouse Square and its duplicates in Los Angeles and elsewhere; and clubs like the famous Dill Pickle Club in Chicago (where hoboes, artists, and intellectuals could meet). All this declined in the 1920s, under the impact of wartime and postwar repression, the "machine age," and the increasingly settled character of communities. Nevertheless, Hobohemia was far from finished by the 1930s, and neither was its left-wing, even anarchist, ethos. Casual workers with the attitudes of Carl Kolins, the steam shovel operator quoted above, were still easy to find, even in the public shelters that functioned so as to beat the spirit out of a man[41]:

> Another thing I don't like about the [*Chicago*] *Tribune* is that they're always rapping Roosevelt. To read the *Tribune* you would think communism was a kind of deadly poisoning. Well, it is to those big fat grafters. They've got all the money they want—that's why they don't want communism or a liberal government. They want to keep us on the bum. [...] [The radio priest Father Coughlin] is pretty good as far as he goes but, of course, he don't want communism, though he is preaching the same thing except that he wants to keep the churches in. Naturally, he would, otherwise that would spoil his racket.[42]

Doubtless the Communist organizers who tried to reach men in shelters and flophouses, and the party newspapers the *Daily Worker* and the *Hunger Fighter*, had something to do with such opinions. And it is true that many other Hobohemians were far from identifying as radicals, whom they called "wobblies," "dirties," and "chiselers." The point is that the ideological background of this swath of shelter inmates was broadly left wing, far more leftist, more laborite, than the Democratic Party under Roosevelt. Even the men who were scornful of "radicals" tended to share their views about how American society operated and how it ought to operate. Understandably disillusioned with the political and economic system, these self-professed patriots would express their alienation by saying things like, "Give the country back to the Indians," and discussing such left-wing ideas as "production for use" with enthusiastic approbation.

Of course, when one is a migratory laborer or a "home-guard" casual worker, politics is not one's primary interest. Consider the following story of a typical immigrant who found himself in Chicago's public shelter system, having run out of ways to "cheat" the institutionalizing momentum of the economic system:

> When I live in Mexico [...] I work on farm. In 1916 I say I come here. I work on Santa Fe railroad in Kansas City. I work there six month and live in a camp. In 1917 I hear an epidemic of flu kill father, mother, and all my family.

---

41. Anderson, *The Hobo*, chapters 13 and 14; Todd DePastino, *Citizen Hobo*, chapter 4, 175–77; Nels Anderson, *Men on the Move* (Chicago, IL: University of Chicago, 1940), chapter 1.
42. Interview of Carl Kolins.

> I earn $1.65 a day on railroad in Kansas City. In winter I go to Montana and work on the Burlington six months. Then I went to Philadelphia on Pennsylvania Railroad. This job hold no more. [...]
>
> In 1921 I get job in Congress Hotel [in Chicago]. I work there eight or nine years washing. In 1930 I still work in Congress Hotel, then I get laid off.
>
> When I work on railroad, I live in camp with all the men. When I work in city like Congress Hotel, I live in rooming house. [...] I start going around to look for work when I no work because I have no money to pay rent. No want landlord put me out. Come out by myself. When I can find no job, I have no place to go, so I go straight to shelter.[43]

The non-Hobohemian portion of the shelter population was similarly heterogeneous, but its members had tended to have more stable work and be less mobile than the others. Still, one cannot draw a firm line between the two categories. Often the non-Hobohemians' path to the shelter had begun with marital problems such as divorce, separation, or the death of a wife, which might result in excessive drinking or depression and the loss of incentives to work. Physical disabilities or injuries were the decisive factor in other cases.[44]

For these people, the decision to apply to shelters was frequently agonizing, signifying as it supposedly did their failure, their complete defeat and "social death." Shelter men were certainly more prone to self-blame than the rest of the unemployed. "If I hadn't been such a fool in the past," a common sentiment went, "I would have had a job at the present time, or at least I would have had some money saved up." "If I had let drink alone I would have been all right." As one of the down-and-out, it was hard not to at least partly absorb the dominant society's contemptuous attitude toward the down-and-out.[45]

And yet, again, the self-blame was usually united with disgust for authority and a blaming of one's problems on the fact that everything was a racket. (This was an idea that Communist organizers and newspapers spread, for example, by arguing that the relief administration was graft-ridden.)[46] One man, for instance, prefaced an expression of self-contempt with a spirited critique of the relief administration:

> As far as the shelter is concerned, it ain't so bad—but the management. They're all a bunch of damn rats, all of them without exception. If you understand the relief system it's all based

---

43. Weinberg, "The Problem of Unattachment of Shelter House Men."
44. Sutherland and Locke, *Twenty Thousand Homeless Men*, 70–86.
45. Ibid., 78, 91.
46. To quote the December 26, 1931, issue of the *Hunger Fighter*:

    > Anyone who knows anything about Chicago business knows that everything connected with it is bound to be a racket of some kind. And so when workers begin to starve and freeze the business of giving them relief becomes another racket. The more underhanded a racket works, the better it is. Now, take Governor Emmerson's Joint Emergency Relief Committee, for instance. First, it collects about nine million dollars from those workers who still have a cent or two left. Then it dishes out big gobs of this swag to all kinds of "charity institutions" for them to hand out as they see fit.

    In some respects, shelter men's cynicism was the cynicism of Communists.

on graft, and all these case workers around here give a damn about is to draw their salary and make it as tough as possible for us, and the more they can squeeze out of us and the less they can give us, that's just that much more for their own pockets. [...] The food is terrible. You have got to line up like a bunch of pigs and wait for hours at a time to get a dish full of that slop they throw at you—self-respecting hogs wouldn't eat it. Though, of course, it's good enough for us stiffs. Who are we anyway? We are nothing.[47]

This was stated by a man familiar with Hobohemia, but it was an attitude that quickly spread to most people after they had entered the shelter. Their former respect for authority—qualified and partial as it was—gave way to a consciousness of being oppressed and exploited (in work relief), and a belief in the fundamental irrationality of a social order that would deprive so many healthy men of productive pursuits. A type of radicalization tended to take place, even without sustained exposure to Communist organizers and publications. If a man felt that he had become a bum, he often blamed it on the shelters, not himself. "The shelters made a lousy bum out of me" was a common refrain. It became a general idea that the profit system had to be changed so as to provide work and security for the laboring class; men who made radical statements were widely applauded, though only a minority subscribed to Communism. (Most took the view that this ideology was unrealistic and its adherents deceived about political possibilities in the United States.) Even those who had once been religious adopted the Hobohemian attitude: "the general consensus [in the shelters]," writes one investigator, "is that all religion is to be classed along with charity organizations as a racket." In fact, some researchers who lived in the shelters as clients were themselves susceptible to the left-wing collective consciousness: "All one hears around this place is a constant discussion of government, the relief racket, and economic conditions until it naturally gets on one's nerves and soon gets him down until he just sits back and waits for something to happen."[48]

And things did happen. In the early years of the Depression, when the Communist Party was most active in organizing the unemployed, well-attended meetings were held at many shelters. For a long time, the auditorium in the Newberry Shelter was the scene of almost nightly meetings of an Unemployed Council committee, which functioned in part as a grievance committee that intervened with management on behalf of the inmates. According to one observer, the Communists had a "large following" among the men and "exercised a potent influence over them." Part of the attraction of the meetings was simply that they provided entertainment and opportunities for self-expression, as well as for solidarity and a sense of belonging. But it is clear that many of the attendees substantially agreed with the ideas on offer—the importance of class consciousness, of fighting for workers' rights, of building a movement against capitalism, and more specifically of fighting to improve conditions in the shelters. "At the conclusion of the meetings," the observer noted, "the radical songs are sung—'Solidarity,' 'We'll Hang

---

47. Interview of Carl Kolins.
48. Sutherland and Locke, *Twenty Thousand Homeless Men*, 152, 159–62.

Hoover to a Sour Apple Tree,' and the 'Marseillaise.' Misguided as it perhaps all is, it is rather a stirring sight to see men and boys stand erect at the end of the meetings and sing these songs with great emotional feeling."[49]

Nor was it only a matter of meeting and singing. Shelter inmates organized to change administrative practices, and sometimes their efforts met with success. One of the few records of such activities is the *Hunger Fighter*, which periodically published short notices on "flophouse" victories. In December 1931, for example, the paper reported that 200 men and boys at one shelter were granted some concessions when they overturned the tables in the cafeteria and threw the "slop" onto the floor, shouting that they wouldn't starve to death quietly. At other shelters grievance committees were formed to present demands to the administration: three meals served every day, a more appetizing menu, the provision of chewing and smoking tobacco twice a week for all men, and 18 inches of space between beds. A couple of months later the paper advertised a few small victories, as when the Salvation Army was forced to fire a chef and serve better food, and when at another shelter the chairman of the flophouse committee showed the superintendent that there were bugs in the food, which convinced him to order healthier meat. In early 1932 a dramatic incident took place: several patrol wagons of police with tear gas and guns forced 500 men out of a shelter run by the Chicago Christian Industrial League after they had voted 493–7 against religious services, which they were being forced to listen to every night. And so it went at shelter after shelter in these years of radical ferment, especially 1930–33. The *Hunger Fighter* and the activities of Communists were well known to, and well feared by, relief administrators, as shown, for instance, by the time when an inmate's clothing was destroyed by sulfur fumigation and he demanded new clothes, to no effect. "Okay," he told the superintendent, "I'll tell the reporter for the *Hunger Fighter* about this." "No, no, not that!" the superintendent replied and found a sweater, shirt, and coat for him.[50]

In May 1932 there was a notable victory: after a shelter on Morgan Street was closed, the 400 homeless people who had lost a place to live sent delegations to the Central Clearing House for Men. The administrators there realized that the men would not be "bulldozed" so easily (to quote the *Hunger Fighter*) and offered to take them all back.[51]

Men did not need Communist organizers to inspire them to take action. Despite the paucity of records of collective action in the shelters, a few suggestive stories remain. Here is one from a report in *The Nation* in August 1934:

> In South Chicago a bunch of sailors did shake off the shackles of the shelters. Twenty-five lake men, on the beach at Calumet Harbor, decided they didn't like the flop-house [i.e., the public shelter]. They protested to the shelter manager, who threatened to call the police. They took their protest to the relief commission and sat down in the commission office, promising to stay there. Lake sailors are big, brawny lads, recruited from the farms of

---

49. "The Drifting Unemployed: A Study of the Younger Unemployed at the Newberry Shelter."
50. *Hunger Fighter*, December 26, 1931, January 9, February 27, and March 12, 1932.
51. Randi Storch, *Red Chicago: American Communism at Its Grassroots, 1928–35* (Chicago, IL: University of Illinois Press, 2007), 109.

Illinois and Michigan and Wisconsin and Minnesota, and the relief commission needed its chairs. Now the seamen have their own shelter in South Chicago, run by themselves, financed by the FERA. Any case worker who goes near it must be prepared to answer rather than ask questions.[52]

There is no telling how many similar incidents of collective resistance took place, even years after the heady days of 1932. On New Year's Day that year, 200 men, disgusted at the particularly bad shelter food that night, went to restaurants and ate large meals without paying. Many of them were arrested, even after railroad workers present had offered to pay for the meals.[53]

The highpoint of Communist influence in the shelters was probably in the spring of 1932, when, according to a former Communist, "it was very easy to organize a demonstration because all you had to do was send word through the flophouses that something is taking place and inside of a half hour you had ten thousand people out in the streets." While surely an exaggeration, this is a telling statement. Almost two thousand homeless people held memberships in shelter committees at this time, and many more attended the meetings. As we'll see in a later chapter, working-class neighborhoods of Chicago in these months and years burst with class consciousness of both explicit and implicit types, which easily spread to—indeed, partly originated in—the Hobohemian districts and even many formerly middle-class people who now lived in them. Few shelter men were committed to a Marxist ideology, but the majority were deeply aware of an antagonism of interests between authorities—economic, political, and administrative—and the working or unemployed poor. Their own experiences had taught them this antagonism; Communist propaganda only drove the point home, heightened their awareness, and encouraged them to act on it.[54]

The whole question of "class consciousness" that comes up in historical scholarship—"How class conscious were the workers?", "Why weren't they more conscious or militant?"—has, perhaps, a rather straightforward answer. While few were educated in the niceties of Marxian theory, the working-class unemployed of Chicago, and the homeless, tended to be quite aware of class, and even, on some level, of the importance of solidarity in order to achieve gains. A researcher of Chicago's shelters in 1935 observed that "if one goes into the assembly room on an afternoon or evening, he will hear men giving the capitalistic system hell in a big way. A dozen cure-alls are suggested as immediate remedies for the depression—communism, socialism, take the profits out of business, immediate payment of the soldiers' bonus, old-age pensions, unemployment insurance, government work projects, and the like." All such ideas were "in the air" at the time, and people were well aware of them and their premise, class conflict. One did not have to have incredible insight or belong to some revolutionary vanguard in order to understand, on some level, one's class interests and the imperative to stand up and

---

52. David Scheyer, "Flop-House," *Nation*, August 22, 1934.
53. *Hunger Fighter*, January 9, 1932.
54. Beasley, "Care of Destitute Unattached Men," 72; Storch, *Red Chicago*, 109, 110.

fight against the "boss class." Franklin Roosevelt's denunciation of "economic royalists," after all, was not exactly an unpopular stance, in light of his crushing victory over Alf Landon in the 1936 presidential election. If most shelter inmates did not engage in continual struggles to influence relief policy or to defend the rights of the poor, it was not necessarily because they were incurably "apathetic"; it was because the task of organizing large numbers of people is not easy, requiring energy and stamina that one no longer possesses after years spent in a public shelter. Furthermore, these people, naturally, were more interested in concrete improvements in their lives than an abstract ideology aimed at a distant future. Thus, to the extent that mass demonstrations and flophouse committee meetings did not substantially improve conditions, men drifted away from them.[55]

But adherence to left-wing ideas and participation in "direct action" were not the only ways of asserting oneself in a demoralizing environment. In fact, the restlessness and protests of shelter inmates in late 1931 and early 1932 led to an important new program that ameliorated boredom: authorities created a Special Activities Division that could provide the men with some recreation and education, thereby, supposedly, rectifying the conditions that caused them to be "the ready prey of the agitator," as an administrator said. Beginning in early 1932, the new department expanded during the next few years to the point that, by 1934, it conducted "motion picture shows, stereopticon lectures, vaudeville shows, boxing and wrestling exhibitions, orchestral entertainment, community songs, educational classes, handicraft activities, athletic competitions, games of various descriptions, libraries, and debates." It operated in each shelter, and not only as entertainment: the homeless themselves staffed the programs—not least because it was discovered that among them were musicians, song-and-dance men, and specialty performers. In fact, in April 1932, these men expanded their performances beyond the shelters, putting on a two-week-running minstrel show for the public called "The Breadline Frolics." Sponsored by 80 civic and social clubs, the show was enormously popular, being covered by newspapers from the *New York Times* to the *Los Angeles Times*. Aside from the thousands of dollars it raised, its most significant function may have been to apprise the public of the very real talent and intelligence that, because of the economy's dysfunction, were consigned to shelters.[56]

The relatively active recreations, especially sports, were most popular with the younger men. During the winter it was ping pong, basketball, and boxing: for example, in two of the shelters "a number of boxing bouts and music and novelty acts staged in one of the congested and ill-ventilated basements would shake the rafters and induce long rounds of spontaneous applause." In the summer it was outdoor sports: four shelters had baseball teams (Newberry had eight of them) and all had at least one softball team, 20 horseshoe courts were maintained, and handball and volleyball games were popular at some shelters.[57]

---

55. Quotation from Sutherland and Locke, *Twenty Thousand Homeless Men*, 13.
56. *Men in the Crucible*, 19–24; Roseman, *Shelter Care*, 28; *The Billboard*, May 7, 1932; *Chicago Tribune*, April 26, 1932; *New York Times*, April 25, 1932; Dees, Jr., *Flophouse*, 63, 64.
57. *Men in the Crucible*, 21.

It was also the younger men who were most interested in discussion groups and classes, especially the vocational ones—typewriting, shorthand, bookkeeping, and so on. All categories of inmates, however, made frequent use of the shelter libraries (sometimes even the city libraries), despite the dim lighting and poor conditions. Thousands of books and magazines were donated every month to the Clearing House, which circulated them among the shelters. Newspapers and pulp magazines were by far the most popular, but technical and scientific literature was not ignored. A sympathetic reporter, impressed by the popularity of reading, pithily summarized its appeal to the homeless: "Reading provides an escape from the sordid and depressing situation of the shelters into the world of imagination. A story enables a man to identify himself with the successful hero of the tale, and serious study enables him to live in the future possibility of a higher and better status." It should be recalled that workers, even the homeless, in the United States had always been avid readers. As the Chicago sociologist Nels Anderson stated in 1923, "The homeless man is an extensive reader. This is especially true of the transients, the tramp, and the hobo. The tramp employs his leisure to read everything that comes his way. If he is walking along the railroad track, he picks up the papers that are thrown from the trains. [...] If he is in the city, he hunts out some quiet corner where he may read." Such traditions continued in the shelters, including among immigrants, who liked to read papers in their native language.[58]

A common practice was for men to leave the shelters early in the morning and walk to the nearest subway station to get the morning newspaper. So many of them had the same idea that they had to stand in line at the station exit, where departing passengers would hand over their own copy. Some of the men collected many papers this way, whereupon they returned to the shelter and sold each for a penny; but most simply took one for their own use, to pass the time, and to maintain some connection to their old life.[59]

Generally, even after the creation of the Special Activities Department, the principal forms of recreation remained extra-institutional and anti-institutional, the activities most conducive to escape from collective anhedonia: drinking, gambling, and visiting prostitutes. In a class-structured world, these were what was left those on the wrong side of the divide.

Gambling, for example, was far more than an act of desperation or despair: it was a positive source of excitement, hope, and intellectual stimulation. Having been exiled from social, political, and cultural life, shelter inmates enthusiastically embraced gambling as one of the remaining means of expressing themselves and resisting the complete extinction of their identity. "The gambling habit has been accentuated since shelter entrance," a researcher writes in 1935. "The men are necessarily limited to small stakes, but they express as much enthusiasm and use as much energy in their gambling as do the patrons of expensive gambling houses." Card playing and, especially, betting on

---

58. Sutherland and Locke, *Twenty Thousand Homeless Men*, 104–107; Dees, Jr., *Flophouse*, 62, 63; Roseman, *Shelter Care*, 29; Anderson, *The Hobo*, 185.
59. Sutherland and Locke, *Twenty Thousand Homeless Men*, 94, 95.

horse races were the most popular activities, the latter being done either among the men themselves—betting with razor blades, cigarettes, and other small items—or at cheap gambling places on West Madison Street. To quote an investigator,

> The men consume much time and energy in doping the races. They pour [sic] over racing literature and racing results in the newspapers and talk for hours on the relative merits of the various horses, the ability of certain jockeys, the condition of the track, the crookedness of the stables and jockeys, and the odds on the horses. On the basis of their reading, conversation, and knowledge of the races, even though they may have little or no money to bet, they have a great time doping out how one should place his bets.[60]

Clearly this activity was engaged in for creative purposes as much as acquisitive ones. As in the case of "policy" among Blacks, elaborate systems were devised for placing the right bets. For some men, gambling became an obsession. "Such men eat horses, sleep horses, and talk horses all day long": in fact, the races gave them a reason to live. "If it wasn't for the fact that the pony players always hope and constantly look for a future change in luck," a shelter inmate observed, "many of them would commit suicide."[61]

There were other comforts too, however, such as visiting prostitutes. Sex starvation was a curse for many of the men. "I tell you that I feel sick when I am away from women," one man said. "I am a married man, a father of children, and even the sight of a woman is helpful to me." One solution, widely adopted, was masturbation. Another was to engage in homosexual practices, though probably less than 10 percent of the men turned to this form of relief. Some were able to drain their dammed lust by going on long walks the entire day, 10 miles out and 10 miles in, which so tired them that they gave little thought to women. Others chose a more immediate type of sublimation: ogling women in parks and on beaches. Oak Street Beach was a mecca for these men; they would spend much of the day there, sitting and dreaming and "wondering if the

---

60. Ibid., 122, 124, 125. In interpreting the significance of gambling for these men, one recalls Noam Chomsky's remarks on spectator sports in contemporary society: a major reason for the incredible popularity of professional sports, and the enormous amount of attention and analysis that people regularly devote to them, is that most other avenues for the exercise of collective intelligence are closed to the public. To quote Chomsky,

    > in our society, we have things that you might use your intelligence on, like politics, but people really can't get involved in them in a very serious way—so what they do is they put their minds into other things, such as sports. You're trained to be obedient; you don't have an interesting job; there's no work around for you that's creative; in the cultural environment you're a passive observer of usually pretty tawdry stuff; political and social life are out of your range, they're in the hands of the rich folk. So what's left? Well, one thing that's left is sports—so you put a lot of the intelligence and the thought and the self-confidence into that.

    Such was the function that gambling served among many thousands of Chicago residents in the 1930s. Peter Mitchell and John Schoeffel, eds., *Understanding Power: The Indispensable Chomsky* (New York: The New Press, 2002), 99.

61. Sutherland and Locke, *Twenty Thousand Homeless Men*, 126–28.

big blonde will come again today." Young men even bought swimsuits and flirted with the girls, their self-confidence intact despite shelter life.[62]

Of course, the most satisfying relief was actual sex, usually with prostitutes. It is impossible to know how many men, and with what frequency, resorted to this expedient, but a study in 1935 of 400 randomly selected men found that 40 percent made visits to prostitutes or other women, the average frequency being about once in six weeks. At between 25 cents and a dollar or two, these were prostitutes of a low status, sometimes middle-aged—but "an old woman isn't so bad after her nose is powdered"—and not rarely willing to rob their clients of whatever they could, even false teeth.[63]

Of the three "vices" in which shelter men most often indulged, drinking was the most widespread. Perhaps even more than gambling, drinking among the homeless was and is widely considered somehow pathetic or stupid, proving them to be worthless bums, since supposedly they should be using the money they get from begging and other sources to buy food or invest in their future. People rarely stop to reflect that after years of discouragement and alienation, one may simply want to feel good from time to time. Ordinarily, for those in the middle class, drinking alcohol is nothing but a means to have fun; for shelter inmates, however, it was more than that. It can be thought of as a form of escape, but a more interesting and fruitful way to conceptualize it is as a type of resistance. One might recall in this context the historian Bruce Nelson's comment, in *Workers on the Waterfront* (1988), about the "drunken sailor" stereotype: rather than being nothing but an expression of a "childlike and irresponsible" nature, seamen's tradition of drinking was "an expression of powerlessness, a reflection of alienation and rebellion, an act of camaraderie among men who lived beyond the pale of bourgeois civility."[64] Again, we must remember that the cynicism and gloomy outlook of most shelter men was not merely a passive reflection of conditions; it was based on a realistic and rational analysis of objective possibilities. Collective resistance could lead to small victories, but it could not change the basic structure of shelter life, nor could it give men jobs. So there was little to be done except try to hold on to some remnant of hope, adapt to reality while yet struggling to maintain one's identity, and rebel against dehumanization in imagination and conversation. Alcohol, like gambling, facilitated these things.

Confidence, courage, and conviviality: three anti-institutional manifestations of one's individuality, and three joys for which alcohol was a uniquely adept midwife. "When I drink I got guts," said one inmate. "When I'm not tanked up I sit quiet and still, but when I'm drunk I can go up and bum anybody, panhandle, or bum from store to store. I can go to a woman, fight, or do anything." While entering the shelter as a stranger in a strange land, an inmate soon learned that "a group of jolly companions could be found around a bottle." Few men drank alone, preferring to share their bottle with friends or anyone nearby. Sometimes several would contribute to a communal fund

---

62. Ibid., 128–32.
63. Ibid.
64. Bruce Nelson, *Workers on the Waterfront: Seamen, Longshoremen, and Unionism in the 1930s* (Chicago, IL: University of Illinois Press, 1988), 24.

with which to "enjoy a real spree" together. They could go to the cheap taverns that abounded in the neighborhoods, or to the "moonshine joints" located in the basements of dilapidated old buildings, or they could buy the even cheaper "derail" that was sold illegally—denatured alcohol diluted with water. Sitting together, they jocularly told tall tales about past conquests of women, or complained about the relief administration, or discussed possible solutions to the economic depression.[65]

As the popular perception was wrong that most homeless men were depressed and alcoholic bums, so it was wrong that most beggars were self-contemptuous failures at life. On the contrary, many treated begging as a job, a craft that required skill and a nuanced understanding of humanity. Some who had practiced the art for a long time complained that it had become much more difficult since the Depression increased the number of beggars and reduced the amount that people gave. And yet it seems that people tended to be surprisingly generous, much more so than business elites were comfortable with. In an earlier chapter we encountered a businessman inveighing, in 1931, against the public's "mistaken ideas of charity," a sentiment certainly shared by a large proportion of the upper class. Under pressure from downtown business interests, police periodically made sweeps of the Loop to round up and arrest as many beggars as they could—83 on one occasion in 1933 (none of them a long-term Chicago resident), 189 on another. Still, despite the risks, the money to be made generally ensured that panhandling was worthwhile—at least if we're to judge by the following experience of a man impersonating a beggar in Springfield, Illinois, in 1933[66]:

[In less than three hours, the man] made 27 contacts, was given aid totaling $1.27 by 10 [people], was taken into a restaurant 4 times and fed, was offered whiskey 6 times, was told by young women [beggars] not to solicit in their territory [...], was invited to meet one of the men next day to be given a shirt, was given 4 lectures on the consequences of being a bum, and received 9 polite refusals.[67]

In New York City, there were reports of professional beggars making $50 a day. Others might make $10 or $15, and still others settled for a dollar or less. On the whole, the relative generosity beggars encountered suggests that the public was rather sympathetic to their plight, and not as utterly contemptuous as one might think from press coverage at the time.[68]

To sum up this discussion of men living in shelters, I would simply suggest, again, that the most fruitful way to think about their situation—like the situation, indeed, of any subaltern group in the modern world—is to focus on the conflict between impersonal,

---

65. Roseman, *Shelter Care*, 33; Sutherland and Locke, *Twenty Thousand Homeless Men*, 113–22; David Scheyer, "Flop-House"; Dees, Jr., *Flophouse*, 117–20.
66. *Chicago Tribune*, February 22, 1931, April 6, 1933; James Finan, "Don't Give to Beggars," *Forum and Century*, June 1938; Sutherland and Locke, *Twenty Thousand Homeless Men*, 141, 142.
67. Quoted in Kusmer, *Down and Out, On the Road*, 200.
68. Finan, "Don't Give to Beggars"; Sutherland and Locke, *Twenty Thousand Homeless Men*, 134, 135, 139.

fundamentally class-determined institutions and the "messy humanity," resistant and resilient, of the people subjected to them. This "dialectic" of the antihuman confronting the human called forth a variety of responses from the subjugated homeless, not all of them pretty or admirable, but none of them uninteresting. The whole project of herding together carpenters, mechanics, shopkeepers, butchers, railroaders, clerks, farm hands, family men and single men, young men and the elderly, and 50 different nationalities can even be called a fascinating social experiment. Unsurprisingly, in such conditions divisions between the men were the norm, not the exception. White Americans, for example, were sometimes so prejudiced against the foreigners in their midst that their anti-Black racism was all but forgotten in comparison. "I don't talk to the Pollacks [i.e., foreigners]," said one American in 1934. "If there is nine hundred men in here, eight hundred men are Pollacks. I get along with them because I stay away from them." "These damn foreigners," complained another. "Why, they are so ignorant and crude. When you are sitting down, they will cough right in your face." Such hostility, on the other hand, could have a constructive effect: it tended to unify the groups who were its targets, encouraging friendship and intimacy among those with a similar cultural background.[69]

In general, it seems that most shelter men understood who their real "enemies" were: the politicians, the administrators and staffers who lorded it over them, the rich businessmen who they knew ruled the country in their own interests. But, physically separated from these enemies, living in animal proximity to fellow unfortunates whom they neither knew nor liked, they did as workers so often have and directed some of their simmering resentment at "alien" groups in their midst. Thus did the squalor of their surroundings divert and pervert their populist indignation.

***

One last group of homeless men remains to be discussed here, albeit only briefly because of the paucity of sources: those men who lived not in shelters but in parks or shantytowns or on streets secluded from the hustle of capitalist society. These people were truly, literally, outcast, unable or unwilling to conform to expected norms and so subject to the physically manifested judgments—punishments—of authorities and the police.

Throughout the 1930s, some men and women inhabited Loop alleys, parks from South Chicago to the North Side, and police stations, where they were often permitted to sleep for a night or two. In times of crisis, as in 1938, their numbers increased, while declining in the middle years of the decade. But this decline was also due to a factor not always emphasized in scholarship: police repression. It is widely known that Chicago had several shantytowns in the early Depression in its parks and railroad yards; less widely known is that the reason they passed out of existence is simply that authorities destroyed them. The largest of them, the Hooverville in Grant Park, was gone as early

---

69. Weinberg, "The Problem of Unattachment of Shelter House Men," 82–84, Burgess Papers, box 184, folder 1.

as 1932, burned to the ground by the police. "The inhabitants were summarily told to get out," a reporter describes, "and thirty minutes later the 'homes' were in ashes."[70]

Until about 1933, one or two hundred men could be found sleeping in the box cars on Navy Pier every night, but the railroad companies grew so tired of this that they wired and fastened the doors of each car shut. The sidewalks, hot air vents, and loading platforms underneath Wacker Drive, likewise, were cleared of homeless men—but not definitively until late 1935, when police were ordered to drive all would-be sleepers away. Around the same time, the police undertook to keep alleys in the Loop clear of sleepers, who were arrested and booked on disorderly conduct charges.

Living in the open air, begging or scavenging or doing odd jobs for food, not having to worry about rent or the other quotidian responsibilities that grind one down year after year, was an existence relatively congenial to many men, even Chicago residents middle-aged or older. They preferred to live outside by their wits rather than be confined to a shelter with its regimentation and lack of privacy. A reporter observed that they considered it more self-respecting to beg in the streets and scavenge food from garbage pails than to be subjected to shelter life.[71]

Admittedly, it is unlikely they were as satisfied as they had been, or would have been, living in "jungles" earlier in the decade, before most of them had been eliminated. The hobo jungle should not be romanticized: it was no paradise. But the appreciative way it was described in an internal Communist Party report of 1933 was not unreasonable:

> There is perhaps no place or institution in the entire world where so much real freedom exists as in the Hobo Jungles. Here there is complete freedom from all inhibitions. No language is considered vile or shocking. No dress is considered inappropriate. No one is condemned for his ideas or habits unless they interfere directly with others present. Laziness is not considered a vice and there is more freedom from labor than elsewhere since a little bumming will supply the necessary needs.[72]

Years earlier, an inhabitant of the jungles had written, "here you share and share alike in true fraternal style. [...] Staple foods are always left behind for the common supply." An extreme democracy reigned, and it functioned well: the camp and everything in it, especially kitchen supplies, were kept clean, and infractions of the rules of etiquette were strictly punished (by expulsion, forced labor, or physical punishment). The jungle, in fact, was an anarchist institution, which, as the Communist writer just quoted said,

---

70. Charles R. Walker, "Relief and Revolution," *Forum and Century*, August 1932; Max Stern, "A Study of Some Aspects of Problems Arising in Connection with the Transfer of Local Homeless Residents from the Service Bureau for Men to Home Relief at the Family District Offices," 9, 10, November 9, 1935, Welfare Council Papers, box 233, folder 6.
71. Max Stern, "The Transfer of Single Unemployed Men to Home Relief in Chicago," *Social Service Review* 10, no. 2 (June 1936): 277–87.
72. "Problem of the Single Unemployed," n.d., Communist Party files, Tamiment Library, microfilm reel 258, #96.

would likely have flourished and expanded had it not been regularly raided and ultimately destroyed by police.[73]

The homeless who lived outside any institutional context did not experience such a mature and organized anarchism, but at least they were free from the despotic regime of the public shelter. Unfortunately, they remained subject to the regime of the broader society, which harassed them and chased them from the visible and comfortable spots in the city. In this respect, they could identify with their fellow outcasts the shelter men, and more broadly with the multitudes too poor to buy social influence, rich only in that mysterious human quality: resilience.

---

73. Kusmer, *Down and Out*, 136; Anderson, *The Hobo*, 19, 21. Anarchy, of course, means simply freedom and democracy (antihierarchy, antiauthoritarianism, etc.). See Peter Marshall, *Demanding the Impossible: A History of Anarchism* (Oakland, CA: PM Press, 2010) and Daniel Guérin, ed., *No Gods, No Masters: An Anthology of Anarchism* (San Francisco, CA: AK Press, 1998).

Chapter Five

RELIEF, PART II: GOVERNMENTS, UNIONS, AND CHURCHES

Two central conflicts broadly determined the quality and quantity of relief for Chicago's unemployed in the 1930s: the class conflict and the political conflict between Cook County and all other Illinois counties (usually referred to as downstate counties). The class conflict, as usual, was by far the more significant one, being largely responsible, at least indirectly, even for the insufficiency of the federal government's aid for relief, but the fierce rivalry between Cook County and downstate counties bore much responsibility for Chicago's many relief crises. Rural counties did not want to pay to relieve Chicago's unemployed, so they regularly lobbied and voted against the city's interests in the state legislature. But the city did not want to pay for its poor either. So in the battle between Cook County and the rest of the state, it was the unemployed who suffered.

This chapter has two purposes: first, to tell the sordid tale of local and state governments' neglect of the poor, as manifested in their meager financing of relief; second, to contrast this miserable record with the more generous one of many unions and churches, which because of their social missions could not act so callously toward the jobless. The section on government in particular supports the Marxian conception of the state as being heavily dominated by the ruling class in its struggle to amass and maintain as much power and wealth as possible.[1] Inasmuch as the disaffected poor tended to share this Marxian attitude, the analysis supports the argument that the supposed cynicism, "apathy," resignation, and diffuse resentment of many of the long-term unemployed were based on a quite rational understanding of the world. Of course, to some very limited extent, the state is capable of neutrality in adjudicating between the poor and the rich, and through popular movements it can be forced to heed certain demands of

---

1. For a non-Marxian account that supports this conception, see G. William Domhoff and Michael J. Webber, *Class and Power in the New Deal: Corporate Moderates, Southern Democrats, and the Liberal-Labor Coalition* (Stanford, CA: Stanford University Press, 2011). The work of the political scientist Thomas Ferguson is equally apt. See, for example, Thomas Ferguson, *Golden Rule: The Investment Theory of Party Competition and the Logic of Money-Driven Political Systems* (Chicago, IL: University of Chicago Press, 1995) and Thomas Ferguson and Joel Rogers, *Right Turn: The Decline of the Democrats and the Future of American Politics* (New York: Hill and Wang, 1986). For an introduction to Marxian accounts of the state, see Clyde W. Barrow, *Critical Theories of the State: Marxist, Neo-Marxist, Post-Marxist* (Madison, WI: University of Wisconsin Press, 1993).

the lower orders. This fact, too, many of the poor understood, as by the millions they pressured government at the local, state, and federal levels to move to the left.

The accounts in this and the following chapter support the analysis given by Frances Fox Piven and Richard A. Cloward in their classic *Regulating the Poor* (1971). As they say,

> The key to an understanding of relief-giving is in the functions it serves for the larger political and economic order, for relief is a secondary and supportive institution. [...] We shall argue that expansive relief policies are designed to mute civil disorder, and restrictive ones to reinforce work norms. In other words, relief policies are cyclical—liberal or restrictive depending on the problems of regulation in the larger society with which government must contend.[2]

We might, however, qualify their argument by noting that relief policies can be expansive and restrictive at the same time, in different respects. And they can never get *too* expansive, for the need to discipline the labor force always remains. Thus, as civil unrest exploded across Illinois from 1930 to 1932, the relief policies and financing of townships, counties, and eventually the state slowly grew more expansive, while yet remaining extremely restrictive relative to the need that existed. In the summer of 1932, the federal government, finally acknowledging the necessity of providing funds to subsidize states' relief efforts, broadened the mandate of the recently created Reconstruction

---

2. Frances Fox Piven and Richard A. Cloward, *Regulating the Poor: The Functions of Public Welfare* (New York: Vintage Books, 1971), xiii. (For discussions of work relief that are broadly consistent with Piven and Cloward's ideas, see William W. Bremer, "Along the 'American Way': The New Deal's Work Relief Programs for the Unemployed," *Journal of American History* 62, no. 3 (December 1975): 636–52, and Chad Alan Goldberg, "Contesting the Status of Relief Workers during the New Deal: The Workers Alliance of America and the Works Progress Administration, 1935–1941," *Social Science History* 29, no. 3 (Fall 2005): 337–71.) Piven and Cloward's arguments have been criticized and debated at great length in many publications since the 1970s. Examples include James Overton, "Public Relief and Social Unrest in Newfoundland in the 1930s: An Evaluation of the Ideas of Piven and Cloward," *Canadian Journal of Sociology* 13, no. 1/2 (Winter–Spring 1988): 143–69; Alexander Hicks and Duane H. Swank, "Civil Disorder, Relief Mobilization, and AFDC Caseloads: A Reexamination of the Piven and Cloward Thesis," *American Journal of Political Science* 27, no. 4 (November 1983): 695–716; Robert B. Albritton, "Social Amelioration through Mass Insurgency? A Reexamination of the Piven and Cloward Thesis," *American Political Science Review* 73, no. 4 (December 1979): 1003–11 (and see the response on pages 112–19); Steve Valocchi, "The Unemployed Workers Movement of the 1930s: A Reexamination of the Piven and Cloward Thesis," *Social Problems* 37, no. 2 (May 1990): 191–205. I cannot settle the debate here, but it is worth noting that prima facie, at least, "the Piven and Cloward thesis" is extremely plausible. Political elites are often apt to give concessions to the masses if pressured sufficiently—including outside of any electoral context—and they are apt to withdraw concessions if they think they can get away with it. "Power concedes nothing without a demand," Frederick Douglass observed. "Find out just what any people will quietly submit to and you have found out the exact measure of injustice and wrong which will be imposed upon them, and those will continue till they are resisted with either words or blows, or with both." From such reasoning as this, it isn't long before one arrives at Piven and Cloward's theses.

Finance Corporation so it could give loans for this purpose. With the initiation of federal involvement, Illinois could continue its niggardly record as regards relief financing without inviting the charge that it was permitting thousands of families to literally starve to death (for the RFC's funds prevented that from happening). Federal relief policies became more expansive with the onset of FERA and then the Civil Works Administration in 1933, while the governments of Illinois and Chicago stayed committed to restrictive policies, preferring to let the national administration be responsible for "muting civil disorder" as the state and city did what they could, in effect, to "reinforce work norms." In retrospect, one can see it was a delicate balancing act that all three levels of government were engaged in: public relief had to be tremendously expanded but not *too* much, lest class structures be upset and the working class become undisciplined.

Once the emergency of civil unrest in the early Depression had subsided, the federal government could abandon its unwonted generosity in the sphere of direct relief and let responsibility for it devolve back to states and localities. This meant that the enforcing of work norms—by keeping public assistance at low levels—would again be the main function of relief. On the federal level, a relatively expansive policy did continue in the form of the Social Security Act and the WPA, but the conservatism and restrictiveness of these measures—even the WPA at its peak aided (with low wages) only about a quarter of the jobless[3]—indicated that their purpose was just as much to reinforce work norms as to prevent and mitigate civil disorder. And so the decade limped to its end in an ever more conservative political environment, the disciplining of the labor force taking greater prominence as a purpose of both direct relief and federal work relief.

It is true that most politicians and officials did not interpret relief in such terms, as being determined by the exigencies of class struggle (the struggle of the rich to control the poor, in the context of the poor's struggles for greater power and dignity). They did not usually see themselves as public servants of the business class. The large majority, surely, were convinced that they were motivated solely by considerations of the general welfare and that regulation of the poor had nothing to do with it. This fact, however, is not an argument against Piven and Cloward's (or my) Marxian interpretation of relief. The self-interpretations and self-reports of institutional actors are highly unreliable guides to the significance of particular political phenomena, for people are expert at deceiving themselves, at embracing high-minded but superficial rationalizations. This is one of the lessons of Marxism, namely that one discovers the broad significance of a phenomenon through institutional analysis, not through analysis of rhetoric or politicians' professed intentions.[4] It is *institutions* that are the main actors here, not individuals

---

3. Piven and Cloward, *Poor People's Movements: Why They Succeed, How They Fail* (New York: Vintage Books, 1979), 83.
4. For an illustration of the anti-Marxian, idealistic method, see, for example, Odd Arne Westad, *The Global Cold War: Third World Interventions and the Making of Our Times* (New York: Cambridge University Press, 2005), which won the Bancroft Prize in 2006. Westad argues, implausibly, that "the United States and the Soviet Union were driven to intervene in the Third World by the *ideologies* inherent in their politics" (my italics), rather than by economic and strategic considerations of power. For instance, after quoting a State Department spokesman on the

somehow isolated from an institutional context—a context that, in fact, structures their actions and determines political possibilities. One might even say, therefore—what I am, in part, arguing in this book—that members of a working class that is typically cynical and suspicious of the motives of the rich and powerful have (to that degree) more honest insight into the workings of society, and are less indoctrinated, than most people who belong to powerful or prestigious status groups that are convinced of their own benignity.[5]

Thus, while it is not hard to find examples of public figures in the early Depression expressing dismay at the thought of widespread suffering and insisting that such suffering alone necessitated huge expansions of relief, this fact is of little interest or importance.

---

reasons for George W. Bush's invasion of Iraq in 2003, Westad states ingenuously that "freedom and security have been, and remain today, the driving forces of U.S. foreign policy" (p. 405), apparently unaware of the countless instances from 1898 to the present of U.S. suppression of freedom and "security" abroad. (See William Blum, *Killing Hope: U.S. Military and CIA Interventions since World War II* (Monroe, ME: Common Courage Press, 2004); David F. Schmitz, *Thank God They're on Our Side: The United States and Right-Wing Dictatorships, 1921–1965* (Chapel Hill, NC: University of North Carolina Press, 1999); Stephen G. Rabe, *The Killing Zone: The United States Wages Cold War in Latin America* (New York: Oxford University Press, 2012).) The intellectual superficiality of idealism is patent. (See my paper "The Significance and Shortcomings of Karl Marx," *Class, Race and Corporate Power* 6, no. 2 (2018). It is rather embarrassing that nearly two centuries after Marx's *The German Ideology*, idealism continues to dominate intellectual culture. But this fact is hardly surprising, given the utility of idealism to the powerful.)

5. Students of U.S. imperialism are especially familiar with the reality of self-deception and hypocrisy among policymakers. To take an example at random, Gillian McGillivray espouses a refreshing realism about U.S. motives in invading Latin American countries dozens of times in the twentieth century when she argues,

> The most common characteristic of these interventions (beginning with Cuba [in 1898]) was the U.S. administrations' need to portray them as motivated by humanitarian generosity when what really drove them was U.S. capitalists' desire for new markets. By the late nineteenth century, many U.S. industrialists were ready to export goods, to import and process primary resources, or to set up export industries abroad. [...] Within this framework, one can understand the contradiction between what U.S. politicians said they were doing and what they actually did in Cuba and the rest of Latin America. The hypocrisy began with the myth that U.S. forces invaded Cuba to help the Cubans win freedom from Spain. The actual goal was to preclude a social and racial revolution ("another Haiti") and to create a new, dependent, and politically moderate Cuba safe for U.S. capital.

Gillian McGillivray, *Blazing Cane: Sugar Communities, Class, and State Formation in Cuba, 1868–1959* (Durham, NC: Duke University Press, 2009), 67, 68. See also, among many others, Noam Chomsky, *Hegemony or Survival: America's Quest for Global Dominance* (New York: Henry Holt and Co., 2003); Noam Chomsky, *Deterring Democracy* (New York: Hill and Wang, 1991); Walter LaFeber, *The New Empire: An Interpretation of American Expansion, 1860–1898* (Ithaca, NY: Cornell University Press, 1963); Walter LaFeber, *Inevitable Revolutions: The United States in Central America* (New York: W. W. Norton, 1993); Gabriel Kolko, *Confronting the Third World: United States Foreign Policy, 1945–1980* (New York: Pantheon, 1988). It is economic interest and power that makes the world go round.

RELIEF, PART II: GOVERNMENTS, UNIONS, AND CHURCHES

We should not conclude from it—as, for instance, the historian Jeff Singleton does—that "the large emergency relief organizations created in the early winter of 1931–1932 do not seem to have been a response to demanding workers [as Piven and Cloward argue] but were produced by a genuine desire to 'prevent starvation.'"[6] Doubtless many officials did have such a genuine desire. The question, however, is whether political and business leaders around the country would have made such a clamor for expansion of relief had the suffering masses remained quietly in their homes, relatively out of sight and out of trouble, or been content to write polite letters to the editor from time to time. If localities and states had not been threatened by multiple types of breakdown—social, political, and financial—it is unlikely that hundreds of representatives of powerful institutions would have pleaded with Congress and Herbert Hoover for federal aid to states (especially considering their earlier abhorrence of that idea). The prospect of mass starvation was useful in lending moral weight to their entreaties, but fundamentally it was threats to institutional stability and the class structure on which it was based that, by mid-1932, provoked a nationwide wave of elite support for federal aid. And it was the perceived disappearance of those threats a few years later that caused such support to recede.

The section on unions is much shorter than the one on government, in part because it is less central to the broader points I want to make in the book. But I'll return to the subject of unionists' radicalism in the following chapter, particularly in the context of their support for the extraordinary Workers' Unemployment and Social Insurance Bill that Representative Ernest Lundeen, of the Minnesota Farmer-Labor Party, introduced in Congress in 1934 and 1935. In this chapter I simply sketch some of unions' responses to mass unemployment and briefly make the not very controversial argument that rank-and-file members of AFL unions tended to be more radical than the higher officials of Internationals, state and local federations, and the national office. I also touch upon the CIO's response to unemployment, which was much more activist than the AFL's.

The section on churches differs from the previous two in that it discusses the unemployed themselves in addition to institutions. What effect did joblessness have on religious attitudes? In what ways did people interact with churches? My emphasis is on the relative generosity and left-wing character of the attitudes that much of the religious community displayed. This emphasis supports the general argument being made that the hegemony of capitalist ideologies, including the belief in the legitimacy of the social order and its ruling authorities, is not necessarily as complete as we may be accustomed to thinking. Wherever there is altruism, compassion, commitment to the principle that every life has dignity, or awareness of the reality of acute conflict between social classes and valorization of the lower class's interests, there is implicit or explicit resistance to the values that guide the dominant institutions of a modern capitalist society, which are demonstrably grounded in the anti-Kantian principle of treating people as means to the

---

6. Jeff Singleton, *The American Dole: Unemployment Relief and the Welfare State in the Great Depression* (Westport, CT: Greenwood Press, 2000), 80. Anthony Badger agrees with this contention when he argues that the evidence does not "support the argument that the New Deal welfare measures were designed to ward off the threat of disorder by the unemployed and the poor." Badger, *The New Deal: The Depression Years, 1933–40* (New York: Hill and Wang, 1989), 302.

end of one's own profit-making and power-accumulating. In the case of churches in the 1930s, this tear in the fabric of "bourgeois hegemony" was quite large.

In fact, the description I give of the lower-income Black church culture permits me to argue that, perhaps paradoxically, one of the central "meanings" of lower-class religion in this era was a type of diverted class struggle. As in the case of other examples of class struggle described in this book, it is not typically *understood* in this way even by the participants. Nevertheless, it is not difficult to discern tendencies that lend themselves to such an interpretation. In certain social contexts, the tendencies blossom into fully fledged struggle between poor and rich, oppressed and oppressors: the case of liberation theology in Latin America between the 1960s and 1980s may be the most obvious example, but aspects of the United States' Civil Rights Movement are another, as are features of the Protestant Reformation itself, and of the very birth of Christianity among the poor and outcast of the Roman Empire.[7] When people of limited means come together to empower themselves, even if not in a directly or explicitly political way, there is reason for the dominant class to be wary. Fortunately for this class, religious institutions are usually integrated into mainstream society and do not pose much of a threat. If they did, they would certainly not be tolerated for long.[8] But the cooperative, compassionate ethic they often preach, and the communitarian essence of many of their institutional practices, should not be seen only as some politically anodyne complement to the Hobbesian market. These tendencies are potentially subversive and must

---

7. See, for example, Christopher Rowland, ed., *The Cambridge Companion to Liberation Theology* (Cambridge: Cambridge University Press, 2007); Charles M. Payne, *I've Got the Light of Freedom* (Los Angeles, CA: University of California Press, 1995); David L. Chappell, *A Stone of Hope: Prophetic Religion and the Death of Jim Crow* (Chapel Hill, NC: University of North Carolina Press, 2004); Robert Craig, *Religion and Radical Politics: An Alternative Christian Tradition in the United States* (Philadelphia, PA: Temple University Press, 1992); Jarod Roll, *Spirit of Rebellion: Labor and Religion in the New Cotton South* (Chicago, IL: University of Illinois Press, 2010); S. G. F. Brandon, *Jesus and the Zealots: A Study of the Political Factor in Primitive Christianity* (Manchester: University Press, 1967); Karl Kautsky, *Communism in Central Europe at the Time of the Reformation* (New York: Russell & Russell, 1959); Karl Kautsky, *Foundations of Christianity: A Study in Christian Origins* (New York: International Publishers, 1925). For a seminal analysis of radicalism in the Black religious tradition, see Gayraud S. Wilmore, *Black Religion and Black Radicalism: An Interpretation of the Religious History of African Americans* (Maryknoll, NY: Orbis Books, 1998). More generally, the historian Matthew Pehl is right that "neither American religious historians nor labor historians have adequately addressed the influence of social class on religious culture." Since class is the primary factor in shaping institutions and the social outlooks of particular groups (for class position broadly determines access to resources, the nature of one's social environment, many of one's values and goals, the conflicts that arise between elite and nonelite groups, etc.), to overlook it or downplay it in the context of religion is absurd. Matthew Pehl, "The Remaking of the Catholic Working Class: Detroit, 1919–1945," *Religion and American Culture: A Journal of Interpretation* 19, no. 1 (Winter 2009): 38.
8. This claim might seem contentious or in need of argument, but it is in fact mere truism. It should hardly be controversial that the dominant class opposes threats to its power. This is why, for instance, business opposes unions. If churches explicitly threatened capitalist power, they would be treated as harshly as unions.

not be permitted to become overtly political or to spread into the broader arena of social and economic relations.

Thus, the first half of the chapter describes the political economy of capitalist atomization, while the second half describes two manifestations of the political economy of solidarity or community. In the following chapter, we'll discuss the clash between the two, in which the poor rose up against the rich.

Money and Politics

It is easy to think that the reason relief was so inadequate in the 1930s is that it was, after all, the Depression. Money was not abundant. In reality, the country had plenty of wealth that it could have spent on the poor, including in the years of greatest crisis. For, of course—among other possibilities on the state level—the federal government *could* have distributed, for the purpose of relief, billions of dollars to individuals, municipalities, and states even in 1932. And it could have afforded to spend many billions more than it did on the WPA from 1935 on. Some members of Congress advocated such policies, as when Senator Robert Wagner sponsored a bill in March 1932 calling for a $1.1 billion public works program to be financed through a bond issue, or when a couple of months later Senator Edward Costigan sponsored a bill permitting a grant of $500 million to states. Hoover and his supporters defeated these and similar measures, unwilling to countenance an unbalanced budget. It is not irrelevant to note that Hoover was utterly in thrall to big banks (which opposed deficit financing), so in thrall that he deliberately faked entries in a "diary" he left historians so as to paint himself as more independent of bankers than he was.[9] Consistent with this orientation, the Reconstruction Finance Corporation was originally created (in January 1932) to lend $2 billion to banks, railroads, insurance companies, building and loan associations, and so on, thus initiating a long tradition of the federal government's bailing out the financial sector when things went awry. The unemployed and the poor got nothing. It was hoped that the RFC's loans would end bank failures, relieve liquidity fears, and allow banks to start lending to businesses again, which would permit them to resume investing on a large scale and so end the crisis. That is, wealth would "trickle down" from banks to industrial firms to employees (the currently unemployed). Needless to say, this did not happen. The bankers who received loans "betrayed" Hoover—as he saw it—by not expanding lending but building up their reserves in case of another liquidity crisis. And so, while the RFC did temporarily stabilize the financial system, industry did not recover.[10]

It was at this point, in the summer of 1932, that Hoover finally relented on the principle of giving loans to states for unemployment relief. The nationwide pressure had become unendurable: constant hunger marches; the beginning of the Bonus March

---

9. Thomas Ferguson, *Golden Rule*, 145.
10. James Stuart Olson, *Herbert Hoover and the Reconstruction Finance Corporation, 1931–1933* (Ames, IA: Iowa State University Press, 1977), 33–39, 56–58, 66; *Barron's*, January 18, 1932; *Chicago Tribune*, July 31, 1932. See also Vincent Gaddis, *Herbert Hoover, Unemployment, and the Public Sphere: A Conceptual History, 1919–1933* (New York: University Press of America, 2005), 107–26.

on Washington (and the organizing of bonus protests in major cities); continual public revelations of mass suffering and social disorder; the impending collapse of relief in Chicago and other cities; intense lobbying by governors, mayors, and businessmen; and considerations of politics in an election year were, in the aggregate, apparently enough to convince Hoover that he should do something. So, after further higgling and haggling with liberal Congressmen, and despite his obsessive fear of anything resembling a national "dole," he signed a bill among whose provisions was that the RFC could lend $300 million to states for direct relief.[11]

And yet even then, this absurdly insufficient amount trickled out to states very slowly, in part because of the stringent conditions a state had to meet (and the vast amount of paperwork it had to submit—every month, for a new loan) before it could receive even a few million dollars. For example, in July 1932, Governor Pinchot of Pennsylvania—a state in desperate straits—applied for a loan of $45 million but was granted nothing, because supposedly the state had not tapped all of its own resources yet. Pinchot tried again in August, arguing that Pennsylvania's good faith had been demonstrated by the General Assembly's recent passage of a $12 million relief bill. Again his request was denied: the state had to do still more before it could get some of the RFC's money. Incensed, Pinchot—a Republican—went public with his disgust, adding his voice to the nationwide chorus of attacks on the RFC for being nothing but a dole to the wealthy. He made a personal appeal to Hoover, asking him to cut the red tape and approve the loan. At last, in late September, the RFC acted: it gave Pennsylvania $2.5 million, which was little better than an insult. Struck by the contrast between the ease and speed with which the RFC had given corporations almost $2 billion and the incredible stinginess with which it approached loans for the purpose of unemployment relief, Pinchot wrote a scathing and well-publicized letter to the head of the RFC, in which he charged that "in giving help to the great banks, great railroads, and great corporations you have shown no such niggardly spirit. [...] [O]ur people have little patience with giving everything possible to the big fellow and as little as possible to the little fellow." Coming from a Republican, this letter did Hoover no favors in the presidential election six weeks later.[12]

Pinchot, incidentally, had distinguished himself months earlier in his willingness to expose all the politicians' cant about America's glorious traditions of rugged individualism, self-reliance, local initiative, neighbor helping neighbor, and the irreparable damage to the national character that would result from federal relief. In an article in January 1932 for the important liberal journal *Survey*, he concluded that the real reason for mainstream opposition to federal relief was "the safeguarding of money in the hands of an incredibly small number of incredibly rich men," a conclusion he backed up with detailed analysis of the polarized economic structure that the 1920s had produced. "The force behind the stubborn opposition to federal relief," he insisted, "is fear lest the taxation to provide that relief be levied on concentrated wealth—fear lest the policy of

---

11. Olson, *Herbert Hoover and the Reconstruction Finance Corporation*, 65–67.
12. Ibid., 80–84; Arthur P. Miles, *Federal Aid and Public Assistance in Illinois* (Chicago, IL: University of Chicago Press, 1941), 25, 26.

years, the policy of shielding big fortunes at the expense of the little ones, should at long last be tossed into the discard." Local, and even state, relief usually meant making the relatively poor pay, as we'll see momentarily, and so was the preferred policy until it was no longer sustainable.[13]

These points would be too obvious to make were it not that historians have tended to focus on policymakers' ideological motivations of localism, voluntarism, and individualism at the expense of the far more important class dynamics out of which such ideologies emerged.

Let us turn now to the state and local levels, which are our main concern. As one historian pointedly states, "the depression years were by no means progressive in the history of state finance." It was in these years that states discovered the sales tax and came to rely on it (together with taxes on alcohol, tobacco, gasoline, and soft drinks) for the majority of their revenue. By 1937, 28 states had a sales tax (and it had been repealed or declared unconstitutional in five other states), up from zero states in 1931. The incredible lucrativeness of consumer taxes accounts for the striking fact that at the end of the Depression decade, states were in a much stronger financial position than at the end of the 1920s, some even showing budget surpluses. "Despite poor economic conditions, states almost doubled their revenues, collecting $2.1 billion from all sources in 1930 and $4.1 billion in 1940." Most states, therefore, could not plead poverty as an excuse for underfunding unemployment relief.[14]

Illinois was an enthusiastic participant in the regressive fiscal trends of these years, by 1938 raising 80 percent of its revenue from four taxes that disproportionately affected the middle and lower classes: a gasoline tax, a motor vehicle registration fee, taxes on alcoholic beverages, and a sales tax. The latter alone, dating from July 1933, provided 43 percent of the state's revenue, a higher proportion than in any other state except West Virginia. On the other hand, while Illinois had a higher percentage of people earning over $5,000 than the United States as a whole, it had no income tax at all, a distinction shared by only 11 other states. (The Illinois Supreme Court had ruled unconstitutional a proposed income tax in 1932.) Nor did it have a state property tax after 1932, since the new sales tax was thought to have made it unnecessary. Cook County and Chicago levied property taxes, but tax delinquency there was "so bad that it is almost impossible to comprehend," an analyst wrote in 1938. "Cook County, Illinois," he declared, "stands out as the only area in the United States where the payment of real estate taxes is more or less a voluntary matter." Such facts as these indicate the degree to which the propertied, in particular those of considerable wealth, were able to mitigate their tax burden in these years.[15]

---

13. Gifford Pinchot, "The Case for Federal Relief," *Survey Graphic*, January 1, 1932.
14. James T. Patterson, *The New Deal and the States: Federalism in Transition* (Princeton, NJ: Princeton University Press, 1969), 97–99.
15. Carl H. Chatters, "Who Pays for Social Services?," in *Social Service Year Book, 1938*, 1–13; Daniel Scheinman, "Financing Unemployment Relief, 1930–38," in *State-Local Fiscal Relations in Illinois*, ed. Simon E. Leland (Chicago, IL: University of Chicago Press, 1941), 186; *Washington Post*, August 3, 1934, December 20, 1935.

Credit for this achievement was due in no small part to organizations like the Civic Federation of Chicago, which was dedicated to safeguarding the taxpayer's purse, especially the businessman's purse. Throughout the decade, it, together with the Better Government Association, the Chicago Association of Commerce, the Illinois Manufacturers' Association, and other such groups, fought against and often defeated such measures as Old Age Assistance, "prevailing rate of wage" laws for public works projects, increased taxes to support Chicago schools, increased assistance for the blind, bond issues for expansions of the overcrowded Cook County Hospital and Oak Forest Infirmary, and additional taxes for poor relief in Cook County and Chicago. Whenever a new tax on property was proposed on the city, county, or state level, the Civic Federation was there to evaluate it and, in all likelihood, lobby against it. Thus, when we read of the hardships of Chicago's poor in the late 1930s, we should not think this state of affairs was something that just happened, an unfortunate product of the Depression and of the complex and inadequate machinery for poor relief that had evolved in Illinois. It was the product of particular policies advocated by particular interests (in addition, of course, to the very structure of Chicago's political economy).[16]

To give another example, the powerful Chicago Real Estate Board was always on hand to press for "drastic economies" in relief administration. In early 1934, for instance, when it looked as though a bond issue would not be sufficient to finance relief for the whole year (as indeed it was not), the president of the Real Estate Board warned the governor that "any attempt to increase taxes on property for emergency relief purposes [...] would certainly meet our most determined opposition. Prompt and determined action must be taken immediately," he admonished, "or all savings to taxpayers, through reduction in public expenditures and through your action in using the proceeds of the sales tax to cover the state budget, will be offset and stultified by the emergency relief and its requirements." He went on to decry the "stubborn opposition" among relief administrators to reducing the number of their employees—a reduction, incidentally, that would have meant disaster, since when the Civil Works Administration ended a month later the relief rolls expanded enormously. But such were the forces that heavily influenced policy.[17]

Early in the Depression, the relief policy that the dominant interests favored was, as ever, voluntarist and privatized. Fundraising drives were organized, and private family welfare agencies were supposed to take the initiative in caring for the unemployed. These sorts of antigovernment dogmas, in fact, were already outdated by the 1920s, for in 1929 the Bureau of Social Statistics had unearthed the striking fact that in the previous year 72 percent of all relief (including mothers' aid, assistance to the blind, etc.) in 15 important cities was from *public*, not private, funds. Nevertheless, when the economic whirlwind struck it was largely up to Chicago's five major private agencies—the United Charities, the Jewish Social Service Bureau, the Catholic Central Charity Bureau,

---

16. Bulletins 123, 126, 127, 137, 147, 161-A, 169-A, Civic Federation of Chicago Papers, UIC Special Collections, box 1, folders 7–9.
17. *Chicago Tribune*, February 25, 1934.

the American Red Cross, and the Salvation Army—to aid the stricken, although hundreds of churches, fraternal organizations, settlement houses, clubs, unions, local relief committees, and schools played in the aggregate an important role as well. The Cook County Bureau of Public Welfare took on many cases, but by 1931 the shares of public and private agencies in total relief activities were the exact inverse of their relative positions in 1928: whereas in that year the public burden of relief was 64 percent and the private burden 36 percent, the opposite was the case in 1931 (36 percent public, 64 percent private).[18]

The only way private agencies were able to so expand their caseload was through state-assisted fundraising. For the first couple of years of the Depression, ad hoc organizations like the Governor's Commission on Unemployment and Relief and the Joint Emergency Relief Fund of Cook County were able to raise some money, though not nearly enough to meet the need. It was primarily the lower middle class that contributed, sometimes in the form of voluntary or involuntary "gifts" that corporations and the state government deducted from the pay of employees.[19]

While the business class could have donated far more than it did (which, by some accounts, was next to nothing), more than enough to solve the relief crisis of the winter of 1931–32, it is true that the Chicago government was not in a position to be of much use. As mentioned in an earlier chapter, even before the Depression hit it was stuck in a fiscal morass due to the profligacy of Mayor "Big Bill" Thompson's administration, excessive political corruption and waste, a drawn-out property reassessment that interfered with tax collection, a tax strike by real estate owners, and in general the inadequate municipal fiscal powers that a hostile state legislature had imposed on Chicago (including debt and tax limits and hundreds of regulations regarding the minutiae of budget matters). Nor was the legislature cooperative in solving the mess it had helped create. As a result, the new mayor Anton Cermak was effectively a captive of bankers and industrialists, whose money he needed in order to keep the city running. "He conducted the business of the municipality," a reporter acidly observed, "not in the council chamber of the City Hall, but in the comfortable quarters of the Chicago and Union League clubs," where the bankers and their friends congregated. As a condition for their loans they demanded Cermak follow a program of ruthless austerity, precisely the opposite of what the relief crisis called for. Thus, during his brief tenure as mayor—he was assassinated in March 1933—Cermak spent most of his time shuttling back and forth between the real centers of power so as to plead for help: business communities in Chicago and New York, the state legislature in Springfield, and Congress, for federal aid.[20]

---

18. Josephine Chapin Brown, *Public Relief, 1929–1939* (New York: Octagon Books, 1971 [1940]), 55; Clorinne McCulloch Brandenburg, "Chicago Relief and Service Statistics, 1928–1931" (MA thesis, University of Chicago, 1932), 39.
19. Brandenburg, "Chicago Relief," 14–16, 20, 21; Brown, *Public Relief*, 72; Mauritz Hallgren, *Seeds of Revolt* (New York: Alfred A. Knopf, 1933), 123, 133.
20. Alex Gottfried, *Boss Cermak of Chicago: A Study of Political Leadership* (Seattle, WA: University of Washington Press, 1962), 247–55; Dwayne Charles Cole, "The Relief Crisis in Illinois

It was in the winter of 1931–32 that Chicago's relief crisis became a climactic emergency, forcing the state legislature to act. This body, dominated by downstate counties, had distinguished itself both for its callousness to the suffering of the unemployed—in 1931 it passed not a single major piece of legislation to alleviate misery in the state—and for its refusal even to reform Cook County's anarchic and archaic tax machinery. The governor called a special legislative session in November 1931 to address these matters, during which bill after bill was introduced to provide state financing for relief. None passed, despite the tremendous pressure coming from public officials and the press in Chicago, where the issue was most urgent. Pleas for action from the Governor's Commission and the Chicago Church Federation were read before the General Assembly, to no effect. By mid-December, the $10 million raised by the Joint Emergency Relief Fund that fall was already approaching exhaustion, and it appeared that relief stations would soon have to close—even as the ranks of the jobless were continuously swelling. There was literally no other recourse but state funding. Nevertheless, having accomplished nothing, the General Assembly adjourned from mid-December until early January. After it reconvened, another bill was introduced, which passed the Senate but died in the House. Incredibly, after this failure, "interest of the General Assembly in the relief problem subsided again," to quote an informed observer. Instead, the legislature finally enacted the long-delayed public finance reform of Cook County and Chicago—after which, again, it adjourned, until early February. "Relief funds in Chicago were only ten days from exhaustion as the state's lawmakers, on whom all hope was pinned, voted themselves a vacation and went home."[21]

For the politically active members of Chicago's elite, who understood the enormity of the crisis, this adjournment in January was the last straw. A few bankers, newspaper editors, relief officials, leaders of the General Assembly, and the governor met in a hotel and, over a few hours, worked out the legislative program that they planned to browbeat the lawmakers into approving. Members of the Assembly were telegraphed to return to Springfield earlier than they had intended. Meanwhile, prominent figures were publicly uttering apocalyptic pronouncements, as when Mayor Cermak spoke of the newly worked out legislation as follows:

> This is civic fire insurance. These communist organizers are not new in our city. We had them in times of plenty. But now they find men more ready to listen to them. I say to the men who may object to this public relief because it will add to the tax burden on their property, that they should be glad to pay it, for it is the best way of insuring that they keep that property.[22]

---

during the Depression, 1930–1940" (PhD diss., St. Louis University, 1973), 4–15; Hallgren, *Seeds of Revolt*, 118–27.

21. Frank Z. Glick, *The Illinois Emergency Relief Commission* (Chicago, IL: University of Chicago Press, 1940), 16–26; Robert Asher, "The Influence of the Chicago Workers' Committee on Unemployment upon the Administration of Relief: 1931–1934" (MA thesis, University of Chicago, 1934), 10.
22. *Chicago Tribune*, January 25, 1932.

RELIEF, PART II: GOVERNMENTS, UNIONS, AND CHURCHES   147

Still the downstate legislators were wary. As the legislation was designed, there was a chance—depending on the outcome of a bond referendum—that the state property tax would be raised in order to pay for the $20 million that was to be allocated to relief. That is, the downstaters worried they and their constituents might end up footing a large part of Chicago's relief bill. Moreover, some members continued to think Chicago had the wherewithal to take care of its own. With some justice, one senator said that "Chicago was proceeding to raise $400,000 for the opera; Chicago had no difficulty in putting up the $300,000 for the national political convention; Chicago was spending millions on the Century of Progress; therefore, Chicago should stop these projects and devote the money to charity." And so the debates continued for another week. Relief funds ran out, but the stations remained open in the hope that legislative action would be forthcoming.[23]

At long last, it was, in early February 1932. Illinois had thus entered the relief business, the fifth state to do so—under extreme duress. The final act was rather dramatic and is worth summarizing, for it was revealing:

> The first effort to pass the [relief] bills was made in the House and many Chicagoans, including the mayor, were present. When the initial roll call was taken on the first of the bills fifty votes were lacking for the two-thirds majority necessary to pass an emergency (immediately effective) measure. At this point the veteran speaker of the House broke his own policy of not speaking to a measure, and said: "There is grave danger now. The federal government has already issued the orders necessary to curb disorder if it arises. The mayor of Chicago is on the rostrum here and he is undecided whether he should agree to calling out the troops tomorrow morning. The armories are under guard now." On a later roll call the bills passed with many votes to spare.[24]

Humanitarianism was not absent, but more importantly, property was in danger.

The legislative program enacted was quite complicated, consisting of five bills that both established the IERC and outlined a convoluted way of funding relief. The essential point, as usual, was not only to protect property but also to protect downstate counties from paying for Chicago's relief (which was just another way of protecting property, namely that of downstaters). The basic method was to make each county responsible for financing its own relief, by diverting its share of the state gasoline tax from highway expenditures to relief expenditures. (In effect, this also meant shifting the burden of relief from property owners to automobile owners, and so, in proportion to wealth, affecting those in the middle and lower classes more than those in the upper class.) It would be cruel to the reader to summarize here the Rube Goldberg legislation, involving tax anticipation warrants, a bond referendum, gasoline tax rebates, and so on; the important thing is that, for the moment, Chicago's relief crisis abated.[25]

---

23. Glick, *The Illinois Emergency Relief Commission*, 20–26; *Chicago Tribune*, February 2, 1932.
24. Glick, *The IERC*, 26; Brown, *Public Relief*, 89–96.
25. Cole, "The Relief Crisis in Illinois," 37–39; Scheinman, "Financing Unemployment Relief," 183; Glick, *The IERC*, 21–25.

The new IERC insisted that public funds should go to public agencies, so the Cook County Bureau of Public Welfare took over control of the Joint Emergency Relief Service—with its many "district relief stations" around the city—that had been organized by the private agencies to care for all the clients who would not ordinarily fall under their purview (in other words, most of the unemployed). Private agencies could now gradually return to something like their pre-Depression caseload, while cooperating with public authorities and sometimes providing crucial aid, as when the relief stations temporarily shut down because of funding problems. The Council of Social Agencies assumed the enormous task of coordinating activities among all the private and public organizations, some of which were yet to be born.[26]

As it happened, within a few months, the relief stations were in danger of closing again, lacking the funds to continue beyond early June. To induce bankers to buy a few more million dollars' worth of tax anticipation warrants and so keep the stations open another month or two, the Unemployed Councils, the Workers Committee on Unemployment, and relief authorities mobilized in May. Public demonstrations, radio and newspaper publicity, telegrams to politicians, and meetings with the mayor and bankers had the desired effect, and at last dozens of Chicago bankers and industrialists held a meeting to buy the remaining warrants. "In other words," recalls an activist, "the starvation date in Cook County was postponed until about July 25." But on this date, the full $20 million that had been appropriated was already going to be exhausted, and there was little hope that the state legislature would appropriate more funds. So Cermak and others redoubled their efforts to get money from the federal government, and this time, as we have seen, met with success, when a bill authorizing the RFC to lend to states was passed. Illinois received $3 million in late July, having asked for $10 million. In August it asked for $23 million and got $6 million. Less than a month later it asked for $37 million to keep the relief stations open until January, and got $5 million. While paltry, these sums were far more than other states received, even though Philadelphia's relief stations had actually been forced to close for the summer, a tragedy that elicited from the RFC only a self-righteous lecture to Governor Pinchot that he ought to have done more to help the victims. Around the same time, incidentally, the Dawes bank in Chicago received a $90 million loan from the RFC, a fact that infuriated unpaid teachers and the unemployed.[27]

---

26. Edward L. Ryerson, Jr., "Out of the Depression," *Survey*, January 1934, 3–7; William Arthur Hillman, "Urbanization and the Organization of Welfare Activities in the Metropolitan Community of Chicago" (PhD diss., University of Chicago, 1940), 60–62; G. D. Jones, "The Local Political Significance of New Deal Relief Legislation in Chicago: 1933–1940" (PhD diss., Northwestern University, 1970), 22. See also Gene D. L. Jones, "The Chicago Catholic Charities, the Great Depression, and Public Monies," *Illinois Historical Journal* 83, no. 1 (Spring 1990): 13–30.
27. Asher, "The Influence of the Chicago Workers' Committee," 17, 18; Edith Abbott, "The Fallacy of Local Relief," *New Republic*, November 9, 1932; *New York Times*, June 28, September 16, 1932.

Through the terrible winter of 1932–33 it was primarily the RFC's advances of money that allowed relief to continue, albeit on an inadequate basis. Indeed, in October the IERC announced a 50 percent cut in that month's relief rations, which were already based on a subsistence level. Disturbances soon broke out all over Chicago in the vicinity of relief stations, as when a crowd of several hundred unemployed went on "strike" by refusing to accept any aid, instead sitting down in various places on the sidewalk (one of the early uses of a tactic that the CIO would make historic use of several years later). A delegation of hundreds went to the city hall to demand more funds, objecting to a sales tax and proposing instead that the police force be reduced and the money saved be used to feed the jobless. A massive hunger march was to happen at the end of the month, even though a permit was denied. All this pressure evidently worked, for at the end of the month the RFC approved a new loan that would permit a resumption of normal relief rations in November. (The march took place anyway, between 30,000 and 60,000 people tramping in pouring rain through the Loop and into Grant Park, where they cheered speakers exhorting them to fight "the bosses of the capitalist class.")[28]

And so Illinois muddled through that winter and spring, living off the largesse of the RFC. So far the state government had, strictly speaking, provided no funds for relief, only diverting local shares of gasoline tax revenues and authorizing county bond issues. This parsimonious phase ended in March 1933 with the inauguration of a state sales tax—which, however, was promptly declared unconstitutional. (The legislature also passed a law requiring relief applicants to sign a "pauper's oath," a tool of humiliation.) RFC loans were set to last only until the middle of May, and none more would be forthcoming because the agency had reached the end of its financial resources. Once again, however, the federal government acted just in time to avert a major crisis, this time by creating FERA, which proceeded to give monthly grants to Illinois from May 1933 to December 1935. The total of these grants was over $200 million, which constituted about 75 percent of Illinois's relief financing, more than most states even though Illinois was one of the wealthiest.[29]

A new, amended sales tax took effect in July 1933, which went some way toward meeting FERA's demands that Illinois do more to finance its own relief. But Harry Hopkins, the head of FERA, was still not satisfied: the tax provided less money than necessary, and starting in 1934 its revenues would not be available for relief anyway. They would go into the state's general revenue fund, making it possible to do away with the property tax. After Hopkins announced in September that federal funds to Illinois would cease unless the state acted more responsibly, Governor Henry Horner called a special legislative session to authorize a new bond issue. Lawmakers were unsympathetic. "The

---

28. Ryerson, "Out of the Depression," 5; Scheinman, "Financing Unemployment Relief," 184, 185; Glick, *The IERC*, 161–64; Asher, "The Influence of the Chicago Workers' Committee," 20–22; *Chicago Tribune*, October 2, 29, 1932; *Washington Post*, October 20, 1932; *New York Herald Tribune*, November 1, 1932; *New York Times*, November 1, 1932; Frank McCulloch letter to Marcia Beales, June 10, 1979, McCulloch Papers, box 7, folder 1.
29. Scheinman, "Financing Unemployment Relief," 185, 186; James T. Nicholson, "Family Relief and Service," in *Social Service Year Book, 1933*, 3; Glick, *The IERC*, 179–86.

impression here," an observer in Illinois told Hopkins, "is that the federal government is going to do it all—let it." After a month of debate and several attempts at the bill's passage, it was finally necessary to fly in Anna Ickes, wife of Secretary of the Interior Harold Ickes, to cast a vote and so get the bill passed by a one-vote margin. The resultant bond issue was the main (albeit insufficient) source of state funding in 1934.[30]

Through the winter of 1933–34, the Civil Works Administration eased the burden on relief agencies and finances, but after it ended in the spring, relief rolls rose again and required still more expenditures than before. Fortunately, FERA was willing to assume the overwhelming responsibility, even when it had to meet more than 90 percent of Illinois's relief needs. Hopkins informed Horner that this could not go on, that in 1935 the state would have to contribute $3 million per month to its relief administration. Otherwise federal aid would cease. But where to get the money? Horner knew the General Assembly would never consent to another bond issue. For the moment, therefore, he asked legislators to allocate for relief the surplus that had accumulated in the treasury from the sales tax, which they did. But this was going to run out by April 1935, after which it would be necessary to find a more permanent solution. This solution, Horner decided, was to raise the sales tax from 2 percent to 3 percent. But there was a problem: while it would not be hard to get a simple majority of the legislature to pass such a measure, the money would not be available until August, whereas Hopkins had insisted that Illinois should provide its monthly quota of $3 million at once. This meant the bill would have to pass as an emergency measure, which required a two-thirds majority. And so the stage was set for an epic battle between Horner and downstate legislators, especially Republicans.[31]

The intricacies of the battle, which provoked one of Illinois's greatest post-1932 relief crises, need not concern us, but they revolved around a couple of different issues. As usual, there was the bitter complaint that the Chicago-based IERC spent a disproportionate amount on Chicago rather than downstate. This complaint had by now fused with resentment of the whole "centralized" FERA system itself as personified in Hopkins, who was hated for his ostensibly autocratic tendencies and contempt for Illinois's lawmakers. It was felt that the state, particularly its non-Cook County portion, was constantly being dictated to, that it was at the mercy of Hopkins's whims and arbitrary demands, for the monthly $3 million was considered excessive. The legislature even sent a delegation to Washington, D.C., to ask Hopkins how he had arrived at that estimate of the state's fair contribution, but he snubbed it by going on a vacation with Roosevelt the night before it arrived. Such treatment only served to make more vituperative the denunciations that Republican politicians heaped on him, especially after he expressed disapproval of two bills to gut the IERC and return relief functions to the local level. "In my present mood," a representative shouted on the floor of the Illinois

---

30. Cole, "The Relief Crisis in Illinois," 121–36; Glick, *The IERC*, 166–68; Jones, "The Local Political Significance," 51, 52.
31. Scheinman, "Financing Unemployment Relief," 187; Glick, *The IERC*, 76, 177; Cole, "The Relief Crisis in Illinois," 254–62; Jones, "The Local Political Significance," 82–100.

House of Representatives, "I am ready and willing to tell Washington to go to hell. [...] Now is the time to determine whether Illinois is a sovereign state or a puppet creature of the Washington bureaucracy."[32]

Hopkins's demand in 1935 for more state money—a perfectly reasonable demand—was but the spark that ignited a powder keg, for the business class's hostility toward public relief had never abated even in the moments of dire crisis. Relief had only been accepted as a necessary evil then, a very temporary necessary evil. Throughout the decade, a relief administrator noted in retrospect, most Illinois newspapers "both shared and reflected a lack of sympathy for the unemployed en masse. [...] The basic assumption seemed to be that the unemployed by and large were ne'er-do-wells who needed discipline as much as public assistance." Interestingly, when the press mentioned particular cases that had come to its attention it frequently criticized the inhumanity of the relief that had been granted (probably as another way to argue that public relief was necessarily bad), but when it dealt in generalities it returned to the criticism that relief was too generous. The *Tribune* expressed a not uncommon attitude in an editorial in early November 1932, in which it declared that "the recipients of unemployment relief are objects of charity [and thus failures]. [...] It was their duty to support themselves and their families and in addition to help support the common government. For one reason or another they have failed to make the grade." The IERC, as the symbol and administrator of public relief, was the target of the most vicious criticism, being subjected to scurrilous and unsupported attacks charging "thievery, swindling, forgery, and plundering," or "THE VILEST KIND OF RACKET," to quote one headline, or waste of funds on a colossal scale. Grand jury investigations uncovered essentially no wrongdoing by the IERC.[33]

Legislative committees, too, conducted investigations of the Relief Commission, for instance in 1934 and 1937–38. The 1934 investigation culminated in a report that was "a vitriolic criticism and little more," "highly biased and largely misinformed." The investigation three years later, which occurred at a time when the Commission had been stripped of nearly all its former powers, was more legitimate, being concerned with the inadequacies of what was by then a system of relief by local governmental units. Indeed, its final report argued that the IERC should regain supervisory authority over local administration of state funds, because the money was being spent wastefully. Nevertheless, it too was somewhat hostile toward unemployment relief, stating, for

---

32. *Chicago Tribune*, March 7, 20, 27, 1935; *New York Times*, March 24, 1935.
33. Jones, "The Local Political Significance," 79–82; Glick, *The IERC*, 137–44. Even the *Chicago Daily News*, not excessively hostile toward the IERC, was quite hostile toward relief in general. To quote one editorial, "[Relief] is a poison, both psychological and moral, that insidiously tempts its victims to succumb, and then destroys the desire and the spirit of enterprise that should grasp every opportunity for a return to independence" *Chicago Daily News*, July 17, 1934. Such an attitude was very common all over the country, including among New Dealers and even the unemployed themselves, who wanted to work. Its seductive appeal was an indispensable ally in the campaigns of conservatives and the business class to roll back and finally destroy federal- and state-administered relief.

example, that "the effort to extend social service as a state-wide function of poor relief [an effort that had been integral to the FERA system of public relief] is an extravagant result of the successful propaganda of a profession [namely, social work] desiring to establish a permanent field of public employment for themselves." All in all, a knowledgeable commentator concludes, "it is apparent that the first state relief administration in Illinois had little or no support from the legislature which had created it." No surprise, then, that it effectively came to an end (albeit temporarily) in July 1936, as we'll see.[34]

Meanwhile, in April 1935 neither the governor nor the downstate opposition forces would back down in their standoff over the sales tax increase. Horner, backed by Hopkins, demanded it immediately, but the Republicans would not grant it. The matter came to a head at the end of April, when funds ran out. The nearly 10,000 employees of the IERC were cut off the payroll (although many continued working as volunteers) and relief stations in most counties closed, leaving the jobless to fend for themselves. Apparently unaware of the irony, politicians and newspaper editors shrieked that Hopkins was "provoking hunger and perhaps even violence" and showing "insolent indifference toward physical suffering," but he did not budge. Some legislators, on the other hand, were not upset by the developments. "For the first time there has been a tightening of the Illinois Relief Commission's purse strings," said one. "They are being forced to purge their rolls of chiselers [i.e., fraudulent relief cases]. The payroll brigade has been laid off and when they get money to start operations again I don't believe they will dare put all their thousands back to work."[35]

Those on relief were of a rather different state of mind. Hundreds of demonstrators marched on the State Capitol waving banners—"United We Eat, Divided We Starve," "Tax Wealth, Not Misery," a criticism of the sales tax (which taxed the unemployed themselves for their own relief). Chicago saw demonstrations as well, at which dozens were arrested. Thousands of eviction notices were posted as rent payments ceased. Later in the month hunger marchers returned to Springfield, this time in the thousands: "unemployed miners, farmers, and laborers in ragged old clothes and overalls, tired and hungry, marched about the capitol building with posters denouncing the sales tax," as "hundreds of state troopers wearing Sam Brown belts studded with bullets guarded the entrance to the capitol." They informed the crowd that machine guns would be turned on them if they tried to enter the building. While the politicians inside attacked one another for their cruelty and callousness, the marchers demanded that relief be restored with money raised by taxes on inheritances, incomes, and the Chicago Board of Trade.[36]

---

34. Glick, *The IERC*, 144–51.
35. Cole, "The Relief Crisis in Illinois," 257–62; Jones, "The Local Political Significance," 94–100; *New York Herald Tribune*, April 28, May 6, 1935; *Washington Post*, May 1, 1935; *New York Times*, May 6, 1935.
36. *New York Herald Tribune*, May 8, 1935; *New York Times*, May 10, 12, 22, 1935; *Chicago Tribune*, May 16, 1935; *Washington Post*, May 16, 1935; Eugene Leslie, "Illinois Creates a Crisis," *Social Work Today*, July 1935.

In late May, finally, the crisis came to an end. It had become clear to Hopkins that a two-thirds majority in the Illinois House was impossible to achieve, so he decided to accept a simple nonemergency measure, according to which the state would resume its financial contributions in August. Horner agreed, having been assured that FERA would finance Illinois's entire relief operation until the rise in the sales tax started to bring in more revenue. For the rest of the year, FERA continued to fund well over three-fourths of the state's unemployment relief.[37]

However, political currents in the second half of 1935 were anything but placid, for major changes in federal policy were in the works. The WPA was slowly being set up in the summer and fall of 1935, in preparation for a dismantling of FERA. In January 1935, Roosevelt had pledged to end federal participation in direct relief, and the gradual disassembling of FERA that fall fulfilled his pledge. Minor "crises" occurred as funding shrank, but the real difficulties for Illinois's administrators were produced by the simultaneous directives to build up the infrastructure of the WPA—which entailed transferring tens of thousands of relief cases to federal work relief—and tear down the infrastructure of FERA. It is something of a miracle that this bureaucratic nightmare did not collapse under the weight of administrative confusion. In fact, the major problems that emerged in the course of the transition, and were not solved in the following years, were financial rather than strictly "administrative": the Roosevelt administration did not request, and Congress did not grant, sufficient funds for the WPA even to hire all the employable ("able-bodied") people on the relief rolls, quite apart from the millions of able-bodied unemployed who were not on relief at all (and therefore could not be hired by the WPA). Governors had been led to expect that nearly all the employable relief cases in their state would be transferred to the WPA and thereby become a federal responsibility, so that the state would no longer have to pay for their direct relief. But because of the inadequate finances of the WPA—which grew even more inadequate after 1935—states ended up being saddled with far more cases than they had expected, which led to even lower standards of care than would have been the case anyway. In Illinois, for example, the "residual" relief caseload (i.e., the number of cases that were not transferred to the WPA) in January 1936 had been predicted to be around 65,000, but it turned out to be 130,000.[38]

Thus, Illinois entered a new, tragic phase, the post-FERA phase of its relief administration. Historians have written about the grim consequences nationwide of this backward step in unemployment relief, the devolution of relief back from the centralized FERA to the states and localities, so we need not dwell on its broad contours. Taking their cue from the federal government, many states quickly shed their relief burden and shunted the responsibility back onto local communities, which in most cases had neither the inclination nor the means to meet the resultant chaos. All too frequently, and as

---

37. *Chicago Tribune*, May 23, 1935; *New York Times*, May 26, 1935.
38. *New York Times*, September 29, 1935; Russell H. Kurtz, "No More Federal Relief?" *Survey*, February 1935; *Biennial Report of the IERC, Covering the Period July 1, 1934 through June 30, 1936* (Chicago, IL, 1936), 149; Margaret D. Yates, "Family Service and Relief," in *Social Service Year Book, 1935*, 13; Singleton, *The American Dole*, 185.

early as January or February 1936, relief sank to old, miserable poor-law standards. "In one eastern community," a relief worker wrote in June 1936, "town officials authorized families to beg their food from merchants and householders when town funds for relief were exhausted. Recently newspapers have reported the encampment of delegations of unemployed in legislative chambers in New Jersey, Pennsylvania, and Missouri protesting the abandonment of state aid for relief, calling to mind the 'hunger marches' of the early period of the depression." During the terrible recession of 1938, a journalist noted that "food, clothing, and shelter budgets for families receiving direct relief have been lopped so drastically and so generally [in the Midwest] that it is impossible to measure the results in human suffering." As may be imagined, conditions were even worse in the South. Dorothy Kahn, director of the Philadelphia relief program, asked in despair, "Have we lived through the agonizing years of depression relief to produce nothing better than this?"[39]

Commentators at the time and subsequently have puzzled over why the Roosevelt administration abruptly ended FERA after only two-and-a-half years. Jacob Fisher, chairman of the National Coordinating Committee of Social Service Employee Groups, was convinced it was the propaganda campaigns and lobbying of the business class that doomed FERA. "The engineers of defeat of the social work program have been the American Manufacturers Association, the Chamber of Commerce, and the Liberty League." There may have been some truth to this, for business at the national and state levels had indeed vigorously opposed high standards of public relief, and much of the media had waged an ideological war against relief. The mainstream culture of the well propertied had never grown comfortable with the idea of the "national dole," especially if it was to last longer than a year or two. But this meant that the Roosevelt administration itself was never comfortable with a national dole, and from the very beginning looked forward to ending it. Indeed, this is why the word "emergency" was in the very name of FERA. Even Harry Hopkins, himself a social worker who was extremely sympathetic to the suffering of the poor, was convinced that relief was a "very demoralizing thing" that encouraged "an unwholesome attitude toward the Nation and the States." Liberals replied to Hopkins and Roosevelt that no one doubted it was better to have work than relief; what was at issue was the inability of the WPA to hire anything close to a majority of the eligible unemployed, who would therefore be thrust back onto the miserable resources and cruelty of states and localities. It was similarly cruel to abandon "unemployables" to their states, even if the provisions of the new Social Security Act were likely to make things somewhat better for them.[40]

---

39. "A New Low in Relief Standards," *Compass*, June 1936, in National Association of Social Workers Papers, Chicago History Museum, box 22, folder 1; Samuel Lubell and Walter Everett, "The Breakdown of Relief," *Nation*, August 20, 1938; Singleton, *The American Dole*, 186; Isidor Feinstein, "Starving on Relief," *Nation*, February 12, 1936; Dorothy C. Kahn, "What Is Worth Saving in 'This Business of Relief'?", *Survey*, February 1937, 38.

40. Jacob Fisher, "The Present Status of Public Relief in the United States," in *Proceedings of the National Conference of Social Work, 1936* (Chicago, IL: University of Chicago Press, 1936), 437; William R. Brock, *Welfare, Democracy, and the New Deal* (New York: Cambridge University

But such pleas were of no use: Roosevelt's personal ideology had been formed in a political economy that overwhelmingly favored the interests of business, so it was basically conservative, committed to fiscal conservatism and a belief that relief was so degrading the federal government should not be involved in it. Reinforcing these convictions was evidence of the "unwholesome attitude" among those on federal relief that disturbed Hopkins: all over the country they had come to think the federal government had an *obligation* to help the needy, and that it was not fulfilling this obligation satisfactorily. "Clients are assuming that the government has a responsibility to provide," a journalist reported, adding that "the stigma of relief has [by 1934] almost disappeared except among white-collar groups." Relief workers noted that many clients even claimed a right to live *comfortably* at the government's expense. We'll return to this important point in the next chapter. Such a defiant attitude was very unsettling to authorities, for in its implications it seemed to demand a wholly new social order. How could capitalism continue—without radically changing—if all the unemployed received generous government support? Average wages would have to rise significantly in order to tempt people to seek work, and wealth would have to be taxed at a very high rate in order to pay for such an expansive welfare state. Society as a whole would become much more statist, and individual states' independence of the federal government would erode significantly. In short, FERA was encouraging attitudes—and social movements—incompatible with America's capitalist economy and federalist political structure. It had to be dismantled lest the pressures for its expansion engulf the nation.[41]

Discipline of the working class, therefore, became the order of the day, an order that Illinois carried out with relish (in effect, if not in intent). To retrace all the political machinations, sectional jealousies, personal rivalries, business lobbying, and popular protests that determined Illinois's relief policies in the following years is a Herculean task that will not be attempted here. But we can draw two main conclusions from the brief overview that follows. First, to quote a relief administrator, "there is no gainsaying the fact that the state and localities could have provided more relief money than they did during the period of FERA grants." This is obvious from the fact that they did provide more money, because they were forced to, *after* the federal government had withdrawn. Second, the welfare of the unemployed was at all times a low priority compared to other issues such as the avoidance of tax increases, the sectional desire to saddle other regions of the state with as much of the relief bill as possible, the determination not to reintroduce a state property tax or pursue any kind of corporate income tax, and the agendas of partisan politics.[42]

It was not a good omen when the underfunding of relief began immediately in January 1936, even though by some accounts the state had an $18 million surplus. Horner called a special session of the legislature, which, after weeks of deliberation,

---

Press, 1988), 259–67; "The New Deal of Lower Wages," *Nation*, January 16, 1935. William Bremer, "Along the 'American Way,'" describes some of the most flagrant inadequacies of both the WPA and New Deal work relief in general.

41. Quote from Brock, *Welfare, Democracy, and the New Deal*, 263.
42. Glick, *The IERC*, 183.

appropriated enough money to keep relief going into the summer. Meanwhile, however, measures had been passed that threatened to throw the entire administrative machinery into chaos: the General Assembly, led by downstate elements (which themselves were largely led by the Illinois Agricultural Association), had decided to gut the hated IERC by that summer and transfer financial and administrative responsibility to the state's 1,454 townships. To make Chicago pay for its own poor, it and all other townships had to levy a property tax in order to be eligible for state funds. Horner, who had often supported Chicago in its battles with downstate counties, signed off on this terrible, hastily conceived legislation because he was at that moment mired in a political battle with the Chicago Democratic machine and had decided to "play rough." He knew, too, that in his fight for reelection downstaters would appreciate an anti-Chicago stance.[43]

Less dramatic than the state's political skirmishes but equally or more real was the continued inadequacy of relief in these early months of 1936. In March, for example, clients' budgets had to be slashed, which meant that the IERC could in but few cases pay rent and electricity bills. Clothing and medical service authorizations, likewise, were restricted to emergency cases. Such curtailments were to recur regularly from 1936 on, even in months of relative financial stability.[44]

Starting in July, the General Assembly decreed that only $2 million of state funds would be available each month—to meet a need of more than twice that amount. The towns were supposed to supply the remainder. Illinois's relief financing and administration entered, then, a period of "truly medieval" decentralization, in which 1,454 authorities existed where formerly there had been one. It was now, much as in the bad old days of "pauper relief," up to townships to determine who would be eligible for relief and how much they would be granted, a system that lent itself to abuses, inefficiencies, local incompetence, and wide variations in relief standards. It is true, however, that there was not a literal return to the Elizabethan poor-law administration of the nineteenth and early twentieth centuries, since the state government did commit to contributing money toward relief and maintained some connection with local institutions (as well as with the WPA and other federal programs). Moreover, Chicago was fortunate in that the new Chicago Relief Administration (CRA) could simply take over the existing networks and professional personnel of the IERC, which had been based there.[45]

On the other hand, the city's poor were *un*fortunate in the degree to which the City Council was subordinate to business interests. The transition to the post-IERC era was going to be difficult in the best of circumstances, but with such a City Council it was utterly chaotic. Even if the council had prepared for the sudden reduction of state funds in July 1936 by passing the required tax levy, a significant cut in relief budgets would have been necessary. But the aldermen refused to do so, hoping to find a way

---

43. *New York Times*, January 4, February 8, 1936; *Chicago Tribune*, January 16, 1936; Cole, "The Relief Crisis in Illinois," 318–26; Jones, "The Local Political Significance," 106, 107; Scheinman, "Financing Unemployment Relief," 188, 189; Glick, *The IERC*, 171, 172. The last four sources are also the main sources for the next paragraph but one.
44. *Chicago Tribune*, March 14, 1936.
45. Lubell and Everett, "The Breakdown of Relief," 173, 174.

to circumvent the state's decree. As neither the city nor the state cared enough to keep relief functioning in Chicago, drastic cuts were necessary beginning in the summer of 1936. Medical and hospital services were discontinued, then rent, gas, electricity, and clothing services, and then food budgets had to be cut. There was not even any money to mail the thousands of grocery orders that families were counting on. For over a week in July, therefore, no food was given. "The total amount of suffering," the *Chicago Defender* observed, "endured during the seven or eight days of absolute destitution by clients will never be known." At last aldermen donated $2,900 to pay for postage to mail the food orders that CRA employees had volunteered (without pay) to fill out.[46]

That week there occurred a dramatic illustration of the Piven-Cloward thesis that (in crude terms) the surest way, and often the only way, for the poor to get consideration is to cause turmoil. Hundreds of people on relief, representing the Illinois Workers Alliance (IWA), the Association of Workers in Public Agencies, and the Revolutionary Workers' League, stormed the City Council chambers and flooded the galleries, loudly denouncing the assembled aldermen as the mayor tried to call the meeting to order. Pandemonium ensued until police dragged the demonstrators into the hallway. With the hundreds of "troublemakers" finally outside, the aldermen were called to order to the tune of "Solidarity Forever" ringing in the halls. This whole affair apparently made an impression, for the City Council promptly voted to levy the property tax it had put off for months. Later that day, grocery orders were mailed to clients.[47]

Unfortunately, the tax could not be collected right away, and no banks would buy the tax anticipation warrants. So local money remained unavailable. A skeleton CRA staff continued to work without pay so that families could receive their grocery orders (the mayor lent $2,500 for the postage), but still no other aid was given. Protest demonstrations continued, as when 10,000 people marched from Union Park to Michigan Avenue to decry the suspension of cash relief and the state's policy of using only one-third of revenue from the sales tax for relief purposes. Conditions were equally bad, or worse, in many other areas of the state, but the governor was on vacation and the legislature was out of session, so nothing was done. Finally, in August, the General Assembly reconvened—under heavy guard, for it was greeted by hundreds of hunger marchers. An anonymous bomb threat heightened the politicians' sense that something should be done. "An infernal machine," the threat said, "will be thrown into the Senate chamber and members of the Legislature will go home in boxes and on stretchers [...] if you don't take up our program first." Obediently they did.[48]

By mid-August, some ameliorations of the statewide disaster had been approved, in particular that for the rest of the year $3 million of state money would be available for relief each month, and that some of the state and local money could be used for administrative purposes (rectifying an oversight in earlier legislation that had necessitated the

---

46. Cole, "The Relief Crisis in Illinois," 348–51; *Chicago Tribune*, June 17, 20, 28, July 2, 1936; *New York Times*, July 12, 1936; *Chicago Defender*, July 18, 1936.
47. *Chicago Tribune*, July 9, 1936.
48. *Chicago Tribune*, July 14, 16, 18, August 5, 1936; Cole, "The Relief Crisis in Illinois," 354–57; *Washington Post*, August 5, 1936; *New York Times*, August 9, 1936.

virtual shutting down of administration). But still only 8 percent of funds could be used for administration in Chicago, an absurd and arbitrary constraint that forced a reduction in the CRA staff from 2,200 to 1,000 and, among other inefficiencies, saddled the remaining caseworkers with 250 cases each. The increased state funds did, at least, allow food budgets to be restored and cash relief to resume, along with semiregular payments for rent, fuel, shoes, and clothing. In December, the state appropriated another $12 million, which carried relief through May 1937—although not without yet more cuts that forced thousands of families off the rolls in Chicago.[49]

And so things went for the next few years, deteriorating significantly during the "Roosevelt recession" of 1937–38. The state kept appropriating more money—usually well after emergency conditions had arisen—but it was never enough. As the conservative backlash against the New Deal gained momentum, the WPA hemorrhaged jobs in 1937, creating dire conditions in Chicago, the rest of Illinois, and indeed much of the country.[50] The CRA was forced, again, to end payments for rent and clothing, as eviction rates shot up in the fall of 1937 and thousands of clients were dropped from the rolls. Desperate parents pleaded with courts to assume guardianship of their children, so that they could receive proper care in foster homes or institutions. By late November, the head of the CRA declared that the city was facing its worst crisis since the winter of 1930–31.[51]

The following year saw a temporary improvement, as relief returned to 80 percent adequacy (as measured by a subsistence budget)—until May, when stations closed

---

49. Cole, "The Relief Crisis," 356–59; *Chicago Tribune*, August 13, 1936; Scheinman, "Financing Unemployment Relief," 189, 190; "The Illinois Relief Imbroglio," *Compass*, October 1936; *Chicago Tribune*, April 30, 1937; Illinois Council on Public Assistance and Employment, "Preliminary Report on Administration of Relief in Chicago," January 25, 1938, in Welfare Council Papers, box 233, folder 6; Fay Herman, "Politics in Illinois," *Social Work Today*, October 1936; letter from Frank McCulloch to Jacob Arvey, April 1, 1937, in Frank McCulloch Papers, box 4, folder 4.

50. It is possible to see the end of FERA as the first moment of the national turn toward conservatism, the initial target of which was public unemployment relief and the second target, a few years later, the spirit of the CIO. From this perspective, ironically, the Social Security Act, approximately coincident with the end of FERA, can be seen as just as much a victory of conservatism as of liberalism, for it constituted but a feeble attempt at state welfarism in comparison to the far more popular Workers' Unemployment and Social Insurance Bill. From these two initial victories, one may see the slowly building conservative "movement" as progressing to even greater triumphs in its vitiation of the potential of the WPA and its halting the social movement momentum of the CIO from 1938 into the war years. Eventually, starting perhaps in 1947 and 1948, it established itself as the dominant political and cultural paradigm. According to this periodization the crucial year was 1935 (not 1938 or the later years that historians have proposed), for it was then that certain radical possibilities were foreclosed, the tide turned against unemployment relief and an expansive welfare state, and the Roosevelt administration definitively revealed its true conservative colors. The die was cast even before Roosevelt's overwhelming electoral win in 1936.

51. Glick, *The IERC*, 174; *New York Times*, September 19, 1937; Cole, "The Relief Crisis," 363–70; *Chicago Tribune*, August 25, September 1, 8, 17, October 14, November 9, 30, 1937; Milton Shufro, "Chicago Spotlights a Crisis," *Compass*, December 1937, 20–22.

again. Tens of thousands of families were shut off from access to life's necessities; for good measure, the Chicago City Council passed a resolution condemning any increase in property taxes. At length, a solution was found to this new emergency, and relief resumed.[52]

But Congress slashed appropriations for the WPA again in 1939, and the relief rolls, yet again, expanded. The CRA and the IERC resorted to the usual measures, for instance discontinuing all relief cases in Chicago (of which there were 190,000, representing 570,000 people) and forcing everyone to reapply and possibly undergo an investigation. To cut the rolls further, the legislature passed a law stipulating that only people who had lived in Illinois for three consecutive years could be granted relief. Despite all these austerity measures, funds kept hemorrhaging. At a time when New York City was contributing 60 percent of the cost of relief, Chicago was supplying about 17 percent.[53]

Nothing noteworthy changed in 1940. In May, labor unions and "a huge host of progressive organizations" such as the Illinois Workers Security Federation (successor to the IWA) sent a resolution to Governor Horner pleading for a special session of the legislature, a resolution that began, "The relief situation in Chicago today is a major emergency. Malnutrition, starvation and disease are appalling in extent. Present WPA cuts will make these conditions even worse." No special session was called. A number of stalwart activists, veterans of unemployed advocacy, valiantly continued the fight in an ever more conservative political climate, but they had little success. Even the most powerful unions were unable to sway the governor or the legislature. For instance, in a letter to the IWSF, the district president of the United Mine Workers lamented that "our Union has done everything humanly possible to bring these matters [of relief] to the attention of the state administration, but, I am sorry to say, without any results." Now that unemployed organizations, victims of conservative backlash, had "shrunk to the vanishing point" (as one activist said), the state had no reason to remember the thousands of unfortunates suffering in their tenements and back alleys.[54]

As we know, what finally saved the unemployed and ended the 12-year-long relief crisis (continuing into 1941) not only in Illinois but all over the country was, perversely, the imperative to kill Nazis in Europe and Japanese in the Pacific. Such an imperative, far from being a threat to the class structures of American capitalism and their distribution of power, was a colossal boon to business, so it was able to become national policy, as

---

52. Cole, "The Relief Crisis," 376–81; Glick, *The IERC*, 175; *Chicago Tribune*, May 18, 27, June 11, 21, 1938; *New York Herald Tribune*, May 19, 22, 1938; *New York Times*, May 22, 26, 1938; Scheinman, "Financing Unemployment Relief," 192; IERC, *The Relief Problem in Illinois: Report to His Excellency, Henry Horner, Governor, and to the Honorable Members of the Sixty-First Illinois General Assembly* (Chicago, IL, 1938).
53. *New York Times*, July 22, 1939; *Chicago Tribune*, January 10, June 2, August 11, 1939; Cole, "The Relief Crisis," 461–76; Jones, "The Local Political Significance of New Deal Relief Legislation," 184–90.
54. Lea D. Taylor et al., "Resolution to Governor Horner on Relief," Frank McCulloch Papers, box 9, folder 4; *Work*, May 23, 1940, 1; letter from UMW District 12 president to McCulloch, May 21, 1940, and letter from McCulloch to Sophonisba Breckenridge, May 18, 1940, in ibid.; *Chicago Tribune*, April 7, June 5, 1940.

adequate unemployment relief never was. Where the New Deal and (in some respects) its humanitarian impulse had failed, global war succeeded.

Unions

One might say that the problem of voluntary organizations such as labor unions, churches, charities, and benefit societies was the opposite of the Illinois government: while the latter had resources but lacked the will to support the unemployed, the former, comparatively speaking, had the will but lacked the resources. It is true that the national, and in most cases state, leadership of organized labor had little will to organize the jobless (though this was less true after the formation of the CIO) and could have lobbied more aggressively for more generous unemployment insurance than it did. Nevertheless, unions generally displayed far more concern for the jobless than governments did. Unfortunately, the weakness of organized labor at the end of the 1920s meant that only a tiny number of workers nationwide belonged to unions that had unemployment-benefit plans for their members: in 1931, for instance, about 65,000 workers were covered by plans jointly administered by companies and unions, while 45,000 were covered by separate union plans. Moreover, these numbers dropped considerably as the Depression progressed and union treasuries depleted.[55]

In Chicago, the most highly developed unemployment benefits plan was that of the Amalgamated Clothing Workers of America. This union had in 1923 set up joint plans with employers in the Chicago area who were engaged in the production of men's clothing in union shops: contributions to the benefit fund were to amount to 1.5 percent of the earnings of union members and 3 percent of the employer's payroll. Involuntarily unemployed workers were to receive 30 percent of their wages per week, for up to three weeks per season. The fund managed to continue through the Depression, even as benefits were slightly increased in 1930 and 1931. But the number of workers the plan covered inevitably dropped: from 19,000 workers in 1926 to 12,500 in late 1933.[56]

A few local unions administered their own benefit plans. Bookbinders Local 8, with 800 members in 1939, paid $5.50 per week to its unemployed members for up to 13 weeks, while Electrotypers Local 3 gave weekly benefits of $15 to journeymen for as long as they were out of work. Photo-engravers Local 5, with 1,500 members, likewise gave benefits indefinitely, although as the Depression dragged on they had to be reduced.

---

55. Anice L. Whitney, "Operation of Unemployment-Benefit Plans in the United States up to 1934: Part 1," *Monthly Labor Review* (June 1934): 1288–318.
56. Ibid., 1313–15; Steven Fraser, *Labor Will Rule: Sidney Hillman and the Rise of American Labor* (New York: The Free Press, 1991), 215–18; Hillman, "Urbanization and the Organization of Welfare Activities," 180, 181; Theresa Wolfson, "Trade Union Insurance—Promises and Realities," *Survey Graphic*, April 1, 1929; "Operation of Unemployment-Benefit Plans in the United States during 1931 and 1932: Part 1," *Monthly Labor Review* (December 1932): 1242, 1243.

Typographical workers, milk drivers, and members of the International Ladies Garment Workers Union were also among the lucky few who received unemployment benefits.[57]

A number of other unions, including among railway carmen, street and electric railwaymen, and in some of the building trades, tried share-the-work schemes early in the Depression.[58] In December 1930, the economist Sumner Slichter described how some of these worked:

> In many railroad shops, on the Baltimore and Ohio, on the Chicago, Indianapolis and Louisville, and on other roads, the men for months have voluntarily been working five days a week instead of six in order to provide jobs for more workers. Under the union regulations, the seniority rule would ordinarily be applied and the junior men laid off. The senior employees in these shops, therefore, are contributing one day's pay a week, *one-sixth* of their income, to the relief of unemployment. This is being done by men who receive eighty cents an hour or less. How many millionaires, or men receiving $5,000 or $10,000 a year, are contributing one-sixth of their incomes to unemployment relief?[59]

A year later, Mayor Harry A. Mackey of Philadelphia declared,

> Up to the present a great proportion of the relief funds has been contributed by the working class. Not one-tenth of our citizens have responded, and it is a lamentable fact, but none the less true, that many of our wealthy men and women have failed to respond, while many others who are rich and well able to do so have sent contributions for insignificant sums. [...] I say to you it is the poor man who has saved the situation up to this time. In other words, the poor man is protecting the interests of the rich man because the poor man is sympathetic.[60]

In fact, according to a study in 1939 by an economist at Columbia University, between 1930 and 1936, Americans with annual incomes of more than a million dollars gave only 3.9 percent of the total that went to private welfare institutions in the country. People earning over $50,000 per year contributed 14.6 percent.[61]

In any event, to address the unemployment epidemic primarily through contributions from wage earners or share-the-work plans was a hopelessly inadequate response. Sooner or later, unions were bound to turn to grander measures to solve the crisis. In particular, the American Federation of Labor's traditional voluntarism could not survive: by 1932, the economic climate had made the AFL's opposition to government-run unemployment insurance

---

57. Anice L. Whitney, "Operation of Unemployment-Benefit Plans in the United States up to 1934: Part 2," *Monthly Labor Review* (July 1934): 1–24; Hillman, "Urbanization and the Organization of Welfare Activities," 182; Kathryn W. Daly, "The International Ladies' Garment Workers' Union in Chicago, 1930–1939" (MA thesis, University of Chicago, 1939).
58. Barbara Warne Newell, *Chicago and the Labor Movement: Metropolitan Unionism in the 1930's* (Urbana, IL: University of Illinois Press, 1961), 38, 39.
59. Sumner H. Slichter, "Doles for Employers," *New Republic*, December 31, 1930.
60. Quoted in Abraham Epstein, *Insecurity: A Challenge to America* (New York: Agathon Press, Inc., 1968 [1938]), 183.
61. *Work*, May 23, 1940, 3.

utterly anachronistic. Its old nostrums of "employment assurance" through a shorter work week, public works, and stable wage levels were little better than a bad joke when nationwide unemployment was approaching 25 percent. However, William Green, head of the AFL, and his fellow officers were not going to give up their voluntarism voluntarily (so to speak). It required a major movement of the rank and file to force the Federation's executive council to change its stance in July 1932, when it finally assigned Green the task of preparing an unemployment insurance bill for introduction in Congress.[62]

The story can be summarized briefly—and is apropos in its anticipation of one of the themes of the next chapter, that people on the "rank-and-file" level tended to be quite radical (much more so than those in positions of authority). Already by late 1930, despite the opposition of the AFL, many constituent organizations and unions had gone on record in support of legislation for unemployment insurance, including eight state federations of labor (not Illinois's), the central labor bodies of nine cities, and the American Federation of Teachers, the Amalgamated Clothing Workers, the ILGWU, the United Textile Workers, and other Internationals. Public pressure continued to mount in 1931, as 52 bills for unemployment insurance were introduced (unsuccessfully) in state legislatures. But at the 1931 AFL convention the leadership was still able to smother the growing demand that the Federation change its voluntarist position. A rank-and-file movement therefore began in January 1932, when Carpenters Local 2717 in New York City called a conference of AFL unions. Representatives of 19 locals passed a resolution to appoint a committee—the AFL Trade Union Committee for Unemployment Insurance and Relief (AFLTU Committee)—that would gauge sentiment and build support among unions for federal insurance, in particular for the Communist-written Workers' Unemployment Insurance Bill. In part because of its activities—and despite its being persecuted by the national office as Communist—by the spring of 1934 over two thousand locals and many central bodies had joined in its endorsement of the radical Workers' Bill that Ernest Lundeen had just sponsored in Congress.[63]

The head of the committee was Louis Weinstock, a Communist and member of the Painters' Union in New York City. To advocate for the Workers' Bill he conducted a national tour in 1934, in each city contacting unionists who helped him organize

---

62. James Lorence, *Organizing the Unemployed: Community and Union Activists in the Industrial Heartland* (Albany, NY: State University of New York Press, 1996), 35; Louis Stark, "Labor's Unemployment Program," *Survey*, November 15, 1930; "Emergency Unemployment Plan of the American Federation of Labor," *Monthly Labor Review* (November 1931): 1044–47; Lewis L. Lorwin, *The American Federation of Labor: History, Politics, and Prospects* (New York: AMS Press, 1970 [1933]), 292–94.

63. Albert Prago, "The Organization of the Unemployed and the Role of the Radicals, 1929–1935" (PhD diss., Union Graduate School, 1976), 217–28; Daniel Nelson, *Unemployment Insurance: The American Experience, 1915–1935* (Madison, WI: University of Wisconsin Press, 1969), 152–58; Mauritz Hallgren, "False Leadership of American Labor," *Modern Monthly* 8 (August 1934): 430; Kenneth M. Casebeer, "Unemployment Insurance: American Social Wage, Labor Organization and Legal Ideology," *Boston College Law Review* 35, issue 2, no. 2 (March 1, 1994): 259–348; "Support of H.R. 7598 Spreads Throughout Rank and File," *A. F. of L. Rank and File Federationist*, March–April 1934.

meetings that were attended by hundreds of workers. Some cities had their own local AFL Committee for Unemployment Insurance, while in others Weinstock helped create one. In reports to the Communist Party he made some telling observations about the left-wing militancy of the local unions he encountered, as contrasted with the conservatism of the Internationals to which they belonged. For example, in Chicago, building trades unions followed the practice of the Communist Unemployed Councils in electing small relief committees to take members to a charity office and demand more relief. They often even united with the Unemployed Councils in these activities, a tendency that, from the perspective of higher union officials, was growing to "alarming proportions" all over the country. Internationals, on the other hand, usually followed the conservative AFL line in its absolute rejection of cooperation with Communists, to the point that members who participated in Unemployed Council demonstrations risked being expelled from the union. In a case in Minneapolis, for instance, a local refused to accept the decision of its International that one of its members be expelled for having taken part in a Communist demonstration. The International replied that unless the union expelled her, it would have its charter revoked.[64]

But already by 1932, sentiment in favor of unemployment insurance had swept the large majority of rank-and-file unionists, in addition, of course, to the long-term unemployed whether unionized or not. Members were radicalizing, growing friendlier with Communists in their disgust at the inaction of union leaders. To quote Mauritz Hallgren, a keen observer of the labor movement,

> although in the early years of the crisis they had tended to drift away from the unions, [jobless members] were in 1932 taking an increasingly active part in union affairs. The fear was expressed that in some organizations the unemployed might even come into control of the bureaucratic machinery. That they exercised a tremendous influence over local unions and city and state central bodies was seen from the avalanche of radical demands that poured in upon the quarterly meeting of the Federation's executive council at Atlantic City in July [1932]. The rank-and-file workers, whether unemployed or not, were no longer to be put off with windy promises of action.[65]

After the powerful United Mine Workers endorsed the principle of government action at its convention in early 1932—which followed endorsements in 1931 by the Teamsters, the International Association of Machinists, and many others—the AFL's executive council saw the writing on the wall. It could prevaricate and postpone no longer; it had to accept, and propose at the next national convention, a version of compulsory unemployment insurance, thereby accepting the idea of government "interference" in the affairs of organized labor. But it could still qualify its endorsement of the principle,

---

64. Prago, "The Organization of the Unemployed," 229; Louis Weinstock, "Report of Tour and Mass Meetings," 1932, Communist Party files, Tamiment Library, New York University, microfilm collection 7548, reel 232; Hallgren, *Seeds of Revolt*, 220; "A. F. of L. Heads Try to Disrupt Weinstock's Tour," *Rank and File Federationist*, March–April 1934.
65. Hallgren, *Seeds of Revolt*, 221.

by proposing only *state* unemployment insurance, not federal. This is what it did at the 1932 convention in November, which was an eventful one as regards the fight between the Federation's left wing and its right wing. After holding a rump convention in Carpenters Hall, the AFLTU Committee sent a small delegation to present to William Green the rank and file's views on unemployment insurance. When they arrived at the convention site, Green refused to meet them. So they sat in the balcony observing the proceedings—until Weinstock climbed onto a chandelier and addressed the convention, which acutely embarrassed the presiding officials. Several were still resolutely opposed even to Green's moderate proposal for legislation, but in the end he was able to overcome their opposition and put the issue to a vote, whereupon the delegates approved his proposal by an "overwhelming margin."[66]

It should be recalled that the years 1931–36 were a time of exceptional "insubordination" in the ranks of labor, as the AFL elite had to fight ruthlessly to contain the "Communism" that was sweeping the masses. The strike wave of 1934 was one manifestation of rank-and-file rebelliousness; the deep conflicts demonstrated at national conventions, culminating in the historic 1935 convention that precipitated the founding of the CIO immediately afterward, were another. At the 1934 convention, to quote a Communist publication, rank-and-file delegates submitted "*62 different resolutions criticizing the policies of the A. F. of L. and proposing a militant program dealing with all phases and problems of the workers in this country*" (italics in original), all of which were rejected by the resolutions committee.[67] The quotation is from the AFLTU Committee's *Rank and File Federationist*, a monthly magazine that proved an effective tool in the committee's ideological guerrilla warfare against the union establishment. So threatened did the establishment apparently feel by this committee (and its affiliates) that it regularly refused its representatives entry to national conventions and in 1936 filed suit with the Federal Trade Commission to have the acronym AFL removed from its name. Similarly, at the 1935 convention, a resolution was approved to "energetically use all means at our command to purge our membership of proven Red termites who are endeavoring to destroy our government and the American Federation of Labor." The influence of the Red

---

66. *New York Times*, November 25, 1936; *Washington Post*, October 5, 1933; "Labor in America," *Social Work Today*, November 1934, 28; Prago, "The Organization of the Unemployed," 229, 230; Franklin Folsom, *Impatient Armies of the Poor: The Story of Collective Action of the Unemployed, 1808–1942* (Niwot, CO: University Press of Colorado, 1991), 394, 395; Nelson, *Unemployment Insurance*, 158–61. The delegates were more conservative than the workers they represented, most of whom would have preferred a more radical measure than Green's.

67. The spread of a militantly progressive spirit in the ranks of the AFL is apparent by comparing the quantity and quality of resolutions introduced at various national conventions. At the 1932 convention, no rank-and-file group was allowed to be represented, and only 90 resolutions were introduced, most of them dealing with conservative and routine issues. At the 1934 convention, by contrast, about 230 resolutions were submitted, over 100 dealing with "rank-and-file issues." The number was still higher at the 1935 convention. "Rank and File Progress in A. F. of L.," *Labor Notes*, November 1935, 5.

termites had, however, at least been indirectly responsible for the AFL's endorsement of the Social Security Act, since the "Communist" Lundeen Bill was anathema.[68]

Meanwhile, the Chicago and the Illinois State Federations of Labor, like their counterparts in other states, were neither ignoring the unemployed nor organizing them. The Executive Board of the CFL debated the question and decided that organization of the unemployed would result in dual unions for existing crafts. The legislative priorities of the CFL and ISFL tended to be such issues as expanding workmen's compensation, establishing state pensions for the elderly and mothers, and regulating the employment of women and children, but the federations did devote considerable attention to the plight of the jobless. With social workers and welfare agencies, they (especially the ISFL) were in the forefront of the push for state funding of public relief, and in their newspapers they regularly published information and stories on unemployment and poverty. For instance, in 1932, the *Federation News*, the CFL's newspaper, published a series of articles on the dreadful conditions at Oak Forest Infirmary just south of Chicago, where over four thousand "poor and needy" were cared for (in a sense). The Federation's investigation uncovered conditions so shocking that the county conducted its own investigation—after which it did nothing to improve the situation, because of the political class's "zeal for economy" (which the CFL and ISFL consistently decried). With regard to unemployment insurance, starting in 1933, the ISFL lobbied for a bill in the Illinois legislature, finally achieving victory in the summer of 1937. Illinois was the last state to establish a system of unemployment compensation—for which most of the unemployed were ineligible.[69]

On at least one occasion the CFL did organize a huge unemployment demonstration, through its affiliated unions. But it was on Labor Day in 1932, incorporated into the festivities (a parade, music, dancing, etc.), so it did not have quite the gravity or rebellious undertone that Communist demonstrations did. In fact, Chicago Communists were convinced, probably with good reason, that it was little more than an attempt to steal the unemployment issue from them and rein in its disorderly tendencies. The CFL's lack of militancy was, of course, perfectly consistent with the orientation of the AFL toward craft unionism, the representation and defense of a small labor aristocracy. For example, in a rather pitiful display of its passiveness, in early December 1932, the CFL reported in the *Federation News* that 30 organizations of the unemployed had recently met in Chicago for the Midwestern Conference of Unemployed Organizations, to lay the foundation

---

68. Philip Foner, "Introduction to *A. F. of L. Rank and File Federationist*"; Edwin Young, "The Split in the Labor Movement," in *Labor and the New Deal*, eds. Milton Derber and Edwin Young (New York: Da Capo Press, 1972), 47–76; "Gag Rule at 54th Convention of A. F. of L. Defeats Rank and File Program," *Rank and File Federationist*, November 1934; *New York Times*, October 22, 1935.

69. Newell, *Chicago and the Labor* Movement, 41; Mitchell Newton-Matza, *Intelligent and Honest Radicals: The Chicago Federation of Labor and the Politics of Progression* (New York: Lexington Books, 2013), 165; Illinois State Federation of Labor, *Weekly Newsletter*, February 1 and December 27, 1930, January 17, 1931, September 10, 1932, March 25, 1933, July 3 and August 21, 1937, in ISFL archives, UIC, box 2, folders 6 and 9; *Federation News*, September 24, October 1, 8, 15, 29, 1932.

for a Federation of Unemployed Workers' Leagues. "The program of the Federation," the article noted, "is of particular interest to organized labor for its deliberate efforts to forestall conflict with organized labor and instead to secure its co-operation." The irony passed unnoticed that the very issue under discussion, namely rampant unemployment, should itself have been of "particular interest to organized labor." And yet not only did the CFL and ISFL have no connection with any of the attending groups: the former had actually refused official support to the Chicago Workers Committee on Unemployment when it was formed in the summer of 1931.[70]

Nevertheless, within the limited sphere of its narrow tactics and excessive conservatism, and notwithstanding exceptions, organized labor did not necessarily acquit itself badly in the unemployment crisis. During Chicago's many relief crises, the ISFL was on hand to aggressively push, through lobbying and press releases, for immediate action by the legislature. In doing so, it sometimes found itself awkwardly placed between the business community and the IWA, a federation of unemployed organizations that was founded in December 1933. During the emergency of May 1935, for instance, ISFL officials were outraged at the stances of both right-wing and left-wing groups, which had curiously merged: the Illinois Chamber of Commerce and its affiliates "deluge[d] the legislature with telegrams against the 'occupational tax'" as the means to fund relief, while the IWA and its affiliates picketed the state capitol in opposition to the same tax, which they called the sales tax because businesses typically passed their so-called occupational tax on to customers. "In each instance," the ISFL observed, "their fire is directed at precisely the same target—the pending bills intended to raise relief funds through what one calls an extension of the 'occupational tax on merchants' and the other calls a 'sales tax on customers.'" After an intelligent critique of each party's proposed solution to the crisis, the press release continued:

> Both are making a political foot-ball out of the miseries and suffering of more than a million of men, women and children. Are they rank hypocrites, brazen mountebanks, or just plain ignoramuses?
>
> Certain of the leaders of one side of this remarkable combination apparently hope that, if the people can be made desperate through hunger, a "revolution" may take place to destroy the other group, some leaders of which seemingly believe that they can "save money" by letting the people starve. What a mess!
>
> Out upon them both! "Go to!" as Shakespeare said. State relief funds must be provided without further delay. Feed the hungry! Have mercy upon the suffering men, women and children for whom the relief agencies are the only source of bread. Pass the pending bills and let them have food.[71]

---

70. *Federation News*, September 3, December 3, 1932; *New York Times*, February 10, 1932; "Report of Resolutions Committee of Midwest Conference of Unemployed Organizations," November 19 and 20, 1932, Raymond Hilliard Papers, Chicago History Museum, box 25, folder 1; Helen Seymour, "The Organized Unemployed" (MA thesis, University of Chicago, 1937), 24, 25. The Chicago Amalgamated Clothing Workers appears to have been the only local union that assisted in the formation of the Workers Committee on Unemployment.
71. "Press Release for Monday papers, May 13, 1935," Illinois State Federation of Labor, in Frank McCulloch Papers, Chicago History Museum, box 4, folder 11.

Inasmuch as the charge leveled at the IWA was largely justified, the ISFL seems in this case to have adopted the most honorable and humane position.

In 1934 and most of 1935, the relations between the IWA and the ISFL were frigid. The latter was hostile, and the former apparently did little to try to improve relations. In the summer of 1934, for example, after hearing reports that Unemployed Councils and IWA members downstate were interfering with work relief and union activities, the secretary-treasurer of the ISFL, Victor Olander, asked union assemblies and federations around the state to send him information on the doings of the "Communist" IWA in their vicinity. By the fall of 1935, one of the leaders of the IWA, Frank W. McCulloch, was so concerned about relations with the ISFL that he arranged to meet Olander and clear up any misunderstandings. Evidently he succeeded, for by 1936, the State Federation was no longer hurling insults at the IWA but rather cooperating with it on issues of mutual interest. Indeed, in November 1936, IWA representatives were even able to appeal to organized labor for financial assistance, noting in their open letter that "in countless instances we have helped trade unions on the picket line, in organizational drives, and have done much to break down resentment to working-class organization in communities where prior to our appearance such a thing was unknown." So, at last, organized labor in Illinois and the organized unemployed were able to overcome their mutual suspicions and join together for common causes.[72]

One such cause—though not one supported by the ISFL—was the establishment in 1935 and 1936 of the Illinois Labor Party. Radical left-wing sentiment was sweeping the country like a conflagration in these years—one need only think of EPIC, Huey Long, Charles Coughlin (not yet a fascist), the CIO, and the Workers' Bill that I'll discuss in the next chapter—and the movement to establish labor parties was one manifestation of it. In 1935, the state federations of labor in Oregon, Utah, and Connecticut endorsed the principle of a labor party, and resolutions for such a party were submitted at the conventions that year of several other state federations. Far more actions to establish labor parties followed in 1936, and they met with far more success, despite the hostility of the AFL's leadership. The CFL and ISFL were similarly hostile. As a result, it was left to unions affiliated with these bodies to independently form, first, the Labor Party of Chicago and Cook County in 1935, and then, with the assistance of the IWA and dozens of other unions around the state, the Illinois Labor Party in 1936.[73]

The platform of the ILP could hardly have been more progressive: a 30-hour week with no reduction in pay; a national minimum wage; abolition of child labor and free primary, secondary, and college education for all; generous unemployment, sickness, and accident insurance, and munificent old-age pensions; permanent legislation

---

72. Frank McCulloch to Victor Olander, September 11, 1935, and other letters from 1934 and 1936, in Victor Olander Papers, UIC Special Collections, box 12, folder 157. It must be said, again, that the "suspiciousness" was usually on the side of organized labor, especially of its state-level and county-level bodies.
73. *Rank and File Federationist*, October 1935; *New York Herald Tribune*, August 16, 1936; *Chicago Tribune*, November 26, 1936; *Daily Worker*, July 18, 24, September 19, November 13, 1935, March 31, April 1, 3, 6, 7, 1936.

against the sales tax; nationalization of banks, transportation, communication, public utilities, and other vital industries; and many more such planks, nearly all of which would have done the Communist Party proud. After its formation the party maintained close relations with the Minnesota Farmer-Labor Party and the Wisconsin Farmer-Labor Progressive Federation, both of which saw huge victories in the 1936 elections. Unfortunately, the ILP did not have such success, even in 1938, after it had had a few years to build support. It simply could not overcome the hostility of the state's political and business establishment (which erected legal barriers even to its participation in elections).[74]

Of all unemployed organizations, the one that secured the most goodwill and cooperation from organized labor was the Workers Alliance of America (WA), founded in 1935. Attendance at the national convention that created it was drawn from 16 states, and organizations in many other states that were unable to attend sent letters of endorsement. Labor unions, too, were interested in this attempt to unite all major unemployed and relief workers' groups in the country, and the convention received greetings from, for example, the ILGWU; the New York Joint Board of Cloakmakers; the Amalgamated Association of Iron, Steel and Tin Workers; and William Green. True national unity was achieved at the 1936 convention, when the Communist National Unemployment Council and A. J. Muste's National Unemployed League joined the Alliance. By the end of 1936, the WA reportedly had 1,600 locals in 43 states, with an estimated 300,000–600,000 members. The federal government had recognized it as a collective bargaining agent for WPA workers. It was a force to be reckoned with—as was indicated by the willingness of organized labor to cooperate with it despite the presence of Communists on its Executive Board.[75]

The CIO, especially, was friendly. In response to the "Roosevelt recession" of 1937–38, CIO leaders began to formulate plans to ensure that union members had access to adequate relief benefits. As historian James Lorence describes, directives were issued "urging all CIO affiliates to establish unemployment committees and uniform machinery to guarantee that union members would be placed on WPA projects and receive

---

74. ISFL *Weekly Newsletter*, October 15, 1938, in ISFL Papers, box 2, folder 10; *Chicago Tribune*, July 5, 1936; Morris Childs, "Forging Unity against Reaction in Illinois," *Communist*, August 1936: 769–83; Clarence Hathaway, "The Minnesota Farmer-Labor Victory," *Communist*, December 1936: 1112–24; Gene Dennis, "The Wisconsin Elections and the Farmer-Labor Party Movement," *Communist*, December 1936: 1125–40; in Frank McCulloch Papers, box 5, folder 11: *Labor Party Voice*, November 1937; "Platform of the Illinois Labor Party, 1938"; George A. Mead, "Call to Labor Party Conference," 1939; "Minutes of the Convention of the Labor Party of Chicago and Cook County," January 31, 1937; Illinois Labor Party, letter "to all trade unions ...," November 1, 1938.

75. Lorence, *Organizing the Unemployed*, 97; Seymour, "The Organized Unemployed," 37–48; *Chicago Defender*, April 18, 1936; Proceedings, Resolutions, and Program of the National Convention of the Unemployed Forming the Workers Alliance of America, McCulloch Papers, box 6, folder 4; Selden Rodman, "Lasser and the Workers' Alliance," *Nation*, September 10, 1938; Anthony Badger, *The New Deal*, 202; *Washington Post*, September 5, 1936.

all unemployment compensation and other benefits to which they were entitled." The CIO undertook to represent unemployed unionists before welfare authorities and lobby Congress for generous relief legislation, and it insisted that jobless members should be able to remain in their union. In Michigan, for example, the United Autoworkers was particularly aggressive in assisting its unemployed members: for instance, dozens of locals established committees to halt evictions, "the employed rally[ing] to defend the unemployed." With the cooperation of the Workers Alliance, the AFL, and WPA workers, the UAW was even able to mobilize over a hundred thousand demonstrators in Detroit's Cadillac Square for more WPA jobs, adequate relief, and a moratorium on debt payments—an event that may have been "the greatest demonstration that was ever staged by one union." The CIO as a whole directed its affiliates to organize their own unemployed members who had taken WPA jobs, in order to keep them within the fold of the union and to fight for such demands as improved working conditions and formal grievance procedures on WPA projects. With the assistance of the Workers Alliance, unions' "WPA auxiliaries" saw notable victories on projects all over the country, including the reform of racist hiring practices and the ending of intimidation of union workers.[76]

The life of the WPA was turbulent: organized and unorganized workers conducted countless demonstrations, sit-ins, strikes, and slowdowns to protest everything from inadequate congressional appropriations to supervisors' misconduct. Chicago did not have such a dominant, progressive union as the UAW, but it was nonetheless a full participant in these national trends. As early as January 1936, the Deputy Works Progress Administrator for Illinois found it necessary to publicly dissuade WPA workers from joining unions, arguing that payment of dues would be a waste of money because organizers could not win changes in working conditions. As elsewhere, it was not mainly AFL affiliates that were organizing relief workers; it was Communists, members of the Workers Alliance, and, eventually, affiliates of the CIO. By 1938, strikes were becoming quite common.[77]

For instance, in early 1938 organizers with the WA facilitated a strike of 7,000 WPA workers at the Chicago airport, which resulted in the granting of their demand for a change in hours. A few weeks earlier, groups of IWA members had staged simultaneous sit-ins at relief stations around the city, forming picket lines after they were ejected. Reminiscent of the early years of the Depression, "pressure groups" filed into stations one by one to make mass demands on behalf of an individual. Both CIO representatives and IWA members were typically found in these groups. Members of the CIO's Steel Workers Organizing Committee who a year earlier had been active in the South Chicago steel mills were now, in early 1938, organizing men on both work relief and direct relief. One tactic was to hold mass meetings at which they urged support of the IWA, the WA, and the CIO, and exhorted their listeners to picket relief stations in order to secure increases in payments for rent, light, gas, and food. The dismay that

---

76. Lorence, *Organizing the Unemployed*, 161–89.
77. *Chicago Tribune,* January 19, 1936.

authorities and the *Chicago Tribune* expressed at the influence of these "outside agitators" testifies to their effectiveness.[78]

With regard to the WPA, the main concerns of the AFL and the ISFL were that wage rates not undermine union wages, and that nonunion workers not take jobs for which union members were eligible. At state conventions, the ISFL regularly stated that neither of these conditions was being met. Delegates at the 1938 convention resolved, for example, that "the expansion of WPA into organized construction fields results in a demoralized industry, making it incapable of reemploying men at full-time jobs." Despite such concerns, however, AFL leaders did not countenance strikes on federal relief projects for higher pay. "The remedy lies with Congress," William Green said in July 1939, "rather than through strikes on WPA projects." This statement amounted to a disavowal of the strikes then occurring all over the country, which had been called not only by affiliates of the Workers Alliance and CIO unions but also by councils and unions affiliated with the AFL. Involving perhaps a hundred thousand relief workers, they were a reaction to Congress's ruling that all WPA employees had to work 130 hours a month with no increase in pay, a ruling that meant that skilled workers, who had previously worked 60 hours or less, would be paid less than half per hour what they had been. The strikers' cause ended in failure.[79]

So, in a sense, the decade ended much as it had begun, with the more militant and rank-and-file-supported aspect of the labor movement vigorously adopting the cause of the unemployed (including relief workers), while the higher officialdom of the AFL and its affiliates took a more distanced and decorous approach to the problem of mass unemployment. This battle between the conservative and the radical strains of organized labor has, of course, been waged through the whole history of industrial capitalism. Nevertheless, even labor's conservative wing was apt to display, as we have seen, a more creditable attitude toward the hungry masses than state and local governments were, and even the federal government. This is hardly surprising. Governments tend to ally with one side of the class struggle, organized labor with the other. It was the misfortune of the unemployed that unions had incomparably fewer resources than business and its political allies.

Churches

The relation of Depression-era churches to the unemployed—that is, the policies and practices they favored—is a massive subject that I can only touch on here. Of course, there was no uniformity between individual churches, denominations, or regions of the country. Nevertheless, without oversimplification it can be said that a large portion of the "religious community" showed a striking degree of compassion and humanity in these years, far more than government regularly did and arguably more than

---

78. Ibid., February 28, 1938.
79. Ibid., September 13, 1935, September 16, 1938, July 18, 1939, August 5, 1939; *New York Times,* July 13, 16, 1939; *Washington Post,* July 9, 1939.

most AFL-affiliated Internationals did. The founder of Christianity would surely have approved of the poor-loving and rich-censuring attitude that many prominent religious organizations displayed.[80]

Father John A. Ryan, head of the Social Action Department of the National Catholic Welfare Conference (NCWC), was speaking for more than a negligible proportion of religious authorities when he thundered, in late 1930, "When I think of what has been happening since unemployment began, and when I think of the futility of the leaders, I wish we might double the number of Communists in this country, to put the fear, if not of God then the fear of something else, into the hearts of our leaders—not only our industrialists but our politicians and statesmen." In cities all over the country, churches and church associations were acting on the basis of such humanitarianism as this. It is widely known that churches were actively in the breadline-and-soup-kitchen business, but other examples can be given. Between November 1930 and early February 1931, with the assistance of the Chicago Church Federation, the 1,200 Protestant churches in Chicago raised $500,000 for emergency relief and found jobs for more than five thousand people. Truckloads of food and clothing were collected and distributed. Indeed, already in the spring of 1930 the 800 Protestant churches affiliated with the Church Federation were (in many cases) appealing to their congregations for help in finding jobs for those out of work. Meanwhile, the well-developed Catholic and Jewish charities, in particular the Central Charity Bureau and the Jewish Social Service Bureau, were aiding many thousands of their constituents. It was not until late 1934 that the Protestant churches formed their own semicomparable entity, the Associated Church Charities, in part to help with financing the tremendous burden being carried by the Protestant charitable agencies.[81]

The ideological orientation of the Chicago Church Federation was consistent with that of the national association with which it was affiliated, the Federal Council of Churches in Christ: both were sharply left wing. And neither was afraid to flaunt its social radicalism. The Federal Council, which represented 135,000 Protestant churches with a membership of 22 million, was considered by many to be notoriously left wing. In 1938, it was condemned at a hearing of the House Un-American Activities Committee (HUAC) for "attempting to spread social radicalism in the various Christian denominations of America." The Reverend John H. McComb spoke for conservative religious groups when he insisted, "The Federal Council is in no sense representative of American Protestantism. It only represents those who use the church as a means to meddle in politics and dabble in sociology." Its meddling and dabbling are illustrated by its adoption

---

80. On Jesus's hostile attitude toward the rich, see, for example, Luke 6:24–25: "But woe unto you that are rich! for ye have received your consolation. Woe unto you that are full! for ye shall hunger. Woe unto you that laugh now! for ye shall mourn and weep." For a description of the remarkably broad cultural appeal of Socialism and Communism in these years, see Arthur M. Schlesinger, Jr., *The Crisis of the Old Order: 1919–1933* (New York: Houghton Mifflin Company, 2003 [1957]), chapter 24.
81. *Federation News*, November 1, 1930, 12; *Chicago Tribune*, April 29 and December 30, 1930, February 14, 1931, December 11, 1934, July 11, 1935.

of a revised Social Creed in 1932, which called for "a wider and fairer distribution of wealth; social insurance against unemployment, sickness, accident and old-age want; social control of the economic process; revision of penal methods and of criminal court procedure," and liberalism with regard to birth control and divorce. HUAC had good reason to be hostile toward the Federal Council.[82]

But even on a less political level, a sort of "communism"—in David Graeber's sense—was at the heart of Christian practice. For this was the meaning of the sympathy and generosity, the powerful (and potentially very subversive) impulse to *share*, that inspired so many thousands of church members in Chicago to donate money and goods to the unemployed and to volunteer their labor for relief services. It is impossible to know the numbers of either donors or beneficiaries—or volunteers—at any time during the Depression, but we can get some indication of the scale of generosity from isolated and anecdotal evidence. Late in 1932, it was estimated, conservatively, that if Protestant organizations suddenly put an end to their permanent relief agencies, at least seven thousand people would have to sleep on the streets that night and twenty thousand would have nothing to eat. But many thousands more were being helped week by week and month by month. The Christian Industrial League alone housed 3,400 people a night and served 12,000 meals every day. A single church on Halsted Street that also functioned as a permanent relief agency gave, with the help of its membership, various forms of relief to more than eight thousand families in its neighborhood. Between 1930 and 1939, the Episcopal Cathedral Shelter provided housing, food, clothing, medical care, and help finding jobs to well over two million people. In addition to such organizations were the hundreds of individual churches that helped their members (and whose members helped each other) in whatever ways they could. The executive secretary of the Church Federation remarked that "unquestionably" the number of people assisted in this way far exceeded that assisted by the relief agencies.[83]

The Catholic Central Charity Bureau was particularly effective at mobilizing volunteers. Under its direction, thousands of men, members of the Society of St. Vincent de Paul, distributed relief to Catholic families, visiting each family once a week. Many of these men were unemployed themselves. A report by the Church Federation on how best to organize its own Associated Church Charities highlighted some of the strengths of this system: "The distributors speak the language of those they serve; they usually live in the same neighborhood and attend the same Church. Their visitations are frequent. [...] Their relief is not alone material; it is friendly, human and spiritual." In 1933, the Society of St. Vincent de Paul directly aided 321,000 people in Chicago.[84]

---

82. *New York Times*, October 15, 1930, December 4 and 8, 1932, December 12, 1938.
83. *Chicago Tribune*, November 6, 13, 1932, October 16, 1939.
84. Angus Hibbard, "Relief Distribution by Protestant Churches," January 23, 1934; Roger J. Coughlin and Cathryn A. Riplinger, *The Story of Charitable Care in the Archdiocese of Chicago, 1844–1997* (Chicago, IL: Catholic Charities, 1999), 214, 215; Raymond Hilliard Papers, box 120, folder 6; *Chicago Tribune*, December 11, 1933. Also see "Central Charity Bureau, Catholic Charities: Study of Work, March 27–April 8, 1933," Welfare Council Papers, box 256, folder "Catholic Charities, 1933–59."

Chicago's Jews, for their part, had, like other ethnicities and religious groups, built a world of relative cooperation, communalism, and mutual aid in the heart of a society ostensibly based on capitalist principles of competition, self-gain, and the impersonal market. In fact, given the relative solidarity and ethnic consciousness that they have traditionally displayed, the Jewish people are an especially powerful illustration of the truth that "communism," far more than capitalism, pervades social relations and human interactions. By 1930, the Jewish Charities of Chicago encompassed 26 organizations and had almost ten thousand subscribers who donated $1.5 million a year. This money helped support the following institutions, among others: two homes for the elderly, two hospitals, two large orphanages, two dispensaries that treated 20,000 annually, a tuberculosis sanitarium, a family welfare agency, and a number of Jewish schools. It also funded a social service bureau that provided legal aid; industrial workshops for the disabled; and assistance for the sick, the poor, the unemployed, and transients. In addition, there were "numberless" charitable institutions not associated with Jewish Charities. And there were the synagogues. What the *Chicago Tribune* had said in 1908 was still largely true a generation later: "with the Jew, his synagogue is the doorway to the satisfaction of his physical needs. Here he gives an account of himself, and establishing his need he is given money in hand to meet these necessities." It was recognized at the time that the (relatively few) Jewish unemployed of Chicago tended to be better taken care of than those of most other ethnicities.[85]

And yet even the least wealthy churches, such as those in the Black Belt, still found ways to feed the jobless. The Immanuel Baptist Church, just north of Bronzeville, almost had to close in 1932 because of the debts it had incurred in its 38 years of feeding the unemployed. Reverend Johnston Myers had established one of Chicago's earliest breadlines in 1895; by 1932, the church had warmed and fed perhaps 15 million people. In the winter of 1932, 3,000 supplicants came every day. "If we go down," Myers said, "it will be with colors flying. Our last penny will go to the needy." The previous year, appalled at the thought that "[even a] single person [should] go hungry in this land of plenty, where fields are running over with things to eat," he organized a program to transport food from farms in Michigan, where crops were rotting in the fields, to Chicago. Contractors donated 15 trucks, farmers charged little or nothing for the food, volunteers picked and loaded the fruit and vegetables onto the trucks, and buildings were donated as food stations. Over several months, thousands of bushels of apples, wheat, and rye, and scores of truckloads of peaches, vegetables, and potatoes, were distributed to the needy. Myers was struck by the abundant generosity that magically appeared as news of the operation spread. A journalist who interviewed him one day noted that the telephone kept him busy. "A thousand bushels of apples are on their way from Benton Harbor and the city council there has voted to co-operate with us," Myers said after one call. "An offer of 300 carloads of potatoes and vegetables," he said a few minutes later, after another call. And again: "I've just had a contribution of $500

---

85. Irving Cutler, *The Jews of Chicago: From Shtetl to Suburb* (Chicago, IL: University of Illinois Press, 1996), 122; *Chicago Tribune*, December 14, 1910, December 29, 1929, March 8, 1908.

promised by one man." Thus did the initiative of one person provide an outlet for the generosity of many.[86]

The institutional tangle of churches and charitable institutions, even in the Black Belt alone (not to mention the entire city), can scarcely be unraveled. With the Great Migration had come an overwhelming need to provide assistance to tens of thousands of Black migrants; the charitable networks that emerged were of use, and were expanded, in the Depression. Huge churches like Olivet Baptist and the Institutional African Methodist Episcopal (AME) had established social service departments long before the 1930s to assist and enrich the lives of migrants, while smaller churches built alliances with secular organizations like the Travelers Aid Society, the Chicago Urban League, and the United Charities. Such alliances helped in the formation, for instance, of the Good Shepherd Community Center in 1936, which was established on the initiative of the Good Shepherd Congregational Church. By 1929, Olivet Baptist, St. Mark's AME, Provident Baptist, Metropolitan Community Church, and others employed full-time social workers and were providing such services as paying for school expenses, caring for widows, giving temporary emergency relief to families, distributing baskets of food to the poor, and "constantly" giving handouts, carfare, lunch, and so on to those who applied for it. Most of this work was financed by taking extra collections from the congregation after the regular church collection every Sunday.[87]

Overall, Protestant institutions were responsible for most of the social agency work done by religious groups in Chicago—four-fifths of it, according to a survey conducted in 1936 by the Federal Council of Churches. The survey found that "of the fifty or more social settlements and neighborhood houses in Chicago, forty are connected with Protestant communions. [...] There are thirteen [Protestant] children's agencies, ten homes for the aged, eight hospitals, fourteen general institutions, [...] twenty-two neighborhood houses, one day nursery, five relief and benevolent agencies, [...] and a few miscellaneous agencies."[88]

As already stated, comparable social consciousness was evidenced at higher levels of Protestant bodies. In fact, the 1930s saw a spectacular revival and radicalization of the Social Gospel, which had declined in the previous decade. In 1932, for example, delegates to the General Conference of the Methodist Church approved a resolution that a journalist described as a "wholesale condemnation of the present social order, and the acquisitive principle on which it is based." That same year, delegates to the Northern Baptist Convention affirmed, among other declarations, "that all wealth and all labor

---

86. *Washington Post*, May 1, 1932; *China Press*, November 25, 1931; *Chicago Tribune*, August 22, 30, 1931.
87. Wallace D. Best, *Passionately Human, No Less Divine: Religion and Culture in Black Chicago, 1915–1952* (Princeton, NJ: Princeton University Press, 2005), 74–84; Helen C. Harris, "The Negro Church on the South Side in Chicago: How It Meets the Problem of the Need for Charity," December 13, 1929, term paper for Sociology 270, Burgess Papers, box 143, folder 5. On the Great Migration, see Isabel Wilkerson, *The Warmth of Other Suns: The Epic Story of America's Great Migration* (New York: Vintage Books, 2010).
88. *New York Herald Tribune*, March 14, 1936; P. Mathew Titus, "A Study of Protestant Charities in Chicago with Special Reference to Neighborhood Houses and Social Settlements" (abstract of PhD diss., University of Chicago, 1939).

power are intended by the Creator for the highest good of all people; that from the cradle to the grave all members of the community are bound to do their best for the common good, and reciprocally are entitled to the best that the community is able to provide for its members in common; that the normal standard of living for any is that which is practicable for all; [...] and that no person can establish a rightful claim upon or within the community for more than a normal living." The Methodist Federation of Social Action was far to the left of the New Deal, as was the Federal Council of Churches as a whole, which was allied with the Workers Alliance. On a local level, the Chicago Church Federation established in 1936 a Department of Social Service, with four divisions: Public Institutions, Race Relations, Civic Relations, and Church and Industry. Such examples of a rejuvenated Social Gospel could be multiplied many times over.[89]

An especially interesting event was the creation, in June 1934, of the Council for Social Action (CSA) by the General Council of Congregational and Christian Churches. The CSA was to be not merely a minor body in the church's structure that would undertake some social advocacy; rather, it was to be a "major society in the denominational structure," to which the entire church should in a sense be subordinated. According to church leaders, its establishment signified a virtual revolution—"the most radical in the history of Protestantism"—namely, the beginning of a turn in Protestantism from "pioneer work in geographical expansion to pioneer work in social reconstruction." The *Christian Century* hailed the creation of the CSA as Christianity's greatest step forward since the establishment of the missionary enterprise. The new social outlook was symbolized by the General Council's passage of a remarkable resolution—which was subsequently very controversial—that demanded the overthrow of the present economic system with its principles of private ownership, which "[depend] upon exploitation of one group by another, create industrial and civic strife, precipitate periods of unemployment, and perpetuate insecurity and all its attendant miseries." The resolution continued:

> We set ourselves to work toward the abolition of the system responsible for all these destructive elements in our common life by eliminating the system's habits, the legal forms which sustain it, the moral ideals which justify it. We set ourselves to work toward the inauguration of a genuinely cooperative social economy, democratically planned to adjust production to consumption requirements, to modify or eliminate private ownership of the means of production or distribution wherever such ownership interferes with the social good.[90]

---

89. Paul A. Carter, *The Decline and Revival of the Social Gospel: Social and Political Liberalism in American Protestant Churches, 1920–1940* (Ithaca, NY: Cornell University Press, 1954), 146, 150–52, 177; Proceedings, Resolutions, and Program of the 1935 National Convention of the Workers Alliance of America, p. 5, McCulloch Papers, box 6, folder 4; Rules and Regulations of the Department of Social Service of the Chicago Church Federation, February 24, 1936, Hilliard Papers, box 120, folder 5. On the radicalism of Methodism in these years, an unusual but interesting source is Elizabeth Dilling, *The Red Network: A "Who's Who" and Handbook of Radicalism for Patriots* (Chicago, IL: Elizabeth Dilling, 1934), 33–38. Dilling, a professional abhorrer of Communists, performed a valuable service for left-wing historians in publishing this compendium.
90. *Chicago Tribune*, June 28, 1934. See also "Chicago Conference on the International and Economic Crisis," May 14, 1934, in McCulloch Papers, box 8, folder 3.

Among other goals, the CSA (headquartered in Chicago and New York) intended to cooperate with the Federal Council of Churches to create a program that would be not only ambitious, staking out left-wing positions with regard to international relations, industrial relations, race relations, and rural conditions, but also "genuinely interdenominational."[91]

The national infrastructure the CSA set up included regional committees, state committees, local church committees, and numerous commissions that were assigned specific tasks. It founded an important bimonthly journal, *Social Action*. The outreach that the CSA undertook to the younger generation involved making contributions to curricula for various classes and clubs; printing pamphlets and leaflets on particular issues such as "Why Men Strike" or "What Makes Communists?"; setting up and supporting institutes, conferences, and seminars; and developing a mailing list of young and adult leaders in local churches. Because church leaders encountered "abysmal apprehension and misunderstanding" regarding the CSA among rank-and-file Congregationalists, who tended to be more conservative than the council, it was deemed necessary to "spend considerable time indoctrinating church members," especially by means of seminars in local churches. How successful these efforts were is unclear, although an "economic plebiscite" of the 1,200,000 church members conducted in 1938 showed that most had liberal views on work relief, labor unions, public ownership of electric utilities, organization of consumer cooperatives, and further social control of the economy. The significance of these findings is limited, however, since only a small fraction of members took part in the plebiscite.[92]

The Catholic Church, likewise, was no pawn in the hands of the business class. In Chicago, in the United States, and internationally, the Church had long had an ambivalent relationship with industrial capitalism, as evidenced by Pope Leo XIII's 1891 encyclical *Rerum Novarum*, which both upheld the rights of private property and inveighed against the social evils of laissez-faire capitalism. Indeed, even if many church leaders had not been offended by the "injustice and oppression and inhuman greed" of big business—to quote Chicago's Catholic newspaper the *New World* in 1904—they would likely have remained skeptical of economic liberalism just because it functioned, they thought, as a solvent of social bonds. Nothing could have been more contrary to the medievalism of the Church, with its conception of society as an organic and harmonious unity, than liberal capitalism. "Justice is allied to cooperation, not competition," declared William J. Dillon, editor of the *New World*, echoing Leo's encyclical. Thus, in the late nineteenth and early twentieth centuries, the American Church

---

91. Carter, *The Decline and Revival of the Social Gospel*, 175–78; CSA By-Laws, McCulloch Papers, box 8, folder 3; CSA Information Bulletin, September 27, 1934, ibid.; *Washington Post*, September 15, 1934; *Chicago Tribune*, June 26, 1934, June 19, 1936.
92. CSA Information Bulletin, September 27, 1934, McCulloch Papers, box 8, folder 3; Harry T. Stock, "Some Opportunities for the Council for Social Action," August 13, 1934, ibid.; letter from Lawrence Wilson to the CSA, August 28, 1934, ibid.; Cyrus Ransom Pangborn, "Free Churches and Social Change: A Critical Study of the Council for Social Action" (PhD diss., Columbia University, 1951), passim.; *New York Times*, January 23, 1939.

often took a rather progressive stand on industrial issues, supporting—as did *Rerum Novarum*—government protection of labor unions, the worker's right to a living wage, and regulation of child labor. It is true that the Church's vehement hostility to socialism significantly tempered its progressivism—most of its leaders, for instance, supported the relatively conservative AFL—and the majority of parish priests certainly could not be called left wing, despite their working-class constituency. On the whole, the Church had a very conservative influence on its mass base. Nevertheless, the social turmoil of the Progressive Era impelled many priests, lay societies, and the Church hierarchy toward ever more leftist positions, culminating in the important Bishops' Program of 1919. This program of social reconstruction, largely the work of the activist Father John A. Ryan but endorsed by the hierarchy through its arm the NCWC, advocated measures that a horrified business community saw as nearly Bolshevik: public housing, control of monopolies, governmental guarantee of workers' right to organize, national minimum wage legislation and a minimum working age, progressive taxation, and insurance against old age, sickness, and unemployment. Had the 1920s not intervened, the stage would have been set for the social agenda of the 1930s.[93]

As it happened, an even more important document set the stage for American Catholicism's definitive move leftward, namely Pope Pius XI's *Quadragesimo Anno*, published in 1931. Received with enthusiasm by American Catholics, this encyclical was quite progressive: it called for redistribution of property, worker participation in management and ownership, a family wage for all workers, state planning of the economy for the sake of "social justice," and, in general, a complete "reform of morals" through a return to the teachings of the Gospel. The appearance of this document greatly enhanced the prestige of John Ryan and his ideas, which were now seen even by many parish priests to have been endorsed by the Pope himself. Catholic spokesmen like Father Charles Coughlin and the more respectable Archbishop John T. McNicholas of Cincinnati were already denouncing "the monstrous abuses of capitalism" (to quote Father Paul Blakely in 1931), and soon they were joined by a nationwide chorus of lay and clerical voices. "The real authors of violent and bloody revolutions in our times," declared the administrative committee of the NCWC, "are not the radicals and communists, but the callous and autocratic possessors of wealth and power who use their positions and their riches to oppress their fellows." "The trouble with us [Catholics] in the past," said Archbishop Mundelein of Chicago, "has been that we were too often

---

93. Charles Shanabruch, *Chicago's Catholics: The Evolution of an American Identity* (Notre Dame, IN: University of Notre Dame Press, 1981), 128–54; Mel Piehl, *Breaking Bread: The Catholic Worker and the Origin of Catholic Radicalism in America* (Tuscaloosa, AL: University of Alabama Press, 2006), 34–53; Neil Betten, *Catholic Activism and the Industrial Worker* (Gainsville, FL: University Presses of Florida, 1976), 3–16, 33–38; Jay P. Dolan, *The American Catholic Experience: A History from Colonial Times to the Present* (Notre Dame, IN: University of Notre Dame Press, 1992), 333–46; Joseph M. McShane, *"Sufficiently Radical": Catholicism, Progressivism, and the Bishops' Program of 1919* (Washington, DC: Catholic University of America Press, 1986). See also Roger Aubert, *Catholic Social Teaching: An Historical Perspective* (Milwaukee, WI: Marquette University Press, 2003).

drawn into an alliance with the wrong side. [...] Our place is beside the poor, beside the working man." Catholic journals like *Commonweal*, *Catholic Charities Review*, *Catholic Mind*, *America*, *Catholic World*, and *Catholic Action* published articles severely critical of capitalism and, after the election of FDR, supportive of the New Deal.[94]

The Social Action Department of the NCWC greatly expanded its activities in the 1930s. Its many publications addressed the Pope's labor encyclicals and the relation of Catholic social thought to the plight of the worker, in particular the scourge of unemployment. It published supportive statements on strikes, and it issued joint statements with Protestant and Jewish bodies supporting organized labor, the Wagner Act, progressive taxation, a shorter work week, and cooperative economic planning. It also organized conferences on reconstructing capitalism that bishops and priests attended, and established schools to train labor priests to agitate among workers. Its guiding spirit John Ryan was nearly ubiquitous in liberal circles: he was vice-president of the National Unemployment League, vice-president of the American Association for Labor Legislation, vice-president of the American Association for Social Security, held several government labor advisory positions, and, like many Catholic leaders, actively supported the CIO. In Chicago, Monseigneur Hildebrand conducted labor seminars at St. Mary's Seminary for priests from industrial districts, frequently inviting labor leaders to give lectures. "The ideology of the Hildebrand school," historian Barbara Warne Newell notes, "placed upon the parish priest, as one of his responsibilities, the encouragement of trade-unionism on the ground that only in this way could the standard of living and the human dignity of man be raised." Chicago's Bishop Sheil provided support to this ideology, notably by harnessing the energies of the Catholic Youth Organization to the crusade being waged by the CIO.[95]

Lay Catholics, too, leapt into labor activism, for instance by forming the Association of Catholic Trade Unionists in 1937, which by 1940 had eight chapters around the country, including in Chicago. Among many other activities, the ACTU helped organize scores of labor schools in 10 cities (in alliance with archdioceses, the Catholic League for Social Justice, and the National Conference of Catholic Charities), conducted mass rallies in working-class parishes, and published a newspaper that vigorously defended the CIO even while consistently attacking communism. The Catholic Worker movement, however, founded in 1933 by Dorothy Day and the French intellectual Peter

---

94. Piehl, *Breaking Bread*, 53; David J. O'Brien, *American Catholics and Social Reform: The New Deal Years* (New York: Oxford University Press, 1968), 17–21, 48; Betten, *Catholic Activism*, 25–31, 46, 47; Anthony Sean Pastor-Zelaya, "The Development of Roman Catholic Social Liberalism in the United States, 1887–1935" (PhD diss., University of California–Santa Barbara, 1988), 160; *New York Times*, January 3, 1938; Robert Brooke Clements, "The Commonweal, 1924–1938: The Williams-Shuster Years" (PhD diss., University of Notre Dame, 1972), 121–74; David O'Brien, "American Catholics and Organized Labor in the 1930's," *Catholic Historical Review* 52, no. 3 (October 1966): 323–49.
95. Betten, *Catholic Activism*, 44–72, 124–34; Aaron I. Abell, *American Catholicism and Social Action: A Search for Social Justice, 1865–1950* (Notre Dame, IN: University of Notre Dame Press, 1963), 258–63; Newell, *Chicago and the Labor Movement*, 244, 245.

Maurin, was far more radical and influential, forming communities across the country that engaged in activism on all issues of the left. Indeed, this movement continues up to the present, so deeply has it resonated among liberal Catholics.[96]

Religion is a complex social phenomenon, however, and local clergy and laypeople were certainly not always as radical as the more visible intellectuals or activists. George Patterson, a Chicago steelworker and organizer with the United Steelworkers in 1937, recalled that the clergy in South Chicago—unlike in the stockyards area—tended to be unsympathetic toward his activism. In part, their reaction was simply good sense: financially, many churches were reliant on the steel mills, so it was unlikely that clergymen would assist organizers or advocate for the union in their sermons. "See the coal down there in the basement?" a priest at St. Michael's said to him once. "[T]he charcoal comes from this mill. See that lumber that's lying outside the window? We're going to build a playroom for the kids. We got that from the steel mills. You don't expect us to bite the hand that feeds us, do you?" Actually, it seems that Protestants were more prone to fierce anti-Communism than Catholics—which is unsurprising, given the typical class composition of the congregations.[97] Patterson had for years been active in the South Shore Presbyterian Church, but as he embraced the labor movement he noticed his former friends shunning him and felt pressure to resign his positions in church groups. When he brought up the union, the response was usually "Reds!"[98]

---

96. Betten, *Catholic Activism*, 44–72, 124–34; Aaron I. Abell, *American Catholicism and Social Action*, 258–63; Steve Rosswurm, "The Catholic Church and the Left-Led Unions: Labor Priests, Labor Schools, and the ACTU," in *The C.I.O.'s Left-Led Unions*, ed. Steve Rosswurm (New Brunswick, NJ: Rutgers University Press, 1992); Pehl, "The Remaking of the Catholic Working Class"; Nancy L. Roberts, *Dorothy Day and the* Catholic Worker (Albany, NY: State University of New York Press, 1984); Francis J. Sicius, *The Word Made Flesh: The Chicago Catholic Worker and the Emergence of Lay Activism in the Church* (New York: University Press of America, 1990); William D. Miller, *A Harsh and Dreadful Love: Dorothy Day and the Catholic Worker Movement* (Milwaukee, WI: Marquette University Press, 2005).

97. Catholic anti-Communism, moreover, was hardly a straightforward matter. Steve Fraser argues that "anticommunism as a mass movement was profoundly anticapitalist insofar as it rebelled against the corporate, bureaucratic, centralizing, and statist tendencies of the modern industrial order." Cultural traditionalism, after all, can be a potent source of "radicalism." Fraser, "The 'Labor Question,'" in *The Rise and Fall of the New Deal Order, 1930–1980*, eds. Steve Fraser and Gary Gerstle (Princeton, NJ: Princeton University Press, 1989), 73. Also see Kenneth J. Heineman, "A Catholic New Deal: Religion and Labor in 1930s Pittsburgh," *Pennsylvania Magazine of History and Biography* 118, no. 4 (October 1994): 363–94. ("[T]he labor priests and laymen," he writes, "were shaping a distinctly Catholic Americanism that was anti-Communist and anti-capitalist.") For a nuanced study of the battles between left-wing and right-wing interpretations of Catholicism in 1930s Detroit, see Matthew Pehl, "'Apostles of Fascism,' 'Communist Clergy,' and the UAW: Political Ideology and Working-Class Religion in Detroit, 1919–1945," *Journal of American History* 99, no. 2 (September 2012): 440–65.

98. Interview with George Patterson, December 1970–January 1971, 55–59, Oral History Project in Labor History, Roosevelt University; Roger Horowitz, "The Path Not Taken: A Social History of Industrial Unionism in Meatpacking, 1930–1960" (PhD diss., University of Wisconsin–Madison, 1990), 258, 259.

In general, despite the examples I have given of an impressive social conscience among the religious, it can hardly be said that most churches, even in Chicago, were as radical or as alive to the sufferings of the poor as the situation called for. Such was the conclusion of a thorough study in 1932, which quoted the opinion of a leader in emergency relief in "a large city" that "not a clergyman in this city has spoken out loud enough to make himself heard against the malnutrition of children." The author of this study observed that "the plain fact is that the well-to-do generally do not want to hear how the unemployed are faring; the subject is unpleasant, and the recital would disturb the peace of a church service." Accordingly, most clergymen tended to avoid the subject in their sermons, and doubtless did not exert as much energy as they could have on fundraising for unemployment relief. Nevertheless, in part through the efforts of such organizations as I have discussed here, even well-to-do church members were not allowed to entirely forget the desolation of long-term unemployment. Every year before Labor Day the Federal Council distributed its Labor Sunday message to 110,000 pastors, with requests that they read it in church. The 1935 message ended with a prayer that concluded, "From ever forgetting the forlorn figure of the unemployed; from failure to see that our social fabric is as shabby as his coat, and that our heads must bow in equal shame with his, good Lord, deliver us. That our consciences may know no rest until unemployment is abolished, we beseech Thee to hear us, good Lord."[99]

It must be said, too, that insofar as churches did not always do as much for the unemployed as one might have wished, this was partly because the Depression had savaged their finances. The pastor of the Mount Meriah Baptist Church, on the South Side, reported in 1934 that the church's current income was 30 percent of what it had been in 1929, and attendance had been cut in half. As historians have argued, such financial troubles meant that social outreach and relief programs suffered: Boy Scout and Campfire Girl programs were cut, social workers had to be laid off, churches could not stay open as many days of the week as previously, and so on. To some extent volunteers were able to take over for paid workers and give assistance to the neediest members of the congregation, but overwhelmingly the indigent masses had to turn to government for help.[100]

***

Thus, while in many respects churches were embracing the poor in these years, the poor were not universally embracing churches. This did not necessarily indicate a loss of religious faith, however; in fact, one study found that most families that no longer attended church professed not to have changed their attitude toward religion. Another

---

99. James Mickel Williams, *Human Aspects of Unemployment and Relief, with Special Reference to the Effects of the Depression on Children* (Chapel Hill, NC: University of North Carolina Press, 1933), 190, 191; *New York Times*, August 26, 1935.
100. "Effect of the depression ... as reported in interviews with the Rev. W. L. Petty, and the Rev. Mary Evans," in Burgess Papers, box 134, folder 1; "Effect of the depression on religion ... as reported in an interview with the Reverend J. B. Redmond," ibid.

study, of families on relief in New York, similarly concluded that the large majority of believers did not "revolt." On the other hand, among all three major religious groups—Catholics, Protestants, and Jews—there *was* in general a "loosening of religious bonds." "Prior to their unemployment," the researchers found that "75 percent of the families had been orthodox; 15 percent, moderate; and the remainder had no religious bonds. Only one was antagonistic. At the time when these families were interviewed, only 40 percent were orthodox; 33 percent, moderate; and 17 percent were without ties. Ten percent were antagonistic."[101]

One reason for the increase of antagonism may have been anger at church practices. Many Catholics in Chicago thought the relief they received from the Central Charity Bureau (of the Catholic Charities) was highly inadequate—when it was given at all. One young couple, for instance, was refused relief on the ridiculous grounds that they lived with the man's mother. A person of some influence in the Polish community insisted, "the worst offenders in the line of skimmed budgets are Catholic Charities." There was also widespread resentment that the Church still expected people to pay parochial school tuition and that some churches still charged fees for performing ritual acts like baptisms, confirmations, and burials. Among Italians on the North Side there was a "definite feeling that the church is always after money, money and more money," an observer stated. "Children, ordinarily too young to make such observations, say when passing the Cardinal's house, 'See what a swell place we pay to keep up.'" Poles on the South Side had similar reactions. One teenage boy colorfully expressed a common attitude: "These fuckers over here at St. Michael's, all they think about is *money*. You should *see* it when the money wagon comes around! They have to wheel it out in wheelbarrows! Anytime you *want* anything, all they think of is, 'Do they get a fin for it?' They'd *never* give a guy a break!"[102]

Such rebelliousness against authority and disgust with the ignominy of the profit motive characterized also much of the Black community on the South Side. The charge of churchly "racketeering" was very common in Bronzeville, especially among non-members. The proprietor of a gambling establishment, for example, remarked, "The church is getting to be too big a racket for me. I'd rather support my own racket." A janitor confided to an interviewer, "You know churches are nothing but a racket." An optometrist commented, "I was baptized in a Baptist church but I don't go regularly. [...] It's just racketeering on people's emotions anyway." A skilled laborer lashed out at preachers: "Blood-suckers! They'll take the food out of your mouth and make you think

---

101. Ruth Shonle Cavan and Katherine Howland Ranck, *The Family and the Depression* (Freeport, NY: Books for Libraries Press, 1969 [1938]), 107; Eli Ginzberg, *The Unemployed* (New Brunswick: Transaction Publishers, 2004 [1943]), 94. American Protestantism, and less so Catholicism and Judaism, had already been experiencing a decline in the 1920s, which continued in the Depression decade. See Robert T. Handy, "The American Religious Depression, 1925–1935," *Church History* 29, no. 1 (March 1960): 3–16.
102. Lizabeth Cohen, *Making a New Deal* (New York: Cambridge University Press, 1990), 224–226; Ginzberg, *The Unemployed*, 97; Mrs. Adamczyne, November 5, 1934, in Ernest Burgess Papers, box 131, folder 3.

they are doing you a favor." Church members grumbled as well. "Ministers are not as conscientious as they used to be," one insisted. "They are money-mad nowadays. All they want is the almighty dollar and that is all they talk about." "I thinks there's only one heaven where we all will go," a woman said, "but the biggest thieves are running the churches, so what can they do about saving us? Nothing!"[103]

Incidentally, such hostility toward the church may not have been entirely justified. Black churches were often deeply in debt from obligations they had incurred before the Depression, and they had to emphasize fundraising just to keep their doors open. Ministerial salaries averaged less than $2,000 a year—although it is true they were higher than what most of the laity earned. One study concluded that on average, 43 percent of the money Black churches raised went to salaries, 21 percent to "benevolence," 23 percent to interest and reduction of debt, and the rest to church upkeep and overhead.[104]

Even white workers in "conservative" Midwestern towns like Muncie, Indiana, sometimes questioned church authority on left-wing grounds. "I don't go to church," a working man told Robert Lynd in 1935, "because the church ought to have something to meet the needs of laboring men, and the laborers feel that the administration of churches is in the hands of wealth." Likely a fairly representative sentiment, this statement already shows a kind of class consciousness—in the heartland of America. On the other hand, an unemployed factory worker from the same town remarked that he and his friends had started going to church because they had no money to go anywhere else, "and we got interested in the teachings and activities and stuck." It may be that they enjoyed the sermons that deprecated lust for dollars, criticized the "practical man" who lived only for the market, and praised kindness, love, and mutual aid.[105]

As was mentioned above, insofar as churches' social service work declined during the Depression, membership tended to shrink. But even when the working-class unemployed continued to attend church, it was not rare for their faith to have been shaken by all the troubles they had seen. The secretary of a Yugoslav Women's Club, for instance, told an interviewer in 1936 that Yugoslavs' religious feeling had weakened. "Slovene people," she said, "are observing religious customs and go to church, of course, but deep in their hearts they are losing faith. They usually say, 'Prayer does not help us any more in this country.'" They attended church less frequently than before and mainly only for its social aspect. Men in particular were most likely to have grown skeptical. "After five years of fruitless prayer," commented a social worker who had had experience with many different nationalities, "[the men] remain to brood in the home, while the women still attend mass." In general, according to an expert on unemployment (writing in 1940), religious activity among "the great masses of workers"—especially men—was

---

103. St. Clair Drake and Horace R. Cayton, *Black Metropolis* (New York: Harcourt, Brace and Company, 1945), 418–22; St. Clair Drake, *Churches and Voluntary Associations in the Negro Community* (Report of WPA Project 465-54-3-386, Chicago, IL, 1940), 199–201.
104. Drake and Cayton, *Black Metropolis*, 420, 421.
105. Robert and Helen Lynd, *Middletown in Transition: A Study in Cultural Conflicts* (New York: Harcourt, Brace & World, 1937), 302. For two representative sermons, see pp. 299, 300.

"more a matter of retaining a nominal contact with a possible source of well-being than a matter of sharing intimately and constantly in the ministrations of the church or the comfort and convictions of religion."[106]

Nevertheless, as an outlet for sociality and a "haven in a heartless world," the church remained an integral part of civic life. A person was not treated there as though he were a mere cog in a machine or an instrument for amassing profit; and to the degree that he thought he *was* treated that way, he rebelled against it and condemned church authorities as base and dishonorable. In church, he was supposed to be not a means to an end but an end in himself, someone with a personal relationship to God and therefore possessing dignity, as contrasted with his condition in society. In fact, one might interpret the entirety of religion itself as, to some degree, manifesting a belief in the illegitimacy of the dominant social order, and as being a potent, durable, and collective form of resistance to injustice. This is approximately how the young Karl Marx saw it in his Introduction to the *Contribution to the Critique of Hegel's Philosophy of Right*: "Religio[n] is, at one and the same time, the *expression* of real suffering and a *protest* against real suffering. Religion is the sigh of the oppressed creature, the heart of a heartless world, and the soul of soulless conditions" (italics in the original). Even in its purely social aspect, as providing a satisfying form of communal participation, one can detect in religion an element of resistance.[107]

Consider the hold that religion continued to exert in these years on Blacks on the South Side of Chicago. While some of the larger, old-line churches saw a drop in attendance, many of the smaller and more "lower-class" churches saw a dramatic increase. The big churches, a housewife said, "don't want you if you haven't any money. [...] I mean that I am recognized in a little church, whereas I wouldn't be in a big church. I'm able to take my place even when I don't have any money, in a little church." By the 1940s, almost 75 percent of the Black Belt's churches were these storefront or house churches, which had an average membership of fewer than 35 people (as contrasted with the 5 largest churches that had a membership of more than 10,000 and sat 2,000 people). There was one on almost every block. They were often Baptist, but a large number were Holiness or Spiritualist churches, which, as Lizabeth Cohen says, "offered worshippers an intense, emotional experience and took little responsibility for anything

---

106. "Mrs. Kushar–landlady–Jugoslavian," Burgess Papers, box 131, folder 3; no title, no name, Burgess Papers, box 131, folder 4; E. Wight Bakke, *Citizens without Work* (New Haven, CT: Yale University Press, 1940), 45.
107. Herbert Gutman was among the first labor historians to analyze the role of religion as a framework to resist economic oppression. See his article "Protestantism and the American Labor Movement: The Christian Spirit in the Gilded Age," *American Historical Review* 72, no. 1 (October 1966): 74–101. For the poor, one historian writes, "otherworldly hope was less about escapism than it was about ultimate vindication." Wayne Flynt, "Religion for the Blues: Evangelicalism, Poor Whites, and the Great Depression," *Journal of Southern History* 71, no. 1 (February 2005): 3–38. This article shows, incidentally, that poor-white churches in Appalachia and the South were remarkably similar to poor-Black churches in urban or rural contexts, characterized, like them, by egalitarianism, democracy, intense community, emotionalism, and resistance to dominant social and cultural norms.

but their souls." The revivalist Cosmopolitan Community Church, for example, saw a 40 percent increase in attendance between 1929 and 1934, apparently because with the arrival of the Reverend Mary Evans it came to be organized in a more intimate and "intense" way. The Holiness church was so named because of its perfectionist doctrine, the doctrine of sanctification. From a writer's description one may well understand the appeal of this church to people whose lot in life was hard:

> [Sanctification] is a concept that makes the guilty guiltless, shields them from that side of life [...] which has become distasteful and repellent. Converts become free from sin, holy, sanctified, and above the world of things. Nothing can touch or harm them. They find complete comfort and perfection of self in union with the person of the Holy Spirit. They find new expression of power. They have refuge from all that they think of as sinful, and from the overpowering forces of immediate social requirements.[108]

At one of these churches in a federal slum clearance area, a domestic worker gave an emotional testimony: "I thank God for being here this morning. I thank God I am saved and sanctified. [...] You and I look up and see God working. You can see how He works and how He guides you. *I was scrubbing the floor last night and I was so tired I couldn't get through. God pulled me through.*"[109]

From waterless tenements and closet-sized kitchenettes, from relief station lines and packed park benches, tens of thousands of people (two-thirds of them women) came to these churches every week, usually multiple times a week. Some churches had services every day. These were not the restrained services that the upper middle class attended, such as the Congregationalist, Presbyterian, Methodist, and Baptist services at the larger churches; they were the ecstatic, Dionysian services that the disinherited craved, simultaneously protest and joyous self-justification. In most churches of this type, the sermons were strikingly democratic: they were simply expositions of scripture read by members of the congregation, a verse at a time, interspersed with elaborations by the minister. In other cases the ministers, or "elders"—who were not infrequently illiterate—expounded, through song, speech, and "speaking in tongues," interpretations of biblical passages and stories. But in these sermons, too, it was not merely an individual addressing an audience of passive listeners; rather, they were *collective* sermons, so to speak, the people participating by giving loud, spontaneous assent in antiphonal fashion. "Amen!" "Preach it!" "Hallelujah!" "Bless God forever!" Or they would emphatically repeat the preacher's dramatic cadences. The collective enthusiasm (pithily referred

---

108. Quoted in Vattel Elbert Daniel, "Ritual in Chicago's South Side Churches for Negroes" (PhD diss., University of Chicago, 1940), 118.
109. Drake and Cayton, *Black Metropolis*, 415, 614; Brian Dolinar, ed., *The Negro in Illinois: The WPA Papers* (Chicago, IL: University of Illinois Press, 2013), 209–16; Cohen, *Making a New Deal*, 226; "Effect of the Depression … as Reported in Interviews with the Rev. W. L. Petty, and the Rev. Mary Evans"; Daniel, "Ritual in Chicago's South Side Churches," 107, 121. Italics in original. On storefront churches, see E. Franklin Frazier, *The Negro Church in America* (New York: Schocken Books, 1963), 53–55.

to as "getting happy") built to the point that the congregation went well beyond the antiphonal tradition of the Greek chorus: in its frenzy it acted out, so to speak, the emotional content of the sermon. According to one reporter, the yelling could grow so vociferous that it sounded like a baseball game. People stood up and raised their hands while praying or speaking in tongues, jumped up and down like a jumping jack, rhythmically clapped and stomped their feet, ran and danced and fainted. In the Holiness sect there were even healing rituals and saint-making rituals. (After being "converted" one could become a "saint," i.e., be sanctified.) One may be inclined to smile at the "superstitious" and wildly popular practice of healing—which was integral to the Spiritualist sect as well—but from innumerable testimonies it seems that remarkable results were sometimes obtained.[110]

Music was at least as essential an element of these lower-class services as of those catering to the upper middle class. But it was a different type of music: gospel, as opposed to the more sober hymns and processionals of the Lutherans and such sects. Even the smaller churches had a gospel chorus. The piano was substituted for the organ, and percussive instruments such as the tambourine, triangle, and drums were introduced. Gospel is a jubilant genre: the songs of these churches more frequently emphasized comfort, joy, and ecstasy than those of the more sedate mainline churches. The most popular gospel hymn of the 1930s, written by a local Chicago Baptist choir leader, went as follows:

> Precious Lord, take my hand,
> Lead me on, let me stand;
> I am tired, I am weak, I am worn;
> Through the night, through the storm,
> Take my hand, lead me on,
> Precious Lord, take my hand, lead me on.[111]

Perhaps as significant as the music's themes of comfort and joy was its swinging and staccato style, and even "the spontaneity with which the music [was] introduced into the service, seemingly anywhere and by anybody." James Baldwin, who grew up under

---

110. Daniel, "Ritual in Chicago's South Side Churches," 25, 40, 41, 80–83; Drake and Cayton, *Black Metropolis*, 619; Dolinar, *The Negro in Illinois*, 211. For examples of the cures of physical ailments that healers were able to bring about, see the reports in Burgess Papers, box 89, folder 10. "Quacks" (as false healers were called) of course abounded, but it does seem that some people had impressive powers of healing. The many thousands of church members (some of them educated and middle class) who were convinced were not merely credulous and irrational; there seems to have been real evidence to back up their faith. To what extent "healing" was due to powerful placebo effects cannot be known, but one hopes that science will someday investigate and clarify these phenomena. (The reader interested in phenomena sometimes called "paranormal" might consult Elizabeth Lloyd Mayer, *Extraordinary Knowing: Science, Skepticism, and the Inexplicable Powers of the Human Mind* (New York: Bantam Books, 2007).)
111. Drake and Cayton, *Black Metropolis*, 622.

the profound influence of the Holiness church (for his father was a storefront preacher), recalled that it was "very exciting. [...] There is no music like that music, no drama like that of the saints rejoicing, the sinners moaning, the tambourines racing, and all those voices coming together and crying holy unto the Lord."[112]

Writer Zora Neale Hurston captured the meaning of all these elements of a Sanctified Church service when she said simply, "The supplication is forgotten in the frenzy of creation." It all amounted to collective *creation*, in fact to drama with music, as Hurston said. "And since music without motion is unnatural among Negroes," she continued, "there is always something that approaches dancing—in fact *IS* dancing—in such a ceremony. [...] It must be noted that the sermon in these churches is not the set thing that [it] is in the other protestant churches. It is loose and formless and is in reality merely a framework upon which to hang more songs. [...] The whole movement of the Sanctified Church is a rebirth of song-making! It has brought in a new era of spiritual-making."[113]

Spiritualist churches, too, proliferated in certain sections of the Black Belt.[114] Patronized even more disproportionately by women than Holiness churches were, they combined religion with fortune-telling and such "heathenish" practices as distributing "lucky" flowers to any member who gave some small amount of money. Aside from the emotional satisfaction that the churches provided, their popularity was due largely to the practical value of being given good luck charms (to help in a job search, for example), lucky policy numbers, messages from fortune-tellers, and messages from departed loved ones. Equally importantly, the Spiritualist sect, unlike other denominations, had no unkind words for card-playing, policy, or dancing. In addition, like the Holiness sect, it was appreciated for its progressive gender norms: ambitious women could rise to the top, could become elders, ministers, healers, mediums, or heads of missionary societies. As historian Wallace Best states, the many women who had high positions in low-income churches "exerted great influence among the city's poor, challenging the male-dominated moral authority and cultural dominance of mainline Protestant black churches." In fact, it was largely women who built and maintained lower-class churches, which were therefore, in effect, a vital terrain of struggle against the dominant society's patriarchal order (even if in many cases they also, inevitably, reproduced patriarchy).[115]

---

112. Daniel, "Ritual in Chicago's South Side Churches," 76–79, 126; Cheryl J. Sanders, *Saints in Exile: The Holiness-Pentecostal Experience in African American Religion and Culture* (New York: Oxford University Press, 1996), 112.
113. Zora Neale Hurston, *The Sanctified Church* (New York: Marlowe & Company, 1981), 54, 104. On the history of music in the Black religious tradition, see C. Eric Lincoln and Lawrence H. Mamiya, *The Black Church in the African American Experience* (Durham, NC: Duke University Press, 1990), chapter 12.
114. Some white immigrants and Americans were also attracted to Spiritualism and Pentecostalism: such churches were scattered all over Chicago in the 1930s. See reports in Burgess Papers, boxes 89 and 90.
115. "A report on the status of spiritualism in the area between 47th, 51st, South Park and the New York Central Tracks, as reported in an interview with R. F. C. Tonelle," Burgess Papers, box 134, folder 1; Drake and Cayton, *Black Metropolis*, 632, 642; Wallace Best,

In a social context as pathological as the one described in earlier chapters, it is hardly surprising that so many people would seek solace, or would express their will to resist, by turning to an institution whose very raison d'être appeared to be love and community: community with God, community with people, and harmony with oneself (by raising oneself up to commune with God and others). It scarcely needs belaboring that the lower-class Black Chicago church, transplanted as it were from the fields of the South, aspired to be a church of love and unity, and racial unity. The following prayer spoken at a Baptist church exemplifies the racial consciousness that infused this religion:

> God, help us all to see the mission field. Help us all to see what Thou hast shown us. Help us to put clothes on the people of Africa. They walk over silver and gold and do not know its worth. They have around them valuable giant trees and do not know how to cut them down. Help us to save our brothers in black. Amen.[116]

On a more intimate level, the congregation was its own community. By participating in a storefront church in particular, one was resisting the atomization of urban life, especially as the vast majority of storefront congregants had recently migrated from the South. Many longed for churches that were "more like the churches in the South," where some congregations were so intimate that if, for example, a woman did not show up to Sunday School they would send someone to her home to see what was the matter. Storefront churches, however, were to some extent able to resurrect this "close and intimate folk culture of the South," as Richard Wright said. Even some larger churches made moves in this direction, as in the case of Mary Evans' Cosmopolitan church. Evans cultivated close ties with her flock, for instance by sending each member a birthday card on his or her birthday; they, in turn, "minded her just like we were children," one recalled.[117]

The "community" aspect of storefront churches was enhanced by their concern not only with the spiritual lives of members but also with the material lives of both members and nonmembers. The overall otherworldly emphasis did not preclude interest in this-worldly struggle. Many of these churches raised money to assist needy families, and sermons not infrequently highlighted issues of clean housing, employment, and education.

Passionately Human, No Less Divine, 67; Cheryl Townsend Gilkes, *"If It Wasn't for the Women ...": Black Women's Experience and Womanist Culture in Church and Community* (Maryknoll, NY: Orbis Books, 2001), 76–91.

116. Daniel, "Ritual in Chicago's South Side Churches," 39, 54.

117. Best, *Passionately Human, No Less Divine*, 65, 158; Richard Wright, *12 Million Black Voices* (reprint, New York: Thunder's Mouth, 1988), 134. For an investigation of the "communal" nature of a Black church in Pittsburgh whose members were rural migrants from the South, see Melvin D. Williams, *Community in a Black Pentecostal Church: An Anthropological Study* (Pittsburgh, PA: University of Pittsburgh Press, 1974). One shouldn't idealize the communal aspect of such a church, since there was, inevitably, conflict and competition for status between members, but one shouldn't underestimate it either. Williams describes, for instance, how it helped sustain defiance against middle-class norms of behavior.

One pastor of a "mixed-type" church, for example, ended a sermon on work with the prayer, "O Father, we are talking about work this morning. We are praying that the people will work as they never have worked before. Give all the needed encouragement and help us to do well." The "mother" of a low-income church prayed, "Gracious Father [...] we come, nothing but filthy rags, this morning. But it is you, the Shepherd, who can help us. [...] We want to pay our bills, my Father. It disturbs us, our Father, when we owe, because you said, 'Owe no man.'" Symptomatic of trends in the 1930s was the sign in front of a Black church in Chicago that a journalist observed: underneath the question "What Must We Do To Be Saved?" was given the answer, "Beset with Rent Hogs, Overcrowded in Hovels, Come to the Housing Meeting, Thursday Noon."[118]

The quintessential example of storefront generosity was that of Elder Lucy Smith, an "elderly, corpulent, dark-skinned and maternal" Georgian who had begun her ministry in a Bronzeville storefront in 1930 but within a few years was so popular that she moved her All Nations Pentecostal Church into a much larger building on a fashionable boulevard. She was practically legendary among the lower classes of Bronzeville (although generally despised by the middle and upper classes for her "ignorant" and "backward" ways).[119] Indeed, so popular was she that in the 1940s she had to build an even larger church, telling an interviewer, "You wouldn't believe that these folks with barely enough to live on are the very people who helped build my new large church." The predominant passion that inspired her, it seems, was to provide aid and comfort to impoverished Blacks and whites—"my people." "The singing in my church has 'swing' to it," she remarked, "because I want my people to swing out of themselves all the mis'ry and troubles that is heavy on their hearts." To concretely ameliorate the misery and troubles of the poor, every Thursday her church distributed food and clothing that had been donated either by congregants or by members of her huge radio audience—for in 1933 she began to broadcast live worship that was carried around the country (the first Black Chicago preacher to do so). Her program *The Glorious Church of the Air* had such influence that she was able to develop fruitful relationships with nearby businesses that heeded her calls for contributions of food and clothing. Poor whites, too, who appreciated her services far more than higher-status Blacks did, came to her church and received help, not only material but also emotional.[120]

---

118. Best, *Passionately Human*, 60, 61; Daniel, "Ritual in Chicago's South Side Churches," 39, 43, 80; James R. McGovern, *And a Time for Hope: Americans in the Great Depression* (Westport, CT: Praeger, 2000), 240.
119. When she died in 1952, more than a hundred thousand people, including some of Chicago's most prominent Black citizens, attended her funeral. It was the largest funeral in Black Chicago's history. Thus, just as the Black Belt's religious practices were transformed by the Great Migration, so its middle and upper classes were eventually compelled to pay at least public homage to the figures who epitomized lower-class religion.
120. Drake and Cayton, *Black Metropolis*, 643–45; Best, *Passionately Human*, 60, 61, 177–83; *Chicago Defender*, June 15, 1935; Herbert M. Smith, "Three Negro Preachers in Chicago: A Study in Religious Leadership" (MA thesis, University of Chicago, 1935), 17, 18.

Apart from all these manifestations of fellow-feeling (as one might call it) that tended to suffuse congregations and animate churchly activities, the human instinct for sociability found further expression in church clubs, as well as opportunities to be elected to some office in the church and to compete for prestige. Clubs were especially common in larger churches (which frequently had many low-income members): while men were rarely very involved in them, women embraced them as being the most satisfying aspect of their social lives. Craft groups, for instance, such as sewing circles, were popular, as were clubs organized along home state lines that were meant to appeal to migrants. There were even "culture" clubs devoted to art, Black history, and the discussion of social problems.[121]

Altogether, as suggested earlier, a fruitful way to interpret lower-class religion may be as, in part, a kind of sublimated class struggle, a spiritualized form of resistance to a political economy that is structured for the benefit of the rich. Whatever the functions or appeal of religious institutions may be for the materially prosperous, it is not implausible to view the religiosity of the poor in class terms. When Chicago's migrant Blacks rejected large churches because of their formality and impersonality, cherishing instead the friendliness and intimacy of storefronts, they were struggling in the most realistic way they could against the isolating and alienating structures of a modern urban capitalist economy. When, having spent the previous day floor-scrubbing in some white domicile or tramping around the city in search of an odd job, they participated in the ecstatic faith and rituals of Pentecostalism with its swinging gospel music, they were repudiating a degrading and racist political economy. The joy that a storefront congregation expressed upon the sanctification of one of its members was an un-self-conscious solidarity of the poor with the poor, against the backdrop of a society that was thought to be money-mad, cruel, and sinful.[122]

The passionate concern that so many Christians evinced in being *good people*, whether "saints" or merely good Christians who tried to minimize their sinning, can be interpreted in these terms. When a Black woman, member of a storefront church, said, "I read the Bible a lot. [...] You see, that's what it's all about. You see I can't teach you not to drink if I sit up in those taverns myself," we must remember that she was sustained by a vital community set against society's vices of pride, greed, envy, intoxication, and

---

121. Drake and Cayton, *Black Metropolis*, 424; Daniel, "Ritual in Chicago's South Side Churches," 108, 141; Sidney Harrison Moore, "Family and Social Networks in an Urban Black Storefront Church" (PhD diss., American University, 1975), 236–52; Drake, *Churches and Voluntary Associations*, 189.
122. "Through its priestly functions," a historian writes, "the Black Church provided comfort, nurture, and care among an outcast people, 'a refuge in a hostile white world' [...] where they could sing, shout, laugh, and cry among those who understood and shared the pain. The weekly worship service gave them the strength to go back to their jobs to survive another day, another week." Lincoln and Mamiya, *The Black Church in the African American Experience*, 272. See also Cheryl Lynn Greenberg, *"Or Does It Explode?" Black Harlem in the Great Depression* (New York: Oxford University Press, 1991), 103–107, and Benjamin Elijah Mays and Joseph William Nicholson, *The Negro's Church* (New York: Institute of Social and Religious Research, 1933), chapter 17.

lust. What such an ethos amounted to was a struggle to raise the moral level of the self and the world such that Christian love is the rule, selfishness has no dominion, the poor are not forgotten or despised, the rich are not beloved for being rich, and people do not treat each other only as means to the ends of amusement or sexual pleasure or financial gain. This radical religious paradigm was the ideal that a large minority of Chicago's Black population—"contradictory" though its "consciousness" necessarily was—tried to uphold in practice.[123]

Blacks, of course, were not the only disenfranchised residents of Chicago who embraced religion in their desire for comfort, community, and education. For example, a large proportion of Mexican migrants belonged to Catholic churches, although some—primarily middle class—were receptive to Protestant proselytizing, including Pentecostalism. Most working-class Mexicans thought of the Protestant church as "little more than a club at which interesting or uninteresting questions are discussed. The use of the beautiful in color, form, action, sound and odor as an aid to religious worship" remained, according to one researcher, integral to the religious practices of most Mexicans in Chicago. In general, another writer reported, "nearly every [Mexican] religious group [had] English classes, settlement activities, entertainments, kindergartens or some other class of work." A single church in South Chicago, known as Tempo de Guadalupe, had 8,000 Mexican members in 1935 and conducted services 4 times a day every day of the week. Adults regularly attended the classes it offered in language, music, sewing, handicrafts, arithmetic, physics, and sociology, and every day well over a hundred children attended the school it ran. The nearby Bird Memorial Congregational Church ran the South Chicago Community Center. In fact, the only part of Chicago's Mexican colony that was not well supplied with places of worship was the Stockyards district.[124]

---

123. Daniel, "Ritual in Chicago's South Side Churches," 105. Sermons in Black churches tended to be infused with a radical, even communistic "humanism"—as indeed was likely the case, to some more limited degree, in most churches generally, given the moral teachings of Christianity. For samples of such communitarian radicalism, see Mays and Nicholson, *The Negro's Church*, chapter 4. One can, of course, also view the moralism of religion as a means of social control, for instance in the characteristic censuring of unconventional sex behavior. This is simply indicative of the ambiguous character of Christianity. It can channel popular resistance even as it permits popular submission. On the church's "social control" function, see Frazier, *The Negro Church in America*, 31–34. For a thoughtful discussion of the interplay between radicalism and social accommodation in Black Christianity—and an overview of the sociological literature—see Gary R. Peck, "Black Radical Consciousness and the Black Christian Experience: Toward a Critical Sociology of Afro-American Religion," *Sociological Analysis* 43, no. 2 (Summer 1982): 155–69. Also see Barbara Dianne Savage, "W. E. B. DuBois and 'The Negro Church,'" *Annals of the American Academy of Political and Social Science* 568 (March 2000): 235–49, and Andrew Billingsley, *Mighty Like a River: The Black Church and Social Reform* (New York: Oxford University Press, 1999).
124. Malachy Richard McCarthy, "Which Christ Came to Chicago: Catholic and Protestant Programs to Evangelize, Socialize and Americanize the Mexican Immigrant, 1900–1940" (PhD diss., Loyola University of Chicago, 2002); "Study of the Religious Life of the Mexicans in Chicago," 1934, Burgess papers, box 134, folder 4; Michael Innis-Jiménez, *Steel Barrio:*

For the long-term unemployed (or their wives) who continued to attend church, certain aspects of religious doctrine could be a source of comfort. Catholics, especially, benefited from their view of God as being merciful and loving: as the sociologist E. Wight Bakke said, the Catholic "'suffering-here–reward-hereafter' formula [was] very nicely suited to producing a more comfortable acceptance of one's lot." The more one suffered, the greater would one's heavenly reward be. (Here, again, we see evidence for the Marxian view of religion as, in part, consolation for the poor. If one cannot wage victorious class struggle in the present, one projects one's victory into the afterlife.)[125]

Despite the continued vitality of religion in the Depression, however, it bears repeating that the urgency of class issues in this time did tend to undermine the authority and hegemony of a semi-"otherworldly" institution. The authors of *Black Metropolis*, written in the early 1940s, considered Chicago's Black Belt to epitomize trends that were operative everywhere:

> Skepticism about the truth of the saga of salvation is general. Mistrust of the motives of the professional religionists is widespread. Often hungry and beset by family troubles, discriminated against by white people and more affluent Negroes, Bronzeville's lower class, during the Depression years, entertained serious doubts of either the necessity or the efficacy of religion. They demanded results in the "here and now" rather than in "the sweet by-and-by."[126]

In Bronzeville as in the United States generally, the majority of the long-term unemployed did not see much hope for "salvation" in religion. Only through individual initiative or *secular* collective action could they wrest from the world what was rightly theirs.

The Great Mexican Migration to South Chicago, 1915–1940 (New York: New York University Press, 2013), 164, 165; Anita Edgar Jones, "Conditions Surrounding Mexicans in Chicago" (MA thesis, University of Chicago, 1928), 89–94; interview with Padre Catatina, December 10, 1936, in *Chicago Foreign Language Press Survey*.

125. Bakke, *Citizens without Work*, 21–24.
126. Drake and Cayton, *Black Metropolis*, 617.

Chapter Six

COLLECTIVE ACTION

Historical scholarship since the 1960s has established that during the Great Depression the long-term unemployed were capable of great militancy, on a broad and sustained scale. Roy Rosenzweig, an expert on the subject, says—in what is likely a considerable understatement—that "easily two million jobless workers engaged in some form of activism at some time in the thirties."[1] Mark Naison's 1983 study *Communists in Harlem during the Depression* shows that the Communist Party was a major force in Harlem the entire decade, in fact in New York City as a whole. James Lorence's *Organizing the Unemployed* (1996) makes it equally clear that across Michigan, from Keweenaw County to Detroit, the jobless actively protested the indignities and hardships that were imposed on them. Late in the decade, the Workers Alliance (WA) was still a "dynamic force" in many counties, and by the spring of 1938 over 80 percent of Michigan's WPA workers were members of the United Auto Workers. Demonstration after demonstration in cities across the country—and Chicago in the first five years of the Depression had well over two thousand such—saw upward of ten or twenty thousand people clamor for action by political authorities, risking police brutality in order to force leaders of business and politics to remember the forgotten man.[2]

At the same time, however, social historians since the 1960s have sometimes been at pains to deny that in these years the masses had much interest in radical ideologies. An image is painted of Americans that seems to attribute to them a sort of cultural inertia, political passivity, a stubborn clinging to individualism and the American political system, and a lack of "class consciousness." Melvyn Dubofsky's 1980 paper "Not So 'Turbulent Years': A New Look at the 1930s," for example, is a classic statement of this perspective. In explaining why (so he argues) "durable working-class radicalism" did not emerge in the Great Depression, Dubofsky invokes the supposed "inability of most workers and their leaders to conceive of an alternative to the values of marketplace capitalism, that is to create a working-class culture autonomous from that of the ruling

---

1. Given the high turnover of participation in Communist and other radical unemployed organizations, and the many hundreds of thousands of people who attended large or small relief demonstrations at least a couple of times, the overall number may well be far higher than Rosenzweig's estimated minimum.
2. Roy Rosenzweig, "'Socialism in Our Time': The Socialist Party and the Unemployed, 1929–1936," *Labor History* 20, no. 4 (Fall 1979): 486; James Lorence, *Organizing the Unemployed: Community and Union Activists in the Industrial Heartland* (Albany, NY: State University of New York Press, 1996), 177, 211; Harold D. Lasswell and Dorothy Blumenstock, *World Revolutionary Propaganda: A Chicago Study* (Westport, CT: Greenwood Press, 1970 [1939]), 44.

class." Workers did not become "a class fully aware of their role, power, and ability to replace the existing system with 'a better, firmer, more just social order [than] the one to be torn down.'" Of the long-term unemployed, Anthony Badger's perspective is not unusual: "the unemployed seem to have been neither rebellious nor the deferential victims of bourgeois hegemony. [...] [E]mployment gave workers many of the values they cherished: status vis-à-vis their fellows, economic security, and a reputation as a good provider. The goal of the unemployed was [nothing more rebellious than] to restore those values." Badger even goes so far as to say, "there was no constituency waiting at the grass-roots for more radical action than Roosevelt offered."[3]

Such interpretations are oversimplified and misleading. Their premise that "radicalism" or "rebelliousness" is measured by the character of one's ideological consciousness, specifically by the degree to which one identifies with Socialism/Communism or has the sort of revolutionary class consciousness of which a Marxist would approve, is flawed. It is an expression of the intellectual's characteristic focus on "consciousness" rather than "social being," to use Marx's terms, particularly of the left-wing intellectual's valorization of his own theoretical understanding of systemic oppression and belief in the possibility of a very different social order. If people do not subscribe to the militant's ideology or to his valorization of rebellious collective action at all costs, they are thought to be rather conservative or perhaps the victims of bourgeois hegemony, as Dubofsky implies. More sensible, though, would be to follow the precept of Marx to concentrate on social being, the social context in which people live and which structures their resistance to authority. From this perspective, one can see that "ordinary people" are frequently rebellious in the ways that are most rational given their situations. As James C. Scott says,

> To require of lower-class resistance that it somehow be "principled" or "selfless" [i.e., "idealistic," ideologically driven] is not only utopian and a slander on the moral status of fundamental material needs; it is, more fundamentally, a misconstruction of the basis of class struggle, which is, first and foremost, a struggle over the appropriation of work, production, property, and taxes. "Bread-and-butter" issues are the essence of lower-class politics and resistance.[4]

It is a confusion to contrast (as does Badger) rebelliousness or radicalism with the commitment to such "conventional," "conservative" values as status and economic security. These are precisely the values that constitute the basis of class struggle.[5]

---

3. Melvyn Dubofsky, "Not So 'Turbulent Years': A New Look at the 1930s," in *Life and Labor: Dimensions of American Working-Class History*, eds. Charles Stephenson and Robert Asher (Albany, NY: State University of New York Press, 1986), 205–23; Anthony Badger, *The New Deal: The Depression Years, 1933–40* (New York: Hill and Wang, 1989), 40, 41, 298.
4. James C. Scott, *Weapons of the Weak: Everyday Forms of Peasant Resistance* (New Haven, CT: Yale University Press, 1985), 296.
5. Scott remarks, contrary to the way of thinking represented by Dubofsky and Badger, that "the rank-and-file actors in most, if not all, revolutionary situations are in fact fighting for rather mundane, if vital, objectives that could in principle—but often not in practice—be accommodated within the prevailing social order." *Weapons of the Weak*, 341.

It can certainly be useful for the sake of achieving greater economic and political power to have a lucid class consciousness. On the other hand, it is unclear what we ought to conclude from the fact that many workers in the United States during the Depression were not as class conscious as a Marxist might have liked. Does this mean they were not opposed to rule by the corporate capitalist class, to the fiscal austerity preached by conservatives, or to violent suppression of labor unions? Surely not. Does it mean they did not have social democratic values or did not desire a society in which the rapacity of capitalism was tamed and ordinary workers had significant input into the political and economic process? No (as we'll see). When in large swathes of the country the Left's organizational resources were very limited, it is no surprise that workers and the unemployed did not always consider it worthwhile to join a union or to get actively involved in politics (possibly with negative consequences for their job and their family). It made more sense to struggle on one's own, with the help of relatives, friends, and neighbors.

The main purpose of this chapter, in short, is to challenge the myth of "ordinary people's" dominant tendency to political conservatism/centrism/apathy. I will start by considering general questions that have received much treatment in historical scholarship, such as the question of whether large proportions of the unemployed blamed themselves rather than, more radically, "the system" for their joblessness. More interesting, however, is the subject of people's political and social views, which I briefly investigate through polls and Depression-era sociological studies.

I also consider the question of why working-class Americans tended to identify themselves as hostile to Communism and argue that *ideological* disagreement was secondary to other causes. This is certainly not the received wisdom or the most obvious interpretation: it would seem, and has generally been assumed by historians, that if people rejected Communism (and even Socialism, in the form, for example, of the Socialist Party) it was mainly because they rejected the views of Communists and Socialists. This interpretation, however, is challenged by statements like the following, from a writer who interviewed members of the famous Bonus Army in 1932:

> A paradox of the Bonus Army is the virulence of their curses at both the bankers and the Communists. They treat the latter roughly whenever they can lay their hands on them. They have to be content with using words to lambast the former. These veterans denounce Hoover, insist it is the right of every citizen to have a job and that the government should take over the industries of the country to make that possible and then, in the next breath, they swear vengeance on "the reds who come in here trying to stir up trouble with their Marxism, Leninism and Bolshevism."[6]

From this observation one should already suspect that popular opposition to Communism and Socialism (to the extent that there was such opposition) was often a rather superficial thing. Apparently even these hard-bitten, patriotic veterans embraced some of the most radical ideas of the left, including absolute denial of the sanctity of

---

6. Gardner Jackson, "Unknown Soldiers," *Survey Graphic*, August 1, 1932, 343.

private property. It was essentially the foreign-sounding *names* "Marxism," "Leninism," and "Bolshevism" to which working-class white Americans objected and the taint of foreignness that clung to certain leftist political parties. When ideas similar to some of the prescriptions, and even the analyses, of Communists and Socialists were put forward by Huey Long, Father Charles Coughlin (at least early on, when his antisemitism was subdued), Upton Sinclair's EPIC movement, the La Follette brothers, and Farmer-Labor parties in the Midwest, millions of Americans became enthusiastic adherents. In fact, from 1930 to 1936 mass support even coalesced around a Workers' Unemployment Insurance Bill that Communists had written and that was much more radical than comparable provisions in the Soviet Union. In the concluding section I'll discuss this support in some depth, because historians have largely ignored it.[7]

A theme of the chapter, then, is that historians have tended to draw unwarranted conclusions about Americans' political values and beliefs from the fact that most have *in name* rejected Marxism and similar "foreign" concepts. Names, and even the analytical niceties of an intellectual system like Marxism, are relatively superficial. On a deeper level, a huge proportion of Americans shared many of the values of Communists, notably collective resistance to the power of the rich for the sake of making society more democratic, egalitarian, and indeed "socialistic" in the sense of radical government interference with the market economy to protect human rights and well-being. Already in 1930 and 1931, millions of people were demanding social-democratic statism.

Most of the chapter consists of an analysis of the two major unemployed organizations in Chicago, the Unemployed Councils and the Chicago Workers Committee on Unemployment. The former has received more attention from scholars, but the latter—including its offshoot the IWA—was almost as successful and important. My focus is not on the structure or the leadership of the two groups, since other historians have treated of these subjects.[8] Instead, I am interested in the participation of "ordinary people" in these groups, the attitudes and actions of the rank and file. While not everyone endorsed the ideology of Communism, even self-declared anti-Communists were, frequently, far from "individualistic" or antistatist.

In the long concluding section on "popular radicalism," I consider several phenomena that more generally illustrate just how "radical" many people were in their attitudes

---

7. For instance, in a book actually called *Voices of Protest* (published in 1983), Alan Brinkley does not devote a single sentence to it. Nor does Robert McElvaine in his standard history of the Depression. David Kennedy devotes half a sentence to it in his Oxford History of the Great Depression, *Freedom from Fear, Part One: The American People in the Great Depression* (Oxford: Oxford University Press, 2004). Neither Jefferson Cowie in *The Great Exception* (Princeton, NJ: Princeton University Press, 2016) nor Ira Katznelson in *Fear Itself: The New Deal and the Origins of Our Time* (New York: Liveright Publishing Company, 2013) mentions it. The list goes on.
8. Randi Storch, Harvey Klehr, Roy Rosenzweig, Daniel Leab, and others have described the elaborate organizational structure of the Councils, and Rosenzweig has discussed the same topic in relation to the Workers Committee.

toward relief, politics, and the economy. The Workers' Bill is the primary case study I use, but I also touch on the Long and Coughlin movements, arguing against a long tradition of scholarship that they were in fact deeply opposed to dominant institutions and ideologies. Even aside from such articulate dissidence, however, millions of relief clients had by 1933 and 1934 (if not earlier) embraced the Communist Party's teaching that anyone who could not find a stable and well-paying job was entitled to a comfortable existence at the government's expense. This is to say that people desired a fundamentally different social order, a hybrid socialistic capitalism such as would be achieved on a less ambitious scale in Western European in the postwar era. The Social Security Act, largely a response to the revolutionary mood of the masses, was but a shadow of this ideal social vision, although in combination with the Works Progress Administration it did somewhat restore the disaffected multitudes' wavering faith in Roosevelt.[9]

***

In the second chapter I briefly discussed the shame that many people felt after being without a job for long stretches of time. Implicit in shame is self-blame, even if *consciously* the ashamed person recognizes that his misfortune is due at least in part to other factors besides his own ability or worth. The fact that shame was rather common is no surprise, not only because of the natural psychological impact of being without a job but also because of the atomized social fabric of the United States, including the weakness of organized labor and the absence of a political party comparable to, say, the Labor Party in Britain. On the other hand, even in Europe, the jobless were very susceptible to the same shame, "passivity," and "apathy" that were thought to characterize Americans. In Britain, Poland, Austria, and elsewhere, writers concluded that the unemployed were "scattered, loose, perplexed and hopeless, [...] *a mass only numerically, not socially*," to quote two Polish sociologists. We should be wary, therefore, of drawing the usual contrasts between "individualistic" attitudes in the United States and "collectivist" attitudes in Europe.[10]

But how common were shame and self-blame in the United States? Until at least the 1980s (and arguably up to the present), it was widely assumed among historians that—to quote a textbook published in 1973—"the average worker in the 1930s blamed

---

9. On the political influence of the working-class urgencies of the early 1930s, see Frances Fox Piven and Richard A. Cloward, *Poor People's Movements: Why They Succeed, How They Fail* (New York: Pantheon Books, 1977); Michael Goldfield, "Worker Insurgency, Radical Organization, and New Deal Labor Legislation," *American Political Science Review* 83, no. 4 (December 1989): 1257–82; J. Craig Jenkins and Barbara G. Brents, "Social Protest, Hegemonic Competition, and Social Reform: A Political Struggle Interpretation of the Origins of the American Welfare State," *American Sociological Review* 54, no. 6 (December 1989): 891–909; and Rhonda F. Levine, *Class Struggle and the New Deal: Industrial Labor, Industrial Capital, and the State* (Lawrence, KS: University Press of Kansas, 1988).
10. Quoted in John A. Garraty, "Unemployment during the Great Depression," *Labor History* 17, no. 2 (Spring 1976): 155. Italics in the original.

his economic hardships on himself and not on the capitalist system."[11] More recent scholars have avoided such categorical statements, but general histories still emphasize (understandably) the shame of unemployment. What are interesting, however, are the many cases of *non*-self-blame. One study published in 1936 had surprising findings: its survey of 2,882 residents of Minneapolis found *less* feeling of inferiority among the unemployed than among employed workers. Those in the former group blamed the economic system, not themselves, for their plight. A study in 1932 of lodgers at the Shelter for Transient Men in Palo Alto, California, found that almost exactly the same proportion blamed the economy for their condition (38 percent) as admitted that they personally bore some responsibility (42 percent). In 1934, interviews with one hundred relief families in St. Louis revealed the following attitudes: 44 men said unequivocally that they deserved help; 14 asked for more work to cover the deficits in their budgets; 10 took relief as a matter of course, saying that since others received help they too expected it; seven were very demanding; and the remainder were either timid or unclear in their attitudes. Still another researcher found in interviews with more than five hundred relief cases in Seattle (in 1935) that 49 percent voiced disapproval of or resistance toward "the system," 12 percent accepted what they could get without thanks or protest, and 39 percent appeared to accept or in some cases approve of the system. Other studies similarly indicated that large proportions of Depression victims did not blame themselves.[12]

Some did, of course. But what does that mean? For one thing, people do not have static or one-dimensional self-conceptions: it is perfectly possible to blame both oneself and broader social forces, and to change one's opinions on this matter over time. Even day to day, one might have a different opinion about who or what is to blame, or one might feel less and more shame depending on circumstances and mood. (For such reasons, every poll or survey on any topic ought to be viewed with some skepticism.) Richard Wright wrote of the burning shame he felt when he thought of going into one of Chicago's relief stations, as if he were making a public confession of his hunger, yet he was certainly aware that his unemployment was not straightforwardly his own fault. In fact, the sociologist E. Wight Bakke observed that even when men found some reason to blame themselves, their perceived personal shortcomings were "robbed of their sting" by the knowledge that others who had presumably *not* made mistakes had lost their jobs as well. Impersonal forces were therefore blamed as much as or more than personal faults.[13]

Secondly, self-blame did not necessarily indicate deep adherence to "individualism" or some conservative ideology, for the simple reason that in many cases there was

---

11. Peter N. Carroll and David W. Noble, *The Restless Centuries: A History of the American People* (Minneapolis, MN: Burgess Publishing Co., 1973), vol. II, 499.
12. Bernard Sternsher, "Victims of the Great Depression: Self-Blame/Non-Self-Blame, Radicalism, and Pre-1929 Experiences," *Social Science History* 1, no. 2 (Winter 1977): 137–77.
13. Richard Wright, *American Hunger* (New York: Harper & Row, 1977 [1944]), 42. E. Wight Bakke, *The Unemployed Worker: A Study of the Task of Making a Living without a Job* (New Haven, CT: Yale University Press, 1940), 101.

rational justification for the belief. To my knowledge, no historian has made this point; all have interpreted "self-blame," implicitly or explicitly, not as a *rational* reaction but as a *culturally produced* one. And yet there is no doubt that in many cases the man was partly right: he had acted irresponsibly in his youth, he had failed to get a good education, he had squandered his earnings on drink and women, he had had too many children or had inadvisably married before settling into a lucrative career. After all, while it is true that he was far from alone in being out of work, a lot of people still had jobs. Evidently, or so it seemed, many of them had made smarter choices, had taken more secure jobs. It was perfectly natural and rational to have regrets, in itself not at all a reflection of ideology.

In extreme manifestations, to be sure, shame and self-blame could, like the emotional depression or lassitude that was often a result of long-term unemployment, interfere with the aggressive defense of one's interests, whether in joint action with others or on one's own. On the other hand, even this debilitating malaise could not prevent, for example, the Bonus March in 1932, in which 20,000 or more veterans descended upon Washington, D.C., to demand early payment of World War I "bonus" they were due in 1945. These men were certainly no revolutionaries: as Mauritz Hallgren observed, they were all in or beyond middle age and had been "thoroughly whipped" by their circumstances. "There is about the lot of them an atmosphere of hopelessness, of utter despair," he said, "though not of desperation." Nevertheless, these harassed and discouraged people had been able to come together from all over the country in pursuit of a common goal. On smaller scales, this phenomenon was constantly occurring in the Depression decade, in cities and towns from coast to coast.[14]

With respect to political beliefs and values, the data from polls and studies conducted at the time are mixed. They do not indicate extreme "class consciousness" among workers and the jobless, but they do not indicate much "individualism" or conservatism either. In their article "Unemployment, Class Consciousness, and Radical Politics: What Didn't Happen in the Thirties" (1977), Sidney Verba and Kay Lehman Schlozman present the results of two national polls that were conducted in 1939 for *Fortune Magazine*. Each survey had 5,214 respondents, over two hundred of whom listed their occupation as "unemployed"—not nearly the same proportion as the unemployed in the general population, but sufficient to allow us to meaningfully distinguish between their attitudes and those of the employed. Table 7 includes some of the more interesting findings[15]:

---

14. Mauritz Hallgren, "The Bonus Army Scares Mr. Hoover," *Nation*, July 27, 1932; Franklin Folsom, *Impatient Armies of the Poor: The Story of Collective Action of the Unemployed, 1808–1942* (Niwot, CO: University Press of Colorado, 1991), 310–22.
15. Sidney Verba and Kay Lehman Schlozman, "Unemployment, Class Consciousness, and Radical Politics: What Didn't Happen in the Thirties," *Journal of Politics* 39, no. 2 (May 1977): 302.

Table 7 Political opinions of Americans in 1939

Percent saying:	Total %	Upper white collar %	Lower white collar %	Wage workers (not salaried) %	Unemployed %
The government should see that everyone is above subsistence	73	59	73	82	86
The government should guarantee job opportunities	61	46	60	73	76
The government should redistribute wealth through high taxes on the rich	35	24	32	44	54
The government should confiscate wealth beyond what people need	15	6	12	24	28
There should be government relief even if it means the end of capitalism	16	7	16	20	32
There should be relief even if it means government assignment of jobs	12	5	12	16	26

These data are even more interesting in light of the fact that, for methodological reasons, Verba and Schlozman chose to exclude Black respondents. Had they been included, the percentages in the last two columns surely would have increased. Thus—according to these surveys—near the end of the 1930s probably a third or more of the jobless thought the government should confiscate wealth, perhaps almost two-fifths were willing to countenance the end of capitalism, and nearly all thought the government should, in effect, guarantee people a living wage. These are strikingly "socialistic" attitudes.

They accord with the findings of a poll of New Haven workers in 1932, before the dramatic entrance of the federal government into the field of relief and social service. Sixty-eight percent of American and Italian workers polled favored "government regulation of wages and hours" and 88 percent favored "other government protection." This is in contrast to the 29 percent who thought that "more individual initiative and thrift" could be a solution to workers' difficulties. In fact, only 13 percent of Americans (as opposed to 45 percent of Italians) agreed with the individualistic solution. Government action was favored by approximately equal percentages of skilled, semiskilled, and unskilled workers: 89, 87, and 91 percent, respectively. (It should be noted, however, that only 19 percent of workers wanted "socialism," a word that had been demonized for decades, to some effect.) In another national survey, a quarter of unemployed workers thought that "a revolution might be a very good thing for this country."[16]

A study published in 1936 found similar attitudes among people on relief in Los Angeles. To the question, "Do you believe in (1) co-operation of members of society for the common

---

16. Bakke, *The Unemployed Worker*, 98–100; Bernard Karsh and Philipps L. Garman, "The Impact of the Political Left," in *Labor and the New Deal*, eds. Milton Derber and Edwin Young (New York: Da Capo Press, 1972 [1957]), 83.

good, or (2) do you feel that each individual's financial and social problems are his own?", 89 favored the first option, 34 the second. Likewise, 86 supported production for use (the plan associated with Upton Sinclair's EPIC campaign), compared to 36 who did not.[17]

National polls found evidence of support for truly radical government action. A *Fortune* poll in 1935 found that 41 percent of the upper-middle class, 49 percent of the lower-middle class, and 60 percent of the poor thought the government should not allow a man to keep investments worth over $1 million. In fact, as late as 1942, 64 percent of people (the poll did not break down respondents in terms of class) thought it was a good idea to limit annual incomes to $25,000. A 1936 survey of 600 Chicago residents found a marked "tendency for the middle-income group to agree with the lower group on questions pertaining to the present distribution of wealth and influence." Thirty-three percent of skilled manual workers and 56 percent of the unskilled and semiskilled favored government ownership of large industries. In 1942, another *Fortune* survey found that almost 30 percent of the nation's factory workers thought "some form of socialism would be a good thing [...] for the country as a whole," while 34 percent had open minds about it—which means only 36 percent thought socialism would be "a bad thing." Given the resources and energy the ruling class had dedicated to vilifying socialism, these findings are striking.[18]

Of course, as noted in the Introduction, such leftist inclinations among the public are precisely one reason why "big business" and government have, since the era of World War I, had to devote colossal resources to indoctrinating people with the proper nationalistic, jingoistic, and capitalistic values. If people already agreed with such values, there would be no need to try to instill them. It is popular tendencies toward *anti*-capitalism and *anti*-nationalism—commitment to values such as compassion, generosity, democracy, local community, social welfare, peace and not war—that have made necessary ubiquitous political and economic propaganda.[19]

---

17. Friendly Sumner Rogers, "The Attitude of the Unemployed: A Survey of Three Hundred Families on Relief" (MA thesis, University of Southern California, 1936), 30, 33. On the EPIC movement, see James N. Gregory, "Upton Sinclair's 1934 EPIC Campaign: Anatomy of a Political Movement," *Labor* 12, no. 4 (December 2015): 51–81.
18. Robert S. McElvaine, "Thunder without Lightning: Working-Class Discontent in the United States, 1929–1937" (PhD diss., State University of New York at Binghamton, 1974), 73, 92–96.
19. Scholarship cited in previous chapters provides support for these ideas. Again, see Alex Carey, *Taking the Risk Out of Democracy: Corporate Propaganda versus Freedom and Liberty* (Urbana, IL: University of Illinois Press, 1997); Elizabeth Fones-Wolf, *Selling Free Enterprise: The Business Assault on Labor and Liberalism, 1945–60* (Chicago, IL: University of Illinois Press, 1994); Susan A. Brewer, *Why America Fights: Patriotism and War Propaganda from the Philippines to Iraq* (New York: Oxford University Press, 2009); Edward S. Herman and Noam Chomsky, *Manufacturing Consent: The Political Economy of the Mass Media* (New York: Knopf Doubleday Publishing, 1988); Kim Phillips-Fein, *Invisible Hands: The Businessmen's Crusade against the New Deal* (New York: W. W. Norton, 2009); Eberhard Demm, *Censorship and Propaganda in World War I* (New York: Bloomsbury, 2019); David Edwards and David Cromwell, *Propaganda Blitz: How the Corporate Media Distort Reality* (London: Pluto Press, 2018). One might argue that values such as compassion and generosity have no ideological or political content, but, as I argued earlier, that is not entirely correct. Popular support for social welfare programs,

Returning to the 1939 *Fortune* polls, questions were also asked about people's class consciousness: specifically, what class they thought they belonged to, and whether they thought the interests of employers and employees were essentially in opposition or essentially the same. Verba and Schlozman's analysis of the results concludes that only 12 percent of wage workers and 10 percent of the unemployed were "fully" class conscious, in the sense of seeing themselves as working class and also believing in class conflict. As for whether this sort of class consciousness correlated with left-wing views, the authors have this to say: "The data indicate that full class consciousness did result in more radical economic views; and it did so to a greater degree when it was coupled with unemployment. Furthermore, the data make clear that working class self-identification was associated with a more radical set of political attitudes only when it was coupled with a perception of conflict among the social classes."[20]

Class consciousness did matter, then, and it was not as widespread as a Marxist would have liked. On the other hand, we should be wary of the temptation to fetishize an inherently atomized and superficial method of understanding popular dispositions just because it deals in easily classifiable quantities. The historian Martin Glaberman criticizes an article by Tom Langford on "strikes and class consciousness" on these grounds:

> In the first place, [in Langford's article] consciousness is defined by verbal statements of belief. This may be appropriate to debates among intellectuals but it is totally irrelevant in ascertaining the dialectical and contradictory nature of working-class consciousness. The nature of working-class consciousness is not easy to document in ways that would be acceptable to academic social science. But occasionally there is a clear-cut example. One such example was a referendum vote in the auto workers union in the waning months of World War II in Canada and the United States. The subject was whether or not the union should retain or abandon its pledge not to strike during the war. The members voted approximately two to one to retain the no-strike pledge. One could easily conclude that workers put patriotism above their own class interest. The problem, however, was that an absolute majority of auto workers went out on wildcat strikes during the very time that the referendum was taking place. Was working-class consciousness reflected in individual thought as each worker filled out a ballot in the privacy of his or her home? Or was working-class consciousness reflected in collective action on the shop floor? There is no way that Langford's methodology [which is that of academic social science] can even begin to deal with that question.[21]

Glaberman also criticizes the very project of "divid[ing] workers up according to the way they think" and notes that the workers who have made or attempted revolutions

---

like popular opposition to imperialistic war, is an outgrowth of basic human values that are in conflict with authoritarian and exploitative structures of capitalism, nationalism, and imperialism.
20. Verba and Schlozman, "Unemployment, Class Consciousness, and Radical Politics," 304–312.
21. Martin Glaberman, "Marxism and Class Consciousness," *Labour/Le Travail* 37 (Spring 1996): 233–37.

from Russia's in 1917 to Hungary's in 1956 and France's in 1968 have, as isolated individuals, had very conservative attitudes (of sexism, chauvinism, antisemitism, etc.). Evidently people who are in many respects "conservative" are capable of acting in revolutionary ways and of having their consciousness transformed thereby.

The very concept of class consciousness is so problematic that an enormous body of sociological literature exists to try to explicate it.[22] Verba and Schlozman's survey-based conception is quite thin and impoverished, given its unavoidable individualist bias, its "exclusive focus on ideation" rather than *practice* (to quote Rick Fantasia), and its hypostatizing assumption that class consciousness is a static thing, something that either exists or doesn't exist, instead of being a dynamic and interactive process of shared understanding that is manifested in the various realms of culture, politics, trade unionism, and the workplace.

More productive than to dwell on the meaning of a highly contested concept is to consider the in-depth observations of investigators. With regard to the unemployed, E. Wight Bakke was one of the best. In his 1940 study, *Citizens without Work*, he observed that most of the unemployed in New Haven, as in other cities, did not get actively involved in radical politics, whether Communist, Socialist, or any other variety. In a sense, he found this puzzling, for agitators in parks and on street corners received sympathetic hearings and garnered large crowds. In Cleveland, for example, the journalist Len De Caux wrote in retrospect, "In hundreds of jobless meetings, I heard no objections to the points the communists made, and much applause for them. Sometimes I'd hear a communist speaker say something so bitter and extreme I'd feel embarrassed. Then I'd look around at the unemployed audience—shabby clothes, expressions worried and sour. Faces would start to glow, heads to nod, hands to clap. They liked that stuff best of all." Urban workers and the jobless in fact tended, on some level, to be quite aware of class: their lives were one long demonstration that the working class was separated by a vast gulf from the upper class, and that the two groups had very different outlooks and interests. As a New Haven machinist said to Bakke, "Hell, brother, you don't have to look to know there's a workin' class!" So why, after a speech by a Communist whose "every word rang true to the experiences men had had," did only a few listeners join him in a march on New Haven's City Hall?[23]

---

22. A few examples include Rick Fantasia, "From Class Consciousness to Culture, Action, and Social Organization," *Annual Review of Sociology* 21 (1995): 269–87; Bertell Ollman, "How to Study Class Consciousness, and Why We Should," *Insurgent Sociologist* 14 (1987): 57–96; Gordon Marshall, "Some Remarks on the Study of Working-Class Consciousness," *Politics and Society* 12 (1983): 289–93; Erik Olin Wright, *Classes* (London: Verso, 1985); Douglas M. Eichar, *Occupations and Class Consciousness in America* (New York: Greenwood Press, 1989); Rhonda Zingraff and Michael D. Schulman, "Social Bases of Class Consciousness: A Study of Southern Textile Workers with a Comparison by Race," *Social Forces* 63, no. 1 (September 1984): 98–116; Alejandro Portes, "On the Interpretation of Class Consciousness," *American Journal of Sociology* 77, no. 2 (September 1971): 228–44. The first two articles make the same points Glaberman does, and many more, in a more richly theoretical way.
23. Len De Caux, *Labor Radical: From the Wobblies to CIO, a Personal History* (Boston, MA: Beacon Press, 1970), 163; E. Wight Bakke, *Citizens without Work* (New Haven, CT: Yale University

From Bakke's account it seems that ideology was not of primary significance. Other factors were more important. First was the very smallness and perceived ineffectiveness of radical political circles. It was thought futile to dedicate oneself to far-left activism, whether Communist or Socialist, when it was bound to have little or no political success. Bakke suspects that a rubber worker was speaking for most men when he said, "I tell you my reason for steering clear of any radical party. [...] I fought enough losin' battles in my life, and, by God, in politics I'm goin' to play a winner if I can. A man can be a Democrat or a Republican and be able to get drunk once in a while on election night because he won. But the Socialists—when do you think they're going to have the chance to get drunk?" There were, after all, very real benefits to being either a Democrat or a Republican: one could receive political patronage through personal connections or from voting the right way, one could socialize and make friends relatively easily on the basis of shared institutions and common interests, one was thought to "fit in" and not be an outsider. Whatever one believed politically, in a time when radical activists constituted a demonized and violently repressed minority the pressures of sociality were, for most Americans, very much on the side of not participating in their movements.

Many thousands of people in Chicago and other cities did join the Communists' Unemployed Councils or even the party itself, for at least a short time. But the historian Daniel Leab is surely right that large numbers "abandoned them when they found out that instead of a larger relief ticket or settlement of their grievances, all their 'radical militancy' got them was a crack on the skull from a police club." As soon as they saw no hope of changing their circumstances through association with Communists, they very sensibly ended such association. Ideology was of little relevance here.[24]

Reinforcing and to some extent coinciding with the pressures of sociality and the belief that radicals were fighting a losing battle was fear of the consequences of joining their ranks. When Bakke asked some men where the Communist office in New Haven was, a Greek immediately warned him to stay aware from there. "This is what happens," he said. "If you are working in a restaurant, dishwashing, and somebody sees you, they will go and say to your boss, 'He's a Communist.'" Similarly, people were unwilling to riot, even when they felt angry enough to do so, because of the possible consequences. For one thing, "You don't have any confidence that if you did riot it would do any good," a textile worker said. "How would you get anything better than what you have?" Even passing out Communist leaflets could get you arrested, as happened often in Chicago.[25]

Perhaps more important than anything else was the fact that "the poor [were] used to being poor," were used to the old ways of dealing with adversity: "put up with it, grin and bear it, and use the common sense and experience you have to pull out." Their lives had consisted of "adjustments to the inevitable," which were even more necessary while unemployed. Indeed, people who were suspicious of the possibility of radical change

---

Press, 1940), 57. This latter book, pp. 55–70, is the main source for the next six paragraphs.
24. Daniel J. Leab, "'United We Eat': The Creation and Organization of the Unemployed Councils in 1930," *Labor History* 8, no. 3 (Fall 1967): 314.
25. Interview of Emil Luchterhand by Kubet Luchterhand, 3, 13, Roosevelt University Oral History Project in Labor History.

arguably showed more realism than the Communists who made a leap of faith into the unknown, being willing to risk personal security for the sake of ideologies and dreams that never had much chance of coming to fruition. The sort of idealism and even recklessness that it takes to try to build a major political movement out of nothing in a society more than willing to violently repress it is a trait that most people lack, having families to worry about and little experience in ideological training. Richard Wright's judgment would have commanded widespread assent: "I liked [Communists'] readiness to act, but they seemed lost in folly, wandering in a fantasy."[26]

In addition to these fundamental "material" and "self-interested" reasons for not joining the Communist Party or participating in collective protests were the secondary ideological reasons. To a large degree, these may have been mere rationalizations for one's disinclination to join a marginalized and maligned minority that demanded extreme commitment in the service of an unrealistic cause, but ultimately we cannot tell how much weight they carried. In any case, historians have amply related these reasons, which included, first and foremost, the hostility to Communists' Russophilia. A boilermaker spoke for probably the majority of white American workers when he said of Communists, "Now suppose they could set us up in that kind of a heaven they tell about. *Suppose* they could I say, because one look, and you know they couldn't. But if they could, would it be America—or would it be Russia? And who the hell wants to live in Russia?"

An argument that the working class in the United States was ideologically opposed to Communism is tendentious insofar as it implies that workers were not left wing enough to be Communists. There is more truth to the way Mauritz Hallgren framed the matter in 1933: "[When Communists] sought recruits for the party, they promptly dropped into a jargon unintelligible to the average American worker. He could have no idea of the meaning of 'rightist deviation,' 'agitprop,' and 'theoretical levels.' [...] The Communists were revolutionists who lacked the courage to discuss revolution in straightforward, realistic terms." The point is not that people were opposed to radicalism but that Communists were opposed to comprehensible and indigenous American radicalism.[27]

Nevertheless, despite all the considerations of rationality and humanity—as opposed to those of ideology and cultural indoctrination—that militated against popular acceptance of Communism, in staggering numbers people came to manifest a radicalism of both thought and deed. Let us turn now to an examination of this popular radicalism.

---

26. Richard Wright, *American Hunger*, 39, 40.
27. Mauritz Hallgren, *Seeds of Revolt* (New York: Alfred A. Knopf, 1933), 336. Even Arthur Schlesinger, Jr., no friend of Communism, remarks that the party's difficulties at attracting a mass membership were due to self-sabotage, not Americans' hostility to the revolutionary vision: "most passed through the party as through a revolving door, finding the discipline unbearable, the dialectic meaningless, and the vocabulary incomprehensible. [...] The Communist vision had been enticing [to new members]; but the facts, even after three years of capitalist decay, remained dull—a clique of dreary fanatics and seedy functionaries, talking to themselves in an unintelligible idiom, ignored by the working class, dedicating their main efforts to witch hunts against liberals and Socialists. The party was sodden, contentious, bureaucratic, and feeble." *The Crisis of the Old Order: 1919–1933* (New York: Houghton Mifflin Company, 2003 [1957]), 222.

Activism in Chicago

Unemployed Councils

Had there been a political party in the United States with the resources and competence to *sustainably* organize the rebellious masses, 6 March 1930 would have been a very good omen. The Comintern had designated this date as International Unemployment Day, which would be marked by demonstrations across the Western world organized by the various Communist parties. The American CP made elaborate preparations for the actions: in Chicago, for example, 200,000 leaflets, 50,000 stickers, and 50,000 shop papers were printed and distributed in the last few days before 6 March, and open-air meetings, lectures, and small demonstrations raised awareness of what was to come. The results exceeded even the party's expectations: while its claim of well over a million demonstrators around the country was an exaggeration, its boast that in the aggregate the protests constituted the single largest workers' demonstration in U.S. history may well have been accurate. Even the *New York Times* reported that 75,000 people participated in Detroit and 35,000 in Union Square in New York. The numbers in Chicago were more modest, between 5,000 and 10,000, with thousands more onlookers. In many cities the day's events ended in sanguinary mayhem, as police forces charged, trampled, and beat up the crowds.[28]

For such a small political party, the events of 6 March were quite an achievement. Party membership in the 1930s is listed in the table below, which includes only those members who had paid their dues in full. (Numbers are unavailable for certain years.)[29]

Table 8 Communist Party membership

Date	National Party	Chicago Party
1930	7,500	683
1931	8–9,000	1,963
1932	12–14,000	2,288
1933	16–20,000	2,417
1934	24,5000	3,303
1935	31,000	—
1936	42,000	—
1937	37,000	—
1938	55,000	5,750
1940	—	5,000

It is true that, nationally, hundreds of thousands more people, most of whom were not Communists, participated in dozens of such "auxiliary" organizations as the

---

28. Lasswell and Blumenstock, *World Revolutionary Propaganda*, 191–94; Roy Rosenzweig, "Organizing the Unemployed: The Early Years of the Great Depression, 1929–1933," *Radical America* 10, no. 4 (July–August 1976): 41; Leab, "United We Eat," 305–308; Prago, "The Organization of the Unemployed and the Role of the Radicals, 1929–1935" (PhD diss., Union Graduate School, 1976), 65–88.
29. Randi Storch, "Shades of Red: The Communist Party and Chicago's Workers, 1928–1939" (PhD diss., University of Illinois at Urbana-Champaign, 1998), 40, 41.

International Labor Defense, the Unemployed Councils, the Young Communist League, the John Reed Clubs, the Young Pioneers of America, and the League of Struggle for Negro Rights. The party itself, though, remained small—in part because of its insufficient finances. A Congressional investigation in the late 1930s determined that the total deposits in 43 bank accounts held by the CP and all its subsidiaries, auxiliaries, and publishing houses were a little over $10 million, in itself an impressive sum (far more than the party possessed before its Popular Front phase) but quite inadequate considering how thinly it was spread. The Illinois budget, for instance, was only $35,000 in 1938, and in huge stretches of the country—including most of its Western half—there was virtually no Communist presence at all. Dues were often not collected, and when they were they sometimes were not turned over to the district office because the lower-level body wanted to keep them for its own needs. Especially in the early 1930s the CP had an acute shortage of organizers and frequently could not afford to pay its functionaries. In the Chicago district, even such basic necessities as mimeograph machines were sometimes luxuries.[30]

Nevertheless, during the 1930s the party did manage to recruit almost 250,000 people, according to historian Harvey Klehr.[31] The problem was that most of them eventually dropped out. Between 1930 and 1934, 60,000 joined the party, but the total increase in membership was only about 16,000. The reasons for this disappointing record had nothing to do with ideology: they had to do with organizational problems and the inner life of the party. For one thing, thousands of people who signed application cards or even paid initiation fees were simply lost, never followed up with. Bureaucratic mismanagement was rife within the CP. Those who were assigned to a local unit, whether a street unit (based on geography) or a shop unit (based on industrial concentration), faced the next hurdle: tolerating the drudgery and dreariness of unit meetings, and the superhuman workload that was imposed on them. The weekly meetings, full of carping criticism and sterile discussion, could last for three or four hours; new members were rarely made to feel welcome. "I can't be everywhere all at once," one member complained. "I must sleep sometimes. I have spent enough energy at inner meetings to overthrow the whole capitalist system. My wife won't stand for it either." Another member pithily summed up the problems: "until our movement [...] realizes that its members are human being [sic] and want to be treated as such and not just a cog in the wheel, our movement will remain small, no matter how many members we attract and recruit."[32]

---

30. Harvey Klehr, *The Heyday of American Communism* (New York: Basic Books, 1984), 105, 374–78, 477; Storch, "Shades of Red," 28, 29.
31. Actually, the number may be higher than this, since the inefficient party bureaucracy bungled untold thousands of applications. Communist organizer Katherine Hyndman estimated that "millions" of people went through the party and its auxiliary organizations. Interview of Katherine Hyndman by Staughton Lynd, 1970, 49, Roosevelt University Oral History Project in Labor History.
32. Klehr, *The Heyday*, 153–58, 413; Nathan Glazer, *The Social Basis of American Communism* (New York: Harcourt, Brace & World, Inc., 1961), 101; H. W., "Human Beings," *Party Organizer*, July 1937, 37, 38; J. Peter, "A Study of Fluctuation in the Chicago District," *Party Organizer*,

All these handicaps did not, however, prevent the CP from facilitating the emergence of Unemployed Councils in dozens of cities already in January and February 1930. While one would not have known this from reading the establishment press—or even subsequent historical accounts—urban areas of the country were in ferment a mere three or four months after the stock market crash. Almost every day the *Daily Worker* reported mass meetings and marches on city halls in cities from Buffalo to Chicago to Chattanooga and beyond, by the spring spreading even to the Deep South. Large-scale actions continued after 6 March, for instance on May Day, which the *Federated Press* reported saw its largest nationwide turnout in 40 years. By the summer, Chicago had 12 Unemployed Councils with a thousand active members and many more peripheral followers, who were regularly carrying out the actions for which councils soon became famous: resisting evictions and protesting at relief stations. While CP leaders were frustrated with the halting progress of the party's unemployed organizing—"[there is] an agitational meeting in a neighborhood or before a factory today and then nothing for a month," Clarence Hathaway reprimanded his comrades—the momentum of the work picked up again in late 1930 and early 1931. The jobless masses were hungry for leadership, and they were happy to have Communists provide it.[33]

For the next couple of years, the continual protests and disruptions that the *Daily Worker* reported—which were inevitably only a fraction of the total—belied intellectuals' impression at the time, transmitted to posterity by historians, that the unemployed (and partly employed) masses were acquiescent and apathetic. In fact, contrary to Irving Bernstein's periodization, the Hoover years were arguably the most "turbulent" of the decade, in some respects more so than the New Deal years. "Hardly a day passed," the historian Albert Prago says, "without some major demonstration [in fact, many] taking place in some town, city, or state capital." It would not be much of an exaggeration to say that society was in upheaval, so riven by rebellion that soon the business class was able to clamor for the hitherto unfathomable: federal unemployment relief and a major public works program. Such a departure from what had been considered the bedrock of capitalists' class interest, namely privatization and social atomization, could only have come about from a general perception that the working class was on the verge of mounting the ramparts and had to be appeased. Moreover, elite panic did not recur on such a broad scale in the later years of the 1930s, despite the birth of the CIO: after 1932, the mayor of Chicago never again came close to pleading for federal armed intervention in his city, as Cermak had. It was the radicalized discontent of those without work

---

October 1934, 20–25; Fraser M. Ottanelli, *The Communist Party of the United States: From the Depression to World War II* (New Brunswick: Rutgers University Press, 1991), 44, 45; District Organization letter, April 3, 1931, Communist Party files, microfilm reel 187, Tamiment Library.
33. *Federated Press*, May 2, 1930; Randi Storch, *Red Chicago: American Communism at Its Grassroots, 1928–35* (Chicago, IL: University of Illinois Press, 2007), 105; James Lorence, *The Unemployed People's Movement: Leftists, Liberals, and Labor in Georgia, 1929–1941* (Athens, GA: University of Georgia Press, 2009), 27; Hathaway, "An Examination of Our Failure"; Lorence, *Organizing the Unemployed*, 28.

that most threatened the foundations of the social order, not the (retrospectively more celebrated) unionizing ambitions of industrial workers.[34]

The occupying and theft of property, for example, were epidemic in the early Depression. Historian Gary Roth describes some of the direct action that was going on in Chicago by 1931 and 1932:

> The unemployed began to use abandoned storefronts for their own purposes. Locks were broken, and the stores became meeting places, with chairs taken from deserted movie houses. [Paul] Mattick[35] estimated that there were fifty or sixty such locales in Chicago, serving as the [unemployed] movement's equivalent of neighbourhood settlement houses. In some areas, there were one or two such places on every street. Mimeograph machines were installed for the production of leaflets and movement literature. Paper was contributed by those still employed, who stole office supplies from their workplaces.
>
> Among the unemployed were many skilled workers, and they procured electricity for the storefronts by running wire from the street lamps. Gas lines were tapped without setting off the meters—something that the plumbers knew how to do, and the gas was used for heating and cooking. Others solicited food in bulk quantities from nearby fruit and vegetable markets, food shops, bakeries, and meat stores, sometimes by threatening the proprietors. Makeshift kitchens were set up in the storefronts and meals cooked around the clock. The homeless also used the storefronts as rudimentary sleeping quarters.[36]

Eviction protests have not always been considered in this light, but, in effect, they were premised on the basically socialist principle that a community was entitled to seize private property to ensure the welfare and dignity of its members. In Marxian language, they expressed class solidarity, even a type of "class consciousness," if by that term we mean not some abstract intellectual awareness of the essence of production relations but rather something more significant, namely, the sort of consciousness that infuses the *practice* of aggressively defending workers and the poor against the predations and depredations of the ownership class (or of authorities in league with the ownership class).

Blacks, not surprisingly, "constitute[d] the most active section of [Chicago's] Unemployed Council" already in mid-1930, according to the *Daily Worker*. From before the beginning of the year Communists had been conducting house-to-house canvasses, literature distribution campaigns, street corner conversations, and mass meetings in the industrial and lower-class sections of the city, not least on the South Side. Interracial marches on the city hall, met by police violence, featured demands for "Work or Wages" ("wages" meant unemployment insurance at full wage rates), "Immediate Relief," and the seven-hour day and five-day week. The unemployed of multiple nationalities attended huge meetings in Musicians' Hall, Ukrainian Hall (in the Back of the Yards neighborhood), and Ashland Auditorium; when the police arrived and arrested scores of

---

34. Prago, "The Organization of the Unemployed," 116.
35. Mattick was an influential Marxist writer and activist, an anti-Leninist who identified with the ideological tradition of council communism.
36. Gary Roth, *Marxism in a Lost Century: A Biography of Paul Mattick* (Boston, MA: Brill, 2015), 97.

participants, Mexicans and Blacks were reported to be the most aggressive in resisting the attacks. (Some of the meetings in fact were organized to protest police brutality—only to elicit more brutality.) Blacks on the South Side were also the most aggressive in fighting evictions, probably for three main reasons: their deprivation was worse than that of other ethnic groups; their racial consciousness sharpened their anger and awareness of grievances; and in general they were not well integrated into the dominant white society, which made them more willing to collectively violate norms of property and propriety.[37]

As Randi Storch and other historians have related, eviction demonstrations sometimes began at Washington Park, where crowds of 50–5,000 listened every day to speakers denounce the injustices of capitalism. Whether here or at the neighborhood Unemployed Council headquarters—a meeting hall where men were always gathered to while away the hours in conversation—someone would show up and inform the others that a person was being evicted blocks away. They would rush over, being joined regularly by hundreds of people. "Whole neighborhoods were frequently mobilized to take part in this mutual assistance," a participant recalled years later. The sociologist Horace Cayton observed one such action in 1931: while eating in a restaurant in the Black Belt he "chanced to look out the window and saw a number of Negroes walking by, three abreast, forming a long uninterrupted line," solemnly marching to a house where a family was being evicted. Frequently confrontations with the police ensued, which were apt to be violent and bloody. The most important of these was in early August 1931, when a crowd of several thousand Blacks and whites marched to protect the home of a woman who lived near Washington Park. Police hurried to intercept them and arrested several of the leaders, as two patrol wagons blocked the crowd in its path. The course of events is uncertain, but the police ended up drawing their revolvers and started shooting, resulting in general tumult. "Thousands of terrified people scattered," a contemporary wrote, "rushing for their lives, tripping, stumbling, stepping on one another. Others fought, slugging with fists, hurling sticks and stones at the police." By the end of the melee, three Black men lay dead and scores of demonstrators were injured.[38]

Within a day of the riot Chicago was thrown into panic and headlines around the country shrieked of the nefarious influence of Reds. Fears of Communist insurrection in Chicago and race riots ran rampant. Scores of squad cars were sent to patrol the district; Mayor Cermak returned early from his yachting vacation; and in the following days enormous meetings of white and Black workers were held in Washington Park to protest the killings. As far as the city's elite was concerned, if the event "had been

---

37. *Daily Worker*, January 27, February 22 and 28, April 24, July 30, 1930; Harold F. Gosnell, *Negro Politicians: The Rise of Negro Politics in Chicago* (Chicago, IL: University of Chicago Press, 1967), 327.
38. Lasswell and Blumenstock, *World Revolutionary Propaganda*, 170, 171, 196–204; Horace Cayton, "The Black Bugs," *Nation*, September 9, 1931; Carl Winter, "Unemployment Struggles of the Thirties," *Political Affairs* 48, nos. 9–10 (September–October 1969): 53–63; Randi Storch, *Red Chicago*, 99–101; *Daily Worker*, August 5–8, 10, 1931.

an out-and-out race riot it would have been understandable," according to the authors of *Black Metropolis*. "But here was something new: Negroes and whites *together* rioting against the forces of law and order." The Renters' Court immediately suspended all eviction proceedings for an indefinite period, which turned out to be several months long. In fact, that summer tenants across the South Side had already been flatly refusing to pay rent, declaring that the Communists would protect them. Landlords had accepted this situation in part because, according to bailiffs, 60 percent of Blacks who were evicted simply looked around the block for the nearest vacant room, broke the locks, and moved in. "Although they are without lights, gas, or water," a bailiff reported, "the squatters remain in their new quarters until evicted again, when they find another vacant flat or are reinstated by the communists. Under these conditions landlords are willing to waive the rent to keep their properties occupied." The hundreds of eviction protests constantly occurring on the South Side that summer had effectively given tenants power to partially dictate the terms of their occupancy.[39]

Meanwhile, the Unemployed Councils and the Communist Party organized a mass funeral and an open-casket viewing of the three fallen men. An estimated 25,000 people filed past the bodies during the two days they were on display—on a stage under a huge photograph of Lenin, the walls adorned with large paintings of a Black and white worker clasping hands—and afterward, even more marchers (almost half of them white) followed the coffins in a slow procession down State Street. As in the many other marches that Chicago saw in these years, placards with such slogans as "Fight Against Lynching—Equal Rights for Negroes!" and "They Died for Us! We Must Keep Fighting!" were generously scattered throughout the parade. In the three weeks that followed the August 3 riot, the Unemployed Councils on the South Side received 5,500 new applications for membership.[40]

While eviction protests were particularly common in the Black Belt, few areas of Chicago were entirely free of them in the early Depression years. We can only guess at how many occurred, but if their frequency in New York City is any indication, there were many thousands: according to one study, of the 185,794 families that received eviction notices in New York in the 8 months before 30 June 1932, 77,000 were saved from temporary homelessness by the efforts of the organized unemployed. Chicago's West Side, for example, had numerous Unemployed Councils by 1931, such as the one on 14th Street near a Greek Workers Club on South Halsted Street. Its proximity to Greektown guaranteed its vitality, for Greek workers were exceptionally militant, as the activist Steve Nelson recalled. "Some were furriers and garment workers, and a few worked in the stockyards, but most were waiters, cooks, and busboys in the city's restaurants. Almost all were single and very militant. Actually, they knew what to do better than I." If they heard of an eviction, they raced over to stop it. The Communist

---

39. *Chicago Defender*, August 8, 1931; *Chicago Tribune*, August 6, 1931; *Pittsburgh Courier*, August 8, 1931; Drake and Cayton, *Black Metropolis*, 87; Horace Cayton, *Long Old Road* (New York: Trident Press, 1965), 182, 183.
40. Lasswell and Blumenstock, *World Revolutionary Propaganda*, 201–204; *Daily Worker*, August 10, 1931; Prago, "Organizing the Unemployed," 108.

organizer Katherine Hyndman remembered a revealing incident worth describing at length, the sort of event that happened continually in these years when "all you had to do was distribute a leaflet and you'd have thousands of people show up [...] not frightened by the police or anything":

> I was on my way to meet the people at the Greek Workers Club when I happened to see a woman and her children. They'd been evicted. They're out there, their furniture, all out in the street. So I hurried over to the Greek Workers Club and got a whole number of people to help break down the door, put in the furniture, and so on. [...] As soon as we got there the police had been in hiding around different buildings, [so they] come there and surround us. And I tried to go up into this small house. [...] So one of the policemen jumps up on the steps of the house with a sawed-off machine gun [...] and he says, "The first son of a bitch that sets foot on these stairs is going to have his head chopped off." Well, you can't let that go unchallenged, you know. So I stepped forward, a young white man steps forward, and a Negro couple. [...] When we four went on the stairs the people came out of their houses. They came swarming out and they surrounded the police. And this policeman [...] just held his gun uselessly in his hand. And the four of us stood triumphantly up at the top of the stairs and were kicking at the door. The policeman who was in charge said [to his fellow officers], "Now, look. We've had hundreds of people arrested [at this location]. It's enough. I've had enough."

The landlord, who had been hiding with the police, decided the family could move back in if a collection were taken up to provide at least a fraction of their rent. So one of the officers passed around his hat, and the family was allowed to return to its home.[41]

In neighborhoods on the North Side where people were paying mortgages on homes, or on the Near North Side where it was most common to live in rooming houses, it was much less easy to organize eviction demonstrations. Instead, as elsewhere in the city, people rallied around demands for less dehumanizing relief. The most dramatic form of activity was the group march on relief stations in response to the ill treatment of, or denial of relief to, a family, or to protest a particular policy. Sometimes the group would occupy the station and refuse to leave until its demands were met; other times it would be less belligerent or would leave in response to threats to call the police. Relief caseworkers' practice of asking invasive and humiliating questions about the private lives of their clients was especially resented, and many demonstrations protested this policy.[42]

---

41. Richard O. Boyer and Herbert Morais, *Labor's Untold Story* (New York: United Electrical Radio and Machine Workers of America, 1972), 261; Steve Nelson, James R. Barrett, and Rob Ruck, *Steve Nelson: American Radical* (Pittsburgh, PA: University of Pittsburgh Press, 1981), 76; interview of Katherine Hyndman by Staughton Lynd, 51–53. On Greek radicalism in the Depression, see Dan Georgakas, "Greek-American Radicalism: The Twentieth Century," in *The Immigrant Left in the United States*, eds. Paul Buhle and Dan Georgakas (Albany, NY: State University of New York Press, 1996), 217–20. Collective defiance of police armed with machine guns seems to have been a not unusual occurrence. See, for example, *Daily Worker*, September 7, 1932.
42. Storch, "Shades of Red," 104; G. P., "Local Struggles and the Building of Unemployed Councils in Preparation for the Hunger March," *Party Organizer*, January 1932, 9, 10; Frank

Examples illustrate protesters' tactics and police responses. In late August 1931, 400 people marched on a United Charities office in Bronzeville. By the time they reached the office the crowd was 1,500 strong, and it proceeded to storm the station. After a police squad arrived, a "general riot" ensued. In March 1932, several thousand people converged on the Humboldt Park relief station to demand that the "box relief" system be changed to cash relief. Police opened fire, though no fatalities ensued. (Soon afterward, the state relief administration announced that it would henceforth give relief in cash.) In early July 1932, hundreds of steel workers and their families stormed a relief station in Kensington because the supply of food had been completely cut off. Police arrived, but the workers broke through their lines and hurled bricks at the windows. "Five more squads of police and a large group of motorcycle reinforcements came up," the *Daily Worker* reported, and "after a vicious battle the men with their women and children were forced to retreat." In September 1932, a huge demonstration occurred at a relief station in Pullman, at which the following demands were made: any three members of the Unemployed Council were always to be recognized as legitimate representatives of relief clients, the police were to be removed from the relief agency's premises, and rent was to be paid for clients. As was often the case, hundreds of women and children were present; police arrested and clubbed many of them. Such spectacular clashes happened most frequently between the summer of 1931 and the early spring of 1933.[43]

Apart from the practical activities of day-to-day struggle against miserable relief, evictions, and the shutting off of gas and electricity in people's homes, the Councils put forward a series of far-reaching political demands. The millions of people who embraced or shared these demands had an "ideology" that was radical indeed, necessitating a total transformation of American capitalism. The centerpiece of the Councils' program was the demand for unemployment insurance, which was raised as early as January 1930. We'll discuss this in more detail later, but judging just by the turnout on 6 March 1930, a large proportion of the unemployed very quickly adopted the Communists' extreme conception of unemployment insurance: full union wages paid by the government with no discrimination against any group, financed by taxes on inheritances, gifts, and individual and corporate incomes of $5,000 a year and over, administered by representatives elected by workers and farmers. Other Council demands, advertised in millions of leaflets, pamphlets, and newspapers, included the seven-hour day and five-day week, free speech and assembly, prohibition of child labor, free employment agencies under workers' control, and demolition of slums and construction of workers' dwellings

---

Z. Glick, *The Illinois Emergency Relief Commission* (Chicago, IL: University of Chicago Press, 1940), 122; *Daily Worker*, March 23, April 24, 1931.

43. Paul Clinton Young, "Race, Class, and Radicalism in Chicago, 1914–1936" (PhD diss., University of Iowa, 2001), 207; Lasswell and Blumenstock, *World Revolutionary Propaganda*, 171; *Daily Worker*, March 14, July 6, September 15, 1932.

to be owned by the city. That these demands were attractive to millions of Americans is hardly surprising.⁴⁴

If Communist Party membership is any indication, the unemployed were sometimes more militant and radical than the employed, despite the very real hardships of the latter. In 1931, about 50 percent of members in Chicago were unemployed, and in a not atypical two-month period in that year, 80 percent of new recruits were without work. This trend was particularly pronounced on the South Side, where, in 1933, 79 percent of party members were unemployed. Nationally, in 1934, Earl Browder, general secretary of the party, estimated that between 60 and 70 percent of the membership was jobless. On the other hand, the numbers were not so disproportionate in later years of the decade, when the Popular Front and the CIO attracted increasing numbers of employed workers to the CP.⁴⁵

The foreign-born, too, were disproportionately drawn to the CP, to the dismay of party leaders. In 1931, two-thirds of the national party and half of Chicago's had been born abroad. In Chicago, Eastern Europeans were overrepresented in the party, while Germans and Italians were underrepresented. Jews were especially prominent: they constituted 22 percent of Chicago's CP in 1931 and 19 percent of the party nationally. Between 1930 and 1935 the CP published daily newspapers in eight foreign languages, in addition to weeklies and the many pamphlets, leaflets, flyers, and shop papers that were constantly being distributed. Some indication of the influence of Communist publications in immigrant communities is given by the percentage of total daily newspaper circulation that was Communist. According to Nathan Glazer, in 1930 half of the circulation of dailies among Croats, Finns, Lithuanians, and Ukrainians was Communist, and about a third among Hungarians, Russians, and Slovaks. This suggests substantial sympathy among these groups for Communist views (particularly since newspapers were likely to be passed around after one person had read them). In Chicago, the CP's many foreign-language federations—principally Workers' Clubs (Jewish, Irish, Italian, Polish, Scandinavian, etc.)—amplified its impact in immigrant communities.⁴⁶

Again, the most striking support for Communism was found in the Black Belt. While it is noteworthy that in 1931 24 percent of Chicago's CP members were Black, more telling are contemporaries' descriptions of the enthusiasm nonmembers displayed toward the radical left. Much as in Harlem, as Mark Naison has described, Communism became a dominant force among Blacks in Chicago under the impact of both the Depression and the Scottsboro campaign to save nine boys in Alabama falsely accused of raping two white women. A series of *Daily Worker* articles by the writer Michael Gold in September 1932 testified to the hegemony the CP had by that time achieved over much of the Black Belt's lower class. With obvious exaggeration, Gold wrote, "Everyone

---

44. "Program of the National Unemployment Conference, New York, March 29–30, 1930," CP records, reel 163, Tamiment; Dorothy Douglas, "Unemployment Insurance—For Whom?", *Social Work Today*, February 1935, 12.
45. Storch, "Shades of Red," 41; Ottanelli, *The Communist Party*, 44.
46. Klehr, *The Heyday*, 162, 163; Storch, "Shades of Red," 43–45; Glazer, *The Social Basis of American Communism*, 81–85; Lasswell and Blumenstock, *World Revolutionary Propaganda*, 73.

on the south side knows and sympathizes with the work of the [unemployed] councils. It has penetrated everywhere." He gave a couple of illustrations: "In a little barbecue restaurant, five truck drivers were at lunch. [...] I heard their talk: they were discussing that morning's editorial in the *Daily Worker* on Germany. On a wooden stoop at sunset sat a group of tall jobless men and their wives. One giant in overalls fingered at a guitar; another was reading aloud to the serious little group out of a pamphlet by Lenin." Observing the crowds at Washington Park and Ellis Park, he wrote, "fathers, mothers, grandmothers from the deep south—all the generations were at the forum, this Communism has become a folk thing. They have taken Communism and translated it into their own idiom." Two months earlier he had witnessed a CP convention at Chicago's Coliseum, 14,000 whites and Blacks from around the country attending, and heard dozens of speakers sound the same theme. "'I love the Communist party,' said Mrs. Laura Osbee, a gaunt stockyards worker in a green shirtwaist, 'because under its banner we are not fighting for a lousy fifteen dollars a week, but for equal rights. This is the comrade party, the others are the boss parties. We Negroes love the Communist party.'"[47]

Such statements invoking freedom and equal rights, which could be multiplied many times over, serve as a salutary reminder that despite the truth of James C. Scott's statement that "'bread-and-butter' issues are the essence of lower-class politics and resistance," the role of *idealism* in animating members of the lower classes should not be discounted. "If we must die," an old man said in Washington Park, "we will die for Communism and a great cause, not like stuck hogs."[48]

Ordinarily idealism and moral consciousness, even revolt against social and economic degradation, found expression in religion. One might think that religion and Communism would be in contradiction, but this was not always the case. It is true that speakers in Washington Park, according to one observer, were "constantly" decrying religious fantasies as being the opiate of the masses, and that under the influence of Communism large numbers of Blacks embraced atheism. Some ministers were so disturbed by the growing materialism of their former flock that they ventured into enemy territory, giving lectures in Washington Park to hostile audiences on such subjects as "Christianism and Communism." The minister of the largest church in the Black Belt did so on one occasion in 1931: when asked by the unfriendly crowd to "explain his presence and to state why he didn't stay in his church, he made the damaging admission that his congregation wasn't coming to his church." His attempts to reconstitute the congregation were fruitless.[49]

---

47. Storch, "Shades of Red," 45; Mark Naison, *Communists in Harlem during the Great Depression* (Chicago, IL: University of Illinois Press, 2005 [1983]); Michael Gold, "The Negro Reds of Chicago," Part II, *Daily Worker*, September 29, 1932; Michael Gold, "The Communists Meet," *New Republic*, June 15, 1932.
48. Gold, "The Negro Reds of Chicago," Part II.
49. Wilson T. Seney, "A Study of the Activities of the Communist Party in Organizing Unrest among the Negroes of Chicago," 19, December 21, 1931, term paper for Sociology 310, Ernest Burgess Papers, box 183, folder 1.

The common attitude on the South Side, as well as in other working-class districts and among men in flophouses and shelters, that everything was a "racket," that ministers and politicians and other public authorities cared only about the almighty dollar and not at all about the woes of the working man, was itself due in no small part to the agitation of Communists, who were preaching exactly that viewpoint. In some ways the popular attitude may even have been more radical than the Communist, for it approached anarchism in its indiscriminate skepticism of all authority (including, sometimes, left-wing authorities like the CP). Religious authority, however, was the easiest target, and old IWW songs like the following, called "Pie in the Sky"—which mocks a preacher's reply to a request for bread—were popular:

By and by, by and by,
Sweat all day, live on hay,
'Cause you'll get pie
In the sky
By and by.[50]

On the other hand, it was the usual policy of CP members not to direct their ire at religion but at economic, social, and political injustices. Many Blacks in fact transferred their religious enthusiasm to Communism, and doubtless did not necessarily see an incompatibility between the sacred and the secular. As Michael Gold said, "At mass meetings [Blacks'] religious past becomes transmitted into a Communist present. They follow every word of the speaker with real emotion; they encourage him, as at a prayer meeting, with cries of 'Yes, yes, comrade,' and often there is an involuntary and heartfelt 'Amen!'" One woman recalled that at least a third of her church at this time was Communist. Prominent ministers began to declare themselves sympathetic to Communism, no doubt primarily for public relations purposes. In mid-1934, for example, Reverend J. C. Austin of Pilgrim Baptist Church, in alliance with the International Labor Defense, invited Angelo Herndon to speak at his church. Herndon was a young party organizer who had become nationally known during his imprisonment in Georgia under the state's old insurrection law, and his visit attracted an interracial crowd of 3,000 people "from every section of the city." Herndon's speech drew wild cheers, but the audience saved its loudest applause for the reverend's remarks. "From all I have learned of Communism," Austin said, "it means simply the brotherhood of man, and as far as I can see Jesus Christ was the greatest Communist of them all. [...] Just a week ago I stood in this church and talked to my congregation from the subject 'Russia, the hope of the Negro.'" A journalist wrote that "fully five minutes" of a "deafening" ovation followed his words (addressed to Communists), "Come here anytime you want to hold a meeting. Not only that, but you will find me always ready and willing to stand shoulder to shoulder with you, preach with you, pray with you, march with you, and, if necessary, die with you for the common good of us all."[51]

---

50. Ibid., 20.
51. Harold F. Gosnell, *Negro Politicians: The Rise of Negro Politics in Chicago* (Chicago, IL: University of Chicago Press, 1967), 338, 341; Naison, *Communists in Harlem*, 57; Storch, *Red Chicago*, 96;

Another illustration of how deeply certain habits and ideas of Communism had penetrated the community is a party leader's remark, in an internal discussion in 1932, that "the word 'comrade' is as popular on the South Side as it is in this Plenum. A Republican and Democratic politician going from house to house collecting signatures on petitions asked Negro workers, 'Will you please sign the petition for comrade so and so?'" Admittedly a trivial detail, the use of this term even by non-Communist politicians reveals the temper of the time.[52]

Popular adoption of the Communist creed extended to the point of continual participation in interracial meetings and actions, despite Chicago's long and violent history of racial and ethnic conflict. It is almost superfluous to give examples, since interethnic and interracial solidarity were very soon the norm rather than the exception. As early as January 1930, Blacks and whites of various ethnicities were marching en masse on City Hall. May Day that year saw a huge march in the vicinity of Haymarket Square, in which thousands of Blacks and hundreds of children participated. In early August, a large crowd attended an antiwar demonstration at Washington Square, at which the Black and white speakers urging interracial cooperation received enthusiastic cheers. "White workers in particular," reported the *Daily Worker*, "cheered the slogan of the speakers that it is up to the white workers to demonstrate to their Negro fellow workers that they will really take up the fight for the Negro workers and fight against lynchings and segregation."[53] In February 1931, a "mammoth" hunger march (as described by the *Chicago Defender*) that proceeded down State Street from 31st to 50th Streets began with a ratio of 20 whites to 1 Black but ended in a rally that was split evenly between the races, at which speakers cried, "Down with the bosses" and for an end to discrimination against Black workers.[54]

Many Unemployed Council locals united ethnicities that had traditionally been mutually hostile. The Back of the Yards council had several thousand members, who gathered bread from bakeries and other food from stores, even meat stolen from packinghouses, to feed more than five hundred people a day. The most spectacular hunger march in this district occurred in April 1932, when thousands of workers marched to the stockyards to present a list of demands to representatives of the Armour, Swift,

---

St. Clair Drake, *Churches and Voluntary Associations in the Negro Community* (Report of WPA Project 465-54-3-386, Chicago, IL, 1940), 260, 261; *Chicago Defender*, September 29, 1934; Charles H. Martin, *The Angelo Herndon Case and Southern Justice* (Baton Rouge, LA: Louisiana State University Press, 1976).

52. Bill Gebert, "The Struggle for the Negro Masses and the Fight against the Social Demagogs [sic]," *Party Organizer*, May–June 1932, 12.

53. Naturally, one cannot always take the words of the *Daily Worker*—or any other newspaper, for that matter— at face value. Exaggeration was a useful device of propaganda. But there is little reason to doubt such a statement as the one just quoted in the text. (Historians sometimes discount the testimony of the *Daily Worker* while taking establishment newspapers more seriously, but in truth, as scholarship has shown and labor organizers can attest to, there is no reason to think the latter are more honest than the left-wing press.)

54. *Daily Worker*, February 22, May 7, August 6, September 9, 1930; *New York Times*, January 30, February 22, 1930; *Chicago Defender*, February 14, 1931; Storch, "Shades of Red," 98.

and Wilson companies. A quarter of the demonstrators were Black, and hundreds of Mexican and Polish workers marched side by side with the American-born. One participant recalled the significance of such experiences. "Polish, Lithuanian, Catholic, Protestant, or whatever, it didn't matter who you were, just that you needed help. Sure some of the old suspicions were there, but they fell away once people saw what they could do together." Mexicans were especially active in Packingtown's unemployed movement, in part because the Catholic Church there did virtually nothing to reach out to them, thus making it easier for them to join left-wing, non-Mexican organizations. Still, they sometimes let caution dictate their moves. In October 1932, members of the University of Chicago Settlement's Mexican Club of Unemployed Men voted against joining thousands of other workers in a hunger march protesting cuts in relief, out of fear that police would label them as Communists and hand them over to immigration officials.[55]

It was not only men doing the organizing and protesting. In Chicago, 15 percent of CP members were women, half of them working and half unemployed. Chicago's party never devoted a lot of resources to recruiting women, but it seems that many did not require much of an external stimulus to activism in any case. To some degree they were held back by the sexism that even egalitarian-minded CP members could not always rid themselves of. An internal party discussion in early 1932 testifies to this fact: "In some of our unemployed branches in Chicago," a member writes, "the women constitute the most active elements in the unemployed branch, yet we find that at a meeting of the City Committee of the Unemployed Councils only one woman delegate is present. The tendency in the unemployed councils is that women can do the technical work, distribute leaflets, fight evictions and appear before charities for relief, *but* women are not eligible as delegates to the City Committee from their respective unemployed branches." Often women were organized in women's councils and mothers' leagues, instead of being drawn into unemployed branches or the block committees that attracted the most militant people in the neighborhood. These female-centered groups engaged in such struggles as demanding pots and pans, bed linen, and clothing from relief agencies and organizing neighborhoods to boycott or picket shops that charged high prices.[56]

---

55. Rick Halpern, *Down on the Killing Floor: Black and White Workers in Chicago's Packinghouses, 1904–1954* (Chicago, IL: University of Illinois Press, 1997), 101–104; *Daily Worker*, April 21, 1932; *Chicago Defender*, April 23, 1932; Louise Año Nuevo Kerr, "The Chicano Experience in Chicago: 1920–1970" (PhD diss., University of Illinois at Chicago Circle, 1976), 106, 107; Gabriela Arredondo, *Mexican Chicago: Race, Identity, and Nation, 1916–39* (Chicago, IL: University of Illinois Press, 2008), 135. On Mexicans' experiences with the labor movement's interracialism in the 1930s, see Michael McCoyer, "Darkness of a Different Color: Mexicans and Racial Formation in Greater Chicago, 1916–1960" (PhD diss., Northwestern University, 2007), 303–29.
56. K. E., "Organize the Work among Women!" *Party Organizer*, January 1932, 26; Storch, *Red Chicago*, 45; *Chicago Hunger Fighter*, February 27, 1932; *Daily Worker*, February 10, 1931. Such picketing was common in Harlem, for example, as in one action in 1935, when "a flying squadron of black housewives marched through the streets demanding that butchers lower their prices by 25 percent." They warned that if they didn't, they could expect a riot. The butchers complied. Lashawn Harris, "Running with the Reds: African American Women

The various social pressures that militated against women's active involvement in the Communist Party did not prevent them from participating en masse in marches and rallies (an act, we should remember, that was always significant because of the threat of police violence). On the one hand, women with children did not necessarily have much time to devote to organizing, and the exigencies of trying to keep a family alive and healthy tended to fix their gaze on issues of relief that many Communists considered relatively trivial. Margaret Keller, the CP's director of women's work in 1933, complained, "it is terrible difficult work among the women, they are very narrow, due to the majority being housewives and can't see anything else but the relief, we hope through education to convince them this is a political struggle."[57]

On the other hand, evidence of women's crucial participation in both employed and unemployed struggles abounds. Historians have shown that women workers and wives in the 1930s (as in other decades) were often extremely militant, but they have devoted less attention to such collective action in the context of unemployment.[58] One has but to peruse newspapers of the time, however, to learn that women were not infrequently *more* assertive than men, or more aggressive in resisting police. To take an example at random, in July 1932, a large meeting was called to protest the expulsion from Douglas Park of people who had no other place to sleep. Led by Chicago's infamous Red Squad, police tried to break up the meeting, driving motorcycles across the sidewalk and into the crowd of men, women, and children. When they seized the speaker, "women led the struggle to get their leader back from the police," which they did successfully. At eviction protests they acted similarly, exhorting crowds to "act like men"—"Hold your places, comrades!"—when attacked by police. Black women were especially prominent in these protests, as in parades and rallies, where they lustily led the singing and chanting.[59]

In December 1934, a correspondent reported in an issue of the CP's *Working Woman* that women from coal mining families in Hillsboro, Illinois, had organized to demand adequate relief. They "held meetings, traveled through the countryside, raised money,

---

and the Communist Party during the Great Depression," *Journal of African American History* 94, no. 1 (Winter 2009): 27.
57. Storch, *Red Chicago*, 126.
58. See Dorothy Sue Cobble, *Dishing It Out: Waitresses and Their Unions in the Twentieth Century* (Chicago, IL: University of Illinois Press, 1991), chapter 4; Jeremy Brecher, *Strike!* (San Francisco, CA: Straight Arrow Books, 1972), chapter 5; Ruth Milkman, ed., *Women, Work, and Protest* (Boston, MA: Routledge & Kegan Paul, 1985); Annelise Orleck, *Common Sense and a Little Fire: Women and Working-Class Politics in the United States* (Chapel Hill, NC: University of North Carolina Press, 1995); Annelise Orleck, "'We Are That Mythical Thing Called the Public': Militant Housewives during the Great Depression," *Feminist Studies* 19, no. 1 (Spring 1993): 147–172; Sharon Hartman Strom, "Challenging 'Woman's Place': Feminism, the Left, and Industrial Unionism in the 1930s," *Feminist Studies* 9, no. 2 (Summer 1983): 359–86; Ruth Susan Meyerowitz, "Organizing and Building the UAW: Women at the Ternstedt General Motors Part Plant, 1936–1950" (PhD diss., Columbia University, 1984).
59. *Daily Worker*, July 27, 1932; Horace Cayton, "The Black Bugs"; Rosemary Feurer, "The Nutpickers' Union, 1933–34: Crossing the Boundaries of Community and Workplace," in *"We Are All Leaders": The Alternative Unionism of the Early 1930s*, ed. Staughton Lynd (Chicago, IL: University of Illinois Press, 1996), 30, 31.

and, in defiance of the male leadership of the Progressive Miners' Association, led demonstrations. As one march began on City Hall, the male demonstrators 'made vain efforts to keep their wives from the front ranks.'" Just as collective action birthed an explicit class consciousness among unemployed men, so it birthed an incipient feminist consciousness among their wives, a sense of female power and a willingness to defy gendered expectations.[60]

In fact, as the historian Annelise Orleck has related, a veritable "housewives' movement" erupted across the country in the 1930s. From large-scale barter networks in Seattle to successful boycotts of high-priced meat in (for example) Detroit and Chicago to lobbying the federal government for price controls, housewives vigorously defended their interests in the most realistic and rational ways available. In Chicago, on one occasion in the summer of 1935, wives stormed meatpacking plants and set on fire thousands of pounds of meat to "dramatize their contention that high prices were not the result of shortages." This was in the context of that summer's nationwide meat strike, organized and coordinated by neighborhood mothers' clubs, church groups, union auxiliaries, and CP-affiliated women's groups from New York to Los Angeles. In the following years the networks that had been forged in 1935 were used to expand the new consumer movement into the realms of political lobbying and electoral politics, as housewives successfully ran for office and pressured governments for further regulation of industry, construction of more public housing, an end to discrimination against female workers, free access to birth control devices, etc. "The uprising of working-class housewives," Orleck sums up, "broadened the terms of the class struggle, forcing male union leaders to admit that 'the roles of producer and consumer are intimately related.'"[61]

By mid-1932, Chicago had 80 Unemployed Council locals with about 15,000 members, in addition to the many block committees and neighborhood committees that sent delegates to these locals. An article in the *Daily Worker* about a "typical" unemployed branch in Chicago (in Lawndale, on the West Side) illuminated the inner life of the councils, in particular the challenges they faced in building a sustainable mass movement. In the two-year history of this council, many hundreds of names had been on its membership books, but at no time more than two hundred. Usually less than fifty attended the branch meetings. "These meetings," the author wrote, "consist mostly of dull routine. Most of the time the agenda has too many points, sometimes as high as 21. [...] The deadly monotony is often broken by squabbles and disorder." The best people were driven away by the long meetings and unnecessary arguments. Moreover, American-born workers were viewed with suspicion—90 percent of the members were Jewish, mostly of foreign birth—and "the talk of stool-pigeons, especially by a Party member, [had] create[d] an atmosphere of distrust." Nearly all the families helped by the council drifted away because there was "no organizational machinery to keep in

---

60. Strom, "Challenging 'Woman's Place,'" 366, 367.
61. Orleck, *Common Sense and a Little Fire*, chapter 6; Orleck, "'We Are That Mythical Thing Called the Public,'" 166..

touch with them and to overcome the influence of the charities which bribe and frighten them away from us." Altogether, the branch was "headless and demoralized."[62]

Party members complained alternately about the absence and the too-strong presence of party control over councils. In 1933, CP leader Israel Amter stated in the *Party Organizer* that there was too much "mechanical" Communist control of the councils. "We think we can remove and appoint and do exactly as we please. The organizers that we put in are responsible to the party but have no responsibility to the masses." Herbert Benjamin had registered a similar complaint a year earlier: "Party organizations, instead of mobilizing the membership for participation in Unemployed Councils and committees, themselves take over the functions of these united front organizations. Where non-Party workers are attracted to our movement in such cases, they find themselves excluded from all participation in the actual work of planning and leading actions." On the other hand, internal documents from the CP's Chicago district periodically lamented the *absence* of functioning party fractions in councils.[63]

In this context of obstacles to the unemployed movement's growth, one must also mention, again, the essential role of police terror. Had there been no police at all, of course, it is likely that most people, not fearing legal repercussions, would have revolted against their rulers, invading stores and warehouses and taking what they wanted. It is easy to underestimate the role of sheer violence (and its threat) in upholding business rule. And violence, as we have seen, was something the Chicago police excelled at. Party member Harry Haywood's retrospective remarks were surely accurate:

> The city administration's answer to this growing [unemployed] movement was unbridled police terror. A tool of the corrupt city government and allied with gangsters, Chicago's police force undoubtedly held the record for terror and lawlessness against workers. They were unsurpassed for sadism and brutality, regularly raiding the halls and offices of the Unemployed Councils, revolutionary organizations and the Party—smashing furniture, beating workers in the halls, on the streets and in the precinct stations.[64]

---

62. Lasswell and Blumenstock, *World Revolutionary Propaganda*, 73, 74; Frank Z. Glick, *The Illinois Emergency Relief Commission* (Chicago, IL: University of Chicago Press, 1940), 118; M. W. Good, "The History of an Unemployed Council Branch," *Daily Worker*, March 15, 1932.
63. Israel Amter, "Low Ebb of Unemployed Work Contrary to Open Letter Line," *Party Organizer*, November 1933, 30–32; Klehr, *The Heyday*, 63; District Organization letter, March 17, 1931, Communist Party files, microfilm reel 187, Tamiment; "Some Material on Our Work among Unemployed," n.d., 4, ibid., reel 232.
64. Harry Haywood, *Black Bolshevik: Autobiography of an Afro-American Communist* (Chicago, IL: Liberator Press, 1978), 444. Consider one example of the horrors that went on continually behind closed doors at the police stations. In August 1937, a 20-year-old African American boy named William Harris was arrested (mistakenly, it turned out) for supposedly stealing a woman's purse a few weeks earlier. As the *Daily Worker* later reported,

> Harris states that [at the police station, two officers] handcuffed his hands behind him to a ladder with his feet on a box. Then [one of them] kicked the box out from under his feet leaving him hanging in the air with the handcuffs cutting his wrists. Harris still refused to confess. He was punched in the stomach, back and sides. At

The Red Squad (the special police force devoted to terrorizing radicals and rebellious workers) constantly surveilled Communists, sending undercover agents to party meetings and periodically stealing or destroying party records. By 1940, the squad's leader, Lieutenant Make Mills, had amassed a file of index cards that included 5,000 local Communists and 75,000 names around the country; the cards specified each person's occupation, nationality, age, and leadership role.[65]

Police tactics changed over several years, but at all times the use of violence as a deterrent, a punishment, and an effective interrupter of protests was crucial. In 1930, with one exception every outdoor demonstration (and many indoor meetings) that Communists organized was cut short by the police. This tendency continued for much of 1931, but eventually it was judged to be simpler and less politically costly (given the continual displays of frenzied brutality) for the police to allow demonstrations, requiring only that a permit be obtained first. When it was denied but the event proceeded anyway, the ensuing police violence could be justified on the basis of the demonstration's "illegality." Participants in such illegal actions sometimes armed themselves with sticks and clubs and filled their pockets with stones; those who did not might follow the CP's instruction to at least use their fists or to try to snatch clubs from officers and use them on the police (in order to protect whoever was speaking). Usually, however, as in the innumerable relief station demonstrations and most eviction protests, the demonstrators were unarmed. This did not stop the police from behaving as they did, for instance, at a March 1932 rally in front of the Japanese Consulate on Michigan Avenue, in protest against Japan's invasion of China and Manchuria: "From Ohio Street," reported the *New York Herald Tribune*, "came the mounted police and machine gun squads. They galloped up the sidewalk, hurtling their mounts into the thick of the crowd. They clubbed left and right with all their strength"—incidentally hitting fellow officers on foot—"while the horses trampled the fleeing demonstrators under foot." As officers shot at demonstrators, bullets ricocheted off the sidewalk and injured passersby.[66]

Spectacular police violence, while less frequent than between 1930 and 1933, continued into the later years of the decade, as the 1937 Memorial Day Massacre attests. In 1935, a South Side demonstration of many thousands against Italy's invasion of Ethiopia

---

last they used a board a foot wide and beat him across the feet, stomach, back and chest about 60 times. Five minutes later they took him back and hung him up again for 15 minutes, beating him again. Then they unlocked the handcuffs and Harris fell face forward to the floor.

Because of this beating, his right arm, wrist, and hand were paralyzed. *Daily Worker*, August 21, 1937.

65. Storch, "Shades of Red," 33; Frank Donner, *Protectors of Privilege: Red Squads and Police Repression in Urban America* (Berkeley, CA: University of California Press, 1990), 50.
66. Frances Fox Piven and Richard A. Cloward, *Poor People's Movements*, 54; A. Verblin, "The Growing Terror in Chicago," *Daily Worker*, August 22, 1930; Lasswell and Blumenstock, *World Revolutionary Propaganda*, 169–80; Chicago Civil Liberties Committee, *Defending Freedom in Chicago*, May 1932, 6, Raymond Hilliard Papers, box 114, folder 1, Chicago History Museum; *New York Herald Tribune*, March 13, 1932; *Daily Worker*, March 15, 1932.

required between 700 and 2,000 police (accounts vary) in order to be broken up. The Red Squad especially discouraged interracial interaction, even in harmless contexts, as was clear from an interview Make Mills gave to (white) University of Chicago students in 1934. After being briefly taken into custody for talking to Blacks on the South Side (the police lectured them about being in a "nigger" neighborhood, telling them to stay out of the Black Belt), they visited Mills to ask if he approved of arrests for such a reason. Evidently he did. "Anytime you go into a nigger district you'll get hit with a club. [...] You've no right to go into any nigger neighborhood." With some exaggeration, the *Chicago Defender* commented that "it is the duty of [Mills'] squad to cruise around the city in search of 'Reds,' as evidenced by a group in which black and white people are found together as friends and not fighting each other. Whenever these squads find such gatherings, they immediately pounce upon the offenders, beat men and women over their heads with clubs, haul them off to stations and put them through 'the works,' which usually consists of photographing and fingerprinting them."[67]

Investigations by the ACLU illuminated the various other means that authorities used to discourage and suppress unemployed radicalism. As a report stated,

> [The unemployed] run up against refusals of permits for meetings and parades, bans by mayors on meetings and parades, refusals of the use of tax-supported meeting places such as school-halls, police orders to landlords to refuse to rent halls, misapplication of ordinances against the distribution of advertising matter by hand bills, refusal of permits to post notices, and rarely, injunctions. Sometimes the welfare authorities themselves are responsible for attempts to hinder or disrupt the organization of the unemployed. Cases are not infrequent where persons active in organization work have been cut off the relief rolls.[68]

In short, throughout the decade the civil liberties of the unemployed were systematically, though not universally, denied. In the words of one article, "Clients protesting inadequate relief [and] workers on relief projects organizing against wage reductions find themselves arrested and in the courts charged with, 'Disorderly Conduct,' 'Malicious Mischief,' 'Assault,' 'Riot,' 'Anarchy,' 'Treason,' 'Criminal Syndicalism,' or even 'Conspiracy to

---

67. *New York Amsterdam News*, September 7, 1935; Haywood, *Black Bolshevik*, 447–57; *Chicago Defender*, May 26, 1934, March 5, 1938. A *Chicago Defender* reporter witnessed the aftermath of the 1935 demonstration:

> If the people who saw the police break up the parade were surprised at the brutality that went on all afternoon on 47th Street they would have been astonished at the downright savageness with which the police amused themselves at the Wabash Avenue Station. The patrol wagons gathered in such numbers in front of the station as to hold up traffic on 48th Street. Prisoners were unloaded in the middle of the thoroughfare. On each side of the wagon formed a long double line of 15-30 police. The unfortunate prisoners were pulled out of the vehicle and forced to run the gauntlet. Their heads, shins and bodies were clubbed by policemen who yelped in glee at the bloody sight.
>
> Haywood, Black Bolshevik, *455*.

68. ACLU, *What Rights for the Unemployed?* (New York: ACLU, 1935), 8.

Overthrow the Government.'" Most common was the charge of disorderly conduct, which could cover everything from leafleting to being in Chicago's Black Belt while white.[69]

But the fact that enormous numbers of the jobless were eager to organize and demonstrate even in the face of repression and police brutality left it to more "benign" authorities to bring about the decline of the Unemployed Councils. As Randi Storch has related, in January 1933 the relief administration declared that it would no longer accept complaints from organized groups at relief stations, instead setting up a Public Relations Bureau downtown where unemployed organizations could register their grievances. Demonstrations were held at the stations in defiance of the new ruling, but the police strictly enforced it. This simple shift in policy did far more than police violence in itself ever could to undercut the councils, because now that adjudication occurred in a relatively routinized manner downtown it was harder for the CP to illustrate to the community the efficacy of mass pressure. Illegal demonstrations grew less frequent, and over the course of 1933 councils in some parts of the city were "almost completely wiped out of existence," according to an internal party letter. "The workers were looking for ACTION," it stated, "[and] when they did not see the actions, they quit the councils."[70]

The other main blow to the councils was the election of Franklin Roosevelt. As Melvyn Dubofsky says, "By frightening the ruling class into conceding reforms and appealing to workers to vote as a solid block, Roosevelt simultaneously intensified class consciousness and stripped it of its radical potential."[71] Internal CP discussions in 1936 acknowledged that the party and its mass organizations had had difficulty adapting to Roosevelt, for instance making the mistake of attacking the Civilian Conservation Corps as fascist and militaristic despite its great popularity. But even had radicals been savvier in their protests against Roosevelt, the fact is that FERA and the various federal work relief programs did improve conditions for millions of people. While maximal demands were not met—of generous social insurance, the wholesale ending of evictions, government guarantee of employment, and no discrimination against Blacks—enough demands were answered in the middle years of the decade for the turbulence of earlier activism to subside somewhat.[72]

One might argue, therefore, that the decline of the councils and their turbulent modes of protest signified their *success* as much as their *failure*. Unemployed activism forced government to intervene in society and the economy on a hitherto unimaginable

---

69. Mortimer Riemer, "The Unemployed—Second Class Citizens: The War against Their Civil Rights," *Social Work Today*, May 1935, 16–18; Wilson Black, "The Fight against Civil Liberties," *Social Work Today*, October 1935, 22, 23; ACLU, *How Goes the Bill of Rights? The Story of the Fight for Civil Liberty, 1935–36* (New York: ACLU, 1936), 25, 27.
70. Lasswell and Blumenstock, *World Revolutionary Propaganda*, 180–82; Storch, *Red Chicago*, 121; William Arthur Hillman, "Urbanization and the Organization of Welfare Activities in the Metropolitan Community of Chicago" (PhD diss., University of Chicago, 1940), 161; "Struggle for Carrying Out the Tasks of the Open Letter," n.d., CP files, microfilm reel 253.
71. Actually, it is simply an assumption on the part of Dubofsky that Roosevelt's rhetoric provoked an "intensification" of class consciousness, an assumption that reflects historians' common belief that most workers are—somehow (because of stupidity?)—unaware of their shared class position with each other and antagonism of interests with "the boss class."
72. Dubofsky, "Not So 'Turbulent Years,'" 221.

scale, and by so doing it undermined the very conditions of its own existence. And yet despite the immense political importance and success of such activism, it is still possible for the volume on the Great Depression in Oxford's History of the United States to include but a single sentence on the Unemployed Councils (and nothing about other comparable organizations).[73] Such is posterity's continuing condescension toward radical groups of this era.

A minority of Chicago's jobless remained quite militant even after 1933. The parks remained full of speakers and crowds, and of thousands of fists held in the air when, for example, a speaker shouted, "A revolution is what we need. A revolution against white bosses and black bosses!" The League of Struggle for Negro Rights continued to be instrumental in stopping evictions on the South Side—although both evictions and protests became less frequent. Despite the prohibition of demonstrations at local relief stations, many continued to occur the whole decade, although the paucity of sources clouds our historical vision. Harry Haywood casually mentions speaking at a relief station demonstration in late 1934, as if such demonstrations were still happening rather frequently. Earlier that year the *Hunger Fighter* reported that Unemployed Council Local 25—and there were still dozens of councils in the city—had organized a small number of people to demand (successfully) their delayed Civil Works Administration checks, clothing, and shoes at the local relief station. A year later, it was reported that locals had recently been winning many grievance cases for relief and were doing such things as organizing neighborhood libraries, performing theater pieces their members had written, and organizing study clubs. It was mentioned in the last chapter that the pace of relief station demonstrations and sit-ins picked up again starting in 1937, with the aid of the WA and the CIO.[74]

In fact, during relief crises, the Unemployed Councils revived on a citywide basis, for a brief time approaching their earlier vitality. In the June 1935 issue of the *Party Organizer*, for example, a correspondent reported that councils in several parts of the city were growing, and overflow meetings were being held on a united front basis (with Socialists and other groups). "Many Sections [of Chicago]," he said, "have correctly linked up the struggle for the opening of the [relief] stations and against the sales tax with the struggle against the high cost of living. In Sections 4 and 11 neighborhood committees are conducting struggle against the high cost of living, participating in all actions for relief and against the sales tax." Demonstrations were also organized in front of the homes of state representatives.[75]

In short, Unemployed Councils existed in Chicago most of the decade, their fortunes waxing and waning in the context of broader political and economic currents. They competed and cooperated with other organizations, most notably the Chicago Workers Committee on Unemployment, to which we now turn.

---

73. David Kennedy, *Freedom from Fear*, 222.
74. Edith Margo, "Chicago's South Side Sees 'Red,'" *Daily Worker*, June 3, 1933; Gosnell, *Negro Politicians*, 331; Haywood, *Black Bolshevik*, 445; *Hunger Fighter*, May 19, 1934, August 1935; *New York Times*, April 11, 1937; *Chicago Defender*, March 5, 1938.
75. B. S., "How the Party Reacted in the Illinois Relief Crisis," *Party Organizer*, June 1935, 13, 14.

Workers Committee on Unemployment

The story of the Workers Committee on Unemployment (WCU) lends support to Hallgren's belief, indicated earlier, that if Communists had had the "courage" to discuss revolution in straightforward American terms, far more people would have rallied to their banner. Founded in the summer of 1931, within a year the WCU had grown to encompass almost 15,000 people divided into 49 local units "meeting in all sections of the city," according to Robert Asher, a young historian who participated in it. Soon it was to have at least sixty locals. Asher emphasized the political radicalism of its members: "The organized unemployed say they are fed up with the Republicans, the Democrats and the system they represent. They are ready [in September 1932] for a complete new deal and will back to the limit any political party with a radical economic program. With this in mind they have made the establishment of a planned economy, in which social security and the right to work shall be placed above the interests of private profit, one of the principal planks in their platform." The rest of their demands, likewise, were similar to Communists': adequate medical, dental, and hospital care; public housing; free public employment exchanges; the five-day week and six-hour day; and unemployment insurance. Had the WCU possessed more resources, its membership could have expanded to far more than the 25,000 people it included by early 1933. But even this number was a substantial achievement for an organization only 18 months old.[76]

The Workers Committee was founded in July 1931 by a small group of people from the Socialist Party and the League for Industrial Democracy (LID) who were fed up with the SP's inaction on the issue of unemployment. Under the leadership of Karl Borders, executive secretary of the Chicago LID, this group of social workers, preachers, professors, and union leaders first agreed on a political program and then set about establishing locals. The Reverend W. B. Waltmire, pastor of the Humboldt Park Methodist Church, organized the first local with 50 unemployed men from his neighborhood, a number that quickly increased to almost three hundred. This group consisted mostly of Scandinavian immigrants; a second local, consisting of Poles, was established at Association House, a settlement house nearby. Three branches were formed at Northwestern University Settlement, and more spread to Chicago Commons, Onward Neighborhood House, and churches on the northwest side of the city. Before long there were 10 branches (containing Greeks, Italians, Americans, and others), and it was decided that delegates from each should meet every two weeks at Association House to discuss their specific problems and work out joint solutions. The original group of Karl Borders and his fellow founders, which had continued to meet downtown, became the Central Committee for the whole organization, and worked together with delegates from the locals to plan activities.[77]

---

76. Robert E. Asher, "The Jobless Help Themselves: A Lesson from Chicago," *New Republic*, September 28, 1932; "Chicago Workers' Committee on Unemployment: Its Purpose and Platform," August 15, 1932; Roy Rosenzweig, "'Socialism in Our Time': The Socialist Party and the Unemployed, 1929–1936," *Labor History* 20, no. 4 (Fall 1979): 491.

77. Robert Asher, "The Influence of the Chicago Workers' Committee on Unemployment upon the Administration of Relief: 1931–1934" (MA thesis, University of Chicago, 1934), 12–14;

Overwhelmingly, the men (and it was mostly men) who joined the Workers Committee were manual laborers. In many cases a few men in a different part of the city heard about the original locals, decided to organize their neighborhood on a similar basis, and then affiliated with the Committee. "Sometimes the initiative came from a Socialist, a LID member, or a minister," Roy Rosenzweig writes, "but most often the unemployed themselves provided the organizing talent. A member of an existing local might, for example, be evicted, move to a new neighborhood, and form a local there." Without the support of settlement houses, however, the movement could hardly have gotten started. They provided facilities, intellectual leadership, connections with political and relief authorities, speakers to periodically address the locals, and morale-boosting encouragement to the discouraged jobless. Frank W. McCulloch, who became one of the leaders of the Workers Committee, remarked later that "the cooperation of the Commons was so constant, its leadership so central a factor in the establishment and maintenance of the CWCOU [...] that I suspect many of us took the Commons—and other settlements—too much for granted."[78]

Indeed, an important reason why Workers Committees were most successful in Chicago and (to a lesser degree) New York City was that settlements there had the political independence necessary to support such a "radical" movement. Unlike in other cities, they were not funded by a central Community Chest, an institution that was dominated by conservative elements from the city's professional and business (particularly banking) elite. The Chest board, in effect, controlled every agency it funded and could prevent settlements from supporting groups of the unemployed and other such class enemies of businessmen. In Chicago, on the other hand, any particular agency might have either a conservative or a liberal board; and if the board was liberal, a settlement could sometimes get away with providing facilities even for Unemployed Council meetings. Chicago Commons and others had such liberal boards—often because one influential liberal who sat on them could outweigh the voices of conservatives. Thus, it was only a slight difference in the politics of repression between Chicago and other cities that opened up the institutional space for a significant unemployed movement to flower there.[79]

Beth Schulman, "'The Workers Are Finding a Voice': The Chicago Workers' Committee and the Relief Struggles of 1932," 1987, 11, McCulloch Papers, box 6, folder 12; Thomas F. Dorrance, "A New Deal Everyday: Civic Authority and Federal Policy in Chicago and Los Angeles during the Great Depression" (PhD diss., University of Illinois at Chicago, 2014), 30–36.

78. Laura Friedman, "A Study of One Hundred Unemployed Families in Chicago, January, 1927 to June, 1932" (MA thesis, University of Chicago, 1933), 8; Rosenzweig, "'Socialism in Our Time,'" 491; Judith Ann Trolander, *Settlement Houses and the Great Depression* (Detroit, MI: Wayne State University Press, 1975), 106.

79. Robert W. Kelso, "Banker Control of Community Chests," *Survey Graphic*, May 1, 1932, 117–19; Trolander, *Settlement Houses*, 150–63. On the ways that a city's conservative business community could manipulate and emasculate an unemployed movement, see Laura Renata Martin, "'California's Unemployed Feed Themselves': Conservative Intervention in the Los Angeles Cooperative Movement, 1931–1934," *Pacific Historical Review* 82, no. 1 (February 1, 2013): 33–62.

Throughout its existence the "higher echelons" of the Workers Committee, with the participation of the rank and file, concentrated on publicizing the plight of the jobless and pressing for legislative action. They worked with the Governor's Commission in 1931 to raise funds for relief, lobbied for a special session of the legislature to deal with unemployment, organized a series of public hearings in 1932 and 1933, represented the unemployed in continual intercessions with relief authorities at local and state levels, and cooperated with other groups to push for state and federal unemployment insurance. On occasion the Workers Committee formed a united front with the Unemployed Councils, but Communists' behavior in the October 1932 hunger march was so sectarian that it poisoned relations for years. The Speakers' Bureau of the WCU arranged debates and open forums, and sent speakers to locals every week in order to stimulate discussion on contemporary issues. For six months in 1933 a newspaper was also published, the *New Frontier*, which had a style and content almost as radical as the Unemployed Council's newspaper the *Hunger Fighter*.[80]

As the unemployed themselves took over increasing control of the Workers Committee in early 1932, the actions that locals engaged in became more militant, focused on immediate problems and not only legislative solutions. (The militancy of the rank and file calls to mind Communists' need sometimes to *dampen* the energy of UC members, by discouraging group looting of supermarkets and violence against property.) Locals established grievance committees that presented cases to relief offices, demanding better treatment of clients. Whatever emergency arose in the neighborhood, Workers Committee members would rush over to remedy it. For instance, they were useful in cases of the "petty persecutions" that landlords resorted to in order to get nonpaying tenants to leave of their own accord. Gertrude Springer, a settlement worker, gave examples in January 1933:

> Mrs. Russo's landlord takes down the door to her flat and carries it off. Come a couple of carpenters from the [Workers Committee] local with a knocked-up packing case and presently Mrs. Russo has a door that answers every practical purpose. Mrs. Kelly's little boy reports breathlessly that his mother's kitchen is flooded—a mysterious hole in a water-pipe and the landlord won't do anything. A plumber, doing his tour of duty on the emergency squad, solders up the hole, obviously punched with a chisel. Mrs. Cohen is being smoked out, "Come a'runnin'." Shock-troopers climb up to the roof, remove a rough and ready layer of bricks from Mrs. Cohen's chimney top, and life goes on.[81]

Such were the tactics of a kind of rudimentary class struggle, which were supplemented by the grander tactics of mass meetings and large demonstrations. Interspersed with these forms of protest were other types of working-class self-activity, including (as with Unemployed Councils) the sponsoring of Christmas parties, dances, picnics, sewing clubs, bands, numerous educational programs, slide shows, a library, and a "Workers' Training

---

80. Karl Borders, "The Unemployed Strike Out for Themselves," *Survey*, March 15, 1932, 663–65; Asher, "The Influence of the Chicago Workers' Committee," 36, 37.
81. Gertrude Springer, "Shock Troops to the Rescue," *Survey*, January 1933, 9–11.

School," all of which led Workers Committee locals to become "part of the fabric of community life, much like the local saloon, church, or fraternal lodge," to quote a historian.[82]

In early 1933, a student at the University of Chicago wrote a case study of a Workers Committee local in South Chicago that describes the trajectory of a typical unit. In early 1932, seven unemployed men drew up plans for a local: they announced in the *Daily Calumet* that the first few meetings would be held in the Bessemer Park clubhouse and invited anyone to attend. A month later the group still had only 45 members, so they mimeographed and distributed handbills and printed more advertisements in the *Daily Calumet* (which ran two or three front-page headliners on the group). So many people began to show up that they had to start using a large auditorium for their weekly meetings, at which speakers from the WCU's Central Committee made presentations on unemployment and the necessity of building a nationwide movement. More than three hundred people of various nationalities regularly attended the lectures, though not everyone was accepted as a member because "no one present could vouch for them." After a few months there was a crisis: Communists started showing up to disrupt the proceedings, on one occasion taking possession of the platform to denounce leaders of the WCU as traitors to the working class. As so often in those years, the Communists could not have been more successful at undermining the Left had they been FBI provocateurs: they antagonized everyone present, and the local actually ceased meeting for a while.[83]

When meetings resumed they were in a smaller location, and membership had to be built up again from a small base. Once a grievance committee was formed in the summer of 1932, however, new members started flooding in, as many as forty a week. One important project of the local was to collect fruits and vegetables from farms for distribution among hundreds of members. This was no simple task: trucks and drivers had to be found, an alderman had to issue letters of introduction to officials of oil and gas companies so they would donate gasoline, letters of introduction to the farmers had to be obtained, and the produce had to be distributed in such a way that everyone received an equal amount. Nevertheless, the project was a great success. Other locals organized similar undertakings, in addition to running cooperative barbershops and doing shoe and furniture repairing for each other.[84]

Since the basis for the Workers Committee's success, however, was its constant interventions at relief stations, the establishment of the Public Relations Bureau in January 1933 was a major blow, as it was to the Unemployed Councils. The WCU's numbers and its spirit began to decline—slowly. "The Workers' Committee continued to use all forms of protest," Robert Asher writes. "It achieved a noteworthy success [in 1933] in mitigating

---

82. Rosenzweig, "Organizing the Unemployed," 45; Rosenzweig, "'Socialism In Our Time,'" 493; *New Frontier,* December 12, 1932, January 8, 1933.
83. Annie Gosenpud, "The History of the Chicago Worker's [*sic*] Committee on Unemployment, Local #24, until Feb. 1933," term paper for Sociology 270, 1933, Ernest Burgess Papers, box 145, folder 7.
84. Ibid.; Trolander, *Settlement Houses,* 101; "Record of the Development of the Clubs for Unemployed Men and Women," 1933, Mary McDowell Papers, box 20, folder 1, Chicago History Museum.

the plight of the single men. Its members marched under their own banners in the 'Save Our Schools' parades. They showed their solidarity with other workers by setting up a labor committee and getting on to strikers' picket lines with signs of 'The Unemployed Won't Scab.'" They continued to call for vastly increased relief and workers' representation on relief agencies, in addition to holding a third series of public hearings in June 1934 and conducting campaigns for cash relief instead of relief in kind. Indeed, the Committee's 1934 annual report stated that in campaigns for decent relief and economic security it had "played an increasingly active and fruitful part" that year, for example helping to organize the Chicago Labor College, agitating for unemployment insurance and a public works program, gathering thousands of signatures on petitions for cash relief, and joining the Unemployed Councils in a gigantic hunger march through the Loop in late November to protest relief cuts and other abuses. Still, as the administration of relief became more centralized in 1933 and 1934, and also in some respects more responsive to the popular will, both the Workers Committee and the Unemployed Councils ceased to be as "menacing [a] threat to the established political and economic order" as they had been.[85]

Accordingly, to magnify its impact the unemployed movement entered its "unity" phase. An attempt to form a Federation of Unemployed Workers Leagues in late 1932 and early 1933, which in its first meeting already had representatives from 35 Midwestern organizations, foundered on sectarian disputes when the Communists and Musteites (in the form of the Congress for Progressive Labor Action) got involved. Much more successful, though more limited in its ambitions and of a different structure, was the IWA, founded by WCU members and allies in December 1933. This organization quickly became one of the most powerful unemployed associations in the country, with locals in over two hundred Illinois towns and cities; miners, a characteristically militant group, were especially attracted to it. As the (unaffiliated) Unemployed Councils lost visibility, the IWA gained it. It played a key role in the establishment of the nationwide WA in March 1935, and managed to survive, albeit in a weakened state, until the United States entered World War II.[86]

In Chicago, the Workers Committee and the IWA were essentially identical: the locals of the former were those of the latter. As before, their main function was the handling of relief grievances. But with the formation of the Public Relations Bureau, the procedure had become harassingly bureaucratic and inefficient. First, the person

---

85. Asher, "The Chicago Workers' Committee," 29, 30; Chicago Workers' Committee on Unemployment, "Annual Report – 1934," Graham Taylor Papers, box 36, folder 1950, Newberry Library; "Jobless Stage Protest March on City Hall," November 24, 1934, Chicago Commons Papers, box 26, folder 1; *Daily Worker*, November 23, 25, 1934; statement by Frank W. McCulloch, *Hearings before a Subcommittee of the Committee on Labor, House of Representatives, on H.R. 2827*, 369.
86. Helen Seymour, "The Organized Unemployed" (MA thesis, University of Chicago, 1937), 33–38; Report of Resolutions Committee of Midwest Conference of Unemployed Organizations, November 19 and 20, 1932, Chicago Commons Papers box 25, folder 1; *Daily Worker*, May 17 and 19, 1933; *New Frontier*, December 12, 1932, April 19, 1933; *Unemployed Union*, March 18, 1935. On the Musteite unemployed movement, which had no presence in Illinois, see Roy Rosenzweig, "Radicals and the Jobless: The Musteites and the Unemployed Leagues, 1932–1936," *Labor History* 16, no. 1 (Winter 1975): 52–77.

with a complaint had to try to resolve it himself at his district relief station; if he failed, the local's grievance committee would take it up. The aggrieved had to sign a statement describing the complaint, after which it was forwarded to the chairman of the central grievance committee at the IWA's office in Chicago, who, like the chairman of the local grievance committee, had to decide whether it was valid. If he thought it was, he placed the seal of the organization on it and forwarded it to the Public Relations Bureau for adjudication as an official complaint. But the Bureau usually did little more than send the complaint back to the original district station for reconsideration, after which the client again had to wait an undetermined amount of time to receive an answer! In most cases the answer was not favorable, or no answer was given at all.[87]

Given the almost Kafkaesque quality of this system, it is no surprise that disturbances by individuals and protests by large groups at relief stations continued the whole decade. Regarding a protest in 1938, when over a hundred people were jammed inside a station in a "sit-in strike," a reporter wrote, "Bitter resentment was evidenced by all against the public relations bureau, and when asked what changes they desired made in that branch, one man shouted, 'None at all. It's prejudiced and incompetent. We want the damn thing abolished!'"[88]

Tens of thousands of members coursed in and out of the IWA. Locals tended to be ethnically rather homogeneous: in Chicago there were locals mainly composed in each case of Italians, Poles, Blacks, native whites, Jews, Austrians, Czechs, and so on. But this was mostly just a consequence of neighborhood demographics, and a number of locals were ethnically mixed. As with other unemployed groups, members were supposed to pay a monthly fee, in this case of one or two cents. Like many another union, the IWA had state conventions to which locals sent delegates, where plans were made on such matters as organizing new areas of the state, launching a "youth movement," affiliating with the national WA, forming a labor party, boycotting newspapers owned by rabid anti-Communist William Randolph Hearst, and "demanding the freedom of all class war prisoners."[89]

By 1936, locals of the Unemployment Councils (as they were called then) were allowed to amalgamate with the IWA. This does not seem, however, to have had much of an impact on the politics or militancy of the IWA, for its members, including in downstate counties, were already quite radical. For example, in Franklin County a protest was organized in July 1934 to demand the resignation of Rosco Webb, chairman of the county relief programs. The letter sent to him read in part as follows:

> We demand a sufficient participation in the wealth which we and our people have created so as to insure to us a decent standard of living. To this as willing workers we are entitled

---

87. Walter C. Hart, "Relief—As the Clients See It" (MA thesis, University of Chicago, 1936); Illinois Workers Alliance of Cook County, Bulletin No. 44, June 15, 1936, Chicago Commons Papers, box 25, folder "I. C. Association," Chicago History Museum.
88. *Chicago Defender*, March 5, 1938.
89. Hart, "Relief," 22–24; *Workers Alliance*, August 15, 1935; "Hearing – Granted by the Illinois Emergency Relief Commission to the Illinois Workers Alliance of Cook County," October 18, 1935, Frank McCulloch Papers, box 4, folder 7.

whether we are employed or unemployed. Our patience and humility are exhausted and we approach the time when we will find it literally necessary to remind you that we are human beings and our anger is fast rising.

Evidently even in relatively rural regions, "class consciousness" was far from unknown. (In fact, as early as the beginning of 1932, the president of the Wisconsin Farmers' Union testified to a Senate committee that "there are more actual reds among the farmers of Wisconsin than you could dream about. [...] They are just ready to do anything to get even with the situation.")[90]

As mass popular movements of the middle years of the 1930s were quashed and the CIO's momentum collided with the obstinacy of reaction, unemployed groups suffered as well. Many of them, however, managed to cling to relative vitality for a long time, up to 1939. Even after renewed hostility between Communists and other political groups caused the WA to split apart in 1939, the unemployed movement did not collapse. We can see evidence of this in the minutes of Cook County-wide meetings of delegates from IWA locals, for instance in the summer of 1939, when massive WPA cuts were starting to take effect and local relief was, as usual, miserly. IWA local 1 was active at relief stations, leafletting, recruiting, and planning a mass meeting the following week; local 16 had 50 members active who were circulating petitions and leaflets; local 35 was bringing in new members, undertaking joint actions with other groups on the South Side, and selling tickets for a huge picnic that the Cook County IWA was organizing. Local 44 was brand new, with an average attendance of 36 but getting new members; it had distributed 2,000 leaflets and was working on the picnic. Other locals were meeting regularly and focusing on grievance work; still others were having a harder time because "summer weather makes attendance generally go down." The West Side, North Side, and South Side district committees were going to work together to plan regional and city-wide protests. The recent conference in Washington, D.C., to form a new national organization, the Workers Security Federation, had gone well; the organizations present—which had split from the WA—represented a total of a hundred thousand people.[91]

A year later, however, the situation was dire. The IWA, which had been renamed the Illinois Workers Security Federation, had fewer members than ever and terrible finances. Only 8 or 10 locals remained in Chicago, with an attendance that varied from 10 to 50. Frank McCulloch, the IWSF's secretary-treasurer, had to resort to begging for money from allies, such as the Juvenile Protective Association and the Federation of Jewish Trade Unions. "We in the Security Federation," he wrote in a letter, "are not strong, for there is great hopelessness and despair—not to say downright physical weakness—in the unemployed group." They had, it is true, "kept together a core of experienced and responsible persons and locals who are working against great odds to

---

90. *Chicago Tribune*, July 17, 1934; Illinois Workers Alliance of Cook County, Bulletin No. 43, mid-May 1936, Chicago Commons Papers, box 25, folder "I. C. Association"; Arthur Schlesinger, Jr., *The Crisis of the Old Order*, 176.
91. "County Delegate Meeting – July 5, 1939," McCulloch Papers, box 4, folder 8.

protect the interests of WPA, low-wage and relief families. But we cannot, alone, meet even office rent and other minimum expenses, not to mention the costs of an effective job and relief campaign." With war looming and conservatives in the ascendancy, the political environment was simply no longer hospitable to the Left.[92]

Perhaps an equally important cause of the withering away of the unemployed movement was that the its constituency in 1940 and later was smaller than it had been earlier in the Depression. Many of the most capable people had found jobs, so the mass base of the movement was less energetic than in, say, 1934.

The WA itself had never become the awe-inspiring force of politics that its organizers had hoped it would be, though for several years it and its affiliates had a vitality that politicians could not afford to ignore. When the Unemployment Councils and National Unemployed League joined in April 1936, one estimate put the Alliance's combined dues-paying and non-dues-paying membership at 800,000, though this was likely too high. Whatever the real numbers were, the organization did a competent job of defending the interests of unemployed and relief workers. One journalist wrote in 1938 that the usual practice of WA groups in New York City, as elsewhere, with regard to relief grievances was, first, to present a formal protest; if satisfactory results were not achieved, the WA would organize a mass demonstration. If that didn't work, then "the organization settles down for a long pull with picket lines around the offices of the offending officials and, when necessary, a walk-out or a sit-down strike." He concluded that "the record is impressive": for instance, in March 1937 3,000 relief clients had sat down in 29 Emergency Relief Bureau offices in New York City. As a result, the mayor granted an open hearing on relief, which led to a much larger relief appropriation by the city council and the speeding up of sluggish bureaucratic procedures.[93]

Whether the WA could have forced more expansive relief policies at the national level "by pushing turbulence to its outer limits," as Piven and Cloward suggest, rather than by cooperating with authorities and cultivating friendly relations with members of Congress and the Roosevelt administration, is impossible to know. What is certain is that the setbacks the movement suffered in the second half of the decade, as federal and state governments retrenched, happened in spite of the aggressive mood and actions of hundreds of thousands of people, who besieged state legislatures, marched on city halls, picketed relief stations, deluged public officials with postcards and letters, and held public hearings. The diminishing returns of such tactics eventually caused the movement to shrink, to the point that by late 1940 it hardly existed at all. All that remained were the memories of how nation-wide class struggles had wrested an incipient welfare state from the ruling class.[94]

---

92. Letter from Frank McCulloch to Jessie Binford, June 11, 1940, McCulloch Papers, box 5, folder 8; McCulloch to Morris Seskind, July 13, 1940, ibid.; McCulloch to Sophonisba Breckenridge, May 18, 1940, ibid.
93. Rosenzweig, "'Socialism in Our Time,'" 499; Nathan Rogg, "The Unemployed Unite," *Social Work Today,* June 1936, 13–15; Prago, "The Organization of the Unemployed," 258.
94. Piven and Cloward, *Poor People's Movements,* 91; *Workers Alliance,* August 1936; *Work,* May 20, 1939, May 23, August 29, 1940.

Popular Radicalism

The kinds of mass behavior that have been described here should put to rest the old notion that victims of the Depression tended to be timid, subservient, primarily self-blaming, and incapable of imagining an alternative social order. Rather, it seems that at least as often they were rebellious, conscious of injustice, and inspired by collectivist ideals. They lashed out against their subjection to callous institutions, braving police brutality in order to force their demands on government and the relief administration. The ease with which Communists were able to mobilize countless numbers across the country already in early 1930—by insisting that relief was a "right rooted in justice rather than a privilege based on charity," to quote James Lorence—testifies to a decidedly nonsubmissive attitude among the public, as does the willingness of millions in the next few years to publicly acknowledge their unemployment by participating in highly visible demonstrations. However discouraged the Depression's victims may have been, and however ashamedly they may have initially approached the relief station, it did not take long for possibly a majority of them to come to the radical conclusion that relief, in fact generous relief, was something to which they were *entitled*.[95]

On a relatively individualized level this attitude, or something like it, was manifested in the "fraud" that relief clients frequently engaged in. The paucity of discussions of relief fraud in historical scholarship is unfortunate, for it was anything but a marginal phenomenon. From the standpoint of the relief administration, this fact was inevitable: since caseworkers were often responsible for more than two hundred cases each, they could hardly investigate every one with the thoroughness that the *Chicago Tribune*, for example, would have liked. (The *Tribune* frequently ran articles alleging fraud of massive proportions among relief recipients.) This means that reliable statistics do not exist. Occasional special investigations, however, had suggestive findings. An investigation by the IERC in 1938 found that a third of relief cases in Springfield were receiving relief through "fraud or inefficiency." Another investigation that year found that nearly half the cases in Granite City, Illinois, evidenced fraud. Indeed, an informant from the IERC told the *Tribune* that "the Illinois Workers' Alliance has been, to all practical purposes, running the administration of relief [in Granite City]." Two studies of fraud in Chicago found that 51 percent of "chiselers" were foreign-born whites and 18 percent were Black.[96]

The resourcefulness with which people cheated the relief administration is revealed by E. Wight Bakke's anecdotal accounts. One caseworker in New Haven who understood Italian was able to eavesdrop on Italian clients' conversations: she would hear the mother call to her son to come see the investigator but to put his old shoes on first, or parents tell someone in the back of the house to put away the wine or food before the investigator came inside. One man who was living with relatives complained to a steam fitter that he could not get on relief. "Did you tell them you're living with relatives?" his interlocutor asked. "Yes." "You *are* a damn fool. You never should have told them that. Tell them you are light housekeeping in a couple of rooms." "It doesn't pay to give them a straight story, does it?" "Oh, Christ!"

---

95. Lorence, *Organizing the Unemployed*, 32.
96. Wayne McMillen, "Client 'Fraud' in Chicago," *Social Service Review* 14, no. 1 (March 1940): 36–60; *Chicago Tribune*, February 28, March 13, 1938.

the steam fitter scoffed. "You'll never get anything if you tell the truth. You gotta be wise, give them a good story." The fact that this was considered utterly obvious, as if one had to be extremely stupid not to know it, suggests how widespread such wisdom must have been.[97]

However mundane and commonsensical relief fraud may seem, in its essence it was not far removed from the eviction protests, relief demonstrations, hunger marches, group thefts, and bootlegging that have received more attention from historians. All such activities constituted a kind of class resistance—resistance against rules and institutions that upheld the power of a dominant class. And all such activities both presupposed and encouraged the attitude that people suffering from material deprivation were entitled to *resist power* for the sake of their dignity and well-being.

A particularly radical form of this belief, or an extension of it, was the conviction that structures of power had to be drastically altered so that *society would provide for those who could not provide for themselves*. Whether elderly or infirm or involuntarily out of work, people were *owed* economic security, and it was to be provided at the expense of the wealthy. In immense numbers, Americans in effect believed and fought for the communist principle, "from each according to his ability, to each according to his need."[98]

An illustration of this fact is the support that Americans gave between 1930 and 1936 to a radical proposal for unemployment and social insurance that was originally authored by the Communist Party. While the proposal took slightly different forms over the years, its essence is captured in the description given at the end of Chapter one of this book. When it was introduced (as the Workers' Social Insurance Bill) in Congress for the last time, in 1936, by Representative Ernest Lundeen of the Minnesota Farmer-Labor Party and Republican Senator Lynn Frazier of North Dakota, it took an even more generous form than before: it included insurance for widows, mothers, and the self-employed, appropriated $5 billion for the year 1936, established a Workers' Social Insurance Commission to administer the system, and elaborated in much more detail than its forerunners had in 1934 and 1935 on how the system would be financed and managed. As before, Congress did not come close to approving the measure. Its provisions were so radical, in fact, that it never had a chance. But what is interesting is the momentum that developed behind it, despite what amounted to a conspiracy of silence from the press and extreme hostility from business constituencies, conservative congressmen, and the Roosevelt administration.[99]

The history of the Workers' Social Insurance Bill (in its various forms), which was to become one of the most popular pieces of legislation of the Depression decade, began in 1930, when the Communist Party proposed its first iteration—an incredible $25 per week to the unemployed and $5 for each dependent—and immediately proceeded

---

97. Bakke, *The Unemployed Worker*, 371–85.
98. It is worth noting that it was not only in the 1930s that this was the case. A poll in 1987 found that 45 percent of Americans considered the quoted principle to be so morally obvious that they thought it was enshrined in the U.S. Constitution! See Jonah Goldberg, "The Will of the Uninformed," *Los Angeles Times*, April 24, 2007.
99. "The New Workers Bill," *Social Work Today*, February 1936, 3; Leo J. Linder, "The New Workers Social Insurance Bill," *Social Work Today*, March 1936, 9–12; *Daily Worker*, January 4, 1936.

to agitate on its behalf. The reception that the unemployed gave this campaign suggests that it did not take long at all for a large proportion of the Depression's victims to reject the voluntarist ideology of the 1920s—not to mention "self-blame" for their troubles—in favor of massive government intervention in the economy for the purpose of income redistribution. By late summer of 1930, the *Daily Worker* was already reporting mass petition signings and continual demonstrations for the bill in scores of cities, including small ones like Indianapolis, Springfield, Belleville, Rockford, Milwaukee, South Chicago, and Gary, Indiana (to speak only of cities near Chicago).[100]

The pace of actions died down a bit in the fall but picked up again in December and January, in preparation for 10 February 1931, when 150 delegates elected from around the country were going to present the bill and its hundreds of thousands of signatures to Congress. Requests for signature lists flooded into the New York office of the National Campaign Committee for Unemployment Insurance from not only the large industrial centers but even towns and farms in the South and West, and Alaska. Metal workers in Chicago Heights got involved in the campaign; railroad workers and section hands in Reno, Nevada, signed petitions; letters like the following were sent to the *Daily Worker*:

> Let me know what I can do to help carry forward the fight for unemployment insurance? This is the greatest need at this hour. I am the only reader of the Daily Worker here in Ashby, Minn., and am one of four Communist votes cast here in the elections. I am a woman of 60 years, living on land; I pass out all my Daily Workers to neighbors and am getting new subscribers. Will help all I can to get signatures for the bill.[101]

Countless united front conferences of workers' organizations took place in cities around the country, for instance Gary, Indiana, where the keynote of one conference was sounded by a Black steelworker and veteran of World War I who said, "It's no use going way over to France to fight. We can demand things here just as good as we can there, fight here just as good as there, and if need be, die here just as good as there. [...] Let's fight for ourselves, right here, now." They fought in Charlotte, North Carolina; Ambridge, Pennsylvania; Wheeling, West Virginia; Minneapolis, Grand Rapids, and San Antonio; Hartford, Buffalo, and San Francisco. City hunger marches were so numerous that the *Daily Worker* could not keep track of them. The Workers' Bill, of course, was not the only or even the most pressing issue addressed by all these actions, but it figured prominently among their demands. On the big day, 10 February, demonstrations and state hunger marches occurred in at least sixty-three cities as the delegation in Washington, D.C., interrupted a session in the House and was forcibly ejected by police. In St. Paul, Minnesota, the type of action occurred that was already becoming rather common: demonstrators broke through police lines around the state capitol and occupied the legislative chambers, announcing that they would not leave until the legislature had acted on their demands.[102]

---

100. *Daily Worker,* July 31, August 2, 13, 18, 20, 1930.
101. Ibid., December 18, 1930.
102. Ibid., January 9, 14, 15, 27, 28, 29, February 2–13, 1931; *New York Herald Tribune,* February 11, 1931; *New York Times,* February 11, 1931; *Chicago Tribune,* February 11, 1931.

In short, even before churches, charities, and benefit societies had conclusively demonstrated their inability to meet the crisis, well over a million people nationwide were actively demanding that the United States become in effect an expansive social democracy. In general, a collectivist orientation among the populace did not have to wait for Roosevelt and the New Deal to act as midwives. It emerged organically on the grassroots level, stimulated both by radical groups and by suffering people's sense that *society*, with all its abundant resources possessed ultimately by the federal government, had to do something to end the epidemic of unjust suffering. Roosevelt and the New Deal were products of the country's growing collectivism more than they were causes of it. And for many millions of Americans, they never went far enough.

Support for the Workers' Bill grew during the next few years. In June 1931, a hunger march of several hundred delegates to Springfield culminated in one of its leaders delivering a speech before the Illinois state legislature demanding enactment of the bill. Other such marches occurred, for example, in April, August, and October of 1933. The two national hunger marches that Communists organized in December 1931 and 1932 gave publicity to the bill; and on 4 February 1932, which the Communist Party had dubbed National Unemployment Insurance Day, hundreds of thousands of people around the country demonstrated for it. Petitions garnered thousands of signatures: according to the *Hunger Fighter*, in just three weeks in March 1932, over 30,000 people in Chicago—in factories, AFL locals, public shelters, and neighborhoods—signed the bill, in preparation for 2 May, when 200 workers "from all important industries from every section of America" were again going to present the petitions to Congress. Across the country, including in Chicago, 1933 saw the organizing of numerous conferences of unemployed groups to coordinate the campaign for unemployment insurance and to prepare for the CP's National Convention Against Unemployment in February 1934.[103]

That February was also the month that Representative Lundeen introduced the bill in the House. While it fared even worse in this session of Congress than it was to fare in 1935, Lundeen's sponsorship increased the momentum of its popularity among the working class. Within just a couple of months of its introduction, 800 more AFL locals had defied the Federation's leadership and endorsed it, joining 1,200 locals that had done so earlier. In Chicago, John Fitzpatrick and other leaders of the Chicago Federation of Labor began to have less success than in previous years preventing unions from endorsing it, as locals of the Railway Conductors, Railway Clerks, Machinists, Painters, School Custodians, Women's Upholsterers, Millinery Workers, and many other unions sent delegates to a Communist-sponsored unemployment insurance conference in the summer of 1934. In July, representatives of 43,000 workers who were organized in fraternal and benevolent societies attended a hearing before the Chicago City Council to

---

103. *New York Times*, June 14, 15, 1931; "Speech of Phil Frankfeld in Name of Delegation for Unemployment Insurance before the Illinois State Legislature," n.d., CP records, microfilm reel 193, #76, Tamiment Library; Unemployed Council of Chicago, Council Letter #16, January 11, 1932, ibid., reel 232; *Daily Worker*, February 5, 1932, April 8, August 25, October 5, December 2, 13, 1933; *Hunger Fighter*, March 26, 1932; Klehr, *The Heyday*, 285.

demand that that body support the bill; committees also visited aldermen in their wards to demand the same. In September, at another conference in Chicago, delegates from the National Unemployed Leagues, the IWA, the Eastern Federation of Unemployed and Emergency Workers Union, the Wisconsin Federation of Unemployed Leagues, and the Fort Wayne Unemployed League—in the aggregate claiming a membership of 750,000—endorsed the measure.[104]

Meanwhile, in January 1934 an organization had been founded that was to play an important role in lending academic respectability to the bill: the Inter-Professional Association for Social Insurance (IPA). While not officially affiliated with the Communist Party, it had close ties to leading party members and coordinated its campaign for passage of the Lundeen Bill with organizations of the Left. Within a year it had dozens of chapters and organizing committees around the country, made up of both individual professionals and representatives of groups—nurses, physicians, actors, teachers, engineers, architects, and so on. The distinguished social worker Mary Van Kleeck of the Russell Sage Foundation led an army of her colleagues in supporting the bill and, in some cases, proselytizing for it in the press and before Congress. Economists and lawyers associated with the IPA testified to the economic soundness and constitutionality of the measure, especially in 1935, when Lundeen reintroduced it as H.R. 2827. Left-wing professionals considered it vastly superior to the Wagner-Lewis bill of 1934 and 1935—which became the Social Security Act. A professor at Smith College, for example, damned the latter as "a proposal to set up little privileged groups in the sea of misery who would be content to sit on their small islands and watch the others drown." The Lundeen Bill was certainly not without flaws, including its vagueness and, arguably, the financial burden it would impose on the country, but evidently its Communist-style radicalism was so appreciated that even experts in their field were willing to overlook its defects.[105]

In fact, it was far more radical than the Soviet Union's measures for unemployment and social insurance. While the Lundeen Bill provided, among other things, for unemployment benefits for an unlimited period of time equal to 100 percent of wages—or much more, since an unskilled laborer with a wife and four children who might be lucky to get $16 a week would get $25 if unemployed![106]—in Soviet Russia only about

---

104. *A. F. of L. Rank and File Federationist*, March–April, August 1934; *Daily Worker*, July 4, 1934; Prago, "The Organization of the Unemployed," 242.
105. Prago, "The Organization of the Unemployed," 234, 235; Klehr, *The Heyday*, 288; Paul H. Douglas, *Social Security in the United States: An Analysis and Appraisal of the Federal Social Security Act* (New York: McGraw-Hill Book Company, 1939), 74–83; "A Social Insurance Spree: Lundeen Bill in Congress Attracts Left-Wing Support," *American Labor Legislation Review* 24 (1934): 67–70; Mary Van Kleeck, "The Workers Bill for Unemployment and Social Insurance," *New Republic*, December 12, 1934; Dorothy W. Douglas, "Unemployment Insurance—For Whom?" *Social Work Today*, February 1935; *New York Times*, April 30, 1934; John A. Fitch, "Unemployment Insurance and the Lundeen Bill," *Catholic Charities Review* 19 (January 1935): 8–11. Whether it indeed was economically unrealistic is debatable, since it would have tremendously raised aggregate demand and thus stimulated the economy.
106. $10 weekly plus $3 for each dependent. To the criticism that under this system malingering would flourish, defenders of the bill answered that this was actually a strength. By

35 percent of the customary wage was paid, and that for a limited time. Moreover, the various forms of insurance that H.R. 2827 would establish (unemployment, old age, maternity, disability, and industrial injury) were to be administered by councils of workers and their representatives, thus embodying "workers' democracy," which the Soviet system certainly did not. In effect, then, the millions of Americans who advocated the measure desired a system that was more authentically communist/socialist than the Soviet one. This is another indication that it was largely the *designation* "Communist" to which many people objected, not the substance of radical doctrines.[107]

A few days after Lundeen reintroduced his bill in early January 1935, the National Congress for Unemployment and Social Insurance was held in Washington, D.C., at the Washington Auditorium. Organized by the CP and its many allies, the congress comprised almost three thousand delegates who had come by truck, jalopy, rail, box car, and on foot from every region of the country and 40 states. To quote one historian, "cowboys from Colorado and Wyoming, black sharecroppers from Alabama, Texas oil hands, Florida housewives, skilled and unskilled workers, employed and unemployed" in the dead of winter made the pilgrimage to the nation's seat of power, guided by visions of an egalitarian society, conscious that in their aggregate they directly represented millions and indirectly represented well over half the country. Unions of all types (professional, AFL affiliated, independent); fraternal organizations and political groups; farm organizations and shop delegates; women's groups, church groups, veterans' groups, and unemployed groups—hundreds of such organizations, in an anticipation of the Popular Front, managed to overcome the congenital sectarianism of the Left and call as one for unprecedented social democracy. A few of the scores of lesser-known unemployed groups that were represented included the Chinese Unemployed Alliance, the Farmer Labor Union, the Italian Unemployed Groups, the Relief Workers League, the United Mine Workers Unemployment Council, the Workers Union of the World, and the Dancers Emergency Association. The National Urban League, which endorsed the bill, also sent delegates.[108]

The legendary socialist and feminist Mother Bloor, who addressed the congress, pithily summed up its significance to a reporter from the *Washington Post*: "'The congress is a success. It's proved a big crowd of people can break down barriers of race, social position, political opinions, and convictions for a common cause. Why, there are white people and yellow people and black people out there.' She nodded toward the mass meeting going on in the auditorium. 'There are Communists and Socialists and Republicans. There's even some Democrats.'" At the congressional hearings on H.R. 2827, the chairman of the

---

withdrawing workers from the labor market, it would force wage rates to rise until they at least equaled unemployment benefits. "The benefits to the unemployed," Paul Douglas noted, "could thus be used as a lever to compel industry to pay a living wage to those who were employed." Douglas, *Social Security in the United States*, 80.
107. Ibid., 79.
108. Prago, "The Organization of the Unemployed," 242–45; *Daily Worker,* January 5, 7, 8, 1935; Elmer Brown, "The Social Insurance Congress," *Rank and File Federationist,* January 1935; *Los Angeles Sentinel,* February 14, 1935.

congress stated, not implausibly, that it had "formed the broadest and most representative congress of the American people ever held in the United States."[109]

The congressional hearings themselves were noteworthy. While the executive secretary of the IPA may have exaggerated when he wrote, "The record of the hearings on H.R. 2827 is one of the most challenging ever placed before the Congress of the United States and probably the most unique document ever to appear in the Congressional Record," that judgment is understandable. Eighty witnesses testified: industrial workers, farmers, veterans, professional workers, women, the foreign-born, and youth. "Probably never in American history," an editor of the *Nation* wrote, "have the underprivileged had a better opportunity to present their case before Congress." The aggregate of the testimonies amounted to a systematic indictment of American capitalism and the New Deal, and an impassioned defense of the radical alternative under consideration. Witness after witness described the harrowing suffering that they and the thousands they represented (in each case) were enduring and condemned the Wagner-Lewis bill as a sham. From the representative of the American Youth Congress, which encompassed over two million people, to the representative of the United Council of Working-Class Women, which had 10,000 members, each testimony fleshed out the eminently "class-conscious" point of view of the people back home who had "gather[ed] up nickels and pennies which they [could] poorly spare" in order to send someone to plead their case before Congress. Most of the Congressmen on the Labor subcommittee they were addressing were strikingly sympathetic.[110]

For example, when Herbert Benjamin, one of the leaders of the CP, had this to say on press coverage (or the lack thereof) of the Lundeen Bill—

> So much has been said in the last few weeks about the Townsend plan [for old-age pensions]. I have discussed this question with a number of Members [of Congress], and they tell me that, outside of California, they received not a single postal card on the Townsend plan, but they received thousands of cards from all over the United States on the Lundeen Bill, asking for the enactment of this bill. Yet the newspapers, by reason of the fact that they really fear this measure and do not fear the Townsend plan, knowing that the Townsend plan can be a very good red herring to draw attention away from social insurance, have given publicity to the Townsend plan, and have yet avoided very studiously any attention to the workers' unemployment and social-insurance measure—

the chairman of the subcommittee, Matthew Dunn, interrupted to say,

> I want to substantiate the statement you just made about the Townsend bill and about this bill. Now, I represent the Thirty-fourth District in Pennsylvania, which is a very large district. May I say that I do not believe I have received over a half dozen letters to support the

---

109. *Daily Worker*, January 7, 1935; *Washington Post*, January 9, 1935; F. Elmer Brown, *Hearings before a Subcommittee of the Committee on Labor, House of Representatives, on H.R. 2827*, 14.
110. Albion A. Hartwell, "America Speaks: The Hearings on the Workers Bill," *Social Work Today*, April 1935, 19, 20; Maxwell Stewart, *Hearings on H.R. 2827*, 681; Herbert Benjamin, ibid., 694. Many opponents of the bill had been invited to testify, but not a single one did. Apparently they had all decided that the best strategy to defeat it was to ignore it.

Townsend bill. [...] [But] I have received many letters and cards from all over the country asking me to give my utmost support in behalf of the Lundeen bill, H.R. 2827.[111]

Incidentally, Benjamin's complaint about press coverage was justified. Overwhelmingly more press attention was devoted to the ridiculous Townsend Plan that made no economic sense at all[112]; virtually no coverage was granted the Lundeen Bill except during and after the subcommittee's hearings, and even then it was mostly local papers that covered it. According to the executive secretary of the IPA, "forty-three news releases to all the news agencies and newspapers of the major cities during the course of two weeks [i.e., during the hearings] were, with few exceptions, suppressed, although in those outlying districts where organization has made the demands of the workers more articulate, some papers carried workers' testimony as front page news." Historians have followed newspapers' lead by ignoring the Lundeen Bill and focusing on the Townsend Plan, in some cases condescendingly interpreting the popularity of the latter as evidence of the credulousness of the American public. This emphasis is unfortunate in that (1) it was the *press* that was significantly responsible for propagating the Townsend Plan (presumably, in part, to divert attention from the Lundeen Bill), and (2) the supposedly simple-minded public had the organizational sophistication and political savvy to build a mass movement around a more reasonable bill premised on both the reality and the valorization of class conflict, not only without help from the press but despite intense hostility from all sectors of power. Under such conditions, for example, organizers' ability to get over five million signatures on their petitions was no mean achievement.[113]

Admittedly, compared to the number of signatures they likely could have collected had they possessed more resources, five million is not terribly impressive. In the spring of 1935, the *New York Post* conducted a poll of its largely working-class readers after printing the contents of the Lundeen, the Townsend, and the Wagner-Lewis bills. Out of 1,391 votes cast, 1,209 readers supported the first, 157 the second, 14 the third, and 7 none of them. Of the 1,073 respondents who were employed, 957 supported the Lundeen Bill, 100 the Townsend Bill, 7 the Wagner-Lewis Bill, and 5 none. It would not be outlandish to infer from these findings that, had they known of the contents of the bills, the great majority of working-class Americans would have much preferred Lundeen's Communist-written one. This is also suggested by the enormous number of letters congressmen received on the measure, such as this one sent to Lundeen:

---

111. Ibid., 173.
112. On the Townsend Plan, see Robert McElvaine, *The Great Depression* (New York: Times Books, 1984), chapter 10; Alan Brinkley, *Voices of Protest: Huey Long, Father Coughlin, and the Great Depression* (New York: Vintage Books, 1983), 222–26; Bruce Mason, "The Townsend Movement," *Southwestern Social Science Quarterly* 35, no. 1 (June 1954): 36–47; Abraham Holtzman, *The Townsend Movement: A Political Study* (New York: Bookman, 1963).
113. Lenore K. Bartlett, "The Attack on the Townsend Plan," *Social Work Today*, April 1936, 11, 12; Hartwell, "America Speaks," 20; *New York Herald Tribune*, October 22, 1935; Klehr, *The Heyday*, 284.

The reason I am writing you is, that we Farmers [and] Industrial workers feel that you are the only Congressman and Representative that is working for our interest. We have analyzed the Wagner-Lewis Bill [and] also [the] Townsend Bill. But the Lundeen H.R. (2827) is the only bill that means anything for our class. [...] The people all over the country are [waking] up to the facts that the two old Political Parties are owned soul, mind [and] body by the Capitalist Class.[114]

Feeling the pressure of this mass movement, both the subcommittee and the House Labor Committee voted in favor of H.R. 2827 that spring, making it the first federal unemployment insurance plan in U.S. history to be recommended by a committee. It had no chance in the House, though. The Rules Committee refused to send it to the floor, although it allowed Lundeen to propose it as an amendment to the Social Security Bill (as a substitute for the unemployment insurance provisions in that bill). It was defeated in April by a vote of 204–52.[115]

As far as its advocates were concerned, the fight was not over. Throughout the spring and summer the flood of endorsements did not stop. The first national convention of rank-and-file social workers endorsed it in February; the Progressive Miners of America followed, along with scores of local unions and such ethnic societies as the Italian-American Democratic Organization of New York (with 235,000 members) and the Slovak-American Political Federation of Youngstown, Ohio. Virtually identical state versions of H.R. 2827 were (or already had been) introduced in the legislatures of California, Oregon, Utah, Wisconsin, Ohio, Pennsylvania, Massachusetts, and other states. Conferences of unions and fraternal organizations were called in a number of states, including the Deep South, to plan further campaigns for the Workers' Bill. That year's May Day was one of the largest in American history, "monster demonstrations" (to quote the *New York Times*) of tens of thousands taking place in New York City, and in many cities, included among the marchers were united fronts of church groups, workers clubs, fraternal lodges, and Communist and Socialist groups parading under banners demanding the passage of H.R. 2827. While the majority of AFL unions never endorsed the bill, perhaps because William Green and the Executive Council were exerting intense pressure on them not to do so, it is probable that most of the rank and file supported it.[116]

As stated above, in January 1936 Lynn Frazier and Ernest Lundeen introduced in their respective houses of Congress a more sophisticated version of the bill, which the Inter-Professional Association had written. Again it was endorsed by unions, labor councils, and other institutions, including the 1936 convention of the EPIC movement

---

114. Both this quotation and the information about the poll are in Kenneth M. Casebeer, "Unemployment Insurance: American Social Wage, Labor Organization and Legal Ideology," *Boston College Law Review* 35, issue 2, no. 2 (March 1, 1994): 294, 295.
115. *New York Times*, April 19, 1935; Klehr, 289.
116. *Daily Worker*, February 19, 22, 23, 26, March 1, 18, 27, 30, April 10, 20, 24, May 2, 25, August 13, September 18, 1935; *Atlanta Daily World*, April 2, 1935; *New York Times*, May 2, 1935; Lorence, *Organizing the Unemployed*, 102.

in California. In New York, "flying squads" from the Fraternal Federation for Social Insurance visited lodges and fraternal organizations throughout the city to secure their support. In Philadelphia, Baltimore, and other cities, united front conferences and committees were organized to campaign for the bill. The hearings before the Senate Labor Committee in April resembled the hearings on H.R. 2827, with academics, social workers, unionists, and farmers testifying as to the inadequacy of the Social Security Act and the necessity of the Frazier-Lundeen Bill. A representative of the National Committee on Rural Social Planning spoke for the millions of agricultural workers, sharecroppers, tenants, and small owners when he opined that this bill was "the only one which is likely to check the fascist terror now riding the fields" in the South (directed against the Southern Tenant Farmers Union and similar organizations).[117]

The fascist terror continued unchecked, however, for the bill did not even make it out of committee. After its dismal fate in 1936, it was never introduced again.

From a certain perspective, one might say that the Workers' Bill, in its radicalism and collectivism, departed from more established patterns of "Americanism," whatever that word is taken to mean. A more defensible perspective, however, would see the bill as something like the apotheosis of collectivist strains that for many decades had been, and would continue to be, embedded deeply in American popular culture. The class solidarity it embodied in its frontal attack on fundamental institutions of capitalism—private appropriation of wealth, determination of wages by the market, maintenance of an insecure army of the unemployed—was hardly an anomaly in the history of the United States.

What one Communist organizer wrote of some workers in a small mining town in southern Illinois can, perhaps, be generalized: "They were filled with capitalist ideology—at the same time being strongly anti-capitalist." Even as many Americans believed, with these workers, that "capitalism had always existed, that it had come into existence peacefully, that capital and labor are equally necessary," their actions revealed a starkly opposed ideology and value system. Farmers and industrial workers, for example, in many cases identified with each other's causes and embraced them. In November 1933, the Farmers' National Relief Conference was held at the Coliseum in Chicago: 700 "frostbitten" delegates from around the country met to coordinate their campaign for a cancellation of all farm debts, including mortgages, crop loans, taxes, and rents. They were greeted and joined by workers from basic industries in Chicago and fed in part by donations of bread from the West Side Jewish Bakers Union. Around the same time, the *Daily Worker* reported that striking farmers in Kankakee, Illinois, and employed and unemployed workers were helping each other: the farmers were distributing hundreds of quarts of free milk to workers who were on strike and to the unemployed, and at the same time workers had joined the farmers on their picket line. A few hundred miles away, in Detroit,

---

117. *Daily Worker*, December 30, 1935, January 2, 4, 27, 29–31, February 5, 7, 8, 13, 22, 27, March 10, 18, 19, 21, 29, April 15, 17, 1936; A. A. Hartwell, "Professional Workers Plan," *Social Work Today*, May 1936, 19. On the "fascist terror" in the South, see, for example, Robin D. G. Kelley, *Hammer and Hoe: Alabama Communists in the Great Depression* (Chapel Hill, NC: University of North Carolina, 2015), chapter 9.

a statewide conference was being held on the Workers' Unemployment Insurance Bill to which both farmers' and workers' organizations had sent delegates.[118]

Historians have recognized that it was essential to the success of the Toledo Auto-Lite strike in 1934 that thousands of the "class-conscious" unemployed, instead of scabbing, joined strikers on the picket lines. But this was only the most dramatic example of a phenomenon that was much more widespread than is commonly recognized. A miners' strike in McKeesport, Pennsylvania, in the fall of 1933 was successful largely because thousands of unemployed men joined it. That October, the municipal unemployment relief committee in Edgewater, New Jersey, tried to use people on relief as scabs in the strike that was going on at the Ford plant nearby, but the unemployed refused to accept the jobs. Instead they joined the picket line and marched in solidarity with the workers on strike. It was noted above that members of the Chicago Workers Committee on Unemployment, not to mention the Unemployed Councils, walked in picket lines with signs proclaiming "The Unemployed Won't Scab." This was the case in, for instance, Milwaukee too, as in the summer of 1934, when the Milwaukee Workers Committee saved the Electric Railway and Light Company strike by organizing mass picketing of the unemployed. That same year, Minneapolis General Drivers' Local 544 recruited unemployed workers for its picket lines during a general strike and even formed a lasting auxiliary called the Federal Workers Section. Robert Asher observed in 1934 that in both Wisconsin and Illinois (and evidently elsewhere), "the cooperation furnished by the unemployed to workers and farmers in industrial and agricultural disputes has been significant." The Musteite Unemployed Leagues were similarly successful in providing solidarity to striking workers.[119]

It is true that in the absence of unemployed organizations, it was rarer for the jobless to join strikes. The CPLA's Executive Committee, allied with the Unemployed Councils, acknowledged this fact in December 1933, when it lamented that recent diversions of cadre from the UCs to other activities had resulted in a decline in participation by the unemployed on picket lines. This is hardly surprising, however, for organization has always facilitated radicalization. The noteworthy thing is that under certain conditions, even people desperate for work were willing and eager to aid their class brothers at the expense of getting a job.[120]

---

118. S. K., "Experiences of a Full-Time Training School in a Mining Center," *Party Organizer*, May 1936, 34–36; *Daily Worker*, November 9, 11, 14, 16, 17, 1933.
119. Israel Amter, "Low Ebb of Unemployed Work Contrary to Open Letter Line," *Party Organizer*, November 1933, 30–32; *New York Times*, September 30, 1933; *Daily Worker*, October 4, 1933; Asher, "The Chicago Workers' Committee on Unemployment," 70, 73; Rosenzweig, "'Socialism In Our Time,'" 499; Charles R. Walker, "A Militant Trade Union," *Survey Graphic*, January 1937, 29–33; Seymour, "The Organized Unemployed," 32; Leilah Danielson, *American Gandhi: A. J. Muste and the History of Radicalism in the Twentieth Century* (Philadelphia: University of Pennsylvania Press, 2014), 186.
120. "Minutes of the National Executive Committee, Conference for Progressive Labor Action, held at national office, December 13, 1933," microfilm reel 258, CP files, Tamiment.

While there is no space to embellish much on this point, we may note that it is not necessary to turn to the Workers' Bill or manifestations of class solidarity between employed and unemployed workers in order to find evidence of a kind of class consciousness and anticapitalism. We can consider, instead, two phenomena that have received a great deal of attention from historians: the mass following behind Huey Long and the mass following behind the "radio priest" Charles Coughlin—at least before his antisemitism overwhelmed the genuinely left-wing content of his message (in the late 1930s, by which time his popularity was a shadow of its former self). The Long and Coughlin movements have been analyzed so often that it is superfluous to dwell on them here.[121] However, a few observations may be worth making, to correct the "anti-left" biases of liberal historians like Alan Brinkley, Anthony Badger, David Kennedy, and Jefferson Cowie.[122]

Brinkley, Robert McElvaine, and others have made the point, but it bears repeating: neither Long nor Coughlin (before 1937 or 1938) was a fascist. A journalist wrote in early 1935 that Coughlin "talk[s] about a living wage, about profits for the farmer, about government-protected labor unions. He insists that human rights be placed above property rights. He emphasizes the 'wickedness' of 'private financialism and production for profit.'" Consistent with these values were the principles of Coughlin's National Union for Social Justice, founded in 1934, including the following: a "just and living [i.e., not market-determined] annual wage which will enable [every citizen willing and able to work] to maintain and educate his family according to the standards of American decency"; nationalization of such "public necessities" as banking, credit and currency, power, light, oil and natural gas, and natural resources; private ownership of all other property, but control of it for the public good; abolition of the privately owned Federal Reserve and establishment of a government-owned central bank; "the lifting of crushing

---

121. See, for example, T. Harry Williams, *Huey Long* (New York: Alfred A. Knopf, 1969); Brinkley, *Voices of Protest*; Anthony J. Badger, "Huey Long and the New Deal," in *Nothing Else to Fear: New Perspectives on America in the Thirties*, eds. Stephen W. Baskerville and Ralph Willett (Manchester: Manchester University Press, 1985), 64–100; David J. O'Brien, *American Catholics and Social Reform: The New Deal Years* (New York: Oxford University Press, 1968), chapter 7; Robert McElvaine, *The Great Depression*; Edward F. Haas, "Huey Long and the Communists," *Louisiana History: The Journal of the Louisiana Historical Association* 32, no. 1 (Winter 1991): 29–46; Charles J. Tull, *Father Coughlin and the New Deal* (Syracuse, NY: Syracuse University Press, 1965); Sheldon Marcus, *Father Coughlin: The Tumultuous Life of the Priest of the Little Flower* (Boston, MA: Little, Brown and Company, 1973).
122. Badger, for instance, argues that the solutions that Long and Coughlin offered "scarcely constituted a radical challenge to the New Deal from the left. They offered instead glib panaceas designed to reassure the discontented that the dramatic benefits that they were promising could be achieved without radical or painful change." Badger, *The New Deal*, 294. Kennedy gives a dismissive analysis of the Long and Coughlin movements in *Freedom from Fear*, 227–244. Cowie, for his part, is convinced that the followers of Long and Coughlin wanted nothing more than "to restore the republic to the little man, resurrect some version of traditional values, and deliver the individual from the crush of mass society." Cowie, *The Great Exception*, 137. The vagueness and idealism of this formulation, which makes no mention of class, is characteristic of liberal historiography.

taxation from the slender revenues of the laboring class" and substituting for it taxation of the rich; in the event of war, "a conscription of wealth as well as a conscription of men"; and the guiding value that "the chief concern of government shall be for the poor." Insofar as Coughlin's tens of millions of fans agreed with this political program, they certainly can be said to have desired *fundamental* reforms in American capitalism, reforms that would have ushered in a much more collectivistic and socialistic society.[123]

Indeed, were it not that Coughlin always remembered to denounce Communism almost as vociferously (though not as verbosely) as he denounced capitalism and Wall Street titans, one suspects that he might have encountered more censorship than he did. This is suggested by an unusual incident in March 1936, when, in order to advertise its supposedly liberal position on freedom of speech, CBS invited Earl Browder to speak for 15 minutes (at 10:45 p.m.) on a national radio broadcast, with the understanding that he would be answered the following night by zealous anti-Communist Congressman Hamilton Fish. This "generosity" toward a Communist created quite a furor among right-wing organizations such as the National Americanization League, which subsequently picketed the CBS building, and many stations around the country refused to air Browder's talk. But it was in fact considerably more tame than Coughlin's diatribes. Browder simply appealed to "the majority of the toiling people" to establish a national Farmer-Labor Party that would be affiliated with the Communist Party but "would not yet take up the full program of socialism, for which many are not yet prepared." He did admit that Communists' ultimate aim was to remake the United States "along the lines of the highly successful Soviet Union": once they had the support of a majority of Americans, he said, "we will put that program into effect with the same firmness, the same determination, with which Washington and the founding fathers carried through the revolution that established our country, with the same thoroughness with which Lincoln abolished chattel slavery."[124]

Reactions to Browder's talk were revealing: according to both CBS and the *Daily Worker*, they were almost uniformly positive. CBS immediately received several hundred responses praising Browder's talk, and the *Daily Worker*, whose New York address Browder had mentioned on the air, received thousands of letters. The following are representative:

Chattanooga, Tennessee: "If you could have listened to the people I know who listened to you, you would have learned that your speech did much to make them realize the importance of

---

123. *New York Times*, March 17, 1935; Marquis W. Childs, "Father Coughlin: A Success Story of the Depression," *New Republic*, May 2, 1934; "Father Coughlin's Preamble and Principles of the National Union for Social Justice," in Brinkley, *Voices of Protest*, 287, 288; Verba and Schlozmann, "Unemployment, Class Consciousness, and Radical Politics," 295. Like the quotation from Badger in the previous footnote, Brinkley's claim that "the Long and Coughlin messages [were appealing because they] avoid[ed] the troubling implications of radical reform" is puzzling, in light of the astonishingly radical reforms Long and Coughlin proposed. *Voices of Protest*, 160.
124. *New York Times*, March 6, 1936; *Washington Post*, March 6, 1936; *Broadcasting*, March 5, 1936; *Variety*, March 11, 1936; *Billboard*, March 14, 1936.

forming a Farmer-Labor Party. I am sure that the 15 minutes into which you put so much that is vitally important to the American people was time used to great advantage. Many people are thanking you, I know."

Evanston, Illinois: "Just listened to your speech tonight and I think it was the truest talk I ever heard on the radio. Mr. Browder, would it not be a good thing if you would have an opportunity to talk to the people of the U.S.A. at least once a week, for 30 to 60 minutes? Let's hear from you some more, Mr. Browder."

Springfield, Pennsylvania: "I listened to your most interesting speech recently on the radio. I would be much pleased to receive your articles on Communism. Although I am an American Legion member I believe you are at least sincere in your teachings."

Bricelyn, Minnesota: "Your speech came in fine and it was music to the ears of another unemployed for four years. Please send me full and complete data on your movement and send a few extra copies if you will, as I have some very interested friends—plenty of them eager to join up, as is yours truly."

Harrold, South Dakota: "Thank you for the fine talk over the air tonight. It was good common sense and we were glad you had a chance to talk over the air and glad to hear someone who had nerve enough to speak against capitalism."

Sparkes, Nebraska: "Would you send me 50 copies of your speech over the radio last night? I would like to give them to some of my neighbors who are all farmers."

Arena, New York: "Although I am a young Republican (but good American citizen) I enjoyed listening to your radio speech last evening. I believe you told the truth in a convincing manner and I failed to see where you said anything dangerous to the welfare of the American people."[125]

In general, the main themes of the letters were questions like, "Where can I learn more about the Communist Party?" and "How can I join your Party?". Some people sent money in the hope that it would facilitate more broadcasts. The editors of the *Daily Worker* plaintively asked their readers, "Isn't it time we overhauled our old horse-and-buggy methods of recruiting? While we are recruiting by ones and twos, aren't we overlooking hundreds?" One can only imagine how many millions of people in far-flung regions would have flocked to the Communist banner had Browder and William Z. Foster been permitted the national radio audience that Coughlin was.

The interpretation that Alan Brinkley espouses as regards radicalism in the 1930s reflects major tendencies in American historiography:

> The failure of more radical political movements to take root in the 1930s reflected, in part, the absence of a serious radical tradition in American political culture. The rhetoric of class conflict echoed only weakly among men and women steeped in the dominant themes of

---

125. *Daily Worker*, March 11, 13, 1936.

their nation's history; and leaders relying upon that rhetoric faced grave, perhaps insuperable difficulties in attempting to create political coalitions.[126]

But this argument is backward. The reason that left-wing leaders have had trouble achieving mainstream success is simply that forces of repression and censorship, emanating from institutions with overwhelming control over resources, have suppressed them and the ideas—or, even more importantly, the *information*—they have tried to propagate.[127] There is no great mystery about it, no need to invoke deep-seated cultural tendencies of individualism or lack of comprehension of "class" (which is a pretty simple notion, after all).[128] When Browder's radio audience heard him discuss class conflict and Marxism, a large proportion of them apparently considered it "good common sense." They did not have to struggle painfully to break free of the shackles of American ideologies, as if liberating their minds from enslavement to a long tradition of bourgeois cultural hegemony. They simply thought, in effect, "this is true, and kind of obvious." But the "grave, perhaps insuperable difficulties" that Communists and others faced in getting information out to tens of millions of Americans had prevented these listeners from learning much about the political ideology they found so commonsensical and even more from getting involved in a radical movement.

Similarly, Brinkley is wrong to argue, in the sentence that follows the above quoted passage, "The Long and Coughlin movements, by contrast, flourished precisely because they evoked so clearly one of the oldest and most powerful of American political traditions [namely, opposition to centralized authority and demands for the wide dispersal of power]."[129] Rather, they flourished for two main reasons: first, in rejecting Communism and Socialism, Long and Coughlin were not quite as anathema to various political and economic authorities as Communists and Socialists, and so were, to some extent,

---

126. Brinkley, *Voices of Protest*, 160, 161.
127. One of the essential functions of the mass media is to suppress information. See Herman and Chomsky, *Manufacturing Consent*, as well as Edward Herman, *The Real Terror Network: Terrorism in Fact and Propaganda* (Boston, MA: Sound End Press, 1982). If great masses of people learn of the horrors that the powerful are constantly inflicting on the subjugated (whether in factories, on farms, in colonial or neocolonial domains, etc.) they will, naturally, try to stop the horrors and make society more democratic and transparent. So it is necessary to prevent them from knowing, for example by excluding Marxist speakers from the airwaves.
128. It isn't hard to comprehend—or to agree with—the idea of a conflict between those who own and those who don't.
129. Elsewhere, Brinkley states that Long, Coughlin, and their followers called for "a society in which the individual retained control of his life and livelihood; in which power resided in visible, accessible institutions; in which wealth was equitably (if not necessarily equally) shared." *Voices of Protest*, xi. One is inclined to reply to this characterization that it is a rather apt, if watered-down, summary of socialism, that is, economic democracy (controlling one's life and livelihood, etc.). So, in effect, even by Brinkley's own admission, it was the socialist ideal that appealed to tens of millions of Americans. (And why shouldn't it, after all? Socialism just means giving power (economic and political) to the people. The extreme dedication of liberals to denying that socialism resonates among Americans is suspicious.)

tolerated and even supported by those with power (such as the Catholic Church in the case of Coughlin and many Louisiana corporations and businessmen in the case of Long).[130] Since they were not constantly censored and suppressed, they were able to get their message out. Second, the two men appealed to the masses by, on the one hand, denouncing the nation's "pigs swilling in the trough of luxury," to quote Long, and on the other hand proposing radical schemes to redistribute wealth. At its core, the matter is as simple as that. Brinkley, characteristically, tries to deflect attention from class and material interests, but sometimes the simplest and most obvious explanation is the right one.

It requires impressive intellectual acrobatics to strongly differentiate the populism of Long and Coughlin from a semi-Marxian populism of class, when, for instance, Long's whimsical retrospective account of his *First Days in the White House*, a book completed a few days before he was shot, describes accomplishments that are so class oriented. As a reviewer summarized Long's postpresidential self-description, "he was the man of action who in rapid succession launched a stupendous program of reclamation and conservation, who planned for scientific treatment of criminals, cheaper transportation and popular control of banking. Higher education for all became fact. Tell every parent, he said to his advisers, 'I will send your boy and girl to college.' There was much more, but all was overshadowed by legislation for the redistribution of wealth [by means of confiscatory taxation]." Such a plan was certainly utopian and therefore, one might say, little more than fantasy, but the Communist vision that inspired Marxists was surely even more utopian and fantastical. In any case, while Long and Coughlin's supporters were not expert in the dialectics of *Das Kapital*, it is clear that most of them dreamed of, in effect, expropriating the expropriators, the great class of propertied magnates, and democratically distributing the proceeds among the middle class and relatively poor.[131]

Given all the protest movements that have been surveyed in this chapter, movements that had been swelling and surging from coast to coast since 1930, officials in the Roosevelt administration should not have been surprised to learn from their roving reporters in 1933 and 1934 that great masses of people had adopted a thoroughly "un-American" attitude toward relief. In August 1933, Lorena Hickock wrote to Harry Hopkins from Pennsylvania, "I still feel, as I felt a week ago, that vast numbers of the unemployed are 'right on the edge,' so to speak—that it wouldn't take much to make Communists out of them." Another reporter wrote that men on relief had become truculent, "more critical, more complaining, more ready to react," and increasingly resentful of investigation and surveillance by social workers. In Ohio, unemployed families were "less and less embarrassed to ask for relief and [...] more and more dependent on it as security against times of unemployment as well as in some cases a bulwark forever." In Flint, Michigan, "all the [relief] workers were unanimous in saying that a large proportion of the relief lists took the 'entitled to it' attitude." The same was true in the

---

130. Badger, "Huey Long and the New Deal," 95; *New York Times*, December 8, 1935.
131. Francis Brown, "Huey Long as Hero and as Demagogue," *New York Times*, September 29, 1935; Raymond Gram Swing, "The Menace of Huey Long," *China Press*, March 30, 1935; Verba and Schlozmann, "Unemployment, Class Consciousness, and Radical Politics," 295.

Stockyards district of Chicago: according to the supervisor of a relief station there, "the clients are less patient than they used to be. They demand relief with more assurance. They criticize more freely."[132]

A leading welfare administrator in New York declared in late 1934 that they could not go on for another year "without being forced to bring in a new social order." The populist pressures were threatening to burst the integument of the old capitalist order. Far from, say, Long and Coughlin's adoring fans not truly desiring radical change, even the average relief recipient apparently wanted the sphere of the market to be severely circumscribed and the federal government to assume the burden of guaranteeing economic security for all. It was Roosevelt's failure to pursue this goal, to vigorously stand up to big business, that caused millions of Americans to turn away from him between late 1934 and early 1935. Historian Charles Beard observed a "staggering rapidity" in the "disintegration of President Roosevelt's prestige" in early 1935, while Martha Gellhorn wrote, "it surprises me how radically attitudes can change within four or five months." Correspondents wrote to Roosevelt that he had "faded out on the masses of hungry, idle people," had served only the "very rich," and proven to be "no deferent [sic] from any other President." "Huey Long is the man we thought you were when we voted for you," a man wrote from Montana. The so-called Second New Deal shored up Roosevelt's popular support, but it was not nearly as left wing as many millions would have liked.[133]

In short, regarding the question whether broad swathes of America could have been called "revolution-minded" in the 1930s, the answer has to be yes, unless one arbitrarily confines the term "revolution" to a collective seizure of the national state and establishment of a so-called dictatorship of the proletariat. Sensibly, most Americans neither hoped for nor attempted such an uprising, which certainly would have been an abortive undertaking. Instead, large numbers of them attempted to carry out the more realistic and democratic revolution of compelling government to provide economic security to everyone, regardless of race, sex, ethnicity, occupation, or age. The radicalism of this ambition was incredible: to realize it on a scale as immense as the United States would have been one of the great achievements of human history. It is no surprise, then, that the project failed. It is up to the present generation and its descendants to take up the battle again, illuminated by the study of past defeats and victories, and to carry it forward to fruition.

---

132. Richard Lowitt and Maurine Beasley, eds., *One Third of a Nation: Lorena Hickok Reports on the Great Depression* (Chicago, IL: University of Illinois Press, 1983), 12; William R. Brock, *Welfare, Democracy, and the New Deal* (New York: Cambridge University Press, 1988), 263, 264; John F. Bauman and Thomas H. Coode, *In the Eye of the Great Depression: New Deal Reporters and the Agony of the American People* (DeKalb, IL: Northern Illinois University Press, 1988), 75; Louisa Wilson, "Report, Flint, Michigan, November 30, 1934," Harry Hopkins Papers, box 66, Franklin Roosevelt Library; Thomas Steep to Harry Hopkins, November 10, 1934, ibid.
133. Brock, *Welfare, Democracy, and the New Deal*, 264; McElvaine, *The Great Depression*, 249, 253, 254. For more examples of popular disillusionment with Roosevelt, see McElvaine, "Thunder without Lightning," 73, 74, 82–88. See also Robert McElvaine, ed., *Down and Out in the Great Depression: Letters from the Forgotten Man* (Chapel Hill, NC: University of North Carolina Press, 2008), chapters 7 and 11.

CONCLUSION

In *The Utopia of Rules* (2015), David Graeber constructs a thought experiment to illustrate why the threat of ruling-class violence is of far more consequence than mass adherence to particular ideologies or "discourses" as an explanation of social "stability." Imagine, he says, that some warlike tribe conquers a group of peaceful farmers. The latter are reduced to working on the estates of the former, who propagate an ideology that holds that the farmers are stupid, ugly, and base and have been cursed by divine powers for some terrible collective sin, while the warriors who have conquered them are beautiful and intelligent, intrinsically superior. Perhaps the farmers come to internalize their disgrace and act as if they believe they are guilty of something. Maybe some of them really do believe it. But on a deeper level, Graeber writes,

> it doesn't make a lot of sense to ask whether they [believe it] or not. The whole arrangement is the fruit of violence and can only be maintained by the continual threat of violence: the fact that the [farmers] are quite aware that if anyone directly challenged property arrangements, or access to education, swords would be drawn and people's heads would almost certainly end up being lopped off. In a case like this, what we talk about in terms of "belief" are simply the psychological techniques people develop to accommodate themselves to this reality. We have no idea how they would act, or what they would think, if the [warriors'] command of the means of violence were to somehow disappear.[1]

Perry Anderson makes a similar point in a discussion of Antonio Gramsci: he observes that, while a kind of "consent" may ordinarily prevail in our society, it is "constituted by a silent, absent force [...]: the monopoly of legitimate violence by the State. Deprived of this, the system of cultural control would be instantly fragile, since the limits of possible actions against it would disappear."[2] It isn't hard to imagine how differently people in the lower classes would act if there were no police forces or military or security guards or prisons.

Control over violence, which rests on control over resources, which itself rests, ultimately, on class position (ownership entails control of resources), is thus the decisive factor. People in subordinate positions may endorse some aspect of a "conservative" ideology or may be integrated in countless ways into the "dominant culture," but as soon as the threat of violent punishment for deviation disappeared, collective rebellions against the ruling class would, surely, break out everywhere. The property of the rich

---

1. David Graeber, *The Utopia of Rules: On Technology, Stupidity, and the Secret Joys of Bureaucracy* (Brooklyn, NY: Melville House, 2015), 58, 59.
2. Perry Anderson, "The Antinomies of Antonio Gramsci," *New Left Review*, I, 100 (November–December 1976): 43.

would be overrun and distributed among the relatively poor, who would have no fear of ending up in prison. There would be no reason for employees to obey employers, for the latter would not be backed by state violence. Social turmoil might ensue, or perhaps new popular authorities would arise to regulate the new society of comparative economic equality. Businesses that had formerly been run by a few capitalists might now be run by the workers themselves. What all this would indicate is the *superficiality* of people's former "consent" to the system of rule, the basically *prudential* nature of their consent. A change in material conditions would bring about a very swift change in behavior and consciousness, and would in fact yield insights into the nature of earlier popular behavior.[3]

This book has constituted, in effect, a case study in these truths, which is to say a study in the realism, resourcefulness, and modes of resistance of humanity—in this case, in a condition of enforced economic idleness. Underneath all the political and cultural indoctrination that abounds, the ethnic and religious hatreds, the social resentments and mistaken political judgments—all of which arise in the context of a violently enforced and seemingly insurmountable system of differential access to economic resources—people have certain basic values: they want a degree of material comfort, control over their work and recreational activities, freedom to express themselves creatively and independently, and a social and natural environment that permits health and mutual recognition. They want not to be shut out of the political sphere, not to be dominated and exploited by entities with interests opposed to theirs, not to have a much lower social status than an esteemed minority, not to be denied their dignity. These are the values that most deeply motivate, and they are the values we have, in the preceding pages, seen manifested by the humblest of Chicago's residents in a time of economic desolation.

People adapt. *Homo sapiens* could almost be defined as the species that adapts. People use the tools and techniques available to them in their lifelong struggle to realize their

---

3. As this book went to press, I came across Vivek Chibber's *The Class Matrix* and was pleased to see that it supports my own "theoretical" perspective. Being a good materialist, Chibber criticizes any approach—Gramscian, Frankfurt School, culturalist, or whatever—that explains the relative stability and longevity of capitalism in terms of cultural hegemony, bourgeois indoctrination of the working class, popular consent to capitalist rule, etc. Instead, he prefers common sense. "A more plausible explanation for capitalism's political stability locates it not in the working class embracing its situation but in *resigning* itself to it—that is, workers accept their location in the class structure because they see no other viable option." People are fairly realistic: to quote Marx, the "dull compulsion of economic relations"—backed by state violence—keeps them doing what they have to do in order to survive and, to the extent possible, advance. "Cultural" considerations (which suggest working-class irrationality, as if workers can't perceive their own true interests) are decidedly secondary. Chibber, *The Class Matrix* (Cambridge: Harvard University Press, 2022), 106. Nicholas Abercrombie et al., *The Dominant Ideology Thesis* (London: George Allen & Unwin, 1980) is another perceptive text in this context; and see the Introduction to my own "Down But Not Out: The Unemployed in Chicago during the Great Depression" (Ph.D. diss., University of Illinois, 2017), which argues against the "Gramscian" point of view in favor of the classical Marxist emphasis on brutally enforced class structures and workers' realism and rationality in adapting to such structures.

deepest values against the interests of dominant groups. Such humble tactics as scavenging streets for coal and wood, selling furniture or wedding rings, stealing clothes from a department store—or sharing resources with friends and relatives, living with a kind neighbor after being evicted from one's home, telling a few lies to a relief worker—or, on a more collective scale, commandeering private property to house a family, demonstrating in the streets for more generous relief policies, lobbying for confiscatory taxes on the wealthy and government-guaranteed economic security for everyone: these were the techniques in the 1930s by which people survived and sought a measure of dignity. When overthrow of the class system was not possible—as was popularly understood, notwithstanding the dreams of Communist activists—people had to settle for what they could get, even if this was only the solidarity of a community of like-minded believers in an urban church.

Historians are free to argue about the various conflicting ideologies and individualisms of even the downtrodden in American history, but ultimately there is no mystery as to popular desires: people want emancipation. They want empowerment. Naturally, they will often feel ashamed if, say, they cannot find employment; this shame ("self-blame") is hardly "pathological" or "individualistic," as one might interpret it in the context of the Great Depression. In such an atomized society as the United States, the feeling of shame may be especially common, just as efforts to build a socialist movement may be less successful than in some vastly smaller country (such as Germany or France) that has not been dominated so ruthlessly for so long by such an exceptionally class-conscious business class.[4] But the facts of class conflict and class struggle remain, and nothing interesting can be inferred from the supposed "individualism" of American "culture" except that the country's business class has had the resources to suppress effective opposition.

People adapt to the circumstances in which they find themselves. If they find that words like "Communist" and "Socialist" are assigned a negative value by the broader society—a fact to which ruling-class propaganda is not irrelevant—they may be reluctant to call themselves Communists or Socialists. They may also, sometimes, be reluctant to join movements or parties led by self-styled Communists. Meanwhile, like many of the proudly anti-Communist veterans in the Bonus Army of 1932, they may continue to hold such socialist views as wanting the government to take over major industries and guarantee people jobs. Why? Because, in their position, that is a rational opinion to hold. In a system of (often unconscious) class struggle, they may adjust their self-conceptions to some of the dominant society's values even as they continue to hold beliefs and values that are radically opposed to the dominant society.

As unemployment in the United States increases in the coming years and decades, activists can draw inspiration from the 1930s' Unemployed Councils, Workers Committees, and Unemployed Leagues, which proved it *is* possible to organize the unemployed. The tactics of such organizations can be profitably studied: for instance,

---

4. See Patricia Cayo Sexton, *The War on Labor and the Left: Understanding America's Unique Conservatism* (Boulder, CO: Westview Press, Inc., 1991).

sweeping ideological appeals tend to be less effective and sustainable than appeals to concrete problems and material needs, on the basis of which positive proposals must be made. This is not because people are "unideological" or insufficiently radical, but simply because they do not live in the clouds: their actual lives are what matter to them, more than utopias and fanciful revolutionary slogans. Admittedly, the "ideology" that motivates them might not have the grandiose pretensions of Marxism-Leninism or some such; it is usually more humble and realistic, consisting, in essence, of the desire for dignity and recognition. But this desire, in the context of an oppressive social system, can be revolutionary, and may well eventuate in dramatic social transformations.[5]

Given the structural parallels that exist between the present and the pre-Depression past, humanity in the twenty-first century can likely look forward to an era of global economic stagnation, generalized conditions of precarious employment, and rampant environmental destruction. We are headed into a long period of nearly apocalyptic conflict between the institutional imperatives of late capitalism and the very different imperatives of human survival. The ever-growing masses of unemployed and insecurely employed people are and will be ripe for organization, as they were in the 1930s, and now that the Soviet Union is gone, Communist Party dogmas and pathologies, so aptly diagnosed by Mauritz Hallgren and others 90 years ago, are not around to interfere with the task of building an indigenous and realistic American revolutionary movement. Organizers preaching the gospel of socialism and economic democracy will not fail, sooner or later, to find a sympathetic hearing, simply because the socialist dream of—in Alan Brinkley's unwitting words—"a society in which the individual retain[s] control of his life and livelihood; in which power reside[s] in visible, accessible institutions; in

---

5. Of course, uglier ideologies, such as nativism and racism, claim many adherents too (in the historically "socialistic" and "class-conscious" Europe no less than the United States). But these sorts of values seem less universal and more the product of ruling-class propaganda meant to divide and conquer the population. It is a historical truism, for example, that employers have exploited race and ethnicity to divide their workforces, and that political parties (e.g., the Republican during and after the time of Nixon's "Southern Strategy"—up to the Trumpian present, in fact) have fomented racism for political gain. It's an unfortunate fact that, in a world in which inequalities of wealth and status are violently enforced and to all appearances insurmountable, people can be susceptible to ideologies of hate, but it is hardly a surprise given the extreme disparity of resources between the business community (and its conservative apologists) and the left. There is a huge literature on the ruling class's use of racism and conservative religiosity for its own ends, but see, for instance, Kim Phillips-Fein, *Invisible Hands: The Businessmen's Crusade against the New Deal* (New York: W. W. Norton, 2009); Theodore W. Allen, *The Invention of the White Race, Vols. 1 and 2* (New York: Verso, 1994 and 1997); Thomas Byrne Edsall and Mary D. Edsall, *Chain Reaction: The Impact of Race, Rights, and Taxes on American Politics* (New York: W. W. Norton & Co., 1992); Michael Perman, *Struggle for Mastery: Disfranchisement in the South, 1888–1908* (Chapel Hill, NC: University of North Carolina Press, 2001); Ian Haney López, *Dog Whistle Politics: How Coded Racial Appeals Have Reinvented Racism and Wrecked the Middle Class* (New York: Oxford University Press, 2014); Elizabeth and Ken Fones-Wolf, *Struggle for the Soul of the Postwar South: White Evangelical Protestants and Operation Dixie* (Chicago, IL: University of Illinois Press, 2015); Bethany Moreton, *To Serve God and Wal-Mart: The Making of Christian Free Enterprise* (Cambridge, MA: Harvard University Press, 2009).

which wealth [is] equitably (if not necessarily equally) shared" is very appealing.[6] In the right circumstances, people can readily be mobilized on the basis of their deeply rooted communistic, mutualist values.

Proper study of the past, of the millions who have fought to overcome the oppressive heritage of their own past, can provide cause for hope. Against enormous odds, people almost barren of resources have won historic, if partial, victories. Through a future succession of partial victories, we may find our way to a more just world.

---

6. Alan Brinkley, *Voices of Protest: Huey Long, Father Coughlin, and the Great Depression* (New York: Vintage Books, 1983), xi. As mentioned in a footnote to the last chapter, Brinkley considered this to be the "anticollectivist" guiding vision of Huey Long and Charles Coughlin's followers, unaware that his characterization was in fact just a somewhat bland restatement of socialist goals. Meanwhile, in our own day, even after more than forty years of neoliberal indoctrination, the ostensibly conservative and individualistic American public has a rather positive view of socialism (whatever that word is taken to mean). According to a Gallup poll in 2019, about half of young adults favor socialism, compared to a third each of Gen Xers and baby boomers. Given the vast public relations industry devoted to demonizing the left, this is a striking finding. Lydia Saad, "Socialism as Popular as Capitalism among Young Adults in U.S.," *Gallup*, November 25, 2019.

INDEX

Note: Page numbers in **bold** refer to tables.

A
activism: Unemployed Councils (*see* Unemployed Councils); Workers Committee on Unemployment (WCU) 226–33; *see also* collective action
administrative practices, shelter men and 124
adult education 99–102
AFL Trade Union Committee for Unemployment Insurance and Relief (AFLTU Committee) 162, 164
alcohol consumption 97, 129–30
All Nations Pentecostal Church 188
Amalgamated Clothing Workers 100, 160, 162, 166n70
American Federation of Labor (AFL) 15, 17, 35, 139, 161–65, 167, 169–71, 177, 237, 239, 242
American Workers Party 34
American Youth Congress 240
Amter, Israel 221
Anderson, Nels 127
Anderson, Perry 251
Angelus Building 72–73
anticapitalist values 5, 36
archery clubs 104
Arkansas 29
Asher, Robert 244
Associated Church Charities 171, 172
Association of Catholic Trade Unionists (ACTU) 178
Austin, J. C. 216

B
Back of the Yards 24, 45, 46, 51, 78, 91, 103, 217
Badger, Anthony 67, 139n6, 194, 245, 245n122
Bakke, E. Wight 74–75, 89, 191, 198, 203–4, 234
Baldwin, James 185–86
bank closings 70
Beard, Charles 250
beggars 119, 120, 130
Benjamin, Herbert 221, 240, 241

Benson, Susan Porter 13, 83, 88
Bernstein, Irving 22, 33, 208
Best, Wallace 186
Better Government Association 144
Binga State Bank 70
Bird Memorial Congregational Church 190
Black Belt 18, 23, 54–56, 214–15; juvenile crime rate 65
Black Metropolis 39, 191, 211
Black women 25; prostitution and 79; regular jobs 79; wage discrimination 78–79
Blacks: as disadvantaged minority 24; discrimination 23, 39; domestic servants 23; employment agencies and 76; Great Migration 18, 174; hardships of 13, 38–39; organized recreation 101–2; population 23; Unemployed Council action 209–10; youth delinquents 65
Bloor, Mother 239
Board of Education 41
Bonus Army 195, 253
Bonus March to Washington 33–34, 199
box cars 132
"Breadline Frolics, The" 126
Brinkley, Alan 7n12, 245, 247–49, 254, 255n6
Brookings Institution 16–18
Browder, Earl 214, 246–48
building trades unions 163
Bulgarian families 24, 59
bull pen 115
Bureau of Public Welfare, Chicago 45, 46, 112, 145, 148
Bureau of Social Statistics 144
bureaucracies 64, 117

C
capitalism 1–2, 170, 176–78, 200, 201, 243; contradictions of 17–19; hegemonic values of 4; as parasitic on everyday communism 5
car thefts 93
Catholic Central Charity Bureau 144, 171, 172, 181
Catholic Church 176–79, 190, 218, 249

Catholic Worker movement 178–79
Catholics/Catholicism 177–79, 190, 191; charities 171; labor activism 178–79
Cayton, Horace 210
Century of Progress 26, 147
Cermak, Anton 28, 55, 77, 81, 145, 146, 148, 208, 210
Chicago 1–2, 63, 81, 83, 193; budget 43; economy 38; as site of unemployed activism 1
Chicago Association of Commerce 144
Chicago Church Federation 146, 171, 175
Chicago Committee on Adequate Relief 50
Chicago Commons 99, 101, 102, 226, 227
Chicago Daily News 84
Chicago Defender 93, 157, 223
Chicago Federation of Labor (CFL) 100, 165–67, 237
Chicago Herald 45
Chicago Leisure Time Service 99, 100
Chicago Relief Administration (CRA) 32, 32n37, 43, 47, 112, 156–59
Chicago Tribune 42, 44, 69, 103, 121, 170, 173, 234
Chicago Workers Committee on Unemployment 33, 148, 166, 226–31, 244
children 57, 59–65, 77, 181; informal recreation 90–95; malnutrition 44; organized recreation 98–102
Children's Leisure Time Service 99–100
Chomsky, Noam 3n4, 8n14, 10n19, 12n22, 128n60
Christian Industrial League 110, 112, 124, 172
churches 10, 26, 64, 139–40, 170–91; attitude and antagonism toward 180–82; breadline-and-soup-kitchen business 171; civic life and 183; clubs 189; community and 187–88; Holiness 183–86; humanitarianism 171; lower-class 183; Mexicans and 190; music 185–86; recreational facilities 91; sermons 184–85; social service work 174, 182; Spiritualist 183, 185, 186; storefront 187–88; working-class unemployed and 182–83
Citizens without Work (Bakke) 203
Civic Federation of Chicago 42, 144
Civil Rights Movement 140
civil society 64
Civil Works Administration (CWA) 28, 137, 144, 150, 225
Civil Works Educational Service 98–99
Civilian Conservation Corps 50, 224
class conflict 1–6, 10, 125, 135, 241, 247–48, 253
class consciousness 2, 14, 67–68, 123, 125, 182, 193–95, 199, 202–3, 209, 220, 224, 232, 245

class struggle 2–4, 14, 50, 112, 120, 137, 140, 189–91, 194, 228
Clearing House for Homeless Men 110, 115, 116, 124, 127
Cloward, Richard A. 136
clubs 100–5, 189, 214, 228
Cohen, Lizabeth 7n12, 63, 70, 85, 183–84
collective action 193–250; activism 206–33; eviction protests 208–13, 218, 219, 225, 235; popular radicalism 234–50
Columbia University 161
communism 121, 164, 172, 205, 214–17; anarchist 5; baseline 5, 82; everyday 6, 82–90; Jews/Jewish people 173
Communist Party 30, 33–36, 123, 132, 163, 168, 193, 197, 205–8, 214–24, 237, 239–40, 254; organizer of unemployed protest 33; *see also* collective action; Unemployed Councils
Communists 9, 36, 253
Communists in Harlem during the Depression (Naison) 193
Conference for Progressive Labor Action (CPLA) 34, 244
Congress of Industrial Organizations (CIO) 14, 139, 149, 158n50, 160, 164, 167–70, 178, 208, 214, 225, 232
Contribution to the Critique of Hegel's Philosophy of Right (Marx) 183
Cook County Bureau of Public Welfare 46, 112, 145, 148
coping 67–105; everyday communism 82–90; informal recreation 90–98; organized recreation 98–105; survival and day-to-day living 67–82
Cosmopolitan Community Church 184, 188
Costigan, Edward 141
Coughlin, Charles 8, 121, 167, 177, 196, 197, 245–50
Council for Social Action (CSA) 175–76
Council of Polish Organizations 105
Council of Social Agencies 101, 148
Cowie, Jefferson 7n12, 12n23, 245
Crane Junior College 98
Creel Committee on Public Information 7
cutting down on expenses 71–72
Czechoslovak community 24, 105

D

Daily Calumet 229
Daily News 37
Daily Worker 37, 121, 208, 209, 213–21, 236, 246–47
Das Kapital 249
De Caux, Len 203
de Man, Henri 16
death rates 49, 50

INDEX

delinquency: *see* juvenile delinquency
Dillon, William J. 176
Division on Education and Recreation of the Chicago Council of Social Agencies 100
Dubofsky, Melvyn 193–94, 224
Dunn, Matthew 240–41

E
Eastern European community 24
Economy 17–20; Communist analyses of 17
Electric Railway and Light Company 244
Emergency Educational Program 99
employment agencies 74–77
employment assurance 162
End Poverty in California (EPIC) 8, 167, 196, 201, 242–43
Episcopal Cathedral Shelter 172
ethnic community, atomization of 63–64
ethnicity 13, 82, 86
Evans, Mary 184, 187
everyday communism 6, 82–90; communist mentality 87; free goods 86; generosity 85–87; gifts 83, 84; goods shared/exchanged 84; local merchant extending credit 85–86; men taking feminine domestic tasks 87–88; sharing of resources 87; sharing of shelter 83
"Everyday Forms of Resistance" (Scott) 4
eviction protests 208–13, 218, 219, 225, 235

F
Fantasia, Rick 4n7, 203
Farmer-Labor Party 246–47
Farmers' National Relief Conference 243
Federal Council of Churches in Christ 171–72, 174–76, 180; Labor Sunday message 180; Social Creed 172; social radicalism 171–72
Federal Emergency Relief Administration (FERA) 28, 29, 32, 46, 49, 55, 111, 137, 149, 150, 152–55, 158n50, 224
Federal Reserve, deflationary policy of raising interest rates 19
Federal Workers Section 244
Federated Council of Professional and Business Women 85
Federation News 165
First Days in the White House (Long) 249
fiscal conservatism 31, 155
Fish, Hamilton 246
Fitzpatrick, John 237
flophouses 9, 45, 108, 114, 119–21, 216
food/meal service in shelters 116–17
Fortune Magazine 199–200, 202, 203
Foster, William Z. 247
Foucault, M. 6, 12n22
Fraternal Federation for Social Insurance 243

Frazier, Lynn 235, 242–43
Frazier-Lundeen Bill 242–43
free junior college 98
freedom/independence 2, 111, 119–20, 132, 215, 252
fundraising 44, 102, 144, 145, 180, 182

G
gambling 92, 96–97, 127–29
gangs 81, 92
gasoline tax 143, 147, 149
Gellhorn, Martha 250
gender roles/norms 59–62, 66, 87–88, 186
General Conference of the Methodist Church 174
General Council of Congregational and Christian Churches 175; *see also* Council for Social Action (CSA)
Glaberman, Martin 202–3
Glorious Church of the Air, The 188
Gold, Michael 214–16
Good Shepherd Community Center 174
Good Shepherd Congregational Church 174
governments 9–10, 46, 135–60
Governor's Commission on Unemployment and Relief 145
Graeber, David 5–6, 82, 172, 251
Gramsci, Antonio 251
Grant Park 26, 27
Great Depression 1, 9, 193; qualitative accounts of 25–26; reasons for 19
Great Fire of 1871 51
Green, William 17–18, 162, 164, 168, 170, 242
Greene, Julie 4n5

H
Hallgren, Mauritz 163, 199, 205, 226, 254
Haywood, Harry 221, 225
health service in shelters 115–16
heavy industry 22
Herndon, Angelo 216
Hickock, Lorena 249
Hobohemia 52, 108–10, 119–23
Holiness churches 183–86
Homo sapiens 58, 252
homosexual practices, shelter men and 128
Hoover, Herbert 45, 141–42
Hoovervilles 26, 131–32
Hopkins, Harry 49, 149–55, 249, 250
Horner, Henry 149–50, 152, 153, 155–56, 159
House Un-American Activities Committee (HUAC) 171–72
household entrepreneurs 77
housing conditions 51–57
H.R. 2827 238–40

Hull House 99, 101–3; neighborhood 51–52
Hunger Fighter 121, 122n46, 124, 225, 228, 237
Hungry School Children's Fund 44
Hurston, Zora Neale 186

I
Illinois Chamber of Commerce 166
Illinois Emergency Relief Commission (IERC) 28, 32, 55, 99, 110, 111, 147–52, 156, 159, 234
Illinois Labor Party (ILP) 167–68
Illinois Manufacturers' Association 144
Illinois Public Aid Commission 32
Illinois State Employment Service 76
Illinois State Federation of Labor (ISFL) 165–67, 170
Illinois State Health Department 50
Illinois Supreme Court 143
Illinois Workers Alliance (IWA) 34, 157, 159, 166–67, 169, 196, 230–32, 238
Illinois Workers Security Federation (IWSF) 34, 157, 159, 166–67, 169, 230–32, 238
Immanuel Baptist Church 173
immigrants 6, 24–25, 53, 61–62, 89, 119, 127
independent enterprisers 64
industrial workers 14, 18, 38, 240–43
Industrial Workers of the World 34; *see also* Unemployed Unions
informal recreation 90–98; entertainment 95; gambling 96–97; policy 96; reading 95; sexual promiscuity 94; stealing 92–93
Institutional African Methodist Episcopal (AME) 174
institutions 2–4, 9–11, 63, 89–91, 98, 112–13, 138–40, 173–75; *see also* churches; governments; unions
Inter-Professional Association for Social Insurance (IPA) 238, 240–41
International Association of Machinists 163
International Ladies Garment Workers Union (ILGWU) 160–62, 168
International Unemployment Day 206
Internationals 139, 163, 171
interrogation by a caseworker 114

J
Japanese Consulate on Michigan Avenue 222
Jewish Charities of Chicago 173
Jewish Social Service Bureau 27, 144, 171
Jewish Vocational Service 76
Jews/Jewish people 173, 181, 214, 220
Jobless-Liberty Party 34
Joint Emergency Relief Fund of Cook County 145

juvenile delinquency 65, 93–94
Juvenile Protective Association 232

K
Keller, Margaret 219
Kelly, Ed 41, 43
Keynes, John Maynard 16
Keyssar, Alexander 72, 86
Klehr, Harvey 207
Kropotkin, Peter 5

L
Labor Notes 30
Labor Research Association 30; numbers of jobless from late 1932 to early 1938 **30**
labor unions 160, 168; government protection of 177, 245; *see also* unions
Langford, Tom 202
League of Struggle for Negro Rights 207, 225
Leo XIII 176
Lepore, Jill 10n18
Leuchtenburg, William 2
life in shelters 112–18; *see also* shelters
Lithuanian Alliance of America 24
Long, Huey 8, 167, 196, 197, 245–50
Loop 15, 26, 52, 108–10, 130–32
Lorence, James 168–69, 193, 234
Los Angeles Times 126
Lundeen, Ernest 35, 139, 162, 165, 235, 237–43; *see also* Workers' Unemployment and Social Insurance Bill
Lynd, Robert 182

M
Mackey, Harry A. 161
Making a New Deal (Cohen) 63, 70
malnutrition 37, 44, 47, 159, 180
marriages 61
Marx, Karl 3, 5, 64, 183, 194
Marxism 137, 195–96, 248
mass adherence to ideologies/discourses 251
Massachusetts 22, 29, 72, 242
Maurin, Peter 178–79
McComb, John H. 171–72
McCulloch, Frank W. 167, 227, 232
McElvaine, Robert 245
McGillivray, Gillian 138n5
McNicholas, Archbishop John T. 177
meatpacking industry: Black workers 38–39; immigrants in 24; share-the-work plans 24; underemployment 38
medical examination in shelters 114
men in shelters 118–33; administrative practices and 124; alcohol consumption 129–30; attitudes 120; class consciousness 125–26; collective action or resistance

124–25, 129; Communist influence 123–25; cultural groups 119; cynicism and gloomy outlook 129; enemies of 131; freedom/independence 119–20; gambling 127–29; Hobohemian 119–20; homosexual practices 128; indifference to religion 120; marital problems 122; nationalities 119; newspapers and pulp magazines 127; physical disabilities/injuries 122; politics and 120–22; radicalization 123; realistic views 120; recreation and education 126–27; restlessness and protests 126; self-blame 122–23; sex starvation 128–29; sports 126; vices 129; visiting prostitutes 128, 129
mental hardship 58–66
Methodist Federation of Social Action 175
Mexicans 24–25, 49, 86, 218; Catholic churches 190; organized recreation 99, 103, 104; Protestant church 190; religious practices 190; removal of 24–25; sports and 104; unemployment rate 24
Michigan 23, 102, 169, 173, 193
Midwestern Conference of Unemployed Organizations 165–66
Mills, Make 222
Milwaukee Workers Committee 244
miners' strike in McKeesport, Pennsylvania 244
Minneapolis General Drivers' Local 544 244
Minnesota Farmer-Labor Party 168
missions 110, 120; *see also* shelters
Montgomery, David 89
mothers' clubs 102
Mundelein, Archbishop George 177–78
Muste, A. J. 34

N
Naison, Mark 193, 214
Nation 80, 124, 240
National Americanization League 246
National Catholic Welfare Conference (NCWC) 171, 177–78
National Committee on Rural Social Planning 243
National Congress for Unemployment and Social Insurance 239–40
National Federation of Settlements, Boston conference of 16
national polls 199–201
National Resources Committee 15, 21
National Union for Social Justice 245–46
Nelson, Bruce 129
New Deal 29–30, 47, 96, 99, 158, 237, 240
New World 176
New York City 22, 78, 130, 159, 211, 233
New York Herald Tribune 222

New York Times 72, 126, 206, 242
Newell, Barbara Warne 178
North Clark Street 52, 109, 119
Northern Baptist Convention 174–75
"Not So 'Turbulent Years': A New Look at the 1930s" (Dubofsky) 193–94

O
Oak Forest Infirmary 165
Oak Street Beach 128–29
Olander, Victor 167
Old Age Assistance 32, 144
Olivet Baptist Church 174
optimism-pessimism-fatalism 59
organized labor cooperation 165–68
organized recreation 98–105; adult education 99; Blacks and 101–2; children 98–99; free junior college 98; Mexicans 103, 104; sports 103–5
Organizing the Unemployed (Lorence) 193
Out of Work (Keyssar) 72

P
part-time and temporary jobs 15, 23, 76–78
Party Organizer 225
Patterson, George 179
Pennsylvania 34, 82, 142, 154, 240, 244, 249
Pentecostalism 189–90
People's History of the United States, A (Zinn) 10
physical disabilities/injuries 122
physical facilities in shelters 114–15
physical hardship 43–57; hunger and disease 43–50; shelter and clothing 51–57
picketing 169–70, 244
"Pie in the Sky" 216
Pinchot, Gifford 142–43, 148
Pius XI 177
Piven, Frances Fox 113, 136–39, 157, 233
Plato 37, 66
Polish community 24, 59, 88; churches and 181
political beliefs and values 199–205
popular radicalism 196, 234–50
poverty 16, 49, 165
Prago, Albert 208
private welfare institutions 124, 144–45, 161
privatization 5, 36, 82, 105, 208
property owners 41, 147
property taxes 143–44, 159
prostitution 79–80, 109; Black women and 79; shelter men and 127–29
Protestant churches and organizations 171–79, 190
Protestant Reformation 140
public parks 101, 104, 131
public school teachers: *see* teachers

262 INDEX

Q
Quadragesimo Anno (Pius XI) 177

R
radicalism: popular 196, 234–50; social 171
Rank and File Federationist 164
rank-and-file unionists 162–64
Real Estate Board of Chicago 144
Reconstruction Finance Corporation (RFC) 28, 41, 136–37, 141, 142, 148–49
recreation 68; informal 90–98; men in shelters 126–27; organized 98–105
recreation room in shelters 114–15
recreational facilities 90–91
Regulating the Poor (Piven and Cloward) 136
Reitman, Ben 108
relief 27–34; federal oversight of 30; private organizations and 27
relief administration 108–12
relief agencies 65, 89, 97, 172
relief stations 3, 13, 49, 146, 148–49, 152, 169, 184, 198, 208, 212–13, 222–25, 229–31
religion 11, 68; as complex social phenomenon 179; lower-class 189; racial consciousness 187; shelter men indifference to 120, 123; as sigh of oppressed creature 183; *see also* churches
Rerum Novarum 177
Roosevelt, Franklin 13n24, 22, 27–29, 31, 42, 98, 121, 126, 153–55, 224, 233, 235, 237, 249, 250
Roosevelt recession of 1937–38 158, 168
Rosenzweig, Roy 193, 196n8, 227
Roth, Gary 209
Ryan, John A. 171, 177, 178

S
sales tax 143, 149–50, 152–53, 166, 225
Salvation Army 15, 27, 74, 81, 110, 112, 124, 145
Sanctified Church 186
savings for survival 69–71
Schlozman, Kay Lehman 199–200, 202, 203
Scott, James C. 4, 194, 215
Second New Deal 250
seeking jobs for survival 74–79
self-blame 12–13, 197–99, 253; men in shelters 122–23; *see also* shame
sermons 179–80, 182, 184–87
Service Bureaus for Men and Women 111–12
sex starvation 128–29
sexual delinquency 94
sexual promiscuity 94
shame 61, 197–99; *see also* self-blame
share-the-work plans 24

Shelter for Transient Men in Palo Alto, California 198
shelter libraries 127
shelters 26, 51–57, 110; buildings used for 26; bull pen 115; food/meal service 116–17; hardships 114; health service 115–16; interrogation by a caseworker 114; life in 112–18; location of 26; medical examination 114; men in 118–33 (*see also* men in shelters); non-white-collar shelters 114; personal services 116; physical facilities 114–15; recreation room 114–15; rule of impersonality 118; sleeping rooms 115; spies 117–18; testimony 113; white-collar clients 114; women 11; work relief 118
shoplifting 81, 92–93
Sinclair, Upton 8, 196
single women on relief 84
Singleton, Jeff 139
sleeping rooms in shelters 115
Slichter, Sumner 161
Slovene National Benefit Society 70
Smith, Elder Lucy 188
Smoot-Hawley Act of 1930 19
Social Action 176
Social Action Department of the NCWC 171, 178
social being 194
social insurance 35, 172
social radicalism 171
Social Security Act 8, 29, 35, 137, 154, 158n50, 197, 238, 243
Social Security payroll tax 31
social service work of churches 174, 182
social stability 6, 251
social workers 62–63
Socialist Party 33, 226
Society of St. Vincent de Paul 172
Some Folks Won't Work 16
South Chicago Community Center 190
South State Street 52, 108
Soviet Union 196, 238–39, 246
Special Activities Division 126, 127
spies in shelters 117–18
Spiritualist churches 183, 185, 186
sports 103–5, 126
starvation 33, 44, 45, 139, 159
states: revenues 143; sales tax 143
Ste. Croix, G. E. M. de 2
stealing/thievery 80–81, 92–93
stock market 18–19, 31
Storch, Randi 196n8, 210, 224
storefront churches 183–89
strangers' kindness 72–73
Strawn, Silas 37

strikes: class consciousness and 202–3; unions 169–70
Sunday School 187
Survey 142
survival and day-to-day living 67–82; bank closings 70; borrowing 70; cutting down on expenses 71–72; hand-to-mouth existence 69; household entrepreneurs 77; part-time and temporary jobs 77–78; prostitution 79–80; raising money 73–74; savings 69–71; seeking jobs 74–76; stealing/thievery 80–82; strangers' kindness 72–73; taking care of appearance 74

T
tax anticipation warrants 41, 147, 148, 157
tax collection 25, 27, 145; suspension of 41
tax delinquency 43, 143
tax strike 41, 145
teachers 37, 41–42, 44
Teamsters 163
technological unemployment 17–18
thievery: *see* stealing/thievery
Thompson, "Big Bill" 145
threat of ruling-class violence 6, 251
Toledo Auto-Lite strike 244
Townsend Plan 240–41

U
Ukrainian Central Committee 105
unattached 9, 108–13
underemployment 24
unemployed: characteristics of 39; by industry in 1931 **40**; numbers of 23; by occupational group in 1931 (men and women) **40**; political beliefs and values 199–201; shame and self-blame 197–99
Unemployed Councils 3, 33, 34, 84, 148, 163, 167, 196, 204, 206–25, 227, 229, 230, 244, 253
Unemployed Leagues 34, 238, 244
Unemployed Unions 34
"Unemployment, Class Consciousness, and Radical Politics: What Didn't Happen in the Thirties" (Verba and Lehman) 199
unemployment benefits plan 160
unemployment insurance 29–30, 35, 162–64, 213, 242
Unemployment Relief Service 112
unions 10, 139, 160–70; access to relief benefits 168–69; employment assurance 162; national unity 168; organized labor co-operation 165–68; rank-and-file rebelliousness 164–65; share-the-work schemes 161; strikes and picketing 169–70; unemployment benefits plan 160–61;

unemployment insurance and 162–64; voluntarism 161–62
United Auto Workers (UAW) 169, 193
United Charities 15, 27, 32n37, 48, 144, 174, 213
United Council of Working-Class Women 240
United Mine Workers 159, 163, 239
United States Department of Labor 44
United Steelworkers 179
United Textile Workers 162
University of Chicago 50, 61, 229
University of Chicago Settlement 50, 61, 101–3, 218
"Urban Famine, An" (WCU report) 44, 51
Urban League 35, 110, 174, 239
Utopia of Rules, The (Graeber) 6, 251

V
vagabonds 108–9
Van Kleeck, Mary 238
Verba, Sidney 199–200, 202, 203
Voices of Protest (Brinkley) 196n7, 248n127
voluntarism 143, 161–62
voluntary organizations 160

W
Wagner, Robert 141
Wagner-Lewis Bill 238, 241; *see also* Social Security Act
Washington Square Park 109, 217
Weinstock, Louis 162–63
West Madison Street 52, 108, 110, 119
white-collar clients in shelters 114
white-collar workers 41
Wisconsin Farmer-Labor Progressive Federation 168
women 25; and activism 218–20; housekeeping 71–72; part-time and seasonal jobs 25; prostitution 79–80; sharing or exchanging goods 84; shelters 11; unemployment rate for 25; wage discrimination against 78–79
Worker Cooperatives and Revolution: History and Possibilities in the United States (Wright) 13–14
Workers Alliance (WA) 34, 100, 168–70, 175, 193, 225, 230–33
Workers' Committee on Unemployment (WCU) 33, 37, 43–44, 226–33
Workers on the Waterfront (Nelson) 129
Workers Security Federation 34, 232
Workers' Unemployment and Social Insurance Bill 8, 35, 139, 238–45
Working Woman 219
Works Progress Administration (WPA) 23, 28–29, 31, 32, 34, 47, 57, 93, 100, 104, 110,

137, 141, 153, 154, 156, 158, 159, 168–70, 193, 232
World War I 7, 19, 201, 236
World War II 17, 23, 38, 72
Wright, Richard 56, 187, 198, 205

Y
YMCA 76, 99–101
young hoodlums 93

youth/young adults 65–66; and crimes 81–82; field trips 102; gangs 92; informal recreation 91–92; juvenile delinquency 65, 93–94
YWCA 76, 99, 101

Z
Zinn, Howard 10, 10n18
Zucman, Gabriel 1